A Constitutional History of Habeas Corpus

Contributions in Legal Studies
Series Editor: *Paul L. Murphy*

Stability, Security, and Continuity: Mr. Justice Burton and Decision-Making in the Supreme Court 1945–1958
Mary Frances Berry

Philosophical Law: Authority, Equality, Adjudication, Privacy
Richard Bronaugh, editor

Law, Soldiers, and Combat
Peter Karsten

Appellate Courts and Lawyers: Information Gathering in the Adversary System
Thomas B. Marvell

Charting the Future: The Supreme Court Responds to a Changing Society, 1890–1920
John E. Semonche

The Promise of Power: The Emergence of the Legal Profession in Massachusetts, 1760–1840
Gerard W. Gawalt

Inferior Courts, Superior Justice: A History of the Justices of the Peace on the Northwest Frontier, 1853–1889
John R. Wunder

Antitrust and the Oil Monopoly: The Standard Oil Cases, 1890–1911
Bruce Bringhurst

They Have No Rights: Dred Scott's Struggle for Freedom
Walter Ehrlich

Popular Influence Upon Public Policy: Petitioning in Eighteenth-Century Virginia
Raymond C. Bailey

Fathers to Daughters: The Legal Foundations of Female Emancipation
Peggy A. Rabkin

In Honor of Justice Douglas: A Symposium on Individual Freedom and Government
Robert H. Keller, Jr., editor

A Constitutional History of Habeas Corpus

~ WILLIAM F. DUKER

GREENWOOD PRESS

Contributions in Legal Studies,
Number 13

WESTPORT, CONNECTICUT
LONDON, ENGLAND

Library of Congress Cataloging in Publication Data

Duker, William F.
  A constitutional history of habeas corpus.

  (Contributions in legal studies ; no. 13   ISSN 0147-
1074)
  Bibliography: p.
  Includes index.
  1. Habeas corpus—United States—History.   2. Habeas
corpus—Great Britain—History.   I. Title.   II. Series.
KF9011.D84   345.73'056   79-6834
ISBN 0-313-22264-9 lib. bdg.

Library of Congress Catalog Card Number: 79-6834
ISBN: 0-313-22264-9
ISSN: 0147-1074

First published in 1980

Greenwood Press
A division of Congressional Information Service, Inc.
88 Post Road West, Westport, Connecticut 06881

Printed in the United States of America

10 9 8 7 6 5 4 3 2 1

To my family
with love and appreciation

-Contents-

-Acknowledgments-

The research for this work was conducted at the incomparable libraries of the University of Cambridge, the Harvard Law School, and the Yale Law School and I would like to express my thanks to the staffs of those libraries. My thanks also to the editors of the *New York University Law Review* for permission to publish chapter 1, which originally appeared in volume 53 of the review. I am extremely grateful for the financial support of *Signum Laudis*, the Institute of Humane Studies, and the Yale Law School. I was fortunate to have secured the typing services of Edna Scott, and I appreciate her good work.

This book benefited from discussions with Kenneth Capalbo, Archibald Cox, Steven Duke, Kenneth Elmsley, Owen M. Fiss, Paul A. Freund, Robert Haws, Morton Horwitz, Harold Hyman, Robert Ihne, Morton Keller, William E. Nelson, David Reiser, Bruce Swartz, and Samuel E. Thorne. I am especially indebted to Oscar Handlin, William Letwin, and J. R. Pole, who read early drafts of this book.

My final tribute is to my wife, Sharon. Although I could have found others to type and proofread early versions of this book, there was and is no substitute for her love and friendship.

A Constitutional
History of
Habeas Corpus

-Introduction-
General Aspects of the Writ of Habeas Corpus

While the meaning of the writs of quo warranto, procedento, mandamus, and certiorari is hidden behind the lawyer's veil of mystery, habeas corpus has long been a part of the vernacular. It is, to lawyer and layman, the great writ of liberty. It is a legal process that has mirrored our substantive concept of liberty. The writ's greatness derives from its function of inquiring into the legality of an individual's confinement. Although the definition of "legality" has changed to meet the demands of a developing concept of liberty, the purpose of the writ has remained the same for several hundred years. Its purpose is neither to compensate the prisoner for past injustice nor to penalize the policeman or judge whose behavior gives rise to the proceeding. Further, it is not concerned with the correction of all errors preceding the challenged confinement. Rather, the purpose of habeas corpus is to insure the integrity of the process resulting in imprisonment. Although it is put into operation by a particular prisoner, whose incentive is his own release, its objective is institutional reform. Habeas corpus is the structural reform mechanism of the criminal justice system, functioning to provide an avenue to vindicate substantive rights.

The focus of this work is the constitutional history of habeas corpus. It is, therefore, a part of the story of the development of liberty. Moreover, since this work is not intended to be a social history of law, it is but a part of a wider story of habeas corpus. Before beginning the part of the story of liberty and habeas corpus to be told here, it is useful to outline the basic principles of the writ.

Prior to American independence, *habeas corpus ad subjiciendum* was a prerogative process for securing the liberty of the subject by affording an effective means of immediate release from unlawful or unjustifiable detention. S. A. DeSmith[1] tells us that the writ was first referred to as a "prerogative writ" in 1620 by Mr. Chief Justice Montague in *Richard Bourn's Case*.[2] At its inception, habeas corpus was a "high prerogative writ" by which the Crown sought to compel the appearance of a subject before its judicial organ.[3] As it developed into a beneficient remedy, its continued association with the king's personal solicitude for the welfare of his subjects was simply sound politics.[4] The Crown was said to have a right to inquire into the cause for which any of its subjects were deprived of their liberty. By the writ of habeas corpus, the High Court and judges of that court, at the instance of a subject aggrieved, commanded the production of that subject, and inquired into the cause of his imprisonment.[5] If there were no legal justification for the detention, the party was ordered released;[6] thus it was often said that habeas corpus is in the nature of a writ of error.[7] In a strict legal sense, "prerogative writ" had become a descriptive term that indicated the writ's extraordinary character; that is to say, habeas corpus issued where the ordinary legal remedies were unavailable or inadequate.[8]

Habeas corpus was a writ of right[9] to which the subject was entitled *ex debito justitiae*.[10] It was not a writ of course.[11] The writ was therefore not available simply for the asking. Although it was said to be a nondiscretionary remedy, the court might refuse to grant it where proper grounds were not apparent. Asked by the House of Lords in 1758 whether by the law as it stood, in cases not within the Habeas Corpus Act of 1679, writs of *habeas corpus ad subjiciendum* ought to issue of course or upon probable grounds verified by affidavit,[12] Mr. Justice Wilmot was of the opinion that they ought to issue upon probable grounds verified by affidavit.[13] He observed:

A writ which issues upon a probable cause, verified by affidavit, is as much a writ of right, as a writ which issues of course.

[The writ of habeas corpus is the] birthright of the people, subject to such provisions as the law has established for granting [it]. . . . Those provisions are not a check upon justice, but a wise and provident direction of it. . . .

There is no such thing in the law, as writs of grace and favour issuing from the Judges: they are all writs of right; but they are not writs of course.

Writs of course, are those writs which lie between party and party, for the commencement of civil suits: and if they are sued without good foundation, the common law punishes the plaintiff for suing out the writ vexatiously, by amercing him "pro falso clamore." And by statute law, he is to pay the costs of the suit.

But the writ of habeas corpus is not the commencement of a civil suit, where the party proceeds at the peril of costs, if his complaint is a groundless one: it is a remedial mandatory writ. . . . And, as all these remedial mandatory writs were, originally, rather the suits of the King than of the subject, the King's Courts of Justice would not suffer them to issue upon a mere suggestion; but upon some proof of a wrong and injury done to a subject.[14]

Once probable ground was shown that the party was committed for no crime, or that he was imprisoned for a crime by a person or an organ lacking jurisdiction, habeas corpus became a matter of right. If doubt existed whether a crime was committed or not, or whether the party was committed by a competent jurisdiction, or there appeared to be a bailable crime, habeas corpus again would be granted as a matter of right. In the former instances, the party would be discharged; in the latter instance, bail was allowed.

The common law of England dealt with this writ so liberally, that the decision of one court or magistrate to refuse to release the prisoner, was no bar to the issuing of a second, or third, or additional writ by another court or magistrate having jurisdiction of the case.[15] The underlying reason for the rule that *res judicata* had no application to habeas proceedings was that since no appeal against a refusal to issue the writ or to discharge the prisoner was available, it would have been intolerable for a person to have the legality of his custody determined conclusively by the first judicial body to hear the matter.[16]

Although the frame of government and the politico-constitutional situation of the American system have necessitated alterations in the scope and function of the writ, its general nature and basic purpose have gone unchanged. Applying the principle that "for the meaning of the term habeas corpus, resort may unquestionably be had to the common law," which he had articulated twenty-three years earlier,[17] Mr. Chief Justice John Marshall, in *Ex parte Watkins*,[18] stated: "The writ of habeas corpus is a high prerogative writ, known to the common law, the great object of which is the liberation of those who may be imprisoned without sufficient cause. It is in the nature of a writ of error, to examine the legality of the commitment."[19] The writ operates precisely as its English model: the writ is directed to a person detaining another, commanding him to produce the body of the prisoner at a designated time and place, to state the day and cause of his capture and detention, to do, submit to, and receive whatever the court or judge awarding the writ shall consider in that behalf.[20] Its "most important result" is that it affords "a swift and imperative remedy in all cases of illegal restraint upon personal liberty."[21] Although prior to its introduction into the legal system of the United States habeas corpus developed most rapidly in response to the abuses of the executive office, it exists in the American structure as a palladium for every person "from being [illegally[22]] detained, restrained, or confined by any branch or agency of government."[23]

The writ does not issue as a matter of course.[24] The court or judge may refuse to grant it where no probable ground for relief is shown in the petition,[25] but where probable ground is shown, the writ of habeas corpus becomes a writ of right, which may not be denied.[26] The principle of *res judicata* does not apply to habeas corpus litigation in the American courts.[27] The courts, however, have found nothing in the tradition of habeas corpus that requires them to tolerate needless litigation, or to entertain collateral proceedings whose only purpose is to vex, harass, or delay.[28] Habeas corpus will be denied where the issues have been previously adjudicated.[29] Moreover, habeas corpus is an "extraordinary" remedy,[30] reserved for those situations where other relief is not practically available.[31]

Before its introduction into the American legal system, habeas corpus had been "esteemed the best and only sufficient defense of personal liberty."[32] Blackstone called it "another Magna Carta."[33] In the United States, the writ continues as the "symbol and guardian of individual liberty."[34] As such, a liberal judicial attitude has been considered appropriate in its administration.[35] The American judiciary has been aware of the progressive development of the writ in England. The writ's propensity for liberal growth was accelerated by the American constitutional and legal system. Mr. Chief Justice Chase, in *Ex parte Yerger*,[36] wrote: "the great spirit and genius of our institution has tended to the widening and enlarging of the habeas corpus jurisdiction of the courts and judges of the United States." Mr. Justice Black a century later observed: "[Habeas corpus] is not now and never has been a static, narrow, formalistic remedy; its scope has grown to achieve its grand purpose—the protection of the individual against erosion of their right to be free from wrongful restraints upon their liberty."[37] Consequently, the Supreme Court in 1973 acknowledged that "[w]hile the 'rhetoric celebrating habeas corpus has changed little over the centuries,' it is nevertheless true that the functions of the writ have undergone dramatic changes."[38]

Despite the fact that the Supreme Court has often looked to legal history for guidance in habeas cases, heretofore no book has been published on the history of the Great Writ. This is not to say that legal scholars have neglected habeas corpus, for the writ inspires many articles every year. Nevertheless, the development of this legal process has not been the subject of a systematic study. In examining habeas corpus, many legal historians have confined their study to identifying the intent of those who formulated the constitutional and statutory provisions regulating habeas corpus.[39] They have viewed history as an event rather than as a process and therefore have failed to take note of the most striking characteristic of the writ of habeas corpus: like liberty itself, the writ is the product of continuous creation.

To fully appreciate this characteristic, it is necessary to begin with an exploration of the origin of the writ of habeas corpus in

English law and to trace the writ's development from a prerogative process into the subject's most celebrated judicial mechanism.
In addition to emphasizing the writ's most important feature, this
discussion is required because many earlier writers have found it
necessary to perpetuate the myth that habeas corpus developed
primarily to protect the liberty of the subject. In fact, the writ's
evolution can be explained by (to borrow from Adam Smith's
Wealth of Nations) the "invisible hand" of constitutional law—
that is, the various departments of English government, by attempting to extend and secure the bounds of their own jurisdiction, enhanced the value of habeas corpus to the subject's liberty.

Before turning to the federal writ, this study will look at the
adoption of habeas corpus by the American colonies and confederation states, for it was during this period that the writ was
cleansed of its peculiar history and recognized as a most efficacious means of safeguarding individual liberty. Further, a study of
the use of the writ in the colonial and confederation periods is
essential to uncovering the original intent of the habeas clause of
the federal Constitution. It is only by knowing the facility with
which the state writs issued at that time that one begins to question today's understanding of the habeas clause.

It is most likely that the framers of the Constitution intended
the habeas clause to restrict *Congress* from suspending *state* habeas
for *federal* prisoners. That meaning, however, can no longer be
ascribed to the clause. The "invisible hand" of constitutional law
has continued to exert an influence on the writ. Political struggles
between the departments of the national government and shifting
notions of federalism have transformed the meaning of the clause
so that today it is generally interpreted as somehow guaranteeing a
federal writ.

Underlying the purpose of the habeas clause was the fear of
federal government. Because state habeas was secured against federal interference, it was unnecessary to provide federal habeas for
state prisoners. To effectuate federal policy, however, federal
habeas was gradually extended to state cases. Thus Congress has
also employed habeas corpus to alter the balance of the federal
structure. To ensure the fine tuning of that balance and to effectuate the goal of finality, the Court created the rule of exhaustion and

has employed that rule to obtain the desired mix of liberty, federal supremacy, and finality.

The transformation of the habeas clause and the extension of federal habeas to state prisoners has been accompanied by the expansion of the use to which habeas corpus has been put. Habeas corpus is no longer confined to questioning the jurisdictional competency of the committing agent. Gradually, the issues cognizable on habeas corpus have been extended to constitutional and some nonconstitutional federal questions. In addition, the use of habeas corpus is no longer confined to release from "custody" as defined in 1789. Not only are forms of custody, not recognized as such at the time the words "habeas corpus" were inserted into the Constitution, now subject to attack by habeas, but the writ today is not limited to effecting immediate or absolute release.

Because I have implicitly conceded the legitimacy of constitutional change, the reader may find confusing the identification of technical errors in many of the Court's opinions. The analysis in no way is intended to challenge the constitutional standing of those decisions but is intended, rather, to highlight the power of constitutional change. In spite of the numerous technical obstacles, habeas corpus has managed to become and to remain the great palladium of individual liberty without the use of the formal amendment procedure. The normative questions concerning the legitimacy of constitutional change are beyond the scope of this work. The question under consideration here is the empirical one: which factors were responsible for the development of the writ of habeas corpus?

NOTES

1. DeSmith, "The Prerogative Writs," 11 Cambridge L. J. 40, 52-53 (1951).
2. 79 Eng. Rep. 465, 466: "that the privilege of the Cinque-Ports, that the King's writ runs not there, is to be intended between party and party; but no such privilege can be against the King: *and this writ is a prerogative writ*, which concerns the King's justice to be administered to his subjects: for the King ought to have an account why any of his subjects are imprisoned: and it is agreeable to all persons and places. . . ." (emphasis added). The Chief Justice was employing the term here to emphasize the extensive territorial ambit of the writ. *See also* 81 Eng. Rep. 975.

3. Chap. 1, *Infra*.

4. DeSmith, "The Prerogative Writs," 11 Cambridge L. J. 40, 53.

5. *See* Wilmot, J., "Opinion on the Writ of Habeas Corpus," 97 Eng. Rep. 29, 43 (1758).

6. *Rex v. Smith*, 27 Eng. Rep. 787 (1736).

7. Joseph Chitty, *A Practical Treatise on Criminal Law* (London: Samuel Brooke, 1826), vol. 1, p. 118.

8. *Rex v. Cowle*, 97 Eng. Rep. 587, 599 (1759).

9. *Rex v. Heath*, 18 St. Tr. 1, 19 (1744).

10. *Jenkes Case*, 6 St. Tr. 1190, 1207-1208 (1676).

11. *Anon.*, 124 Eng. Rep. 928 (1671).

12. Wilmot, "Opinion," 97 Eng. Rep. 29.

13. Ibid., p. 32.

14. Ibid., pp. 32, 33, 36.

15. *See Bonham's Case*, 77 Eng. Rep. 658 (1609).

16. R. J. Sharpe, *The Law of Habeas Corpus* (Oxford: Oxford Univ. Press, 1976) p. 195. Cf. however, *In re Hastings* (No. 2) [1959] 1 Q. B. 358 (1958), and 8 and 9 Elizabeth II c. 65, sect. 14(2) (1960).

17. *Ex parte Bollman*, 4 Cranch 75, 94 (1807).

18. 3 Peters 193 (1830).

19. Ibid., p. 202.

20. *Price v. Johnston*, 334 U.S. 266, 283 (1947). *See also In re Dierks*, 55 F.2d 371 (1932); *Doss v. Lindsley*, 53 F. Supp. 427 (1944); *In re Rowland*, 85 F. Supp. 550 (1949); *Brooks v. State of Tennessee*, 256 F. Supp. 807 (1966), rev'd on other grounds 381 F.2d 619 (1967); *Harvey v. State of South Carolina*, 310 F. Supp. 83 (1970).

21. *Price v. Johnston*, 334 U.S. 266, 283 (1947). *See also Fay v. Noia*, 372 U.S. 391 (1963); *Carafas v. LaVallee*, 391 U.S. 234 (1968); *Prieser v. Rodriguez*, 411 U.S. 475 (1973); *Morgan v. State of Tennessee*, 298 F. Supp. 581 (1969).

22. *See* chap. 5, *infra*.

23. *Scagges v. Lt. General Stanley Larsen*, 396 U.S. 1206, 1208 (1969).

24. *Ex parte Frederich*, 149 U.S. 70 (1892). *See also In re Boardman*, 169 U.S. 39, 43 (1898).

25. *In re Keeler*, 14 Fed. Cas. 173 (1843); *In re Taylor*, 23 Fed. Cas. 728 (1879).

26. *In re Winder*, 30 Fed. Cas. 288 (1862).

27. *See* authorities cited in *Fay v. Noia*, 372 U.S. 391, 423; Cf. however, 28 U.S.C. section 2244 and John J. Parker, "Limiting the Abuse of Habeas Corpus," 8 F. R. D. 171, 174 (1948).

28. *La Clair v. United States*, 241 F. Supp. 819 (1965).

29. *Harris v. Tahash*, 353 F.2d 119 (1965).

30. *Goto v. Lane*, 265 U.S. 393 (1924).

31. *Hensley v. Municipal Court, San Jose—Milpitas Judicial District*, 411 U.S. 345 (1973); *United States ex rel. Caputo v. Sharpe*, 282 F. Supp. 362 (1968). *See also Aubut v. State of Maine*, 431 F.2d 688 (1970); *Bernier v. Moore*, 441 F.2d 395 (1971).

32. *Ex parte Yerger*, 75 U.S. 85, 95 (1868).

33. William Blackstone, *Commentaries on the Law of England* (Oxford, 1770), vol. 3, p. 136.

34. *Peyton v. Rowe*, 391 U.S. 54, 59 (1968).

35. *Steward v. Overholser*, 186 F.2d 339 (1950).

36. 75 U.S. 85, 102 (1868).

37. *Jones v. Cunningham*, 371 U.S. 236, 243 (1963).

38. *Hensley v. Municipal Court, San Jose—Milpitas Judicial District*, 411 U.S. 345, 349 (1973).

39. *See e.g.* Mayers, "The Habeas Corpus Act of 1867: The Supreme Court as Legal Historian," 33 U. Chi. L. Rev. 31 (1965); Oaks, "Legal History in the High Court," 64 U. Mich. L. Rev. 451 (1966); Pascal, "Habeas Corpus and the Constitution," 1970 Duke L. J. 605.

English Origins of the Writ of Habeas Corpus: A Peculiar Path to Fame

INTRODUCTION

This chapter searches out the origin of habeas corpus and traces its development through the seventeenth century. It is a study that finds a precept compelling appearance being transformed into a great writ of liberty. This transformation was, for the most part, the result of the unconscious forces of constitutional law. In an effort to correct the injustices of the inferior courts, during the fourteenth century the central courts utilized the thirteenth century summoning process, along with an order requesting the cause of imprisonment. The commands eventually united to form the *habeas corpus cum causa.* This writ was in turn used by the superior common-law courts in the fifteenth, sixteenth, and seventeenth centuries to counter the encroaching jurisdiction of the equity and ecclesiastical courts and the various councils. The arguments developed in those cases were later enhanced and employed by the parliamentary leaders in their struggle for power against the Crown during the seventeenth century. That habeas corpus was not developed primarily for "the liberty of the subject" is at no time more obvious than in the latter years of the seventeenth century.

THE HUMBLE ORIGINS OF THE GREAT WRIT

The noted seventeenth-century legal commentator Sir Edward Coke observed that, by the writ of habeas corpus, "it manifestly appeareth, that no man ought to be imprisoned but for some certain cause: and these words, Ad subjiciend' Et recipiend', &c. [to do, submit to, and receive whatsoever the judge or court awarding such writ shall consider in that behalf] prove that cause must be shewed: for otherwise how can the Court take order therein according to Law."[1] In tracing the origin of habeas corpus, subsequent legal scholars—ignoring Coke's role in the transformation of this "high prerogative writ"[2] into the "great and efficacious writ"[3] used as the "engine for defeating the king's own orders"[4]—have perpetuated the myth that the writ of habeas corpus originated and developed primarily to protect the English subject from illegal imprisonment.[5] The writ's putative origins were further colored by its modern function as the guardian of individual liberty.[6]

In 1902, Edward Jenks published a short article advancing a "most embarrassing discovery."[7] Jenks suggested that "the writ of *Habeas Corpus* was originally intended not to get people out of prison, *but to put them in it.*"[8] Jenks was wrong.[9] His mistake, however, has alerted us to begin our investigation of "the most celebrated writ in the English law"[10] not by rehearsing the rhetoric that extols it, but rather by examining the meaning of the words "habeas corpus."[11]

The words "habeas corpus" indicate a command by some individual in authority requiring that the recipient of the command, presumably a person having the capacity to exert control over the subject of the precept, bring a certain party before the directing officer. In early Anglo-Saxon England, when justice was dispensed under the principles of the "blood-feud," satisfaction for the transgression of a perceived right was exacted by the injured party or, in the event he were killed, by the next of kin.[12] As the social unit shifted from the family to the clan, the clan patriarch became the de facto magistrate to whom the jurisdiction of protection belonged.[13] His duty was to warrant the safety of the clan unit and to insure the vindication of a wrong done any of his clansmen.[14] Conversely, if one of the clan was the aggressor, the clan chief and clan had either to surrender the offender or to bear the feud.[15] As the notion of the overriding interest of the "state" in keeping the peace began to emerge, the "blood-feud" was gradually replaced by the system of *wergeld* (the price set upon the life and bodily faculties of a man), and a system of compensation replaced revenge.[16] Gradually, judicial procedures developed to implement the *wergeld* system.

In the laws of King Ine (688-725 A.D.), the general principle of the new order was laid down: "If anyone exacts redress, before he pleads for justice, he shall give up what he has taken, and pay as much again, and 30 shillings compensation."[17] The aim of the Anglo-Saxon code in general was to restrain private vengeance.[18] Even a thief caught in the act could not be summarily dealt with[19] unless he resisted appearing before the judicial body or tried to escape from custody.[20] Implementation of the new order required that a mechanism be developed to ensure appearance before the "courts of law" and to guarantee the payment of *wergeld*. To meet this need the *borh* (pledge or surety) system, founded upon the traditional principles of the blood-feud, began to emerge: one man became responsible for the appearance and compliance of another.[21]

Because the success of the *wergeld* system entirely depended on the individual's submission to the judicial tribunal, his appearance before the court was essential. If an individual, when summoned, failed to attend the *gemot* (court) three times, he was obliged to pay the king's *oferhyrnes* (fine for contempt).[22] If he continued to disregard the authority of the *gemot* and refused to pay the *oferhyrnes*, the chief men, belonging to the *burh* (fortress), were to distrain him of his property and place him in *borh*.[23] Indicative of the importance that the Normans later attached to presence before the court were the *Leges Henrici Primi*, which stated that: "No judgment shall be given in a doubtful case or when the accused is absent."[24]

NORMAN CENTRALIZATION OF THE JUDICIAL SYSTEM

When the Normans arrived in England in 1066, they found no central court system.[25] Even the "national system of local courts" was largely overshadowed by the small private franchise units.[26] The absence of a central administration was discordant with the Norman notion that justice flowed from the king. To implement this notion, William the Conqueror introduced the *Curia Regis* (king's council) and the royal *missi* (itinerant justices),[27] but left the local courts standing.[28] Broad civil and criminal jurisdiction was given to the *Curia*,[29] which was therefore eventually able to transcend the former localized court system.[30]

For William's centralization of the court system to be effective, uniform procedures, including a standard form of precept to compel a defendant's appearance, were necessary. Such a precept, or *breve*,[31] was not a novel instrument.[32] Originally, it was a short, written command issued by an official, and tested (signed) or sealed by him in proof of its authenticity.[33] The King's *breve*, established after the conquest, soon replaced all inferior writs.[34] It was directed to the sheriff of the county where the defendant lived and commanded him to summon the party to appear at a particular court.[35]

The *missi*, as the administrators of the King's justice, were first sent out on circuit by William.[36] Initially, their circuits were irregular, but under Henry II the *missi* became an organized body of legal administrators traveling regularly throughout the country.[37] They were to administer the Assize of Clarendon[38] (1166) and the Assize of Northampton[39] (1176).[40]

In the Assize of Clarendon, the first great legislative enactment of Henry II, the visitation of itinerant justices was made regular.[41] Moreover, there one finds an early version of the command "have the body":

> 4. And when a robber or murderer or thief or receiver of them has been arrested . . . if the justices are not about to come speedily enough into the county where they have been taken, let the sheriffs send word to the nearest justice by some well-informed person that they have arrested such men, and the justices shall send back word to the sheriffs informing them where they desire the men to be brought before them; and let the sheriffs bring them before the justices.[42]

The form of the judicial communication was most probably written and sealed. Thus, the sheriff was to be ordered, probably *via* writ judicial, to have the body of the accused brought before the justices. The Assize of Northampton added forgery and arson to the crimes enumerated in the Assize of Clarendon warranting arrest.[43]

The Crown, probably motivated by the emoluments accruing,[44] developed an intense interest in having those accused of the above crimes present before its justices. In addition, the failure of the suretyship of the tithing[45] to maintain the peace undoubtedly played no small part in the extension of sovereign control.[46] Most infractions, however, remained offenses against the individual. An accusation charging commission of crime was, for the most part, still a private matter, and although the procedure was coordinated by the rules of the Crown's courts, the complainant was master of his own process.

The extension of judicial control, through the fiction of the King's Peace, was evident in the civil jurisdiction as well as the criminal. The most striking indication of the development of the Crown's control in the civil area was the use of writs of liberty. Among the remedies available to an individual seeking deliverance from imprisonment of a public or private nature were the writ *de Homine Replegiando*, the writ *de Manucaptione*, and the writ *de Odio et Atia*.[47]

Another manifestation of the expansion of the Crown's power was the strict procedure followed in the mesne process in personal actions. This process, implemented shortly before the thirteenth century,[48] is described in Bracton's *De Legibus et Consuetudinibus Angliae*.[49] The primary step in the process was a writ of summons. If the defendant failed to answer it, the sheriff was directed to put him under gage (bail) and pledges (sureties) so "that he should appear before our justiciaries at Westminster" on a specified day.[50] If he failed to appear after the first attachment, a writ to attach by better gage and pledges was issued.[51] Upon the third default, the procedure, in Bracton's words, continued as follows:

> A. presented himself on the fourth day against B., and B. did not come, &c., and made several defaults, so that he was at first attached through C. and D., and secondly through E. and F., and accordingly all the sureties are amerciable [subject to fine], and there is reason, because they are not to be further summoned in order to show wherefore they have not produced him as they pledged themselves to do; and then let it be enjoined to the viscount [sheriff] that he produce his body ["et tunc praecipietur vicecomiti quod habeat corpus"] on another day by a writ of this kind: The king to the viscount greeting. We enjoin you that you produce before our justiciaries, &c. on such a day the body of A., to answer to B.

> concerning such a plea . . . , according to the form of the
> original writ, and at the end is added this clause, in order to
> hear his judgment concerning several defaults, and produce
> there his writ.[52]

After the third default the sheriff was thus made responsible for
the production of the defendant's body before the court through a
writ of *habeas corpus ad respondendum* (have the body to answer.)[53] If the sheriff could not find the defendant, he returned the
writ: *"non inventus est"*[54] (he is not found). This writ of *habeas
corpus ad respondendum*[55] was firmly established by 1230.[56]

STREAMLINING THE PROCESS

The process described by Bracton continued to function until
the middle of the thirteenth century.[57] In the mid-1250s, however,
recognition that the Bractonian process was too slow inspired the
courts to begin consolidating the procedure.[58] In the year 1256, on
the assize rolls for the county of Northumberland, the following
mandate directed to the sheriff appears: "quod distringat eum per
omnes terres . . . Et quod habeat corpus. . . ." (to distrain him of
all [his] lands and [in this way] have [his] body.[59] Numerous
examples of this union of habeas corpus and distraint are to be
found in *Placitorum Abbreviatio.* [60]

The trend toward aggregation of the steps in the Bractonian
process was continued by the executive and legislative branches
in the Statute of Marlborough.[61] For example, the sanction applied
against those lords who should act contrary to the law in one
type of action[62] was as follows:

> [T]he Lords shall be attached to appear in the King's Court
> at a short Day, to make answer thereto, and shall have but
> one Essoin [excuse] therein, if they be within the Realm; and
> immediately the Beasts, or other Distresses taken by this
> Occasion, shall be delivered to the Plaintiff, and so shall re-
> main, until the Plea betwixt them be determined. And if the
> Lords of the Courts which took Distresses, come not at the
> Day that they were attached, or do not keep the Day given
> to them by Essoin, then the Sheriff shall be commanded to

cause them to come at another Day; at which Day, if they come not, then he shall be commanded to distrain them by all their Goods and Chattels. . . .[63]

The Statute of Marlborough also provided that in pleas of *Quare impedit* (wherefore he hinders), if the disturber defaulted on the first day of the summons and cast no essoin, he was to be attached.[64] If the attachment proved ineffective, he was distrained by the "grand distraint" (distraint of all goods and chattels).[65] The chapter went on to provide that "The same Law, as to the making of Attachments, shall from henceforth be observed in all Writs where Attachments lie, as in making Distresses, so that the second Attachment shall be made by better Pledges, and afterwards the last Distress" (grand distraint).[66] The movement to curtail the lengthy mesne process continued in the reign of Edward I. His first major piece of legislation, the Statute of Westminster I, provided:

Concerning Delays in all Manner of Writs and Attachments, it is thus provided, That if the Tenant or Defendant, after the first Attachments returned, make Default, that incontinent the [grand] Distress shall be awarded; and if the Sheriff do not make sufficient Return by a certain Day, he shall be grieviously amerced. . . .[67]

Although the process was substantially streamlined, its objective remained the same, namely, to secure the appearance of an unwilling defendant. The grand distress was effective against defendants such as Hugh of Eure who in 1273, in a plea commenced by William de Valencia on a claim that Hugh wrongfully detained him of five hundred marks, failed to come to the court on the day appointed; after several defaults, the sheriff was ordered to "distrain him by all his lands . . . and to have his body here in the quindene of St. John the Baptist."[68] But distraint could hardly compel the appearance of a reluctant, propertyless defendant, and so the *capias ita habeas corpus* (arrest and in this way have the body) developed to complement *quod distringat . . . et habeas corpus* (distrain [him of his lands] and [in this way] have [his] body).

In the 1245 case of *Rad de Planaz v. Galfr Page*,[69] for example, after the defendant failed to answer the summons and then defaulted on the attachments, the sheriff was ordered "capiat eu, &c. & salvo, &c. Ita qd habeat corpus, &c. in octab, &c." (arrest him, etc. and keep him safely, etc. and in this way have his body, etc. in October, etc.).[70] The writ thus instructed the sheriff to have the body of the defendant before the justices and also provided the sheriff with directions on how to accomplish the task—that is, by arresting him.[71]

Under the earlier habeas corpus, the sheriff alone was responsible for the defendant's appearance. If the sheriff released the party to sureties, that fact would not provide a legitimate return, and the sheriff would be amerced.[72] The sheriff, however, could easily afford the occasional expense of such a system for he had learned to insure himself against such business losses by demanding payment for releasing individuals to surety.[73] Under the new form of habeas corpus *(capias ita habeas corpus)*, the sheriff fulfilled his responsibility upon arrest. This new writ thus legitimized the return by the sheriff that he was unable to do as the writ instructed because he had let the defendant to mainprise or bail, since the common law gave the sheriff discretion to allow mainprise or bail in such cases.[74] If the defendant were released to surety, the names of the pledges were supplied to the court on return of the writ of habeas corpus and in cases of non-appearance they were amerced.[75]

HABEAS AND CAPIAS

A difference of opinion exists as to the breadth of the common law's authorization of arrest and imprisonment. While it has generally been accepted that in crimes alleging force the common law did provide for arrest and imprisonment, early legal commentators maintained that in actions where force was not alleged there was no such process.[76] In 1784, John Reeves, in his *History of the English Law*, argued that these earlier writers were mistaken.[77] He equated the third step in the Bractonian process, *habeas corpus ad respondendum*, with the writ of capias.[78] Reeves' thesis received support many years later when Professor Edward Jenks agreed that "under the more familiar name of *Capias,* the writ of *Habeas Corpus* plays a normal part in almost every personal action."[79] The

Reeves-Jenks assertion highlights a question that must be answered in order to understand correctly the development of the habeas writ: did habeas corpus at some period serve the same function as capias—that is, the arrest and imprisonment of an individual?

Jenks' argument was inspired by his apparent failure to locate examples of *habeas corpus ad respondendum* in the late thirteenth century and during a great part of the fourteenth century.[80] He maintained that the writ, in its habeas corpus form, was supplanted for a time by its form as a capias.[81] He found support for his thesis in the existence of *alias* (second) and pluries (third) habeas corpus, arguing that they developed when the writ existed in the form of a capias because arrest was difficult to accomplish and so repeated orders had to be issued.[82] Jenks concluded that, "whatever may have been its ultimate use, the writ of *Habeas Corpus* was originally intended not to get people out of prison, *but to put them in it.*"[83]

Sir John C. Fox rejected the Reeves-Jenks theory and contended that *habeas corpus ad respondendum* and capias, by their very terms, were dissimilar:

> Under the *capias* . . . the sheriff arrests the defendant, and detains him in a safe place until he brings him into Court. This involves imprisonment, subject to bail, for some days may elapse before the defendant is brought into Court. Bracton points to the distinction between *habeas corpus* and a writ which authorizes imprisonment when, in describing the errors that a sheriff may fall into, he suggests by way of example that, having been ordered to produce the defendant's body *(quod habeas corpus)*, the sheriff may return that he has attached him by pledges or *has committed him by his bailiff.* The *habeas corpus* is for the protection of the defendant, not for his punishment; it requires the sheriff to bring him into Court because the law considers that justice cannot be done between the parties in the absence of either of them.[84]

It is true that the Bractonian process did not expressly provide for any imprisonment upon mesne process—there were no instructions given to the sheriff to "arrest" the body; the precept was "to have the body." Pollock and Maitland noted, however, that although there was no provision for imprisonment at common law in cases where no force was alleged, "the *Habeas corpus* would . . . justify the sheriff in arresting the defendant when the court-day was approaching in order to bring him into court."[85] Indeed, the importance the common law attached to the appearance of a defendant before the court, illustrated by the mesne process, suggests the likelihood of arrest at *any* time before the court-appointed day. At the third stage in the mesne process the court was applying the power of the office of sheriff to ensure the defendant's appearance.[86] If habeas corpus allowed seizure only as the court day was approaching, as Pollock and Maitland suggested, it would have failed to invest the sheriff with sufficient power to perform his responsibility: given such a warning, the defendant could easily arrange to be beyond the reach of the writ just as the court day approached.[87]

Seizure pursuant to a writ of *habeas corpus ad respondendum* was thus not arrest in a technical sense; it did not order imprisonment, and therefore a return by the sheriff informing the court that he could not produce the seized party in court because he had let the party to pledges was insufficient.[88] Although the court recognized that due to the cost, trouble, and frequent impossibility of keeping prisoners secure pending trial[89] the sheriff would allow the party to remain at large if sufficient pledges were available, this recognition did not provide the sheriff with a legitimate excuse for the party's absence on the appointed day. Releasing the party to pledges merely provided the sheriff with insurance to cover the amercement that would be levied on him in the event he did not produce the seized party.[90] By contrast, capias,[91] which had existed independently before it was united with habeas corpus in some cases in the mid-thirteenth century, operated together with habeas corpus to provide explicit directions to the sheriff for accomplishing the task of producing the defendant assigned to him by the court.[92] It therefore legitimized the return that the body was not brought because the seized party had been released to pledges. The pledges were now made directly responsible to the court.[93]

Although *habeas corpus ad respondendum* and capias shared a certain resemblance and at certain periods interacted, they were thus distinct. Jenks' reasons for equating capias and habeas corpus were unfounded: his inability to find habeas corpus during the first half of the fourteenth century was merely a limitation of his day, as an examination of the plea rolls now available attests.[94] Moreover, Jenks was mistaken in arguing that, "whatever may have been its ultimate use, the writ of *Habeas Corpus* was not to get people out of prison, *but to put them in it.*"[95] Although that was one possible outcome of a trial, the intended purpose of the writ itself was merely to secure appearance after more lenient methods had failed. An investigation not limited to the records of the court of common pleas reveals that the purpose of the command "habeas corpus" was broader than that ascribed by Jenks. The barons of the exchequer court employed habeas corpus for the same purpose as did the court of common pleas in the mesne process in personal actions.[96] Such was also the intended purpose of courts when the command was used to gather a jury.[97] Obviously, the habeas corpus in this case was not to put the jurors in jail.

As the Assize of Clarendon indicates, habeas corpus was also employed in the public sector from an early date.[98] The *Case of Aldus uxor Otte Flandrensis*[99] and *Baldwin Tyrel's Case*[100] provide examples. Aldus Flandrensis was arrested in Lincoln on a charge of possessing counterfeit currency.[101] She escaped and fled to York, where she was rearrested and delivered to the gaoler of York.[102] A writ was then issued to "have the body" of Aldus Flandrensis returned to Lincoln so that justice might be done.[103] The writ served here as a document of extradition. In the course of Baldwin Tyrel's trial, three varieties of the writ of habeas corpus were used. The first directed the sheriff to produce Tyrel before the court to answer the charge of " 'denouncing' the King's death," levied against him by Ranulf of Devonsby and Gilbert of Girmunville.[104] The sheriff was also told to summon Ranulf and Gilbert so that they might prosecute their appeal.[105] On the court day, the sheriff produced Tyrel; however, Ranulf and Gilbert failed to appear.[106] Because the suit concerned the king's person, and because Tyrel had paid twenty shillings in order that a record of the appeal initiated against him might come before the justices at Westminster, along with the record of appeal that he had earlier brought against the same Ranulf and Gilbert and others for breach of the king's peace, the sheriff was ordered to have a record of the appeal made at Westminster on the first Sunday of the Lent Term and to have the bodies of Ranulf and Gilbert brought before the court to prosecute their appeal.[107]

From the record of the trial, it appears that Ranulf and Gilbert initiated their appeal to impede an earlier claim alleging false imprisonment and breach of the king's peace brought against them by Tyrel.[108] After testimony substantiating Tyrel's claim was taken in the county court, Ranulf and Gilbert were assigned to the custody of Henry of Pomeroy and Alan of Dunstanville, codefendants in the case brought by Tyrel, and their bodies, lands, and tenements were attached.[109] Upon being summoned into court, Ranulf and Gilbert *essoined* themselves but the court held that because they were in custody, no *essoin* lay.[110] The sheriff was therefore ordered at the bench, orally and by writ judicial, "to have the bodies of Gilbert and Ranulf at Westminster."[111] The *Tyrel* court thus made use of the precept "habeas corpus" to command the presence of a defendant, in the custody of the sheriff, and that of the accusers required to prosecute the suit and, finally, to command the sheriff to produce the bodies of individuals in the custody of pledges. Examples are also found during this period of the writ of habeas corpus issuing to private persons, commanding them to bring before the court the bodies of persons under their control.[112]

In sum, the two-word command "habeas corpus," which was issued by the various judicial officers of the Crown, was directed to both ministerial officers and private persons, and was relied on in both public and private law. Its objective was a simple one: to compel appearance. It was, indeed, the Crown's prerogative writ.

HABEAS CORPUS IN THE FOURTEENTH CENTURY: A STEP FORWARD FOR THE SUBJECT'S LIBERTY

During the fourteenth century, the purpose of the writ of habeas corpus remained unchanged, and it continued to be very much the Crown's prerogative writ.[113] But a new development, best illustrated by case law, was taking place. In the Year Books of Edward

III for the year 1340, one discovers a very early example of the combined use of the writ of habeas corpus and the writ of certiorari.[114] The case concerned a recognizance on the Statute of Merchants[115] made to the plaintiff by three persons.[116] The plaintiff sued for a certification, and the sheriff was directed to arrest the three.[117] Although the sheriff had to return that two of the defendants could not be found, one was arrested and imprisoned.[118] The imprisoned defendant petitioned for a writ of certiorari to bring the matter into Chancery, alleging that the plaintiff had executed a release to him.[119] In response to the petition, a writ of habeas corpus was issued by Chancery, directed to the sheriff, commanding him to have the body of the defendant brought before the justices on a certain day, "if he [the defendant] be detained for that reason and no other."[120] A writ also issued for the sheriff to summon the plaintiff and to cause the defendants at large to come.[121] On the appointed day, the sheriff produced the imprisoned defendant as instructed.[122] The plaintiff was also present, but the other defendants were not.[123] After submitting his plea, the defendant was released to sureties to await trial.[124]

The purpose of the writ issued in this case was similar to that of the *habeas corpus ad respondendum* in that it commanded the sheriff "to have the body" of the defendant. But there were two critical differences: first, the proceeding was instituted on the petition of the prisoner; and second, it was implicit in the court's action that it intended to examine the cause of the imprisonment.[125] The court thus assumed a right to inquire into the nature of an incarceration, and the inference is inescapable that it intended, on the basis of its findings, to do what it deemed just.

Again in 1343, on the petition of a prisoner, the Chancery issued a writ of habeas corpus.[126] The prisoner had petitioned for an *audita querela* (initial process in an action brought by a defendant to obtain relief against the consequences of an adverse judgment) and the court responded by directing the sheriff "d'aver le corps icy" (to have his body here).[127] Again, the prisoner's body was ordered to be brought before the court at his own request. By the middle of the fourteenth century, the use of habeas corpus in response to petitions on behalf of prisoners that they might be presented before the court was sufficiently common to have become a distinct form of habeas corpus: *habeas corpus cum causa*, or simply, *corpus cum causa*.[128] The writ ordered the sheriff to have the body of the prisoner brought before the court along with the cause of his arrest and detention.[129] Its significance is that it presupposed a detention. Although the writ of habeas corpus demanding the presence of a prisoner had issued to sheriffs as early as the thirteenth century,[130] whether the defendant was incarcerated had been irrelevant before the origin of the *cum causa* form of habeas corpus.

Habeas corpus cum causa was, in fact, an aggregation of two existing writs: habeas corpus, and a writ questioning the cause of a prisoner's custody. The latter writ surfaced in cases as early as the mid-1320s. In a 1326 case, the King's Bench issued a writ to the sheriff demanding the cause for detaining a prisoner.[131] The cause was found insufficient and the prisoner was let to mainprise.[132] Significantly, the body of the prisoner was not ordered brought before the court. In 1327, the Parliament directed a writ to Johem de Glenton, demanding him to "show cause" why he had arrested the Abbot de Jude.[133] The writ concluded with the precept: *"Et si comperiatur quod causa non fuit rationabilis, tunc deliberetur, ..."* (And if it is learned that the cause is not rational, then he will be delivered).[134] In 1332, the King's Bench issued a writ asking the cause of Peter of Hangleton's imprisonment.[135] The writ was returned explaining that Peter was accused of murder. [136] Because the court had no record of any murder indictment, or of any other cause for which Peter could be arraigned, the steward, marshal, and coroner were instructed to search their rolls, and if any indictment were found, to send it before the court.[137] In the meantime, Peter was released to sureties.[138]

The use of the new aggregate writ, *habeas corpus cum causa*, is illustrated by cases in 1351, 1383, and 1388. In 1351, a prisoner held at Newgate sued out an *audita querela*.[139] The court then issued a writ of *habeas corpus cum causa* to the sheriff of London.[140] At this time there was no explicit statement of what the court intended to do beyond examination of the cause. In the second case, a *corpus cum causa* was directed to the mayor of London on March 2, 1383, ordering him to send one Peter Gracyan of

Lombard, then imprisoned at Newgate, before the Council at West-minster, together with "the cause of his taking and detaining."[141] The writ was returned stating that Peter had been imprisoned in August 1382 in a plea of account between himself and Luke Braga-dyn, merchant of Venice, for default on a debt,[142] and that he was therefore detained "in accordance with the custom of the city and the law merchant."[143] In 1388, in the third case, John Milner peti-tioned the court for a writ of *corpus cum causa*, alleging that he had been the beneficiary of a pardon, and further, that prior to this present petition he had had a writ of Privy Seal directed to the mayor of London for his deliverance.[144] But before the writ was delivered to the mayor, Milner was tricked into signing a confes-sion.[145] He therefore petitioned the court to have the bodies of all parties involved in the case brought before it, so that the court might "examine . . . and . . . search out the truth of this matter, and thereupon to do what law and right demand. . . ."[146] In re-sponse to the petition, the Chancery directed the following writ to the sheriff of London:

> We command you, firmly enjoining you that all other matters laid aside and all excuse whatsoever wholly ceasing, you do have before us in our Chancery on Monday next . . . John Milner . . . now detained under arrest . . . in our prison of Newgate, . . . together with the cause of his arrest and de-tention. . . .[147]

Although this writ did not disclose what the court intended to do upon the arrival of the prisoner and the examination of his arrest and detention, the petitioner's request indicated that he, at least, expected the court "to do what law and right demand."[148]

The cases of the mid-fourteenth century in which the writ of habeas corpus was used show that one role of the higher judicial tribunals was emerging. In the later years of the century, the poli-tics of the bench became more transparent and as the century drew to a close, the development of the writ of habeas corpus was largely attributable to the superior courts' desire to extend and secure their jurisdiction. The writ of habeas corpus, especially in its form *cum causa,* proved to be a strategic weapon during this campaign,[149] and its effectiveness was considerably enhanced by its association with the writs of certiorari and privilege.

THE SUPERIOR COURTS VERSUS THE LOCAL COURTS: UNINTENTIONAL PROGRESS

THE OFFENSE

Originally, the prerogative writ of habeas corpus was a judicial mechanism by which the sheriff or other custodian was commanded to "have the body" of some person before the court. Its purpose was simply to secure the presence of the party; the dispensing of justice by the sovereign, it was reasoned, required the submission of the subject to the King's judicial authority through his presence before the King's courts. From the mid-fourteenth century until the mid-sixteenth century, the same judicial writ that had facilitated the sovereign judicial power was often employed by the central courts to deprive the local courts of their ultimate sanction in the course of the judicial process—imprisonment.

That the writ of *habeas corpus cum causa* originated in the mid-fourteenth century in the Court of Chancery is not surprising. The development was generated by the same characteristic of the common law responsible for the fission of the courts of law and equity: its propensity for rigidity.[150] The equity powers of the Chancellor were often required to rectify unjust decisions of the inferior tribunals.[151] Used in conjunction with the writ of certiorari,[152] *corpus cum causa* was a useful device in bringing about this objective. By the writ of certiorari, the proceedings of the lower court were removed to the forum of the superior court,[153] and if a party in the case were imprisoned, he could be brought before the court by habeas corpus.[154]

The use of the writ of *habeas corpus cum causa* as a means of correction is well illustrated by three cases decided in the latter part of the fourteenth century.[155] In 1389, the Chancery directed a writ of certiorari to an inferior court in London demanding the records and the process of actions brought by John Reymes and John Payn against John Botelesham, and the judgment against Botelesham's sureties.[156] After examining the documents, the Chancery issued a writ of *corpus cum causa*, followed by a writ *sicut alias* (a second *corpus cum causa*) and a writ *sicut pluries* (a third such writ), commanding that the sureties imprisoned in connection with the action be brought to bar, together with the cause of their taking and detention.[157] In a 1397 case, the writ of *corpus cum causa* was directed from Chancery to the mayor and alderman of London requiring them to bring to bar the body of John Walpole,[158] who was being held prisoner for speaking dangerous words.[159] During an earlier imprisonment at Ludgate, Walpole had, in 1388, complained that the keeper and clerk of the Ludgate prison ruled it "extortionately and evilly."[160] His petition had been delayed by the officers of the prison so that it would reach the mayor when he was too busy to consider it.[161] Meanwhile, Walpole had been put in stocks and irons for five weeks in punishment for the petition.[162] During this period, a grant of forty shillings had been made for his deliverance.[163] The money was detained by the keeper and Walpole was transferred to the prison at Newgate.[164] Further, all of his clothes and other property were confiscated.[165] After he was finally freed he sought out the mayor and complained of these matters.[166] When he was rebuffed, he shouted in public, "[M]ayor, do me justice, or I will bring such a mob about you that you will be glad to do justice," for which he was imprisoned.[167] He then petitioned for and was granted a writ of *corpus cum causa* by the Chancery.[168] The writ is particularly significant because it goes much further than demanding the presentment of the prisoner's body together with the cause of his taking and detention, in that it includes an explicit statement of the court's intention upon examination: "in order that the king might give order for his delivery according to right and the law and custom of the realm."[169]

This method of defeating the jurisdiction of the lower courts was soon recognized as an avenue whereby debtors could secure release on bail to the eventual loss of their creditors and the unconscionable defeat of the lawful judgments of the local courts.[170] Parliament responded to this perversion of process in 1414 by providing

That if any . . . Writ of *Certiorari,* or *Corpus cum causa,* be

granted . . . and upon the said writ if it be returned, that the
prisoner which is so holden in prison is condemned by judge-
ment given against him, that presently he shall be remanded,
where he shall remain continually in prison according to the
law and custom of the land, without being let to go by bail
or by mainprise against the will of the said plaintiffs, until
agreement be made to them of the sums so adjudged.[171]

The statute had little effect, however, and writs of *corpus cum
causa* continued to issue from Chancery almost as a matter of
course.[172] In 1433, further legislation attempted to correct the
abuse of the writ.[173] The object of this second statute was to prevent
the use of the writ in a two-step process whereby recognitors (obli-
gors) held under the process of inferior tribunals could defeat their
recognizance (obligation to be in court at a certain time). After
securing release from the control of the inferior courts via *corpus
cum causa* issued by Chancery, the recognitors would sue out writs
of *scire facias* (a writ requiring the party against whom it is brought
to show cause) against their recognizance in order to defeat the
lower court proceedings entirely.[174] The legislative remedy for
these abuses was equally unsuccessful in curbing the laxity preva-
lent in Chancery: clerks were all too willing to increase their business, and the *corpus cum causa* provided them with a most market-
able item.[175] Not until the following century was issuance of the
writ by Chancery brought under control. In 1545, the Chancellor,
wishing to put his house in order, decreed that neither injunctions
nor writs of *habeas corpus cum causa* nor certiorari could be issued
from Chancery by anyone except the Chancellor himself, or in
his absence by the Master of the Rolls, who could issue the writs
only in open court and only if he signed them.[176] Five years later,
Chancellor Riche ordered that no clerk or other person writing in
the Chancery could thereafter issue a *corpus cum causa* or certiorari, upon pain of fine and imprisonment,[177] unless it were cosigned
by the Lord Chancellor.[178] The order was reissued in 1619 under
the chancellorship of Bacon.[179]

Although to a lesser extent than Chancery, the courts of common law also began to use the *corpus cum causa* to extend their
jurisdiction by bringing the body of the petitioner, as well as the

record of the case, before them. In 1406, for example, the barons of the Exchequer issued a writ of *corpus cum causa* to the sheriff of London directing him to have the body of one John Rede brought before them.[180] The sheriff's return stated that the said Rede had been arrested and committed to prison for certain causes pending before the mayor.[181] The barons then issued a writ of certiorari ordering the mayor to certify the cause of John Rede's taking, arrest, and commitment.[182] The justices of the King's Bench[183] and Common Pleas[184] used the writs in a similar manner.

In 1554, legislation was enacted that resembled the measure Chancery had imposed on itself nine years earlier. It provided

> That no writs of *habeas corpus* or *certiorari*, shall be hereafter granted to remove any prisoner out of any gaol, or to remove any recognisance, except the same writs be signed with the proper hands of the chief justice, or in his absence, one of the justices of the court out of which the same writs shall be awarded or made. . . .[185]

Late in the reign of Queen Elizabeth another legislative attempt to limit the writ was enacted.[186] The act sought to correct the practice whereby defendants would obtain writs of certiorari and *corpus cum causa* and then delay in asserting the benefit of the writs until after the jury was sworn and the case had proceeded to the stage at which the plaintiff had given testimony and had presented his witnesses and other proofs.[187] Pleas of debt or other actions, plaints, and suits levied in the lower court were thus brought before the courts of record at Westminster for "no other purpose . . . [than] to impugn those proofs which the plaintiffs have openly made by their witnesses and proofs, which is a great cause of perjury and subordination of perjury, and great expenses to the plaintiffs."[188] It was therefore enacted:

> That . . . no writ or writs of *habeas corpus*, or any other writ or writs sued forth . . . by any person or persons whatsoever, out of her Majesty's courts of record at Westminster, to remove any action, suit, plaint or cause, depending . . . in any court or courts within any city or town corporate, or else-

> where, which have or shall have jurisdiction, power or authority to hold plea in any action, plaint or suit, shall be received or allowed by the judge or judges, or officer or officers of the court or courts wherein or to whom any such writ or writs shall be delivered . . . except that the said writ or writs be delivered . . . before that the jury which is to try the cause . . . have appeared, and one of the said jury sworn to try the said cause.[189]

Additional legislation in 1623 enhanced the right of lower court magistrates to refuse to recognize *corpus cum causa* and certiorari.[190] The statute permitted lower-level judicial officers to ignore such writs once they had become seised of the case and possessed jurisdiction.[191] The aim was to correct the abuse of judicial machinery by defendants whose action for removal would result in "*the intolerable delay of justice . . .* [at the] great expences of [the plaintiffs]."[192] Before the enactment of this statute, however, the triumph of the superior courts had long since been complete, and the high courts were now anxious to rid themselves of the mass of petty litigation that made up the spoils of victory.[193]

THE DEFENSE

From early times, certain classes of people were above the ordinary mechanisms and processes of the legal system.[194] At about the same time as the writ of *corpus cum causa* began to develop, an act appeared on the statutory rolls concerning the notion of privilege.[195] While the writ of *corpus cum causa,* in conjunction with the writ of certiorari, was being awarded by the superior courts in an effort to augment their power, an expansion in the concept of privilege was also taking place.

In addition to the clergy, individuals involved in the affairs of the Crown were in certain ways exempt from the authority of judicial tribunals: members of Parliament, ministers of the King, and clerks and officers of the various Crown courts were the chief beneficiaries of this exemption.[196] The theory behind the writ of privilege was that those classes should be tried for violations of the law in their own courts, where they were needed to carry on the affairs of the Crown.[197] The writ of habeas corpus proved an able device to enforce the notion of privilege.[198]

In the first third of the fifteenth century the notion was expanded dramatically to protect suitors in a superior court, so that if they were arrested on the process of an inferior tribunal while on the way to appear before the superior court, they were entitled to be removed by a *corpus cum causa*.[199] In 1430, for example, a writ of habeas corpus was issued in favor of Alice Hemyngford, who had been arrested and detained in prison by the sheriff of London when she was on her way to the Court of Common Pleas in Westminster to sue a certain John Wroxhale.[200] In 1440, a writ of *corpus cum causa* specifically recited "that all lieges of the king are under his protection when coming and going to his court of the Bench."[201] By the mid-fifteenth century this theory was firmly embedded in English jurisprudence.[202]

The combined use of the writs of privilege and *corpus cum causa* provided the ideal deterrent to encroachments on the jurisdiction of the superior courts. Inevitably this mechanism of defense was used by some as an offensive weapon to disrupt the just operation of the lower courts.[203] Determined to enjoin this abuse, the superior courts would refuse to grant a writ of *corpus cum causa* based upon privilege if they perceived that the petition was an attempt by the applicant to evade his lawful obligations.[204] Soon after the expansion of the concept of privilege, it was decided that the writ would lie only when the person arrested by the process of an inferior court was at the time engaged in the business of his case in the superior court.[205] It followed that if an application for *corpus cum causa* based on privilege were made during the court's vacation, it would fail.[206] The writ would also be denied if the superior court case were commenced subsequent to the arrest and detention complained of.[207] Those who abused the system were dealt with severely.[208] Nor would the writ be granted to petitioners actually engaged in the business of their case if they were committed at the suit of the King.[209] The rationale behind this denial was that the Crown's prerogative writ should not issue to defeat the King's personal, though purely formal, interest in the case. Moreover, one arrested by order of the Parliament could not have benefit of privilege or *corpus cum causa* against the legislative body's superior privilege.[210]

In sum, the superior courts' efforts to maintain and extend their jurisdiction had the unintended effect of changing the nature of the prerogative writ of habeas corpus; for in so using the writ, the superior courts were questioning the validity of an imprisonment. This "liberalization" of the writ was accelerated when the jurisdictional contest shifted from the arena of the local courts to that of the superior courts. It was during the contests among the rival superior courts, which will be described next, that the writ of habeas corpus was displayed as a formidable weapon to protect the liberty of the English subject.

JURISDICTIONAL BATTLES AMONG THE SUPERIOR COURTS

THE COMMON-LAW COURTS VERSUS THE CHANCERY

The writ of habeas corpus was to assume a vital role in the jurisdictional battles among the superior judicial tribunals that arose in the late fifteenth century and continued into the seventeenth century.[211] The development and implementation of *corpus cum causa* by Chancery had done much to expand its jurisdiction. The growth of its power was not applauded by the courts of common law, nor appreciated by the lawyers of common law, who viewed Chancery as an office that robbed them of potential fees.[212] This attitude was expressed in an unsuccessful petition on the parliamentary rolls in 1422 requesting that two judges of the common law be required to certify that no remedy was available at common law before a party could be given standing in Chancery.[213]

Most distressing to the common-law judges and lawyers was the manner in which the Chancellor was to exercise power. Since the goal of equity was to provide the flexibility that the common law lacked, the Chancellor was governed only by the dictates of his conscience in administering justice.[214] For the rigidity of the common law to be mitigated by the principles of equity, it became essential that the Chancellor be able to restrain the operation of the common law. The device employed for that purpose was the writ of injunction.[215] The common-law lawyers marveled at the authority this writ bestowed on the Chancellor.[216] By means of the injunction the Chancellor could, in effect, suspend the operation of the common law in individual cases.[217] In response to this power, the Court of King's Bench in 1483, *per* Mr. Justice Fairfax, asserted that if a case fell within its jurisdiction, it could prohibit the parties to the case from resorting to any other jurisdiction.[218] Later that year, Mr. Chief Justice Huse held that if the Chancellor committed a suitor for breach of an injunction that sought to restrain the party from suing his case at common law, King's Bench could release him by means of a writ of habeas corpus.[219]

The controversy between the courts of equity and common law continued through the sixteenth century,[220] interrupted only during the chancellorship of Sir Thomas More, a common-law lawyer himself, who succeeded Cardinal Wolsey after the latter's impeachment for, among other things, an excessive use of writs of injunction.[221] Upon coming to office, More invited all the judges of the courts of Westminster to dinner and explained to them his reasons for issuing many injunctions immediately after assuming office.[222] After examining the injunctions, his guests were forced to confess that they themselves, in like cases, would have acted no differently.[223] The truce was imperfect, however, for the judges would not agree to mitigate the severity of the common law in return for More's pledge to curtail the issuance of writs of injunction.[224]

The conflict between the courts of common law and equity continued to escalate, climaxing during the reign of James I.[225] In 1605, Chancery attempted to assert the benefits of privilege for one of its clerks against a suit in the King's Bench.[226] The attempt failed because it was held that King's Bench was the superior court.[227] It followed that the writs of privilege and habeas corpus could not issue against King's Bench by Chancery to remove the party once King's Bench was seized of the case, even though the suitor was an officer of Chancery. The King's Bench responded similarly in *Addis' Case*[228] in 1610, when a writ of habeas corpus was returned that the prisoner was committed by a warrant of the Chancellor of England "for certain matters concerning the King."[229] The King's Bench held the return insufficient, "for it shews not for what causes he was committed, for it might be a cause which would not hinder him of his privilege."[230]

In *Glanville v. Courtney*,[231] the King's Bench bailed an individual committed for contempt by the Chancery.[232] In the common-law courts, verdict and judgment were awarded the plaintiff-creditor.[233] The defendant, alleging fraud, proffered a bill into Chancery, and there obtained an order for a stay of proceedings.[234] For contempt in attempting to disregard the order, Glanville, the creditor, was committed.[235] In letting the prisoner to bail, King's Bench, per Lord Coke, ruled that if a case arose in law and in equity and it was decided initially in law, it should not subsequently be reversed in equity.[236] Glanville was subsequently recommitted by the Lord Chancellor and again, on a writ of habeas corpus, released on bail by the King's Bench.[237]

In 1615, in *King v. Dr. Gouge*,[238] Coke reiterated this rationale[239] upon releasing an individual committed for contempt by virtue of an order of Chancery "for his contumacy and contempt, in refusing to answer unto a bill there exhibited against him."[240] In these cases, the King's prerogative writ issued to defeat, technically that is, the King's own authority as embodied in the Chancery.

THE COMMON-LAW COURTS VERSUS THE ECCLESIASTICAL COURT

Although Coke's dismissal in 1616 curtailed the enthusiastic issuance of the writ, habeas corpus continued to be used in the conflict throughout the next several years.[241] While the courts of common law were embroiled in the battle with Chancery, they were waging a similar campaign against the Court of High Commission. The roots of this ecclesiastical tribunal reach back to 1535 when Henry VIII declared himself the supreme head of the Church of England.[242] Among the members of the early Commissions were the Lord Chief Justice, one of his colleagues, and the Attorney General.[243] As the year 1580 approached, the attendance of these formerly active and influential common-law members declined.[244] With its transformation into an ecclesiastical tribunal complete at about the same time[245] and the representatives of common law no longer present, the Commission inevitably assumed the position of a rival court.[246]

Unlike the Court of Chancery, the High Commission was a recent creation and the bounds of its jurisdiction were therefore un-hampered by precedent. The common-law judges employed the writs of prohibition and habeas corpus to check this court's "usur-pations" of the affairs of the common-law courts. The writ of pro-hibition was issued to enjoin the ecclesiastical judges from con-tinuing the trial of a given case on the ground that it involved tem-poral matters.[247] The writ of habeas corpus issued to free those imprisoned by the Commission.[248] The courts of common law main-tained that the Commission had no authority to fine or imprison even for purely ecclesiastical offenses.[249] This claim, however, was not successful in the case of Nicholas Fuller in 1607.[250] Fuller had been the barrister for two defendants who had been imprisoned for refusing to take an oath ex officio required by the Commission.[251] They were brought before the King's Bench on writs of habeas cor-pus where Fuller argued in their defense that the detentions were illegal.[252] He submitted that prior to 1559 the bishops did not have power to fine or imprison.[253] Further, he averred that the bishops " 'did proceede in these dayes by taking an ell whereby they had but an ynch granted them, and in examining men upon their oaths at their discretion and indiscretion as such their dealings were not lamentable.' "[254] Fuller's bold statements in defense of his clients aroused the wrath of the Commissioners, and he was arraigned upon a list of " 'scandalous' things he had 'factiously and falsely' affirmed."[255] Fuller requested and was granted a writ of prohibition by the King's Bench.[256] The justices of the King's Bench took coun-sel with their brethren of the Common Pleas and of the Exchequer, and shortly after the consultation the case was released back to the Commissioners,[257] who after hearing further arguments imprisoned Fuller and fined him £200.[258] The King's Bench then granted him a writ of habeas corpus, but in the end sustained his detention.[259]

Fuller's arguments fared better than he himself did. Coke's *Re-ports* contain the substance of an after-dinner discussion among the judges and sergeants of Sergeant's Inn in 1607, when the ques-tion was raised whether the High Commissioners could imprison in ecclesiastical cases.[260] The group resolved that the King could not alter his temporal or ecclesiastical laws by his grant or com-mission, and therefore that the High Commissioners did not have authority to fine and imprison since they had not been granted such authority by act of Parliament.[261]

The following year, this view was implemented in *Sir Anthony Roper's Case*.[262] Roper was brought before the High Commissioners at the suit of Bulbrook, the vicar of Bentley,[263] and was imprisoned after he refused to comply with the order of the Commission.[264] A writ of habeas corpus was then granted by the justices of the King's Bench, who unanimously decided that the act allowing Queen Elizabeth, her heirs, and successors the power to assign Commissioners to exercise and execute all matter of spiritual jurisdiction[265] did not include the power to fine and imprison.[266]

In 1611 a writ of habeas corpus was granted to Lady Throgmorton, who was committed by the ecclesiastical Commissioners because, in the words of the return, "she had done many evil offices betwixt Sir James Scudamore and her daughter the Lady Scudamore, wife of the said James, and to make separation betwixt them, and detained her from her husband: and upon her departure after sentence before the Commissioners, for divers centemptuous [sic] words against the Court, saying, that she neither had law nor justice there."[267] Bail was allowed because her actions in attempting to bring about a separation between her daughter and son-in-law did not constitute an offense; because, for detaining her daughter, there was a remedy at common law; and because by the return, it did not appear that the "centemptuous" [sic] words were spoken in the Court.[268]

The following year, in the case of *Sir William Chancey*[269] who was imprisoned by the High Commission for adultery, cohabitation with a woman other than his wife, failing to provide his wife with proper maintenance, and "contempt of His Majesty" in failing to obey the orders of the Commissioners was released upon a writ of habeas corpus.[270] The justices ruled that the Commissioners had no jurisdiction to punish for adultery nor any power to imprison in this case.[271] Mr. Justice Walmsley noted that "although [the Commissioners] have used by 20 years to imprison in such case, without exception taken, yet when it came before them judicially, they ought to judge according to law."[272] The justices bailed the prisoner and unanimously resolved "that when upon the return it doth appear, that the imprisonment is not lawful, the Court may discharge him of imprisonment; but in this case, the Court thought fit rather to bail."[273] Following *Chancey's Case*, the King ordered all of the justices of England to assemble in the Council Chamber at Whitehall[274] to discuss the jurisdiction of the Court of High Commission and the issuance of writs of habeas corpus by the courts of common law. After hearing arguments the King announced that he would reform the ecclesiastical court,[275] but the conference seems to have had little, if any, effect on the course of judicial activity during the next several years.

In *Bradstone v. High-Commission Court*,[276] upon a writ of habeas corpus, the imprisonment of the petitioner was adjudged to be illegal, and his detainment for adultery and failure to pay alimony was relieved by bail.[277] In the case of *Codd v. Turback*,[278] decided one year later, the return of a writ of habeas corpus stated that the petitioner had been committed by the Commission for refusing to maintain his wife properly and for speaking "diversa opprobriosa verba" (assorted insults).[279] It was held insufficient because "the cause of the commitment in this return, ought certainly to appear, [and] it is here altogether uncertain, the time uncertain when the words were spoken, it might be in the time of Queen Eliz. and so the same pardoned."[280] Coke continued, with reasoning he would employ thirteen years later in the parliamentary debates following *Darnel's Case*,[281] "By the law of God, none ought to be imprisoned, but with the cause expressed in the return of his imprisonment, as appeareth in the Acts of the Apostles."[282] He went on, in *Codd*, to observe that "[t]his kind of imprisonment is much to be disliked, being a very great grievance and vexation to the subjects."[283] In that same year, a certain Hodd, who was imprisoned for using "divers contemptuous and reproachful words, touching [the Court of High Commission's] proceedings" was granted a writ of habeas corpus and was subsequently discharged.[284] The Court, again *per* Coke, held: "[I]t doth not appear by the return, what the words were which he spake, and they may be such as ought to be determined by the common law; for this cause the return is not good. . . ."[285] The controversy continued throughout the next several years.[286] As late as 1641, the year in which the clause of the Act of Supremacy that empowered the Crown to exercise its supremacy in ecclesiastical affairs through Commissioners was repealed,[287] remnants of the dispute survived.[288]

THE COMMON-LAW COURTS VERSUS THE COURTS OF ADMIRALTY AND REQUEST

The common-law courts' jealousy of all jurisdictions other than their own was felt also by the Court of Admiralty.[289] By the mid-sixteenth century, Admiralty was hearing a constantly increasing number of cases.[290] This naturally aroused the courts of common law.[291] The Admiralty Court was successful at first in resisting the common-law courts' employment of writs of habeas corpus.[292] In *Dolphyn v. Shutford*,[293] for example, Sir John Russell, the Lord High Admiral, refused to honor a writ of habeas corpus issued by Mr. Chief Justice Montague ordering that the body of Shutford be brought before him.[294] Russell believed that to honor the writ would be a transgression of the law and prejudicial to the King's prerogative.[295] In 1553, a writ of habeas corpus and *supersedeas* from the Court of Exchequer received a similar return.[296]

At the turn of the century, however, the writ proved effective in controlling the jurisdiction of Admiralty. In *Thomlinson's Case*,[297] the prisoner had been committed for refusing to answer under oath certain interrogatories put to him by the Court of Admiralty.[298] The Common Pleas granted a writ of habeas corpus, which was returned that he had been committed for contempt.[299] Because the return failed to specify the cause for which the party was examined, it was held to be too general and insufficient.[300] Likewise in *Hawkeridge's Case*,[301] a return of a writ of habeas corpus by the marshal of the Admiralty Court was held insufficient, and he was ordered to amend the return and to show the cause of a delay in the petitioner's sentencing.[302] When he failed to amend the return, the marshal was ordered to deliver the prisoner to bail.[303]

The common-law courts also used the writ of habeas corpus against the Court of Requests.[304] In the 1572 case of *Humfrey v. Humfrey*,[305] the Court of Requests ordered the holder of a judgment rendered by the Court of Common Pleas not to execute it.[306] He disobeyed Request's order and was committed to the Fleet, a London prison.[307] He petitioned the Court of Common Pleas, which released him upon habeas corpus, noting that if its judgment holder were again imprisoned, it would again issue a writ of habeas corpus to free him.[308]

One finds, then, that in the efforts of the common-law courts to guard the bounds of their jurisdiction, the rhetoric used to disguise the pursuit was itself assuming a lofty eminence. The common-law courts' selfish designs are also evident in their struggle, described below, with obnoxious "administrative agencies," that is, the various Councils. In their battle with these partially judicial, partially executive bodies, the writ moved yet closer to its role as a safeguard against the arbitrary power of the Crown itself. This development was completed when the legislature emerged the victor from its power struggle with the executive.

DELINEATING THE EXECUTIVE POWER

The fiction that the writ of habeas corpus provided the English subject with a palladium against arbitrary government pressed closer to reality when the courts of common law began to resist what they perceived as interference from the Privy Council. In a sense both a successor of the Curia Regis and a predecessor of the modern-day administrative agency, the Council was the organ through which the King carried on the work of government.[309] Under Henry VII, the Council, which possessed both executive and judicial powers, helped bring about a more efficient and effective government than any since the reign of Henry II.[310] With the Council's aid, the Tudor monarchs were able to bring the anomie of the preceding era under control.[311] As late as 1577, the common-law courts were expressing a tolerance for the delicate position of this executive agency. In that year, upon a writ of habeas corpus, a certain Hinde was brought before the Court of Common Pleas along with a return stating that he was committed to prison by commandment of the Commissioners for "causes ecclesiastical."[312] As the preceding discussion suggests,[313] the return was held invalid for its failure "to certifie the cause for which he was committed; ... upon the return the Court ought to examine the cause if it be sufficient or not."[314] The court went on to note, however, that "if one be committed to prison, by the commandment of the Queens

Privy Council, there the cause needs not to be shewed in the return, because it may concern the state of the realm, which ought not to be published."[315]

THE COMMON-LAW COURTS VERSUS THE PRIVY COUNCIL

The growing jurisdiction of the Council and the creation of various subordinate councils throughout the realm,[316] the end of a period of widespread lawlessness, the tone and temper of Queen Elizabeth's administration, which displayed itself in a "vigilant execution of severe statutes,"[317] the jealous nature of the common-law courts, and the successes of the arguments against arbitrary imprisonment developed by the common-law lawyers and judges to conceal their selfish pursuits produced a greater receptivity on the part of the courts of common law to the arguments voiced against commitments by the executive Council in the latter years of Queen Elizabeth's reign.[318] The first indications of the common-law courts' readiness to question the authority of the Privy Council appeared in cases holding that, in the absence of cause shown, a person held at the command of individual Council members would be released. In 1587, in *Hellyard's Case*,[319] a return stating only that the prisoner was committed "per mandatum Francisci Walsingham, militis unius principalium Secretariorum Dominae Reginae" (by order of Francis Walsingham, principal military secretary of his majesty's household), but showing no cause, was held insufficient by Common Pleas.[320] In that same year, one William Peter, who came to London to prosecute an action for debt and was afterwards committed to the Marshalsey by order of Lord Hunsdon, chamberlain of the Queen's household and a member of the Privy Council, was granted a writ of habeas corpus by Common Pleas.[321] Because the return stated only that he was held at the command of Lord Hunsdon, "there to remain and to answer before the Lords of Her Majesties Council to such matters," Peter was discharged.[322] The following year, in *Howel's Case*,[323] a return similar to that in *Hellyard's Case* was made.[324] Again the return was adjudged inadequate for want of sufficient cause shown.[325] An amended return stated that Howel was committed by "totisus concilii privati cominae reginae" (the entire Privy Council of her majesty).[326] This time the Court of Common Pleas accepted the return: "where one is committed by one of the Privy Council . . . the cause of the committing ought to be set down in the return; but contrary where the party is committed by the whole Council, there no cause need to be alleadged."[327] It insisted, however, that the prisoner should always be produced so that if the argument against detention seemed valid the court could allow the imprisoned party his privilege.[328]

The same term produced a case that does not fit easily into the pattern just described. A writ of habeas corpus issued from the Court of Common Pleas to the steward and marshal (inferior members of the Queen's household) for one William Search.[329] Search had been arrested and detained for having himself earlier arrested a certain John Preston, surety of John Mabbe.[330] Mabbe had obtained letters patent from the Queen protecting himself and his sureties from arrest.[331] The letters patent provided that "if any person should arrest, or cause to be arrested the said John Mabbe or any of his sureties, that then the marshal . . . might arrest every such person, and detain them in prison until such person should answer before the Privy Council for the contempt."[332] Upon return of the habeas corpus, the Common Pleas discharged Search.[333] He was subsequently rearrested,[334] whereupon the court issued an attachment against his captors.[335] The court seemed to be denying the Queen power to imprison by letters patent.

In 1591, the judges of the King's Bench and Common Pleas and the barons of the Exchequer Court assembled to discuss their dissatisfaction with the practices of the Council.[336] The judges complained that the monarch's councillors commanded imprisonments contrary to law, and so the courts attempted to release those unlawfully imprisoned by means of the writ of habeas corpus.[337] When the writs were returned and no legal cause for the commitments could be shown, they ordered that such prisoners should be delivered.[338] But, continued the judges, many of those so delivered were reimprisoned—this time in "secret [prisons]," so that "the Queens Courts cannot learn to whom to direct her Majesties Writs."[339] Moreover, those who attempted to execute the writs judicial were often intimidated.[340] It was therefore resolved that:

if any person be committed by her Majesties commandment from her Person, or by order from the Council-board, or if any one or two of her Council commit one for high treason such persons so in the case before committed may not be delivered by any of her Courts without due tryal by the Law, and Judgment of aquittal, had.

Nevertheless the Judges may award the Queens Writs to bring the bodies of such persons before them, and if upon return thereof the causes of their commitment be certified to the Judges as it ought to be, then the Judges in the Cases before ought not to deliver him, but to remand the prisoner to the place from whence he came.

Which cannot conveniently be done unless notice of the cause in generality or else specially be given to the Keeper or Gaoler that shall have custody of such prisoner.[341]

The resolution thus specifically sanctioned commitments *per speciale mandatum* (by special order) of the Queen or the entire Privy Council, or by members thereof in cases of high treason. The judges, however, asserted power to issue the writ of habeas corpus in all cases and demanded that a specific return to the writ be made in all but the special instances stated, in which a general return would suffice. The resolution was therefore no more than an accurate restatement of the existing case law[342] (excepting, perhaps, *Search's Case*).[343]

The rules of the resolution and supporting case law were strictly interpreted and adhered to by the courts of common law throughout the early seventeenth century. Even Coke, champion of the "progressive" rhetoric, at times sustained the legality of a commitment by the monarch or Council on a return lacking details of the cause of commitment.[344] Therefore, in 1627, when the *Case of the Five Knights*[345] (*Darnel's Case*) was presented before the King's Bench, a return stating that the prisoner was held "by the special command of his majesty"[346] would seem to have been valid. The arguments presented by defense attorneys Bramston, Noye, Selden, and Calthorpe were emotionally appealing indeed; they were not, however, congruent with case law as it had developed by 1627.

Sir Thomas Darnel, Sir John Corbet, Sir Walter Earl, Sir John Heveningham, and Sir Edmund Hampden had been imprisoned for refusing to submit to King Charles' forced loan.[347] They petitioned for and were granted writs of *habeas corpus cum causa*.[348] There being some delay, an *alias* was sued out.[349] The warden then returned that they had been committed "by special command of his majesty."[350] Counsel for the five knights argued eloquently that such a return was insufficient:

> [T]he Writ of Habeas Corpus is the only means the subject hath to obtain his liberty, and the end of this Writ is to return the cause of the imprisonment, that it may be examined in this court, whether the parties ought to be discharged or not: but that cannot be done upon this return: for the cause of the imprisonment of this gentleman at first is so far from appearing particularly by it, that there is no cause at all expressed in it.[351]

The writ was portrayed by the barristers as the only check against the arbitrary occurrence of imprisonments of indeterminate length. The argument, in effect, embraced a more balanced government by emphasizing an independent judiciary.

Such an argument was far in advance of the constitutional law in England at this time. All justice still flowed from the king; the courts merely dispensed that justice.[352] It was on this institutional principle that Attorney General Heath based his argument on behalf of the King—the same principle on which the extrajudicial opinion of the common-law judges in 1591[353] was based, and, in the end, it was that principle the court adopted in remanding the prisoners.[354] Under the circumstances, the justices could have done no differently.[355]

PARLIAMENT VERSUS THE KING

By the late 1620s, the conflict that had been brewing for a generation between the legislative and executive branches was responsible for effectuating the advancement of the writ of habeas corpus. The aggravated state of Crown finances forced the King, in the year following *Darnel's Case*, to assemble a Parliament.[356] Immediately after the business of organization was completed, Parliament moved to consider the grievances growing out of the illegal levies of the Crown.

After heated debates[357] the Commons passed three resolutions in support of the liberty of the subject,[358] which provided, in substance, that no one should be imprisoned without a showing of cause, that habeas corpus should be available in all cases to examine the cause, and that if the writ were returned without cause shown, a prisoner committed by the King or Privy Council should be released.[359] The Commons argued that the writ of habeas corpus was an instrument springing naturally and inevitably from the Magna Carta.[360] But the legislators, especially Coke, were certainly aware that the statutory and case history hardly compelled the conclusion they were arguing for. Indicative of this awareness was their rejection of the King's offer merely to reaffirm these statutes.[361] Instead, the legislators demanded that the King affirm the bill delivered to him in the form of a Petition of Right.[362] The Petition of Right[363] abolished the king's power to imprison by special command without showing cause.[364] Although this advance in the status of the writ of habeas corpus was not a natural development, neither was it an illogical one. By means of "progressive" rhetoric and faulty historical analysis, the legislators were building on the arguments voiced during the jurisdictional court battles of previous years.

The parliamentary session ended with the commencement of the *Six Members' Case*,[365] which illustrated how easily the King could follow the letter of the Petition while debasing its spirit entirely. The cause for the commitment of the six members of Parliament given in the return to the writ of habeas corpus was " 'for notable contempts . . . against our self and our government, and for stirring up sedition against us.' "[366] Counsel for the prisoners argued that the return was insufficient within the terms of the Petition of Right.[367] In response, Attorney General Heath stated:

> A Petition in parliament is not a law, yet it is for the honour and dignity of the king, to observe and keep it faithfully; but it is the duty of the people not to stretch it beyond the words and intention of the king. And no other construction can be made of the Petition, than to take it as a confirmation of the ancient liberties and rights of the subjects. So that now the case remains in the same quality and degree, as it was before the Petition.[368]

The Attorney General's argument, in one blow, rendered the parliamentary effort of the previous year a mockery.[369]

In that same year, the *Chambers's Case*[370] came before the King's Bench. Chambers, a London merchant, refused to submit to the payment of tonnage and poundage.[371] For his "contempt" he was summoned to appear before the Privy Council.[372] Before the Lords of the Council, Chambers declared that "such great Customs & Impositions were required from the Merchants in England as were in no other place, and that they were more screwed up than under the Turk,"[373] and for these words he was committed to prison.[374] Chambers petitioned for and was granted a writ of habeas corpus out of the King's Bench.[375] The return to the writ stated only that he was committed to prison by the Lords of the Council "for insolent behaviour and words spoken at the Council table."[376] The court held the return insufficient and advised the marshal to amend it.[377] After examining the amended return, the court let Chambers to bail.[378] Rushworth reports that Lords of the Council were dissatisfied with the judicial decision and sent for the justices, who explained that the law required that they let Chambers to bail.[379] The members of the Council then told the justices that "it was necessary for the Preservation of the State, that the Power and Dignity of the Council-Table should be preserved, and that it could not be done without Correspondency from the Courts of Justice."[380] Rushworth gives no further details of the meeting other than to note that "they parted in very fair Terms."[381] Chambers was afterwards charged in the Star Chamber, where he was fined £2,000.[382] In default, he was committed to the Fleet, from which he was again brought before the King's Bench upon a writ of habeas corpus.[383] It was argued on his behalf that the Court of Star Chamber had no authority to punish for words only.[384] The argument was rejected and the court held that "the Court of Star Chamber was . . . one of the most high and honourable Courts of Justice; and to deliver one who was committed by the decree of one of the Courts of Justice, was not the usage of this Court."[385]

Chambers's Case confirmed that the writ of habeas corpus had assumed a new role. No longer was it primarily an instrument employed by the common-law courts to protect their jurisdiction. The questioning of the validity of commitments, previously an incidental effect of the writ, now became the major object. It was at this point, then, that the writ of habeas corpus embarked upon its journey as "the highest remedy in law, for any man that is imprisoned."[386] Even during what Jenks refers to as "eleven of the blackest years in the history of English law"[387] (the suspension of Parliament from 1629 to 1640), the writ was used to check the illegal confinements of the Council.[388] *Chambers's Case*, however, also pointed up a potential obstacle in the path of the subject's liberty: the Court of Star Chamber, acknowledged by the *Chambers's* court as a "high and honourable Court of Justice," could still be employed by the executive branch to execute its will. To remove this obstacle, the legislature enacted the "Act for the regulating of the privy council, and for taking away the court commonly called the star-chamber," known also as the Habeas Corpus Act of 1641.[389] In addition to abolishing the Court of Star Chamber,[390] which had "been found to be an intolerable burthen to the subjects, and the means to introduce an arbitrary power and government,"[391] the Act provided that if anyone were imprisoned by any court claiming like jurisdiction, or by command or warrant of the King or his Council or any of its members, he was to have a writ of habeas corpus upon demand to the judges of the King's Bench or Common Pleas, "without Delay."[392] The custodian of the party so committed was

> at the return of the said writ, and according to the command thereof, upon due and convenient Notice . . . to . . . bring or cause to be brought the body of the . . . party so committed . . . and shall then likewise certify the true cause of such . . . imprisonment, and thereupon the court, within three court-days after such return made . . . shall proceed to examine and determine whether the cause of such commitment appearing upon the said return be just and legal, or not, and thereupon do what to justice shall appertain, either by delivering, bailing or remanding the prisoner. . . .[393]

Moreover, the Act declared that any judge acting contrary to the "true meaning" of the Act was liable in treble damages to the person offended.[394] Unsatisfied with the legislative remedy alone, however, the Commons later that year issued a stinging indictment of the King for his past malfeasance.[395] This so-called Grand Remonstrance complained, among other things,[396] of the Crown's disregard of the Petition of Right and of the capricious and arbitrary imprisonment of the members of Parliament.[397]

TOWARD THE FAMOUS ACT OF 1679: A PERIOD OF HYPOCRISY

Neither the Habeas Corpus Act of 1641 nor the Grand Remonstrance could heal the divisions, at which those documents hinted, in the English constitutional system at this time. The conflicts grew more inflamed until civil war broke out in 1642. Charles was defeated, and the victors were, in theory and often in fact, more "liberal" in their social and political ideas than he had been.[398] One of the first acts of the victorious party, however, illustrates the conflicting tone of the new administration. The King was executed after a trial by a court of commissioners, fundamentally similar to the Court of Star Chamber that the victors had earlier helped to abolish but had then revived, cloaked in the rhetorical disguise that "the people are, under God, the original of all just power."[399]

THE WRIT OF HABEAS CORPUS UNDER CROMWELL

The interregnum government did much to democratize the writ of habeas corpus in the civil sector. In December 1649, the same year in which Charles was executed, "An Act for discharging from Imprisonment poor Prisoners unable to satisfie their Creditors" was enacted.[400] The Act provided that for those imprisonments that originated for debt or breach of promise, contract, or covenant, a *habeas corpus cum causa* could be granted, and that upon the prisoner's taking an oath that

> he or she is not worth in Possession, Reversion, Remainder of any Estate Real or Personal, except onely the Debts due to him or them from the Parliament, for the service of the Commonwealth, to the value of Five pounds, besides necessary wearing Apparel, and Bedding for himself, Wife and Children, and Tools necessary for his Trade or Occuption,[401]

the justice of the peace was to certify "without delay" to the court from which the process of imprisonment had issued that the prisoner had been examined on the oath he had taken.[402] The court of process was then to issue a *scire facias*, with an order of *non omittas propter aliquam libertatem* (not to be disregarded because of some liberty [privilege]), directed to the sheriff of the county in which the party lived by whose action the prisoner was held, requiring that party's appearance so that cause could be shown why the prisoner should not be free.[403] If sufficient cause were wanting or if the persons who initiated the imprisonment proceedings failed to answer the summons, the imprisoned party was delivered.[404] Four months later the procedure was further liberalized by an act that permitted the prisoners in the above cases to be let to sureties pending the return day of their case or such time as was established by their temporary release order.[405]

The government was determined to survive, however, and when it recognized that habeas corpus, acting in conjunction with certiorari, issuing out of the Upper (King's) Bench, could interfere with matters of public policy, such as its strict control over "the buying, selling, searching, viewing, ordering or disposing of any Corn, Wine, Beer, Ale, Fish, Flesh, Salt, Butter, Cheese, or other dead Victual whatsoever . . . ," it enacted that no such writs were to issue in the above cases, and where they were granted, the prosecutor and informers were empowered to ignore them.[406] Moreover, in political matters, Lord Protector Oliver Cromwell and his Parliament's liberal propensities were no stronger than those of the King and Council they had replaced. For example, in 1653 one John Streater was imprisoned "for publishing of seditious Pamphlets against the State."[407] He was brought before the Upper Bench on a *habeas corpus ad subjiciendum*, where it was returned that he was committed by Parliament and the Council of State.[408] Streater argued that the return was defective because it failed to name the books or pamphlets alleged seditious, and because the time or place of the crime was nowhere stated:[409]

My lord, seeing, as I say, that the Parliament did at first declare that they would be tender of our Rights and Privileges; and seeing the law saith, 'That if there be no cause, there shall

> be no imprisonment;' and in regard there is no cause shewn, why I should be a prisoner: I do aver that the parliament cannot have greater dishonour put upon them, than for anyone to alledge that they intended imprisonment to me, if there should no cause in law appear.[410]

Attorney General Prideaux apparently felt no need to meet the argument and merely informed the court that the prisoner was committed by command of the Parliament.[411] The information was found sufficient. The court conceded that the return was inadequate but nevertheless refused to question the legislative authority and remanded the petitioner.[412] The following term Streater again petitioned for habeas corpus, arguing that since Parliament had been dissolved, the validity of its commitment order had expired.[413] After habeas corpus and alias habeas corpus, he was once more brought before the Upper Bench.[414] Prideaux argued that the prisoner could not be delivered except by order of Parliament.[415] Streater rejoined that if orders of Parliament were binding in succession there would be no need for acts of Parliament.[416] The Court was persuaded and the prisoner was delivered.[417]

The following year, a request for a habeas corpus was filed on behalf of a captured outlaw accused of a felony.[418] The Protector intervened personally in the case, requesting that the writ not be issued "because the prisoner stands committed for divers felonies and rapes."[419] Mr. Chief Justice Rolle nevertheless granted habeas corpus, although he noted that the prisoner would immediately be remanded for trial upon the reversal of the outlawry.[420]

These cases testify to the salience of an independent judiciary in safeguarding against executive power. During Cromwell's time, however, judicial independence was difficult to maintain, as *Cony's Case* indicates.[421] Cony, a London merchant, had refused to pay a customs duty he considered illegal.[422] When the duty was forcibly taken from him, he initiated an action at common law against the collector.[423] Cromwell then summoned Cony to appear before him,[424] where Cony responded to the Protector's plea that he abandon his opposition by quoting one of Cromwell's own remarks: " 'that all, who submitted to them, and paid illegal taxes, were more to blame, and greater enemies to their country, than they who had imposed them; and that the tyranny of princes could never be grievous, but by the tameness and stupidity of the people.' "[425] Seeing that Cony could not be persuaded to drop the action, Cromwell had him committed, whereupon the Upper Bench indicated that it would grant a writ of habeas corpus.[426] Cromwell then sent for the judges of the court and reprehended them for allowing Cony's counsel to question the Protector's authority.[427] When they humbly mentioned the law, especially the Magna Carta, Cromwell replied that " 'their Magna F**** should not controul his actions,' " which were designed for the safety of the Commonwealth.[428] He then asked " 'who made them judges [and] whether they had any authority to sit there, but what he gave them' " and noted that " 'if his authority were at an end, they knew well enough, what would become of themselves.' "[429] They therefore were advised " 'to be more tender of that which could only preserve them' " and cautioned " 'not [to] suffer the lawyers to prate what it would not become them to hear.' "[430]

When Cony's barristers attempted to prosecute his suit against the collector, Cromwell, who wished to avoid such a dangerous precedent, had them imprisoned in the Tower.[431] They were released a few days later after petitioning for their liberty, acknowledging their fault and promising never again to appear as representatives in such actions.[432] Since his lawyers had been intimidated, Cony pleaded his own case and referred the matter to the Upper Bench.[433] The issue before the court was whether the tax, which was not authorized by Parliament, ought to be paid.[434] Mr. Chief Justice Rolle, who feared Cromwell but was unable to rule against his conscience, resigned from the bench before the matter proceeded to decision.[435] Shortly thereafter, Cony withdrew from the case.[436] Meanwhile, Sir Peter Wentworth, a member of the Long Parliament, had caused a collector to be arrested and forced a similar issue before the courts.[437] Wentworth was unable to secure legal representation and so attempted to prosecute his own suit, but Cromwell had received notice of the prosecution, sent for him and ordered him to withdraw his action.[438] Wentworth was forced to obey.[439]

Such abuse continued after the death of Cromwell. During Richard's reign, certain prisoners who had been detained in the

Tower by Cromwell's order had been sent by his successor to Jersey and other places overseas.[440] Those sent beyond the reach of the writ sent a complaint to Parliament alleging that they were falsely imprisoned.[441] Their gaoler was sent for and, having been requested to show by what authority he kept those persons imprisoned, produced a paper, fully written by Cromwell: " 'Sir, I pray you seize such and such persons, and all others whom you shall judge dangerous men; do it quickly, and you shall have a warrant after it is done.' "[442] Parliament voted that these commitments were "illegal, unjust and tyrannical" because:

(1) the warrant by which they were committed was by the "Chief Magistrate"; (2) the warrant displayed no cause for the commitments; and, (3) the sending of prisoners beyond the reach of the writ of habeas corpus was, in effect, a banishment, and by law no Englishman could be banished by any authority other than an Act of Parliament.[443]

But before the prisoners could be set at liberty and the lieutenant of the gaol punished for obeying so unjust a warrant, the Parliament was dissolved.[444]

During the interregnum, then, great advances occurred in the application of the writ of habeas corpus to the civil sector. At the same time, the new administration of England approached the use of the writ in politically sensitive criminal cases in a way that differed markedly from the rhetoric of the revolution and that, in fact, differed little from the approach of the regime the Protector had deposed.

THE HABEAS CORPUS ACT OF 1679

This divarication continued after the return of the Stuarts. The passage of the Habeas Corpus Act of 1679,[445] which, with the exception of the Magna Carta, is probably the most famous statute in the annals of English Law, overshadowed much of the oppressive activity of the body responsible for its passage. While the Act was being conceived, nurtured, and weaned, the actions of both houses of Parliament and of the executive branch of government presented an interesting contrast to the spirit of the Act.[446]

The weakness of the writ as a safeguard against executive power was demonstrated by the impeachment of the Earl of Clarendon, Lord High Chancellor of England.[447] Among other charges, the articles of impeachment presented against Clarendon alleged that

> he hath advised and procured divers of his majesty's subjects to be imprisoned against law, in remote islands, garrisons, and other places, thereby to prevent them from the benefit of the law, and to produce precedents for the imprisoning any other of his majesty's subjects in like manner.[448]

Although the Commons were condemning Clarendon's disregard of individual liberty, they had initially sought to have him sequestered on a general charge of treason, promising to present specific articles "in convenient time."[449] The Lords, however, rejected the move and forced the lower house to present particular articles of impeachment.[450]

The recognition of the type of abuse engaged in by Clarendon brought about the introduction the following year of a bill that would assure the availability of the writ of habeas corpus,[451] but the bill died in committee. One year later, a bill to prevent the transportation of English subjects "beyond the sea" was sent out of committee and given a hearing before all the Commons.[452] A vocal opposition feared that such a bill would dangerously diminish the Crown's power.[453] Juxtaposed against such apprehension was the argument voiced most concisely by Sir Thomas Lee:

> He that is sent to Jersey or Guernsey, may be sent to Tangier, and so never know what his crimes are, and no *Habeas Corpus* can reach him. All convictions must be by a Plebian Jury, which now they cannot have. . . . [I]t does not take away the King's power at all, but secures the subject.[454]

The bill passed the House by the narrowest of margins, 100-99,[455] but it failed to withstand the scrutiny of the Lords.[456]

The year 1670 did not prove a complete loss to the advancement of the security of the subject's liberty, for in that year the celebrated *Bushell's Case*[457] was decided by Common Pleas. To understand *Bushell's Case* one must first consider the trial from which it resulted

—that of William Penn and William Mead.[458] Penn and Mead had been arrested for assembling "unlawfully and tumultuously," which resulted in "the disturbance of the peace."[459] As the trial began, Penn prayed that the court grant him two requests: first, "[t]hat no advantage may be taken against me, nor I deprived of any benefit, which I might otherwise have received," and second, "[t]hat you will promise me a fair hearing, and liberty of making my defence."[460] The court naturally agreed but proceeded to conduct a travesty of a trial.[461] When asked for the verdict of the jury, the foreman answered that the defendants were "Guilty of speaking in Grace-church Street."[462] For this verdict the jurors were "vilif[ied] . . . with most opprobrious language."[463] The court refused to accept such a verdict, and the jury was sent out again for a more acceptable one.[464] The same verdict was once again returned.[465] The jury was again sent out, and sent out three more times after that, until finally they were fined forty marks per man and imprisoned until it was paid.[466] Among the jurors imprisoned was a certain Bushell, who applied for and was granted a writ of habeas corpus.[467] Although the court's favorable decision on Bushell's petition is more important to a history of the jury,[468] the rhetoric of the court in allowing the writ is relevant to an analysis of its origin since the court, *per* Mr. Chief Justice Vaughan, adopted the language of liberty that Coke, Selden, and others had employed over forty years earlier to define the nature of the writ: "The Writ of *habeas corpus* is now the most usual remedy by which a man is restored again to his liberty, if he have been against law deprived of it."[469]

Meanwhile, the Commons continued their attempt to draft an acceptable bill that would correct the defects in the procedure for obtaining the writ of habeas corpus. In 1673, a bill to prevent imprisonments beyond the sea was again reported out of committee. It was debated early the following year,[470] passed, and sent to the Lords as "An Act to prevent the illegal Imprisonment of the Subject."[471] It was introduced in the upper chamber,[472] but Parliament was prorogued before the Lords voted on the bill.[473] On June 3, 1675, the Commons passed and sent to the Lords "An Act for preservation of the liberty of the King's subjects."[474] Once again the end of the Lords' session intervened.[475] While this latest bill was being debated in the Commons,[476] a struggle between the two houses, which came to involve the writ of habeas corpus, was in progress.

On June 1, 1675, Sir John Churchill, Mr. Serjeant Peck, Mr. Serjeant Pemberton, and Mr. Charles Porter, counsellors at law assigned by the House of Lords to represent Sir Nicholas Crispe against a member of Parliament, Mr. Dalmahoy, and others, were summoned before the Commons. They were asked to explain their appearance before the bar of the Lords, in breach of an order of the Commons, in the prosecution of a case against Mr. Dalmahoy.[477] They claimed to have received no notice of the order of the Commons, but admitted that they had heard of it in general conversations.[478] Knowing that Mr. Dalmahoy was involved, they explained, they had at first declined to appear; but an order of the Lords was served on them and they complied.[479] The Commons found their excuse unsatisfactory and ordered that they be taken into the custody of the serjeant of the lower house for breach of privilege.[480] The Lords protested and called the imprisonment "illegal [and] arbitrary"[481] and "a transcendent invasion on the right and liberty of the subject, and against *Magna Charta*, the Petition of Right, and many other laws."[482] They further informed the Commons that in pursuance of those laws they had sent the Gentleman Usher of the Black Rod to transmit their order to set those imprisoned at large and to prohibit "the Lieutenant of the *Tower*, and [all] other keepers of prisons, [and] jailers, and all persons whatsoever, from arresting, imprisoning, detaining, or otherwise molesting, or charging, the said gentlemen, or any of them, in this case."[483] The Commons were infuriated by the actions and allegations of the Lords. Mr. Swynfin, as if searching for past injustices to justify the present evil, raised examples of illegal imprisonments initiated by the Lords and queried "where the Petition of Right and *Magna Charta* [were] then."[484] On June 7, four days after their transmission to the Lords of "An Act for preservation of the liberty of the King's subjects," the Commons, fearing that the Lords might employ the writ of habeas corpus, ordered "that the Lieutenant of the *Tower* . . . not deliver the prisoners, till he has the Order of the House for it."[485] The following day, Sir John Robinson, Lieutenant of the Tower, appeared before the Commons and informed them that Black Rod had arrived with an order from the Lords demanding that the prisoners be released; but because they had been committed by order of the House of Commons, and in view of the vote in that chamber the preceding day, Robinson had refused to deliver them.[486] The Lieutenant further informed the lower house that after he had refused to submit to the Black Rod, four writs of habeas corpus, under the Great Seal, were delivered to him.[487] In response to this information, the House of Commons resolved:

> That no Commoners of *England*, committed by Order or Warrant of the House of Commons for Breach of Privilege or Contempt of that House, ought, without Order of that House, to be by any Writ of *Habeas Corpus* or other Authority whatsoever, made to appear, and answer, and do and receive a Determination in the House of Peers, during that Session of Parliament, wherein such Person was so committed. . . .[488]

and further,

> That the Order of the House of Peers, for the issuing out of Writs of *Habeas Corpus*, concerning [the four counsellors] . . . , is insufficient and illegal; for that it is general, and expresses no particular Cause of Privilege. . . .[489]

and, to protect the Lieutenant of the Tower from fine and amercement in the event of his need to disregard a pluries habeas corpus,

> That the Lieutenant of the *Tower*, in case he hath received, or shall receive, any Writ, [Warrant,] Order, or Commandment, to remove or deliver, any person, or persons, committed for breach of Privilege, but any Order or Warrant of this House, shall not make any return thereof, or yield any obedience thereunto, before he hath first acquainted this House, and received their Order and Directions how to proceed therein.[490]

The King failed to see any other way of resolving the differences between the two houses and terminated the parliamentary session.[491]
    Shortly after the end of the suspension of Parliament, the case

of Francis Jenkes was presented before the King's Bench.[492] The case underscored another defect in the procedure for receiving the benefits of the writ of habeas corpus. Jenkes was committed by the Lords of the Council for attempting "in a most seditious and mutinous manner" to stir those listening to his speech to go to the Lord-Mayor and urge him to call a Common-Council for the purpose of requesting the King to call a new Parliament.[493] When Jenkes' friends attempted to act as sureties for him, Lord Chief Justice Rainsford refused to entertain a writ of habeas corpus because it was out of term.[494] The following day, they moved Lord Chancellor Finch for the writ, citing in support of their request Coke's *Second Part of the Institutes*, which stated:

> The like Writ is to be granted out of the Chancery, either in the time of the Term, (as in the King's Bench) or in the Vacation; for the Court of Chancery is *officina justita*, and is ever open, and never adjourned, so as the Subject being wrongfully imprisoned, may have justice for the liberty of his person as well as in the Vacation time as in the Term.[495]

Finch replied, "The lord Coke was not infallible."[496] He reasoned that even if habeas corpus were granted, obeyed, and returned, the prisoner still could not be bailed or discharged until after the return was filed, which could not be done in vacation.[497] He also indicated that 16 Charles I, c. 10 "would have taken some notice of the Chancery and have provided against the delays of *habeas corpus* there as in other courts"[498] if that court had been a proper court for the issuance of the writ during the vacation.[499] Finally, the Lord Chancellor pointed to the bill of the Commons of June 3, 1675, which, if Coke were correct, would have been "needless."[500] A remedy at law was never afforded Jenkes, although he was released to bail by informal means.[501]

The case displayed one further flaw in the procedure, and when Parliament met the following year the movement to mend this and other defects, through which *the executive* could defeat the effect of habeas corpus, continued. In March 1677, a bill was sent from the Commons to the Lords.[502] It was considered in Grand Committee on the fifth of April, when several amendments were suggested;[503] further consideration, however, was prevented by adjournment.[504]

While the Lords were considering the bill, the Earl of Shaftesbury was imprisoned in the Tower by order of the House of Peers for the unspecified charge of "high contempts."[505] After four months of confinement on a general charge, Shaftesbury's case was brought before the King's Bench on a writ of habeas corpus.[506] On his behalf it was argued that the return was insufficient, "for the general allegation of high contempts is too uncertain, for the court cannot judge of the contempt, if it doth not appear in what act it consists."[507] In addition, it was noted that the return was uncertain as to the place and time of the alleged offense and as to whether the commitment was on a conviction or accusation only.[508] Although the court agreed that the return was illegal, it ordered that the prisoner be remanded: "This Court cannot meddle with the transactions of the most High Court of Peers in parliament."[509] The following February, the Lords considered Shaftesbury's appeal to the King's Bench for a writ of habeas corpus and resolved: "That it is a breach of the privilege of this House, for any Lord committed by this House to bring a Habeas Corpus in any inferior Court, to free himself from that imprisonment during the session of parliament."[510] The writ was thus unable to overcome an illegal commitment insulated by the concept of privilege, the same concept that in earlier times had been a catalyst in the transformation of the king's "prerogative writ" into a writ of liberty.

A large part of the 1678-1679 legislative schedule following the Shaftesbury affair was consumed with further debate on a bill to amend the procedure for obtaining the benefits of the writ of habeas corpus and with the impeachment of Thomas Earl of Danby, Lord High Treasurer of England. After a decade of failure, a bill, which passed the Commons after amendments, conferences, and compromises, managed to win the approval of the Lords and to receive the assent of the King.[511] Its passage has been attributed to "one misteller [in the House of Lords], guided by the justice of Heaven"[512] —a fitting climax to a singular history of advance.

BEYOND THE HABEAS CORPUS ACT: THE FINAL HYPOCRISY

It is unnecessary to recite the many provisions of the Act here, for its fame has assured that it is readily available for examination. Nor is added commentary on its contents and shortcomings compelled.[513] It is necessary, however, to proceed beyond passage of the Act a few more years to see the story of hypocrisy continued.

While the final debates on the habeas corpus bill were taking place, the two houses of Parliament were involved in an equally powerful constitutional debate over the impeachment of Thomas Earl of Danby.[514] The Commons resolved to impeach Danby of high treason and other high crimes and misdemeanors on December 20, 1678.[515] Prior to a vote on the Articles of Impeachment presented against Danby in the lower house, the King granted Danby his royal pardon.[516] Parliament was thus faced with the question whether an impeachment could be prevented by a pardon. The issue set the two houses at loggerheads and before any resolution could occur, Charles prorogued Parliament.[517] While the issue awaited resolution, Danby remained confined in the Tower on a general charge of treason, untried and fully pardoned.[518] After three years of confinement, there being no Parliament sitting to which he could apply for liberty, Danby sought a writ of habeas corpus in the King's Bench in order to be bailed.[519] He claimed that he had been accused and committed without oath or affidavit made against him for any particular crime whatsoever, that there was no particular treason mentioned in the articles against him, that his imprisonment was in violation of the royal pardon he had received, that his counsel had been threatened if he dared to plead the matter at law, and that he had been confined for over forty months without prosecution.[520] The judges agreed with many of Danby's arguments but could offer him only compassion, for he had been "imprisoned by an higher hand . . . where they had no power to intermeddle."[521] The Court held: "Whether their lordships had cause, or not cause, to commit his lordship, they could not suspect; but that they ought to believe that his lordship was justly committed; and that their lordships, in their mature deliberation, would do nothing unjustly."[522]

Undoubtedly, the decision had been influenced by debate in the Commons on the case of a Mr. Sheridan,[523] involving many of the same legislators responsible for the passage of the Habeas Corpus Act of 1679. Sheridan and Day had been committed by the Commons in December 1680.[524] The consensus of the House was that the scope of the Habeas Corpus Act never intended to comprehend Parliament, but only inferior courts. "[I]t was for the growing evils of removing men out of the reach of *Habeas Corpus*, that this Bill was formerly brought in. . . . [I]t was never intended against Commitments of the House of Commons."[525] This opinion was reinforced by the judiciary in the 1704 case of *Regina v. Paty*.[526] The defendants in the case had been committed to the prison at Newgate by the House of Commons "for having commenced and prosecuted an action at law against the constables of Aylesbury, for refusing their votes in the election of members of Parliament, in contempt of the jurisdiction and open breach of the known privileges of the House of Commons."[527] The case was brought before the King's Bench on habeas corpus.[528] The Court ruled the commitments lawful, noting that "the House of Commons [was] the proper [judge] of [its] own privileges."[529]

An interesting dissenting opinion by Holt saw the actions of the defendants as no breach of privilege and stated further that

> when the House of Commons exceed the legal bounds and authority, their acts are wrongful, and cannot be justified more than the acts of private men: that there was no question but their authority is from the law, and as it is circumscribed, so it may be exceeded: to say they are judges of their own privileges and their own authority, and no body else, is to make their privilege to be as they would have them.[530]

Neither Holt's view on judicial review nor on the privileges of Parliament has been accepted by the courts in England.[531] Thus, each chamber of the Parliament asserted a power to imprison arbitrarily —a power that Parliaments during the earlier part of the century had struggled to eliminate from the executive branch.

The final division of the century to be considered here occurred in the year 1689. It was, by far, the most significant split, if only because over the years the two divergent governmental principles involved had both become firmly established components of the same system: one congruent with the concept of limited government, the other entirely contrary to that notion. One of the loopholes in the Habeas Corpus Act was that it allowed the judges almost absolute discretion in the setting of bail.[532] This flaw was mended in 1688 by the Bill of Rights, which provided, among other things, that "excessive bail ought not to be required."[533] While the Bill of Rights was being debated, Mr. Hampden brought the following message to Parliament:

> I am commanded by the King to acquaint the House, that several persons about the Town, in Cabals, conspire against the Government, for the interest of King *James*: Some the King has caused to be apprehended and secured, and thinks he may see cause to do so by others. If these should be set at liberty, 'tis apprehended we shall be wanting to our own safety, the Government, and People. The King is not willing to do any thing but what he may be warranted by Law; therefore, if these persons deliver themselves by *Habeas Corpus*, there may arise a difficulty. Excessive Bail you have complained of. If men hope to carry their great design on, they will not be unwilling to forfeit their Bail. The King asks your Advice. . . . I forgot to tell you, some are committed on suspicion of Treason only.[534]

In effect, the new monarch was requesting the suspension of the Habeas Corpus Act. The principle underlying the division of those for and against acceding to his request was simply that those who favored suspension saw those who threatened the government as the greater evil;[535] those opposed to the suspension feared more the precedent that would be established and suggested, as an alternative to suspension, that greater security be taken to insure the appearance of those let to bail.[536] A three-month suspension was finally imposed.[537] In May, Hampden moved for an extension of the period of suspension.[538] To this motion Sir Robert Napier replied, "This Mistress of ours, the *Habeas Corpus* Act, if we part with it twice, it will become quite a common Whore. Let us not remove this Landmark of the Nation, for a curse attends it."[539] Sir Robert Cotton, of Cambridgeshire, continued:

> As an *Englishman*, I am jealous of our Liberties, and will not give my Vote to betray them. The difference betwixt a Subject

and a Slave is, that one has the benefit of Law, the other is used at pleasure. . . . You are told, "This Bill is necessary as long as the Government is unsettled." *Lewis* XI of *France* desired only liberty to raise Money till the next Parliament did sit; and he never called a Parliament, and they have raised Money without Parliaments ever since. I am jealous of a thing of so high importance to preserve our Liberties, not to put the Subjects in such a condition as to suspend their liberty for an hour.[540]

Such arguments proved unconvincing, the motion passed, and those who found the existing laws somehow incompatible with a state of emergency carried the day.[541] To paraphrase Montesquieu,[542] the spring of government lost a bit of its elasticity, the imagination grew a little more accustomed to the severe as to the milder punishment, and the precedent was established.

CONCLUSION

Habeas corpus originated as a device for compelling appearance before the King's judicial instrumentalities. It is easy to conceive of the writ as a process that could be used by a repressive government to divest an individual of personal freedom. It was, therefore, in the nature of the developing view of the individual in society rather than in the nature of the writ itself, that an otherwise antilibertarian instrument (that is, one *compelling* appearance) was transformed into an instrument that safeguards individual freedom.

What might be referred to as the unconscious forces of constitutional law crystallized the basic function of the writ as we know it today. From the fourteenth to the seventeenth century, habeas corpus was a convenient weapon wielded by the courts of England in their maneuvers to increase and to safeguard their jurisdictions. A subject imprisoned by one court could be released by means of the writ issued by a rival court on the holding that the committing court lacked jurisdiction in the case. Release had nothing to do with the guilt or innocence of the party confined.

In the seventeenth century, the jurisdictional battle line divided the executive and legislative branches. As long as the executive retained authority to imprison arbitrarily, Parliament remained subordinate. In the name of individual liberty, Parliament, adopting the rhetoric of the judiciary's battles, fought to restrict the Crown's powers. The hypocrisy of the remaining years of the seventeenth century confirms the view that the development of habeas corpus can largely be attributed to the unconscious forces of constitutional law. Fortunately, rhetoric overcame reality. The writ became a viable bulwark between the powers of government and the rights of the people in both England and the United States, although Congress, in "Cases of Rebellion or Invasion," when required by the "public Safety,"[543] has the power to remove that fortification.

NOTES

1. Edward Coke, *The Second Part of the Institutes of the Laws of England* (5th ed. London, 1671, 1st ed. London, 1628), p. 53.

2. In English law, "prerogative writ" was the name given to certain judicial writs issued by the courts only upon proper cause shown, but never as a mere right. De Smith, "The Prerogative Writs," 11 Cambridge L.J. 40, 42-44 (1951). Other examples of prerogative writs include the writs of certiorari, prohibition, and mandamus. Ibid., p. 40.

3. William Blackstone, *Commentaries on the Laws of England* (Oxford, 1770), vol. 3, p. 141.

4. Edward Jenks, "The Story of the Habeas Corpus," 18 Law Q. Rev. 64 (1902).

5. The best example of this can be found in F. Solly-Flood, *Abridged History of the Writ of Habeas Corpus Cum Causa as a Remedy Against Unlawful Imprisonment* (1887) (Mss. Royal Historical Society), a tightly handwritten manuscript of 570 pages. The most extensive history available today on the origins of habeas corpus, this manuscript treats the writ as a writ of liberty from its inception. *See also, Fay v. Noia*, 372 U.S. 391, 399-405 (1963).

6. *See* 28 U.S.C. sections 2254-2255 (1970).

7. Jenks, "The Story," p. 65.

8. Ibid.

9. *See* text accompanying notes 85-112 *infra*.

10. Blackstone, *Commentaries*, p. 129.

11. Robert Walker, *The Constitutional and Legal Development of Habeas Corpus As the Writ of Liberty* (Oklahoma State University Publications, 1960), pp. 12-13; Maxwell Cohen, "Some Considerations on the Origins of Habeas Corpus," 16 Can. B. Rev. 92, 103 (1938).

12. Paul Vinogradoff, *Outlines of Historical Jurisprudence* (New York: Oxford University Press, 1920), vol. 1, p. 320; George E. Howard, "Development of the King's Peace, and the English Local Peace-Magistracy," 1 Neb. U. Stud. 235, 236 (1890).

13. Howard, "The King's Peace," 1 Neb. U. Stud. 235, 240.

14. Ibid.

15. Ibid.

16. Elsa De Haas, *Antiquities of Bail: Origin and Historical Development in Criminal Cases to the Year 1275* (New York: Columbia University Press, 1940), p. 4; William F. Duker, "The Right to Bail: A Historical Inquiry," 42 Alb. L. Rev. 33, 35 (1977).

17. Laws of Ine, c. 9, F. L. Attenborough, ed., *The Laws of the Earliest Kings* (New York: Russell and Russell, 1963), p. 39 (footnote omitted).

18. *See* Howard, "The King's Peace," 1 Neb. U. Stud. 235.

19. "He who captures a thief shall have 10 shillings. The thief shall be given up to the king, and his kinsmen shall swear that they will carry no vendetta against him." Laws of Ine, c. 28, Attenborough, *Laws of the Earliest Kings*, p. 45.

20. "He who kills a thief shall be allowed to declare with an oath that he whom he killed was a thief trying to escape, and the kinsmen of the dead man shall swear an oath to carry on no vendetta against him." Ibid. c. 35, p. 47. The laws of Ethelstan (925?-939? A.D.) provided that if the thief tried to defend himself or attempted to flee, "he shall not be spared." Ibid., 2 Laws of Ethelstan, c. 1, sect. 2, p. 127 (footnote omitted).

Individual justice was not, however, absolutely abolished. For example, the laws of Canute (1017-1035 A.D.) provided that no one could distrain another's property until he had sought redress, without satisfaction, three times in the hundred court. 2 Laws of Canute, c. 19, A. J. Robertson ed., *The Laws of the Kings of England from Edmund to Henry I* (Cambridge: Cambridge University Press, 1925), p. 183. The statute continued:

> 1. If on the third occasion he does not obtain justice, he shall go on the fourth occasion to the shire court, and the shire court shall appoint a day when he shall issue his summons for the fourth time.
>
> 2. And if this summons fails, he shall get leave, either from the one court or the other, to take his own measures. . . .

Ibid. c. 19, sects. 1-2, p. 183 (footnote omitted).

21. This development occurred in the laws of Kings Hlothaere (673-685 A.D.) and Eadric (685-687 A.D.). Laws of Hlothaere and Eadric, cc. 1-16, B. Thorpe (ed.), *Ancient Laws and Institutes of England* (The Commission on Public Records of the Kingdom, 1840), vol. 1, pp. 27-35. Elements of feudalism are readily apparent. Chapter I provided that "If any one's 'eshe' [servant] slay a man of an 'eorl's' [nobleman's] degree, whoever it be, let the owner pay with three hundred shillings, give up the slayer, and add three 'man-wyrths' [male workers] thereto." Ibid. c. 1, p. 27 (footnotes omitted). If the slayer escaped, a fourth *man-wyrth* was added to the fine, and it was incumbent upon the master to prove that he could not find the slayer. Ibid. c. 2, p. 29. In addition:

> If a man entertain a stranger for three nights at his own home, a chapman or any other who has come over the march, and then feed him with his own food, and he [the stranger] then do harm to any man, let the man [the host] bring the other to justice. . . .

Ibid. c. 15, pp. 33-35 (footnote omitted).

22. Ibid., Laws of Ethelstan, c. 20, p. 209.

23. Ibid. The law continued:

But if any one will not ride with his fellows, let him pay the king's 'oferhyrnes.' And let it be announced at the 'gemot,' that the 'frith' [peace] be kept toward all that the king wills to be within the 'frith,' and theft be forgone by his life and by all that he has. And he who for the 'wites' [fines] will not desist, then let all the chief men belonging to the 'burh' ride to him, and take all that he has; and let the king take possession of half, of half the men who may be in the riding; and place him in 'borh.' If he know not who will be his 'borh,' let them imprison him. If he will not suffer it, let him be killed, unless he escape. If any one will avenge him, or be at feud with any of them, then be he foe to the king, and to all his friends. If he escape, and any one harbour him, let him be liable in his 'wer' [wergeld] unless he shall dare to clear himself by the 'flyma's' [outlaw, that is, a man who has fled from the law] 'wer,' that he knew not he was a 'flyma.'

Ibid., pp. 209-11; see ibid. c. 1, pp. 199-200. For examples of similar provisions, see ibid., Laws of Edward the Elder, c. 1, pp. 159-61, c. 5, p. 163, c. 10, p. 165; ibid., Laws of Canute, c. 29, p. 393.

24. Laws of Henry I, c. 5, sect. 2a, L. J. Downer ed., *Leges Henrici Primi* (Oxford: Clarendon Press, 1972), p. 85. If when summoned to the hundred court, however, an individual refused to come without "any genuine and compelling reason," he was fined thirty pence for each default, ibid. c. 29, sect. 2, p. 131; see ibid. c. 51, sect. 1, p. 167. The legal *essoins* (excuses) that excused the noncompliance with a summons were: "sudden illness or . . . necessary service to his lord or . . . military duties or . . . the operations of his enemies or . . . lawful detention by a justice of the king. . . ." Ibid. c. 59, sect. 1a, p. 181. Unless one of the aforesaid reasons detained the summoned party, a default on the third appointed time would give rise to a verdict of guilty on the accusation levied against him, ibid. c. 133, sect. 3a, p. 133, and he would be required to pay the full *wite* (fine), ibid. c. 51, section 1, p. 167. For nonappearance in the face of a summons issued by the county court, the individual was held guilty of *overseunesse* (contempt) toward the king. Ibid. c. 53, sect. 1, p. 169. If he refused to pay the fine for *overseunesse*, his property was distrained and, if need be, he was placed under surety. Ibid. c. 53, sect. 1b, p. 171. If his defiance continued, he forfeited all that he owned, and he was seized and imprisoned unless he could produce sureties. Ibid. c. 53, sect. 1c, p. 171. If he resisted arrest, and it became necessary, he was killed. Ibid. c. 53, sect. 1d, p. 171. If his resistance was successful and he escaped, he was outlawed, that is, placed outside the protection of the king. Ibid. c. 53, sect. 1e, p. 171.

25. W. S. Holdsworth, *A History of English Law* (London: Methuen and Co., 1956), p. 3.

26. Ibid., pp. 3-4.

27. Ibid., pp. 33-35; F. Pollock and F. W. Maitland, *The History of English Law Before the Time of Edward I* (Cambridge: Cambridge University Press, 2nd ed., 1968), vol. 1, p. 513.

28. Ibid., p. 88.

29. This was accomplished during the reign of Henry II. 1 Holdsworth 47-48.

30. Ibid., p. 9; 1 Pollock and Maitland 532.

31. Undoubtedly the precept was so termed because it was a "brief" communication of the state of the case.

32. *See*, George Burton Adams, *The Origin of the English Constitution* (New Haven: Yale University Press, 1912), pp. 76-77; T. A. M. Bishop and P. Chaplais ed., *Facsimiles of English Royal Writs to A.D. 1100* (Oxford: Clarendon Press, 1957), p. ix; F. E. Harmer, *Anglo-Saxon Writs* (Manchester: Manchester University Press, 1952), p. 1; Edward Jenks, *Law and Politics in the Middle Ages* (London: John Murray, 1898), p. 123; Doris M. Stenton, *English Justice Between the Norman Conquest and the Great Charter* (London: American Philosophical Society, 1964), p. 17; Naomi Hurnard, "The Jury of Presentment and the Assise of Clarendon," 56 Eng. Hist. Rev. 374, 376-78 (1941).

33. Edward Jenks, "The Prerogative Writs in English Law," 32 Yale L.J. 523 (1923).

34. *See* A. H. Thomas ed., *Calendar of Early Mayor's Court Rolls (1298-1307)* (Cambridge: Cambridge University Press, 1924), pp. xviii-xix.

35.   The necessity of such *brevia* was very obvious; . . . when suits were commenced in the king's court, at a great distance from the habitation of the parties, and process was to issue to him merely as an officer, who knew nothing more of the matter than what the precept explained, it was necessary that something more particular should be exhibited to him; and therefore, that the precept should be *written*.

John Reeves, *The History of English Law* (London: Reeves and Turner, 1869; 1st ed. London 1784), p. 147 (emphasis in original).

36. 1 Holdsworth 49.

37. Ibid., p. 50; *See* W. Farrer ed., *The Lancashire Pipe Rolls* (Liverpool: Henry Young and Sons, 1902), p. 17.

38. David Douglas and George W. Greenaway eds., *English Historical Documents* (London: Eyre and Spotteswoods, 1953), pp. 407-10.

39. Ibid., pp. 411-13.

40. 1 Holdsworth 50. In the thirty-first year of Henry II's reign, the sheriff of York was amerced (fined) for causing an accused, saved from the ordeal of cold water, to abjure the realm without the authority of the justices. 31 Hen. 2, 34 Pipe Rolls 70, r. 5, m. 1d (1184-1185).

41. Douglas and Greenaway, *Documents*, pp. 408-10.

42. Ibid., p. 408. For the latin version, *see* William Stubbs ed., *Select Charters and Other Illustrations of English Constitutional History* (Oxford: Clarendon Press, 1895), p. 170.

43. Ibid., p. 411; compare, Douglas and Greenaway, *Documents*, p. 408.

44. *See* Farrer, *Lancashire Pipe Rolls*, p. 17.

45. The tithing was a local governmental unit that had the responsibility for the apprehension of those accused of crimes. For an explanation of the relationship between the functions of the tithing system and the *borh* system, *see* Duker, "The Right to Bail," 42 Alb. L. Rev. 33, 38 n.28.

46. William Alfred Morris, *The Frankpledge System* (London: Longmans, Green and Co., 1910), p. 151.

47. For the definition of these three writs, *see* Duker, "The Right to Bail," 42 Alb. L. Rev. 33, 43 n.63. *See* De Haas, *Antiquities of Bail*, pp. 51-127;

Cohen, "Origins," 16 Can. B. Rev. 92, 96-102; Jenks, "The Story," 18 Law Q. Rev. 64, 66-67.

48. The process was probably implemented in the final decade of the twelfth century. It seems to have been well established by the first decade of the thirteenth century. When Glanvill's treatise was written (probably between 1187 and 1189, by an author whose identity is now uncertain, C. D. C. Hall ed., *The Treatise on the Laws and Customs of the Realm of England Commonly Called Glanvill* |Nelson, 1965|, pp. xxx-xxxiii) however, the procedure that Bracton later describes was not yet in operation. The Glanvill process operated in the following manner:

> On the appointed return day the party summoned either comes or does not. . . . If he neither comes nor sends anyone, the other party who is claiming against him should appear before the justices on the appointed return day and present his case against the tenant; and he shall wait three days in court. If the tenant does not come on the fourth day, but the summoners appear and allege that he has been properly summoned and offer to prove this in whatever way the court may decide, then the court shall direct that the tenant be summoned again by a further writ to come on a return day at least a fortnight later. This writ shall direct him to come and answer both as to the principal plea and as to his not coming at the first summons.
>
> Three summonses shall be sent out in this way. If the tenant neither comes nor sends anyone at the third summons, then the land shall be taken into the lord king's hand, and shall remain thus for a fortnight; if the tenant does not come within the fortnight, seisin shall be adjudged to the other party, and the tenant shall not be allowed to reopen the issue except on the question of property by a means of a writ of right. If, however, the tenant comes within the fortnight and wishes to replevy the tenement, he shall be ordered to come on the fourth day, when he shall have justice done to him; and so, if he comes then, he can get back his seisin.
>
> If the tenant does come at the third summons and admits the previous summonses, he immediately loses his seisin unless he is able to save the previous return days by royal warrant. . . .

Ibid., pp. 5-6 (footnotes omitted); *see* ibid., pp. 8, 12, 20, 40, 42, 44, 48, 49, 63-64, 105, 110, 117, 131, 142, 143.

49. Sir Travers Twiss ed., *Bracton, De Legibus et Consuetudinibus Angliae* (London: Longmans and Co., 1883), pp. 465-81. The Bractonian process was the general procedure. *See* Donald W. Sutherland, "Mesne Process upon Personal Actions in the Early Common Law," 82 Law Q. Rev. 482, 482-84 (1966). But cf. 2 Pollock and Maitland 593 ("Bracton has drawn up a scheme which in his eyes is or should be the normal process of compulsion; but we can see both from his own text and from the plea rolls that he is aiming at generality and simplicity, and also that some questions are still open.") (footnote omitted). However, the courts often permitted plaintiffs to skip steps. Sutherland, "Mesne Process," 82 Law Q. Rev. 482, 484. As Bracton observed:

The solemn order of attachments ought not to be observed . . . in all personal actions as well on account of the privilege and favour of those who have vowed a crusade, whose affairs require readiness and instance . . . Likewise an account of the cause or the necessity . . . Likewise on account of the thing itself . . . Likewise in an action for an injury . . . Likewise on account of the persons against whom the injury has been done. . . .

6 *Bracton* 503-05. For examples, *see Brianus de Insula v. Agatham de Sancto Jeorgeo*, Mich. 16-17 Hen. 3, 14 Curia Regis Rolls 525, no. 2428, r. 110, m. 19 (1232); *Abbas de'Stratford v. Ricardum de Monte Ficheti*, Mich. 16-17 Hen. 3, 14 Curia Regis Rolls 522, no. 2411, r. 111, m. 21d (1232); *Radulfus de Clere v. Jordanum de Wakervill'*, Mich. 14-15 Hen. 3, 14 Curia Regis Rolls 168, no. 836, r. 107, m. 20d (1230); *Ricardus de Ratlesden v. Ricardum de Hautevill'*, Mich. 14-15 Hen. 3, 14 Curia Regis Rolls 147, no. 729, r. 107, m. 15 (1230); *Thomas Filius Willelmi v. Aliciam de Paheham*, Mich. 14-15 Hen. 3, 14 Curia Regis Rolls 147, no. 727, r. 107, m. 15 (1230); *Magister militie Templi v. Johannem de Normanvill'*, Mich. 14-15 Hen. 3, 14 Curia Regis Rolls 119-20, no. 604, r. 107, m. 8 (1230); *Rogerus de Antreuen v. Robertam la Gard*, Trin. 14 Hen. 3, 14 Curia Regis Rolls 41-42, no. 210, r. 106, m. 8d (1230); *Stephanus de Farnberg' v. Simonem personam de Crumdel*, Trin. 14 Hen. 3, 14 Curia Regis Rolls 15-16, no. 95, r. 106, m. 3d (1230). Working against this expedition of the process were delays in the sheriff's returns. Sutherland, "Mesne Process," 82 Law Q. Rev. 482, 485. This necessitated the issuance of *sicut alias* (second) and *sicut pluries* (third) writs. Ibid.; *see* 2 Pollock and Maitland 593.

50. 6 *Bracton* 469; Sutherland, "Mesne Process," 82 Law Q. Rev. 482, 482-83.

51. 6 *Bracton* 471-73.

52. Ibid., pp. 474-77.

53. *See* note 56 *infra*; text accompanying notes 72, 88-90 *infra*.

54. Sutherland, "Mesne Process," 82 Law Q. Rev. 482, 483 n.6. Upon that return, there followed a series of distraints, 6 *Bracton* 477-81, possibly leading to outlawry. Bracton remarked:

[T]here is no greater crime than contumacy and disobedience, for all persons within the realm ought to be obedient to the lord the king and within his peace, and when having been called or summoned by the king they have contumaciously omitted to come they make themselves outlaws, and accordingly ought to be outlawed. . . .

Ibid., p. 481. But cf. John C. Fox, "Process of Imprisonment at Common Law," 39 Law Q. Rev. 46, 50 (1923) ("No record has ever been cited to show that outlawry applied at common law to injuries without force.").

55. *See* Eas. 14 Hen. 3, Memoranda Roll 62-63, m. 8 (1230-1231).

56. Early case law illustrates the writ's use and development in both public and private law. In the private sector, habeas corpus, as just stated, was the third step in the tedious mesne process. In *Tebbaldus de Bilton' v. Willelmun fratrem suum*, Trin. 8 John 1, 4 Curia Regis Rolls 153, r. 42, m. 8 (1206), four individuals were sent to examine the validity of an *essoin*, based upon ill health, pleaded by one Tebbaldus de Bilton' in lieu of appearance on a summons. The defendant and the four recognitors (jurors) were sum-

moned to appear on a certain day, but the five failed to do so. Ibid., p. 153. Attachments by pledges and better pledges also failed to elicit compliance with the court order. The court then commanded the sheriff to "habeat corpora eorundem" (have the bodies of those five [before it]). Ibid.

In *Magister Henricus de Legha v. Abbatem et Priorem de Muchelnye*, Trin. 4 Hen. 3, 3 *Bracton's Note Book* 339, pl. 1370 (1220), the defendants failed to appear on the summons. Ibid., pp. 339-40. They were then attached by Rogerus, Priur de Pleministro. Ibid., p. 340. Upon a second default, they were attached by Hugo de Montesorelli and Thomas de Dreyton. Ibid. Hugo and Thomas were also unsuccessful in bringing the Abbot and Prior to court and, therefore, the sheriff was ordered to have both the Abbot and the Prior brought before the court at a certain day and the first and second pledges fined for their default. Ibid. In the same year, Bracton reports an action brought by Rogerus de S. Dioneses and his wife Sarra against Isaac the Jew of Norwich. *Rogerus de S. Dionisio et Sarra uxor v. Isaac Judeum de Norwico*, Trin. 4 Hen. 4, 3 *Bracton's Note Book* 342, pl. 1376 (1220). There were no attachments following the unheeded summons because Isaac, as a Jew, could not own property. Ibid., p. 342. The sheriff was therefore ordered by "consilium curi[a]e" to have his body at a certain day. Ibid. In *Hugo le Butiller v. Rannulfum de Sheltona*, Trin. 4 Hen. 3, 3 *Bracton's Note Book* 361, pl. 1407 (1220), a writ of habeas corpus did not seem to issue until "many" pledges and "several" attachments proved fruitless. In another case, following the sheriff's return of the writ of habeas corpus, informing the court of his unsuccessful attempt to locate the defendant, it was ordered that the sheriff distrain the defendant by his land and chattels. *Robertus de Insula v. Willelmun filium warini*, Trin. 4 Hen. 3, 3 *Bracton's Note Book* 361, pl. 1408 (1220); *see Radulfus Musand v. Willelmum de Gardino*, Trin. 4 Hen. 3, 3 *Bracton's Note Book* 395, pl. 1446 (1220); *Willelmus prior de Leghe v. Rogerum filium Osberti*, Eas. 15 Hen. 3, 14 Curia Regis Rolls 282, no. 1331, r. 108, m. 6d (1231). In a case where the defendant was unable to secure pledges, the court required the sheriff to assume responsibility for assuring the court appearance of the defendant on the appointed day. *Walterus Driwe v. Josceam et Margeriam filias Roberti*, Trin. 4 Hen. 3, 3 *Bracton's Note Book* 374, no. 1420 (1220). In an action commenced by William, the brother of Benedict, the sheriff was directed to have the bodies of the defaulting parties before the court so that they could hear their judgment and show "quare non fecerunt sicut eis preceptum fuit" (why they had not done as they were often ordered). *Willelmus filius Benedicti v. Edwardus le Aungele et Josceum filium Ricardi*, Trin. 4 Hen. 3, 3 *Bracton's Note Book* 374, no. 1421 (1220). A similar directive is found on the Curia Regis Rolls in the same year. *Henricus de Legh' v. Eliam le Bule*, Eas. 4 Hen. 3, 8 Curia Regis Rolls 308, r. 72, m. 18 (1220).

In 1224, in *Prior de Bridelinton' v. Willilmum de Fortibus*, Mich. 8-9 Hen. 3, 11 Curia Regis Rolls 459, no. 2303, r. 87, m. 6d (1224), a writ of *haberet corpora* was issued to the sheriff. His return stated that he was unable to produce the body because he had let William to pledges. Ibid., p. 459. The pledges, however, were unsuccessful in securing his appearance. Ibid. A *sicut prius habeas corpus* issued immediately. Ibid. The court in this third step of the mesne process was applying the sanction of the sheriff's power; pledges had already failed to satisfy the court. The court held, therefore, that the sheriff's return was not a legitimate explanation for his failure to produce the body. Ibid. This principle was also illustrated in *Andreas de Fauhebergh v. Willelmum filiam Theme*, Hil. 14 Hen. 3, 13 Curia Regis Rolls 578, no. 2739, r. 104, m. 22 (1230), in which, upon a *haberet corpora*, the sheriff returned that he had "distringat eos per terras et catalla" (distrained them by land and chattels). Ibid., p. 578. The court then ordered the sheriff to come to bar and hear judgment on why he failed to bring the defendants' bodies. Ibid. Again, the sheriff's return was not a valid one, for it was incompatible with the rationale for this phase of the mesne process—that is, applying the power of the sheriff's office.

This is not to say that the sheriff, after receiving the writ of habeas corpus, could not require the defendant to supply pledges or mainpernors to guarantee his appearance. *Vide Henricus de la Bergh' v. Mattheum de How*, Trin. 15 Hen. 3, 14 Curia Regis Rolls 385, no. 1797, r. 109, m. 11d (1231). The pledges were, however, in such instances, responsible only to the sheriff, who in turn was solely responsible to the court. Moreover, if the defendant would not supply pledges to guarantee his appearance, the sheriff might distrain him by his land and chattels. In *Henricus Buqueinte v. Willelmum de Reymes*, Hil. 14 Hen. 3, 13 Curia Regis Rolls 582, no. 2756, r. 104, m. 22d (1230), the court implicitly sanctioned this method when it commanded the sheriff of Essex to have the defendant's body because "Willelmus non habet terram in comitatu Midd' per quam distringi potest nisi servicium, sed habet terram in comitatu Essex' " (William does not have land in the County of Middlesex by which he can be distrained except by feudal service, but he does have land in the county of Essex). Ibid., p. 582. In a case the following year, *Willelmus prior de Leghe v. Rogerum filium Osberti Radulfum*, Eas. 15 Hen. 3, 14 Curia Regis Rolls 280, no. 1331, r. 108, m. 6d (1231), involving a dispute over the judgment of the justices in an *assize de mortis antecessoris*, the sheriff was directed to have before the King's Court the bodies of the lower court justices "ad certificandum justiciarios de sacramento quod inde fecerunt, et quod haberet predictum Oliverum ad audiendum recordum illud et ad faciendum inde quod curia domini regis consideraverit" (to certify their judgment in the case and to have Oliver [the victorious party in the lower court] to hear the record and to do whatever the King's council shall decide). Ibid., p. 280. Unable to apply the more "inartistic" methods of compliance, due to the lower court justices' "libertatem" (privilege), the sheriff distrained the justices of their land and chattels, in order to assure their obedience to the writ of habeas corpus. Ibid. Thus, the cases seem to imply that in instances where the sheriff could take the defendant into custody—that is, in all cases except those involving privilege, those in which the defendant resided in a jurisdiction beyond the reach of the writ or, as noted earlier, those in which the defendant could not be found, *see* text accompanying note 54 *supra*— habeas corpus justified the seizure of the defendant in order to warrant his appearance on the courtday. *See* Sutherland, "Mesne Process," 82 Law Q. Rev. 482, 483 n.9; text accompanying notes 85-87 *infra*.

57. *See* 6 Calendar of Close Rolls 359, m. 11d (1250).

58. Undoubtedly because delay brought in money, there was great reluctance to hasten the process. *See* John Parker ed., *Plea Rolls of the County Palatine of Lancaster* (Chetham Society, 1928), pp. xiii-xiv.

59. William Page ed., *Three Assize Rolls For the County of Northumberland* (Surtees Society, 1891), pp. 51-52; 59-60. For examples in the year 1269, *see* ibid., pp. 178; 199-200.

60. *See e.g.* [1260-1261] Placitorum Abbreviatio 152; [1268] ibid., pp. 170, 171; [1218] ibid., pp. 173, 174, 175; [1268] ibid., p. 177.

61. 52 Hen. III c. 9, sects. 8-9 (1267).

62. The statute provided that in an action brought by a class of feoffers, the lord of the fee should bring only one suit, and should exact inheritance for one suit and not a separate exactment for each individual involved in the class action. Ibid. section 6.

63. Ibid. sects. 8-9.

64. Ibid., c. 12, sect. 3.

65. Ibid.

66. Ibid. sect. 5. The following chapter, attempting to expedite matters at a later stage, provided that after an issue was joined there should be but one essoin, or one default,

> so that if he [the defendant] come not at the Day given to him by the Essoin, or make Default the second Day, then the Enquest shall be taken by his Default, and according to the same Enquest they shall proceed to Judgement. And if such Enquest be taken in the County, before the Sheriff or Coroner, it shall be returned unto the King's Justices at a certain Day; and if the Party Defendant come not at that Day, then, upon his Default, another Day shall be assigned to him after the Discretion of the Justices; and it shall be commanded to the Sheriff, *that he cause him to come* to hear the Judgement, if he will, according to the Enquest; at which Day, if he come not, upon his Default they shall proceed to Judgement. In like manner it shall be done, if he come not at the Day given unto him by his Essoin.

Ibid. c. 13, sects. 1-2 (emphasis added).

67. Statute of Westminster I, 1275, 3 Edw. I, c. 45, sects. 1-2. In an attempt to eliminate the delays and false returns of writs by sheriffs, ten years later, in the Statute of Westminster II, it was provided that because the sheriffs

> make also many Times false Answers, returning that they could not execute the King's Precept for the Resistance of some great Man . . . And if per case the Sheriff when he cometh do find Resistance, he shall certifie to the Court the Names of the Resisters, Aiders, Consenters, Commanders, and Favourers, and by a Writ judicial they shall be attached by their Bodies to appear at the King's Court. . . .

Statute of Westminster II, 1285, 13 Edw. I, c. 39, sects. 22, 24.

68. A. Hamilton Thompson ed., *Northumbrian Pleas from De Banco Rolls 1-19* (1-5 Edward I) (Surtees Society, 1950), p. 12, pl. 32; *see also* William Huse Dunham ed., *Casus Placitorum and Reports of Cases in the King's Bench* (Seldon Society, 1952), *Ralph of Normanville v. Lucy of Kyme* (1275), pp. 52-54.

69. [1254] Placitorium Abbreviatio 137; *see* [1268] ibid., p. 169; [1268] ibid., p. 174; [1268] ibid., p. 176.

70. Ibid., p. 137.

71. Thompson, *Northumbrian Pleas*, p. 6, pl. 20.

72. *See supra* note 56; text accompanying note 53 *supra*, notes 89-90 *infra*.

73. Duker, "Right to Bail," 42 Alb. L. Rev. 33, 42.

74. Ibid., p. 43. For an explanation of the distinction between bail and mainprise, *see* ibid., p. 61, n. 152.

75. Sutherland, "Mesne Process," 82 Law Q. Rev. 482, 488; *see* text accompanying notes 88-89 *infra*.

76. *Foster v. Jackson*, 80 Eng. Rep. 201, 210 (K.B. 1613); 3 Blackstone, *Commentaries*, p. 281; P. W. Crowther, *The History of the Law of Arrest in Personal Actions* (London: J. and W. T. Clarke, 1828) p. 2; Fleta, Book 2, c. 65, in 72 Seldon Society 216-17 (H. Richards and G. Sayles eds. 1955); Mathew Hale, "A Discourse Concerning the Courts of King's Bench and Common-Pleas," in Francis Hargrave ed., *A Collection of Tracts Relative to the Law of England* (Dublin, 1787) vol. 1, p. 359. Coke stated:

> But the common law, which is the preserver of the common peace of the land, did abhor all force as a capital enemy to it; and therefore against those who committed any force, the common law did subject their bodies to imprisonment, which is the highest execution, by which he loses his liberty till he agree with party, and pay a fine to the King. . . .

Harbert's Case, 76 Eng. Rep. 647, 656 (Ex. 1584). Such a procedure is also described in Glanvill, *Treatise*, pp. 171-72. *See also* Fox, "Imprisonment," 39 Law Q. Rev. 46, 48-52.

77. Reeves, *History of English Law*, vol. 1, pp. 52-55; ibid., vol. 2, pp. 309-11.

78. Ibid.

79. Jenks, "The Story," 18 Law Q. Rev. 64, 67.

80. *See* ibid., pp. 67-69. *See also*, Maxwell Cohen, "Habeas Corpus Cum Causa—The Emergence of the Modern Writ—I," 18 Can. B. Rev. 10, 11 (1940).

81. Jenks, "The Story," 18 Law Q. Rev. 64, 68.

82. Ibid., pp. 67-68.

83. Ibid., p. 65 (emphasis in original).

84. Fox, "Imprisonment," 39 Law Q. Rev. 46, 54.

85. 2 Pollock and Maitland 593 n. 4.

86. *See Willelmus prior de Leghe v. Rogerum filium Osberti Radulfum*, Eas. 15 Hen. 3, 14 Curia Regis Rolls 280, no. 1331, r. 108, m. 6d (1231); *Henricus Buqueninte v. Willelmum de Reymes*, Hil. 14 Hen. 3, 13 Curia Regis Rolls 582, no. 2756, r. 104, m. 22d (1230); *Prior de Brindleton' v. Willilmum de Fortibus*, Mich. 8-9 Hen. 3, 11 Curia Regis Rolls 459, no. 2303, r. 87, m. 6d (1224).

87. Sutherland, "Mesne Process," 82 Law Q. Rev. 482, 483 n. 9. This theory conforms to the ancient notion of the seriousness of disobedience to the King and the summons of his courts, as illustrated by the Anglo-Saxon laws regarding *oferhyrnes*, *see* text accompanying notes 22-23 *supra*, the Norman laws regarding *overseunesse*, *see* note 24 *supra*, and the thirteenth-century attitude toward contempt displayed in Bracton's text, *see* note 54 *supra*.

88. *See* note 56 *supra*; text accompanying notes 53, 72 *supra*.

89. Duker, "Right to Bail," 42 Alb. L. Rev. 33, 41-42.

90. *See* text accompanying note 73 *supra*.

91. For examples of capias, *see Anon.*, Y. B. Mich. 11 Edw. 2, pl. 31 (1317), *reprinted in* 61 Seldon Society 114, 114-15 (J. Collas and W. Holdsworth eds. 1942); *Anon.*, Y. B. Mich. 5 Edw. 2, pl. 79 (1311), *reprinted in* 63 Seldon Society 270 (G. Turner ed. 1947); *Anon.*, Y. B. Mich. 4 Edw. 2, pl. 82 (1310), *reprinted in* 22 Seldon Society 195, 195-96 (G. Turner ed. 1907).

92. *See* text accompanying notes 69-71 *supra*.

93. *See* text accompanying note 75 *supra*. This development was in complete congruence with the emerging policy that sought to curtail the abusive utilization of the bail system by sheriffs. *See* Duker, "Right to Bail," 42 Alb. L. Rev. 33, 45-47.

94. *See* text accompanying notes 96-112 *infra*.

95. Jenks, "The Story," 18 Law Q. Rev. 64, 65 (emphasis in original).

96. In the early Memoranda Rolls of Henry III's Exchequer Court, the writ of habeas corpus is discovered side by side with writs of summons, *venire facias* (cause to come), *pone per vadium* (put to bail), and distraint. *Select Cases in the Exchequer of Pleas*, in 48 Seldon Society, p. xxxiii (H. Jenkinson and B. Formay eds. 1932); *see* Eas. 14 Hen. 3, Memoranda Roll 62-63 (1230-1231). In 1231, an entry on the Pipe Rolls indicates the issuance of a writ of habeas corpus to the sheriff ordering him to "have the body" so that the military honors of Lancaster could be received. Eas. 14 Hen. 3, Pipe Rolls 37, m. 5d (1231). In three 1236 cases, the *habeas corpus ad respondendum* was employed by the barons of the Exchequer Court. *Exchequer of Pleas*, pp. xlvi, xlviii-xlix. In the mid-thirteenth century there are examples of the use of habeas corpus by the barons on the Memoranda Rolls. Ibid., pp. lvii-lviii.

In the formative years of the exchequer court, a writ original or judicial could be directed in the form of a bill when the officer to whom the writ was directed was an official of the City of London or the County of Middlesex. Ibid., p. cxxxi. Thus, at this time, bills of habeas corpus are also found. Ibid., p. cxxxii.

97. The precept was often necessary because, as Bracton wrote "although the parties may be present, and put themselves on the assise, the jurors nevertheless, who ought to declare the truth, may be absent, and therefore of necessity the assise is respited from default of recognisors." 4 *Bracton* 143.

The form of the precept directing the sheriff to have the jurors was not unlike the *habeas corpus ad respondendum*: "[Y]ou [sheriff] have &c. the bodies of A., B., and C., as recognisors of an assise of last presentation which has been summoned in court, &c. between A. as plaintiff, and B. . . . ." Ibid., p. 9; *see* Charles Travis Clay ed., *Three Yorkshire Assise Rolls* (Yorkshire Archeological Society, 1911), pp. 84-85 (case of Abbat of Byland against John son of Robert de Alwaldeley (1251)).

98. *See* text accompanying note 42 *supra*.

99. Doris M. Stenton ed., *The Earliest Lincolnshire Assize Rolls, A.D. 1202-1209* (Lincoln Record Society, 1926), p. 162, pl. 980, r. 492, m. 8 (Pleas of the Crown at Lincoln 1202).

100. *Case of Baldwinus Tyrell*, Trin. 16 John 1, *Select Pleas of the Crown*, in 1 Seldon Society 67, pl. 115 (1214) (F. Maitland ed. 1888).

101. Stenton, *Earliest Lincolnshire*, p. 162, pl. 980.

102. Ibid.

103. Ibid.

104. 1 *Select Pleas of the Crown* 67.

105. Ibid.

106. Ibid.

107. Ibid., pp. 67-68.

108. Ibid., p. 72.

109. Ibid., pp. 70-71.

110. Ibid., p. 74.

111. Ibid., pp. 74-75.

112. In 1199, one Walterus de Ferlinton was commanded by the Justices at Westminster "quod tunc habeat Wimarcam uxorem suam ibi" (to have your wife here at that time). Hil. 1 John 1, 1 Curia Regis Rolls 165, r. 20, m. 13d (1200). In 1217 one Falkes de Breaute was ordered to produce the bodies of the defendants to answer Roberto, the claimant, why "against our peace they robbed him." 1 Rotuli Litterarum Clausarum 301.

113. As it was the Crown's prerogative writ, *see* note 2 *supra*, no privilege could impede the return of the writ. To illustrate this fact, Sir Matthew Hale pointed to the punishment of the Bishop of Durham in 1305 for refusing to execute a writ of habeas corpus out of the King's Bench. Matthew Hale, *The History of the Common Law*, vol. 2, p. 43 (C. Runnington ed. London 1794). The case also suggests that Jenks was mistaken in claiming that the writ of habeas corpus was completely supplanted by capias in the first half of the fourteenth century. *See* text accompanying notes 79-83 *supra*.

114. Y. B. Trin. 14 Edw. 3, f. 20, pl. 12 (1340), *reprinted in* Year Books 204 (L. O. Pike ed. 1888).

115. A recognizance was a security for a debt acknowledged to be due, entered into before the chief magistrate of some trading town pursuant to the *Statutum de Mercatoribus*, 11 Edw. 1 (1283) by which the debtor's goods could be seized in satisfaction of the debt, ibid. sects. 7-8, or the debtor imprisoned, ibid. sect. 14.

116. Y. B. Trin. 14 Edw. 3, at f. 20, pl. 12.

117. Ibid.

118. Ibid.

119. Ibid.

120. Ibid.

121. Ibid.

122. Ibid.

123. Ibid.

124. Ibid.

125. Cohen, "Modern Writ," 18 Can. B. Rev. 10, 13.

126. Y. B. Trin. 17 Edw. 3, f. 37, pl. 9 (1343), *reprinted in* Year Books 484 (L. O. Pike ed. 1901).

127. Ibid.

128. Cohen, "Modern Writ," 18 Can. B. Rev. 10, 13. Jenks, in contrast, was unable to locate this new form of the writ before the fifteenth century. Jenks, "The Story," 18 Law Q. Rev. 64, 69.

129. *See* Cohen, "Modern Writ," 18 Can. B. Rev. 10, 13.

130. *See* text accompanying notes 99, 101-03 *supra. But cf.* Cohen, "Modern Writ," 18 Can. B. Rev. 10, 13 (the writ may have first emerged in the fourteenth century).

131. 4 *Select Cases in the Court of King's Bench*, in 74 Seldon Society 164, pl. 58 (G. Sayles ed. 1957).

132. Ibid., p. 165.

133. 2 Rotuli Parliamentorum 431, no. 21 (1327).

134. Ibid.

135. 5 *King's Bench*, in 76 Seldon Society 70, 70-71, pl. 30 (G. Sayles ed. 1958).

136. Ibid., p. 71.

137. Ibid.

138. Ibid. For another example, *see* 6 ibid., in 82 Seldon Society 72, 72-73, pl. 47 (G. Sayles ed. 1965). In 1351, a writ was issued by the king to one of his justices to ascertain the cause of imprisonment of certain poor prisoners. Ibid., p. 72. The justice examined the cause and returned that one Donatus of Florence was imprisoned for allegedly quarreling. Ibid., p. 73. The justice issued a writ to the keepers to have the prisoner brought before him. Ibid. The prisoner was released because no evidence of an indictment against him could be found. Ibid., p. 74.

139. Y. B. Trin. 24 Edw. 3, f. 27, pl. 3 (1351).

140. Ibid.

141. [1383] A. H. Thomas, ed., *Calendar of Select Pleas and Memoranda of the City of London* (Cambridge: Cambridge University Press, 1932), p. 40 (1381-1412).

142. Ibid., p. 41.

143. Ibid.

144. [1388] *Select Cases in Chancery*, in 10 Seldon Society 8, 8-9, pl. 8 (W. Baildon ed. 1896).

145. Ibid., p. 9.

146. Ibid.

147. Ibid.

148. *See William Culne's Case*, [1394] *Select Cases in Chancery*, p. 80, pl. 87. The request in the case read:

> May it please your most gracious Lordship to grant a writ to cause the said John [Shortegrove, who had arrested Culne] to come before you at a certain day and on a certain pain, bringing with him the said William, who is in his keeping, to answer touching the matters aforesaid, and further [please you] to do grace unto the said William, and to ordain that he may be delivered [out of prison] by sufficient mainprise, to await what right and reason demand in this case. . . .

Ibid., p. 81, pl. 87.

149. In the meantime, the writ of habeas corpus without cause remained in use during the fourteenth century. In 1356, one John Redeswelle, who was detained in the prison of the bishop of London at Stortford, was brought before the King's Bench on a writ of habeas corpus. Bertha Haven Putnam ed., *Proceedings Before the Justice of the Peace in the Fourteenth and Fifteenth Centuries* (Ames Foundation, 1938), p. 59. Redeswelle pleaded not

guilty to the charge levied against him; nevertheless, he was convicted and hanged. Ibid. The case provides an example of the use of the *habeas corpus ad testificandum*. This same type of habeas corpus was used in the case of *Walter de Shirland and Joan atte Flete*, Rosamond Sillen ed., *Records of Some Sessions of the Peace in Lincolnshire 1360-1375* (Lincoln Record Society, 1936), p. 117. There, the said Joan had been indicted at two different sessions of the peace for burglarizing the home of John Pardoner of Scotter in 1373. Ibid., p. 117. Walter was indicted for felony on the separate charges of having "received and maintained [Joan]," knowing her to have committed the felony, and of having raped her. Ibid. Prior to Joan's conviction, Walter received a pardon for all felonies. Ibid., p. 118. The court held, however, that this absolved him only of the rape and not of the charge as an accessory to burglary, Joan not yet having been tried or pardoned for the crime. Ibid. Pending Joan's trial, Walter was let to mainprise but, upon suit by one of his sureties for a debt of twenty pounds, he was imprisoned at Newgate by the sheriff of London. Ibid. He was therefore unable to appear before the court on the criminal charge until the court of criminal jurisdiction issued a writ of habeas corpus to the sheriff. Ibid., pp. 118-19.

Beside *habeas corpus ad testificandum*, *habeas corpora* continued to be employed for the summoning of juries. *See* e.g., Y. B. Hil. 12 Edw. 2 (1319), *reprinted in* 14 Year Books of Edward II 66, in 70 Seldon Society 66 (J. Collas Ed. 1953); Y. B. Hil. 12 Rich. 2 (1388), *reprinted in* 6 Ames Foundation 117, no. 8 (G. Deiser ed. 1914); Y. B. Hil. 12 Rich. 2 (1388), reprinted in ibid. at 127, no. 18.

In addition, the writ of *habeas corpus ad respondendum* continued to issue. In 1377, the Chancery granted John Wallingford's petition for a writ of habeas corpus to have one John Dodeford brought before Parliament to respond to a charge levied by Wallingford. *Select Cases in Chancery*, p. 104. In the *Year Books* of Richard II, there is reported a 1388 case involving an ex-sheriff who was sued by a woman "to have the body" of a certain prisoner whom he had arrested while still sheriff, under a writ of *capias vtagatum* (you take the outlaw) at the same woman's suit. Y. B. Eas. 11 Rich. 2, pl. 20 (1388), *reprinted in* 5 Ames Foundation 244 (I. Thornley ed. 1937). The ex-sheriff, by attorney, came before the court in response to a writ of distress. Ibid. His attorney informed the court that after having arrested the prisoner on the *capias vtlagatum*, the sheriff had been unable to present him, the prisoner being too ill to be moved at that time. Ibid. This return was allowed. The ex-sheriff's attorney argued further that since his client had left office in the meantime and his prisoners had been delivered to his successor, this present action should be dismissed. Ibid. The court, however, ruled that "the sheriff could not be discharged by attorney, but it behoved him to come in person." Ibid., p. 245. For a further example, *see Select Cases from the Coroner Rolls*, in 9 Seldon Society 116-17 (1366) (C. Gross ed. 1896).

150. 1 Holdsworth 446-47.

151. *See* ibid., pp. 457-58.

152. Cohen, "Modern Writ," 18 Can. B. Rev. 10, 14; Jenks, "The Story," 18 Law Q. Rev. 64, 69-70, 72.

153. *See* De Smith, "The Prerogative Writs," 11 Cambridge L. J. 40, 45-48; Jenks, "The Story," 18 Law Q. Rev. 64, 69.

154. *See* text accompanying notes 114-29 *supra*.

155. For further illustration of this corrective use of the writ, *see* text accompanying notes 114-48 *supra*.

156. [1389] Calendar (1381-1412), p. 161.

157. Ibid.

158. [1397] ibid., p. 242.

159. [1395] ibid., p. 228.

160. [1388] ibid., p. 159.

161. Ibid.

162. Ibid.

163. Ibid.

164. Ibid.

165. Ibid.

166. [1395], ibid., p. 229.

167. Ibid.

168. [1397] ibid., p. 242.

169. Ibid.

170. *See* Cohen, "Modern Writ," 18 Can. B. Rev. 10, 14.

171. Statute of Leicester, 1414, 2 Hen. 5, stat. 1, c. 2, sect. 4.

172. *See e.g.*, [1432] *Calendar of Plea and Memoranda Rolls (1413-1437)*, pp. 262, 266, 269 (A. Thomas ed. 1943); [1431] ibid., pp. 252, 256; [1430] ibid., pp. 236, 241; [1429] ibid., p. 227; [1428] ibid., pp. 215, 219; [1427] ibid., p. 210; [1425] ibid., p. 179; [1421] ibid., p. 88; [1420] ibid., p. 84; [1419] ibid., pp. 67, 72; [1417] ibid., p. 64; [1416] ibid., pp. 46, 51; [1415] ibid., p. 38.

173. 11 Hen. 6, c. 10 (1433).

174. *See* Cohen, "Modern Writ," 18 Can. B. Rev. 10, 14-15; Jenks, "The Story," 18 Law Q. Rev. 64, 70.

175. *See e.g.*, [1462] *Calendar of Plea and Memoranda Rolls (1458-1482)*, p. 23 (P. Jones ed. 1961); [1456] *A Calendar of the White and Black Books of the Cinque Ports*, p. 36, f. 25 (F. Hull ed. 1966); [1452] *Calendar of Plea and Memoranda Rolls (1437-1457)*, pp. 122-23, 124 (P. Jones ed. 1954); [1448] ibid., p. 109; [1447] ibid., pp. 97, 100-02; [1446] ibid., pp. 91, 93-95; [1445] ibid., pp. 65-69, 72-74, 82; [1444] ibid., pp. 55-56, 60-62, 64; [1442] ibid., pp. 49, 50; [1441] ibid., p. 42; [1440] ibid., pp. 23, 25-29, 34-35; [1439] ibid., pp. 15-17; [1437] *Calendar (1413-1437)*, pp. 297-98; [1436] ibid., pp. 291-92, 294; [1435] ibid., p. 292; [1434] ibid., pp. 272, 275.

176. George William Sanders ed., *Orders in the High Court of Chancery* (London: A. Maxwell and Son, 1845), pp. 8-9.

177. Ibid., p. 10.

178. Ibid.

179. Ibid., p. 120; *see* De Smith, "Prerogative Writs," 11 Cambridge L. J. 40, 43.

180. [1406] *Calendar (1381-1412)*, p. 275.

181. Ibid.

182. Ibid.

183. *See, e.g.*, [1517] *Cinque Ports*, p. 170, ff. 171-171v; [1444] *Calendar (1437-1457)*, p. 61; [1414] *Calendar (1413-1437)*, p. 14. For an interesting case brought to light by a petition of Parliament in 1429, *see* 4 Rotuli Parliamentorum 357-58 (K. B. 1429).

184. *See* [1427] *Calendar (1413-1437)*, p. 218.

185. 1 and 2 Phil. and M., c. 13, sect. 7 (1554).

186. 43 Eliz. 1, c. 5 (1601).

187. Ibid. sect. 1 (2).

188. Ibid. sect. 1(3).

189. Ibid. sect. 2. This legislation was extended by 3 Car. 1, c. 4, sect. 22(11) (1627), and by 16 Car. 1, c. 4 (1640).

190. 21 Jac. 1, c. 23 (1623).

191. Ibid., sect. 2.

192. Ibid., sect. 1(2) (emphasis in original).

193. 9 Holdsworth 109.

194. Jenks, "The Story," 18 Law Q. Rev. 64, 70.

195. 18 Edw. 3, stat. 3, c. 7 (1344).

196. Cohen, "Modern Writ," 18 Can. B. Rev. 10, 16.

197. Ibid., pp. 16-17; *see Hutchins v. Player*, 124 Eng. Rep. 585, 594 (K. B. 1663) [describing Andrew de Vine's case (1456)].

198. This can be illustrated by two early cases. In 1398, a writ of habeas corpus issued to the mayor and alderman of London from the barons of the Exchequer to have the body of Ralph Gronyly, *scrutator* (bailiff of a river) in the port of Plymouth, brought before the bench. [1398] *Calendar (1381-1412)*, p. 260. Gronyly, having no property in the city that might be attached, had previously been arrested to answer a certain Perynanton de Blay on a bill of complaint. Ibid. The writ declared that it was a royal prerogative that debts to the King should be paid before satisfaction was made to others. Ibid. Another example of a writ reciting the King's prerogative of being satisfied from a debtor's goods before other creditors appears in [1415] *Calendar (1413-1437)*, pp. 31-32. The writ demanded that Thomas Leycestre, deputy of Thomas Morstede, the King's *scrutator* in the port of London, and William Sawce, controller of the *scrutator*, imprisoned in one of the city's prisons whereby they were

> prevented from attending to their duties and rendering account for the issues of their scrutiny, be brought before the barons of the Exchequer at Westminster with the cause of their taking and detaining and the tenor of any inquisitions concerning them, and that proceedings against them in the city be stayed. . . .

Ibid. For further examples, *see* [1443] *Calendar (1458-1482)*, p. 53; [1442] ibid., p. 48.

199. Jenks, "The Story," 18 Law Q. Rev. 64, 71.

200. [1430] *Calendar (1413-1437)* p. 241; *see* [1436] ibid., p. 292.

201. [1440] *Calendar (1437-1457)*, p. 25; see [1437] *Calendar (1413-1437)*, p. 296.

202. *See Vandevelde v. Lluellin*, 83 Eng. Rep. 910, 910 (K. B. 1661); *Peter's Case*, 74 Eng. Rep. 628, 628 (K. B. 1587); *Skrogges v. Coleshil*, 73 Eng. Rep. 386, 386 (K. B. 1560); Y. B. Mich. 4 Hen. 6, pl. 22 (1403); Y. B. Mich. 9 Hen. 6, pl. 40 (1408).

203. For an example of the type of abuse to which the concept was subjected, see the petition of Robert Shirbourne, 5 Rotuli Parliamentorum 106-07 (K. B. 1444).

204. In a 1487 case, the court insisted upon the presence of the petitioner at bar so that he could be examined as to the nature of his privilege. *Anon.*,

145 Eng. Rep. 113, 113 (Ex. 1487); *see Peter's Case*, 74 Eng. Rep. 628, 628 (K. B. 1587).

205. Y. B. Pasch. 9 Hen. 6, pl. 16 (1408).

206. Y. B. Hil. 39 Hen. 6, pl. 15 (1438), aff'd Y. B. Mich. 2 Hen. 7, pl. 6 (1501). An interesting case decided in 1649 rejected an application for a writ of habeas corpus (based on the privilege of a witness) shortly before the end of the term, with the Court of King's Bench holding: "[W]e will grant no *habeas corpus*, for this is but a trick of the party himself to gain his liberty that he may go a hawking and hunting this long vacation." *Anon.*, 82 Eng. Rep. 584, 584 (K. B. 1649).

207. Y. B. Mich. 8 Edw. 6, pl. 23 (1280).

208. For example, in a 1485 case, a prisoner who was committed to a London prison for debt solicited someone to bring a charge against him in the King's Bench for trespass so that he might be released from his commitment via habeas corpus. The writ of habeas corpus based upon privilege was granted. He confessed the trespass, and the Exchequer Chamber ruled that although the indictment was by his own procurement, he should be fined for the trespass and committed to the Marshalsea for the said fine and for his execution in London. *Anon.*, 145 Eng. Rep. 111, 111 (Ex. 1485). For another example, *see* Y. B. Mich. 16 Edw. 4, pl. 5 (1288).

209. Y. B. Hil. 22 Hen. 6, pl. 34 (1421).

210. Y. B. Pasch. 2 Edw. 4, pl. 8 (1463).

211. *See* generally W. Jones, *The Elizabethan Court of Chancery* (Oxford: Clarendon Press, 1967), 449-98 (1967); Cohen, "Modern Writ," 18 Can. B. Rev. 10, 20-25.

212. Goldwin Smith, *A Constitutional and Legal History of England* (New York: Charles Scribner's Sons, 1955), p. 211.

213. 4 Rotuli Parliamentorum 189-90 (1422).

214. Reeves, *History of English Law*, p. 552.

215. 1 Holdsworth 459.

216. *See* "Two Pieces Concerning Suits in Chancery By Subpoena," in 1 Hargrave (ed.), *A Collection*, pp. 321, 325.

217. *See* 1 Holdsworth 457; "Two Pieces," 1 Hargrave, *A Collection*, p. 325.

218. Y. B. Pasch. 21 Edw. 4, pl. 6 (1483).

219. Y. B. Mich. 22 Edw. 4, pl. 21 (1483). Undoubtedly, Justice Fairfax, who concurred in the opinion, must have failed to see the implications of the synthesis of these two decisions: the writ of habeas corpus was, of course, equally available to the Chancery in nullifying the prohibitions of the King's Bench. *See Carie v. Denis*, 74 Eng. Rep. 134 (K. B. 1589), in which upon a *latitat* (a writ that issued in personal actions on the return of *non inventus est*) to a bill of Middlesex, the sheriff returned that by virtue of the said process, he had arrested the body of the defendant. Ibid., p. 134. The defendant, however, was subsequently discharged upon a writ of habeas corpus issued by Chancery. Ibid., p. 135. Although the discharge was clearly legal, the King's Bench reprimanded the Master of the Rolls for discharging the prisoner.

> for we oftentimes have persons here upon habeas corpus who are also arrested by process out of the Exchequer, or of the Common Pleas,

but we will not discharge them before they have found sureties for their appearance, & and so the [Court of Chancery] use to do reciprocally. . . .

Ibid., p. 135.

220. *See* 1 Holdsworth 460.

221. Articles 20 and 21 of the bill of impeachment (no doubt relatively insignificant articles) complained of the frequency with which Wolsey issued injunctions:

20. Also, the said lord cardinal hath examined divers and many matters in the Chancery, after Judgment thereof given at the common law, in subversion of your laws; and made some persons restore again to the other party condemned, that they had in execution by virtue of the Judgment in the common law.

21. Also, the said lord cardinal hath granted many injunctions by writ, and the parties never called thereunto, nor bill put in against them. And, by reason thereof, divers of your subjects have been put out of their lands and tenements. And, by such means, he hath brought the more party of the sutors of this your realm before himself, whereby he and divers of his servants have gotten much riches, and your subjects suffered great wrongs.

Proceedings against Thomas Wolsey (1529), 1 *A Complete Collection of State Trials* 367, 376 (T. Howell ed. 1816).

222. Creasacre More, *The Life and Death of Sir Thomas More* (Menston, England: Scolar Press, 1971; 1st ed. 1630), p. 295.

223. Ibid.

224. Ibid., pp. 218-19.

225. 1 Holdsworth 461-63.

226. *Anon.*, 72 Eng. Rep. 883, 883 (K. B. 1605).

227. Ibid.

228. 79 Eng. Rep. 190 (K. B. 1610).

229. Ibid., p. 191.

230. Ibid.

231. 80 Eng. Rep. 1139 (K. B. 1615). The case originated from an action of debt upon a bond for the nonpayment of money used in the purchase of certain jewelry. Ibid., p. 1139.

232. Ibid.

233. Ibid.

234. Ibid.

235. Ibid.

236. Ibid.

237. Ibid., pp. 1139-40.

238. 81 Eng. Rep. 98 (K. B. 1615).

239. Ibid., p. 99.

240. Ibid., p. 98.

241. *See,* e.g., *Blackwell's Case*, 73 Eng. Rep. 1057, 1058-59 (K. B. 1626); *Apsley's Case*, 72 Eng. Rep. 940, 940 (K. B. 1616); *Russwell's Case*, 81 Eng. Rep. 445, 445-46 (K. B. 1616). The conflict itself lingered on during the rest of the seventeenth century. 1 Holdsworth 463-65.

242. Roland G. Usher, *The Rise and Fall of the High Commission* (Oxford: Clarendon Press, 1913), pp. 15-20 (1913). *See* ibid., pp. 11-31.

243. Ibid., p. 149.

244. Ibid.

245. Ibid., p. 64.

246. Ibid., p. 149. For a history of the Court of High Commission, *see* 1 Holdsworth 605-11.

247. *See* Usher, *High Commission*, pp. 159-61.

248. *See* Cohen, "Modern Writ," 18 Can. B. Rev. 10, 21-22.

249. Usher, *High Commission*, p. 168.

250. *Fuller's Case*, 74 Eng. Rep. 1091, 1091 (K. B. 1607); *Nicholas Fuller's Case*, 77 Eng. Rep. 1322, 1323-25 (1607); *see* Leonard W. Levy, *Origin of the Fifth Amendment* (New York: Oxford University Press, 1968), pp. 229-65.

251. Usher, *High Commission*, pp. 170-71.

252. Ibid., p. 172.

253. Ibid.

254. Ibid., pp. 172-73.

255. Ibid., p. 173.

256. Ibid.

257. *See Nicholas Fuller's Case*, 77 Eng. Rep. 1322 (1607).

258. *See* ibid., p. 1325.

259. *Fuller's Case*, 74 Eng. Rep. 1091, 1091 (K. B. 1607). It is possible that undue influence was brought to bear on the judges. In a letter of November 27, 1607, to the Earl of Salisbury, Sir Thomas Lake wrote:

> His Majesty came in late this evening, and so it was late before he read your letters concerning Mr. Fuller, which have exceedingly contented him; and after he uttered his liking he repeated that which I advertised you before that he had said, and bound it with an oath: that the Judges had done well for themselves as well as for him, for that he was resolved if they had done otherwise, and maintained their habeas corpus, he would have committed them.

M. S. Giuseppi ed., *Historical Manuscripts Commission, Calendar of the Manuscripts of the Most Honourable The Marquess of Salisbury* (Historical Manuscripts Commission, 1965), pt. 19, pp. 343-44; *see* Levy, *Fifth Amendment*, p. 239; R. Usher, *High Commissions*, p. 177.

260. "Q. If High Commissioners Have Power to Imprison," 77 Eng. Rep. 1301, 1301-02 (1607).

261. Ibid.

262. 77 Eng. Rep. 1326 (K. B. 1608).

263. Ibid., p. 1328.

264. Ibid.

265. 1 Eliz. 1, c. 1, section 18 (1558).

266. 77 Eng. Rep. at 1328; *see Nicholas Fuller's Case*, 77 Eng. Rep. 1322, 1323-25 (1607).

267. *Lady Throgmorton's Case*, 77 Eng. Rep. 1347, 1347 (K. B. 1611).

268. Ibid.

269. 77 Eng. Rep. 1360 (K. B. 1612).

270. Ibid., pp. 1360-61.

271. Ibid., p. 1361.
272. Ibid., p. 1360.
273. Ibid., pp. 1360-61.
274. *See* Coke, *High Commission*, 77 Eng. Rep. 1361, 1361-63 (1612).
275. Ibid., p. 1362. In response to King James' announcement, Coke stated: [I]t was grievous to us his Justices of the Bench, to be so severed from our brethren, the justices and Barons, but more grievous that they differed from us in opinion, without hearing one another; and especially forasmuch as we have proceeded in the case of Sir William Chancey, and other cases concerning the power of the High Commissioners in imposing of fines and imprisonment judicially in open Court, upon argument at the Bar and the Bench, where it was resolved by us, that the High Commissioners cannot fine and imprison, but in certain cases; and the judicial course ought to be judicially reversed: but . . . when we the Justices of the Common Pleas see the commission newly reformed, we will, as to that which is of right, seek to satisfy the King's expectation. . . .
Ibid., p. 1363.
276. 80 Eng. Rep. 1138 (K. B. 1615).
277. Ibid., p. 1138.
278. 81 Eng. Rep. 94 (K. B. 1616).
279. Ibid., p. 94.
280. Ibid.
281. *Proceedings on the Habeas Corpus, brought by Sir Thomas Darnel, Sir John Corbet, Sir Walter Earl, Sir John Heveningham, & Sir Edmund Hampden,* [K. B. 1627] 3 *State Trials*, 1; *see* text accompanying notes 345-51 *infra*.
282. 81 Eng. Rep. 94.
283. Ibid.
284. *Hodd v. High Commission Court*, 81 Eng. Rep. 125, 125 (1616).
285. Ibid.
286. *See*, e.g., *Deyton's Case*, 72 Eng. Rep. 940, 940 (K. B. 1617); *Brokes Case*, 72 Eng. Rep. 940, 941 (K. B. 1617); Sir Bulstrode Whitelocke, *Memorials of the English Affairs* (2d ed. Oxford 1853—1st ed. London 1682), vol. 1, pp. 36-37 [describing *Huntley's Case* (1629)].
287. 16 Car. 1, c. 11 (1641).
288. In *Torle's Case*, 79 Eng. Rep. 1100 (K. B. 1641), five prisoners were brought before the King's Bench by a writ of habeas corpus and there let to bail from a commitment for contempt arising from their failure to obey an order of the ecclesiastical Commissioners to pay a parishclerk's wages. Ibid., p. 1100. That same year, however, neither discharge nor bail was awarded an individual committed by order of the Exchequer for failure to pay a fine of £50 levied against him by the ecclesiastical Commissioners. *Anon.*, 79 Eng. Rep. 1097, 1097 (K. B. 1641). In this case, although the cause for the fine was not given in the return, the return was held valid because the commitment was by order of a temporal judicial tribunal. Ibid.
289. Cohen, "Modern Writ," 18 Can. B. Rev. 10, 22.
290. *See* 1 Holdsworth 547, 549, 552.

291. Ibid., p. 553.

292. *See* 2 *Select Pleas in the Court of Admiralty,* in 11 Seldon Society xli (R. Marsden ed. 1897).

293. Ibid., p. xlvi (Adm. 1542).

294. Ibid., pp. xlvi-xlvii.

295. Ibid., p. xlvii.

296. *In re Pyke,* ibid., pp. xlvii, xlvii (Adm. 1553); *see In re John Andrewes,* ibid., pp. xlv, xlv (Adm. 1538).

297. 77 Eng. Rep. 1379 (C. P. 1605).

298. Ibid., p. 1379.

299. Ibid.

300. Ibid.

301. 77 Eng. Rep. 1404 (C. P. 1617).

302. Ibid., p. 1404.

303. Ibid. But *see Anon.,* 82 Eng. Rep. 585, 585 (K. B. 1648); *Scadding's Case,* 80 Eng. Rep. 91, 91 (K. B. 1609) (per curiam).

304. Cohen, "Modern Writ," 18 Can. B. Rev. 10, 22. For a discussion of the battle between the common-law courts and the Court of Requests, *see* 1 Holdsworth 414.

305. 135 Eng. Rep. 291 (C. P. 1572).

306. Ibid., p. 291.

307. Ibid.

308. Ibid.

309. 1 Holdsworth 477-78.

310. Ibid., p. 492.

311. Ibid., p. 492. *See* generally Geoffrey R. Elton, *The Tudor Constitution* (Cambridge: Cambridge University Press, 1960), pp. 87-93.

312. *Hinde's Case,* 74 Eng. Rep. 701, 701 (C. P. 1577).

313. *See* text accompanying notes 297-308 *supra.*

314. 74 Eng. Rep. 701.

315. Ibid.

316. On the use of the writ of habeas corpus as a means of interfering with the various subordinate Councils, *see Case of the Lords Presidents of Wales and York,* 77 Eng. Rep. 1331, 1333-34 (1608); R. R. Reid, *The King's Council in the North* (London: Longmans, Green and Co., 1921), pp. 315, 343, 355, 358-59, 411, 426.

317. Henry Hallam, *The Constitutional History of England* (London: Alex Murray and Sons, 1870), p. 137.

318. Ibid., pp. 139-40.

319. 74 Eng. Rep. 455 (C. P. 1587).

320. Ibid., p. 455.

321. *Peter's Case,* 74 Eng. Rep. 628, 628 (C. P. 1587).

322. Ibid.

323. 74 Eng. Rep. 66 (C. P. 1588). In this case, Walsingham was also identified by the return as a member of the Privy Council. Ibid., p. 66.

324. Ibid.

325. Ibid.

326. Ibid.

327. Ibid.

328. Ibid.

329. *Searches Case*, 74 Eng. Rep. 65, 65 (C. P. 1588).

330. Ibid., p. 66.

331. Ibid.

332. Ibid.

333. Ibid.

334. Ibid. For a very early example of a *corpus cum causa* being employed to test the validity of a recapture, *see* Y. B. Mich. 13 Hen. 7, pl. 1 (1497).

335. 74 Eng. Rep. 66. That anyone again imprisoning a person released by habeas corpus was liable to attachments was reemphasized by Coke in *Case of the City of London*, 77 Eng. Rep. 658, 658 (K. B. 1610).

336. In *Anderson's Reports*, the product of the assembly is dated 1592. 123 Eng. Rep. 482, 483. But *see* Hallam, *Constitutional History*, p. 140.

337. 123 Eng. Rep. 482.

338. Ibid.

339. Ibid.

340. Ibid.

341. Ibid., pp. 482-83. Compare this with the version in Hallam, *Constitutional History*, p. 140, which is probably an early draft of the resolution, but which aids in the interpretation of the version in *Anderson's Reports*.

342. *See* generally F. W. Maitland, *The Constitutional History of England* (Cambridge: Cambridge University Press, 1908), pp. 274-75.

343. 74 Eng. Rep. 65 (C. P. 1588); *see* text accompanying notes 329-35 *supra*.

344. *See Sir Sam. Salkingstowes Case*, 81 Eng Rep. 444-45 (K. B. 1616). There the return stated only that the party was "commit per le Privie Counsell." Ibid., p. 445.

345. *Darnel's Case*, 3 State Trials 1 (1627).

346. Ibid., p. 3.

347. Ibid., pp. 1-2. *See* generally Christopher Hill, *The Century of Revolution 1603-1714* (London: Sphere, 1969), pp. 11, 53; Frances Helen Relf, *The Petition of Right* (Ann Arbor: University of Michigan Press, 1917), pp. 1-2; J. R. Tanner, *English Constitutional Conflicts of the Seventeenth Century* (Cambridge: Cambridge University Press, 1928), pp. 60-61, 270-72.

348. *Darnel's Case*, 3 State Trials 2-3.

349. Ibid.

350. Ibid.

351. Ibid., pp. 6-7. Barristers for the five knights argued that such action was repugnant to A Statute of Purveyors, 25 Edw. 3, stat. 5, c. 4, sect. 2 (1350), which provided that "none shall be taken by petition or suggestion made to our lord the King, or to his council, unless it be by indictment or presentment of good and lawful people of the same neighbourhood where such deeds be done, in due manner, or by process made by writ original at the common law," and to the Statute of Westminster, 42 Edw. 3, c. 3, section 2 (1368), which, because of accusations induced by revenge, provided that "no man [shall] be put to answer without presentment." *Darnel's Case*, 3 State Trials 7. Apparently, the framers of those statutes did not contemplate the immediate case.

352. *See* Paul Vinogradoff, "Magna Carta, c. 39," in *Magna Carta Commemoration Essays* (H. Malden ed. 1917), pp. 93-94.

353. *See* text accompanying notes 336-43 *supra*.

354. It was argued that the charge, coming prior to trial and conviction, was simply an accusation and thus bail should be allowed: "[I]f this return shall be good, then [the] imprisonment shall not continue on for a time, but for ever; and the subjects of this kingdom may be restrained of their liberties perpetually. . . ." *Darnel's Case*, 3 State Trials 8. In response, the Attorney General conceded that acceptance of the argument based upon the sovereign's power would mean that many might suffer wrongful imprisonment, but he maintained that was not reason enough to deliver all those who were imprisoned by "special command of his majesty" without a more specific charge. Ibid., pp. 36-44. Heath pointed to the overriding interests of the government and suggested that the King's position was best for balancing the interests of society and of the individual. Ibid., pp. 45-46. It was this line of reasoning that the court adopted in deciding to remand the prisoner: "[The Attorney General has said] that the King hath done it, and we trust him in great matters, and he is bound by law, and he bids us proceed by law, as we are sworn to do, and so is the king. . . ." Ibid., p. 59. Heath later employed this argument during the parliamentary debates following the case. "Proceedings in Parliament Relating to the Liberty of the Subject," [1628] 3 State Trials 59, 154. Of course, it was not well received. *See* ibid., pp. 159-60 (Glanvile's remarks).

355. Although Charles clearly had the weight of the law on his side, he was taking no chances. Prior to the trial, Sir Randolf Crew, who displayed no zeal for the forced loan, was removed from the seat of Lord Chief Justice and replaced by Sir Nicholas Hyde, who, in the words of Lord Campbell, was "elevated to the bench that he might remand to prison Sir Thomas Darnel." John Campbell, *The Lives of the Chief Justices of England* (New York: J. Cockcroft and Co., 1874), p. 1.

356. *See* Tanner, *English Constitutional Conflicts*, pp. 59-61. Darnel and the many others who were imprisoned for the same reason were released on January 2, 1628, three months before the King assembled a Parliament. Many of those who had suffered confinement because of their refusal to defray the unconstitutional appropriation were elected to Parliament. In fact, of the seventy-six prisoners, twenty-seven were elected. Tanner, *English Constitutional Conflicts*, p. 61.

357. *See* "Proceedings," 3 State Trials 59-82.

358. Shortly afterwards they met in conference with the Lords. Most members of the Commons felt that the concurrence of the Lords was unlikely. Charles H. Firth, *The House of the Lords During the Civil War* (New York: Longmans, Green and Co., 1910), p. 48. Immediately preceding the decisive debates, the King had bolstered his camp by the appointment of five new members to the upper house. Ibid.

359. The resolutions provided:

> I. That no Freeman ought to be detained or kept in prison, or otherwise restrained by the command of the king or privy-council, or any other, unless some cause of the commitment, detainer or restraint be expressed, for which by law he ought to be committed, detained or restrained.

> II. That the Writ of Habeas Corpus may not be denied, but ought to be granted to every man that is committed or detained in prison, or

otherwise restrained, though it be by the command of the king, the privy-council, or any other, he praying the same.

III. That if a Freeman be committed or detained in prison, or otherwise restrained by the command of the king, the privy-council, or any other, no cause of such commitment, detainer, or restraint being expressed, for which by law he ought to be committed, detained, or restrained, and the same be returned upon an Habeas Corpus, granted for the said party; then he ought to be delivered or bailed.

"Proceedings," 3 State Trials 82-83.

360. By juxtaposing chapter 29 of the Magna Carta, 9 Hen. 3 (1225), and 28 Edw. 3, c. 3 (1354), which provided that "no Man . . . shall be put out of Land or Tenement, nor taken, nor imprisoned, nor disinherited, nor put to Death, without being brought in Answer by due Process of the Law," see 7 Rich. 2, c. 4 (1383); 42 Edw. 3, c. 3 (1368); 37 Edw. 3, c. 18 (1363); 37 Edw. 3, stat. 2, c. 3 (1363); 2 Rotuli Parliamentorum 280 (1363); ibid., p. 239 (1352); ibid., p. 228, no. 19 (1351); 25 Edw. 3, stat. 5, c. 4 (1350); 5 Edw. 3, c. 9 (1331), the Commons concluded that the "law of the Land" and "due process" clauses were synonymous. "Proceedings," 3 State Trials 86. Next, to prove that the dictates of due process were ascendant before, as well as during, the trial, the Commons pointed to 25 Edw. 3, stat. 5, c. 4 (1350), see note 351 supra. "Proceedings," 3 State Trials 86-87. Heath rebutted by arguing that such statutes referred not to "First Commitment, or putting into safe Custody" but rather to "a Legal Proceeding to Judgment or Condemnation." 3 H. L. Jour. 754 (1628). In addition to this flaw in reasoning, there was a technical problem with the argument of the Commons. Bail was a jailer of one's own choosing. See Charles Petersdorff, A Practical Treatise on the Law of Bail in Civil and Criminal Proceedings (London: Butterworth and Son, 1824), p. 7. Thus, it was incongruous to argue that imprisonment without cause shown was unconstitutional and that therefore the accused was entitled to bail. Duker, "Right to Bail," 42 Alb. L. Rev. 33, 61 n. 152.

361. "Proceedings," 3 State Trials 186.

362. The document read in part:

III. "And whereas also by the statute called, 'The Great Charter of the Liberties of England,' it is declared and enacted, That no Freeman may be taken or imprisoned or be disseised of his freehold or liberties, or his free customs, or be outlawed or exiled, or in any manner destroyed, but by the lawful judgment of his peers, or by the law of the land.

IV. "And in the 28th year of the reign of king Edward 3, it was declared and enacted by authority of parliament, That no man, of what estate or condition he be, should be put out of his land or tenements, nor taken, nor imprisoned, nor disinherited, nor put to death, without being brought to answer by due process of law.

V. "Nevertheless, against the tenor of the said statutes, and other the good laws and statutes of your realm, . . . divers of your subjects have of late been imprisoned, without any cause shewed; and when for their deliverance they were brought before your justices, by your majesty's Writs of Habeas Corpus, there to undergo and receive as the court should order, and their keepers commanded to certify the causes of their detainer; no cause was certified, but that they were detained by your majesty's special command, signified by the lords of your privy-council, and yet were returned back to several prisons, without being charged with any thing to which they might make answer according to the law.

Ibid., pp. 222-23. It was therefore declared "that no freeman in any such manner as is before mentioned, be imprisoned or detained." Ibid., p. 224.

363. Many of the defects of the writ of habeas corpus that were the subject of legislative action later in the century were noticed at the time of the Petition of Right. *See* Thomas P. Taswell-Langmead, *English Constitutional History* (London: Stevens and Haynes, 1875), p. 590. Legislative reform of the writ of habeas corpus was attempted on two occasions prior to the Petition of Right. In 1593, a bill was introduced in the Commons by James Morice, which provided:

Whereas the bodies of sundrie [of] her Majesty's subjects without anie suite, or Lawful process or Arrest or without sufficient warrant or ordinary and due course and proceedings in Lawe onlie uppon some sinister and unjust accusacion or informacion and by the procurement of some malitious persons have bene committed to prison and ther remaine to their grevous and intollerable vexacion and contrary to the great Charter and aunchent good Lawes and statutes of this realme. For remedy whereof be it enacted &c. That the provisions and prohibicions of the said great Charter and others Lawes in that behalfe made be dulie and inviolatelie observed. And that no person or persons be hereafter committed to prison but yt be by sufficient warrant and Authoritie and by due course and proceedings in Lawe uppon paine that he or thei that shall so procur anie person to be committed or imprisoned contrarie to the Lawes aforesaid and the true meaninge of this Acte shall forfeite to the partie so imprisoned his treble damage susteyned by reason of anie suche imprisonment. . . . And that the Justice of anie [of] the Queens [Majesties] Courts of Recorde at the common Lawe maie awarde a writt of habeas Corpus for the deliverye of anye person so imprisoned and yf the keeper of the prison or his duputie shall after notice of such writt deteyne the bodie of such person so committed he shall forfeit and loose to the partie so greaved xlli of Lawfull englishe money and shall answear to the . . . case Bill pleint of Informaccion in anie of the Queenes [Majesties] Courtes of Recorde wherein no essoyne proteccion or wager of Lawe shalbe admitted.

Faith Thompson, *Magna Carta: Its Role in the Making of the English Constitution 1300-1629* (New York: Octagon Books, 1972), pp. 394-95. Interestingly enough, Edward Coke, the speaker of the House, skillfully shelved the bill by asking leave to consider it. Ibid., p. 224. Although Coke promised to keep its contents secret, the Queen was informed of the bill and sent back a message with Coke commanding "that no Bill touching the said matters of state or reform in Causes Ecclesiastical be exhibited." Ibid., p. 225. Morice was reprimanded and temporarily suspended. Ibid.

A bill introduced in 1621 by Sir William Fleetwood providing for the better securement of the subjects' liberty contrary to chapter 29 of the Magna Carta, 1 H. C. Jour. 653 (1621), likewise failed. The bill allowed the recovery of ten times damages for imprisonments contrary to the Great Charter. Wallace Notestein, Francis Helen Relf, Hartley Simpson ed., *Commons Debates 1621* (New Haven: Yale University Press, 1935), p. 226. Further, it required that the cause of commitments must be expressed in the *mittimus* (commitment papers) and that a copy of the *mittimus* be given the prisoner on pain of £40. Ibid. Moreover, it stated that no judge should deny a *corpus cum causa*. Ibid. The bill excepted only the cases of treason and commitment by members of the Privy Council when it was specified that the imprisonment was for matters of state not fit to be revealed. 5 *Commons Debates* 1621, 226; 1 H. C. Jour. 653 (1621). Reasons for the bill's failure are given by Pym in his Diary. *See* 4 *Commons Debates* 382.

364. *See* note 362 *supra*.

365. *Proceedings against William Stroud*, [K. B. 1629] 3 State Trials 235.

366. Ibid., p. 240. In fact, the prisoners were committed for preventing the speaker from communicating the King's prorogation order so that a remonstrance against the King's collection of tonnage and poundage fees without parliamentary sanction could be voiced. Ibid., pp. 235-37.

367. Ibid., pp. 241-42.

368. Ibid., pp. 281-82.

369. For other examples of the King's disregard of the Petition of Right, *see Ship-Money Case*, [1637] 3 State Trials 825, 1237; John Forster, *The Debates on the Grand Remonstrance* (London: John Murray, 1860), p. 221n.

370. 79 Eng. Rep. 717 (K. B. 1629).

371. John Rushworth, *Historical Collection* (London, 1721) vol. 1, p. 639.

372. Ibid.

373. Ibid.

374. Ibid.

375. 79 Eng. Rep. 717.

376. Ibid.

377. Ibid.

378. Ibid.

379. Ibid., p. 640.

380. Ibid.

381. Ibid.

382. *Chamber's Case*, 79 Eng. Rep. 746, 746 (K. B. 1630).

383. Ibid.

384. Ibid.

385. Ibid., p. 747.

386. "Proceedings," 3 State Trials 95.

387. Jenks, "The Story," 18 Law Q. Rev. 64, 76.

388. *See* Petition of Anne Baron (1641), reported in *Fourth Report of the Royal Commission on Historical Manuscripts app.*, pp. 66-67 (1874); *Freeman's Case*, 79 Eng. Rep. 1096, 1097 (K. B. 1640); *Case of Seeles*, 79

Eng. Rep. 1080, 1080 (K. B. 1639); *Wolnough's Case*, 79 Eng. Rep. 1075, 1075 (K. B. 1639); *Thomas Barkham's Case*, 79 Eng. Rep. 1037, 1037 (K. B. 1638); *Lawson's Case*, 79 Eng. Rep. 1038, 1038 (K. B. 1638).

389. 16 Car. 1, c. 10 (1640).

390. Ibid. sect. 3.

391. Ibid. sect. 2 (3).

392. Ibid. sect. 8 (3).

393. Ibid. sect. 8 (4)-(5).

394. Ibid. sect. 7.

395. *See* Firth, *The House of Lords*, pp. 98-99.

396. The document contained 204 articles of complaint. Samuel R. Gardiner (ed.), *The Constitutional Documents of the Puritan Revolution* (Oxford: Clarendon Press, 1906), pp. 202, 208-32.

397. Ibid., p. 209, art. 11, 12, 14, 15.

398. *See* generally Tanner, *English Constitutional Conflicts*, pp. 144-48.

399. G. W. Brothers and E. M. Lloyd, "Presbyterians and Independents," *The Cambridge Modern History* (Cambridge: Cambridge University Press, 1906), vol. 4, p. 355. *See also* Gardiner, *Documents*, pp. 357-58, 371-74.

400. C. H. Firth and R. S. Rait ed., *Acts and Ordinances of the Interregnum (1642-1660)* (London, 1911), vol. 2, p. 321.

401. Ibid., pp. 321-22.

402. Ibid., p. 322.

403. Ibid., pp. 322-23.

404. Ibid., p. 323. The prisoner could take benefit of the act *in forma pauperis*. Ibid., p. 324.

405. Ibid., pp. 378-79. No fees were taken for such sureties. Ibid., p. 378.

406. An Act touching the sale of Corn and Meal, 1650, ibid., pp. 442-43.

407. *Case of Captain John Streater*, [U. B. 1653] 5 State Trials 366, 371.

408. Ibid.

409. Ibid., pp. 376-79.

410. Ibid., p. 385.

411. Ibid., p. 386.

412. Ibid., pp. 386-88. As he left the courtroom, Streater provided a summary of the proceedings: "I desire I might be bailed . . . and if not bailed, I may be a prisoner a hundred years." Ibid., p. 387.

413. Ibid., p. 388.

414. Ibid., pp. 389, 391. After the report of Streater's first appearance before the court, there is an entry pertaining to another case of some importance to the development of the writ of habeas corpus, particularly when examining the policy of the interregnum government toward the writ. The entry records the appearance of Colonel Barksted before the court. Ibid., p. 371. He had been directed to have the body of Lieutenant Colonel John Lilburne brought before the court, but was unable to do so, as he explained:

> According to my orders, my lord, and the Return of the Habeas Corpus, I brought the body of lieut. col. John Lilburne on Monday to the court; at which time I was ordered to attend the court again with him here as this day. But this morning I received an order from the Council of State to the contrary. . . .

Ibid. The order merely commanded Barksted not to bring Lilburne. Ibid. No cause for the precept was included. Ibid. Lilburne's counsel protested: "My lord, on Monday it was agreed that they should bring him again on Wednesday; and I have no instruction from my client, for I have no access to him, nor he to me." Ibid. He then moved the court for alias habeas corpus. Ibid. Barksted defensively replied: "I have only learned, my lord, to obey orders, and I shall obey them." Ibid. To which the judge answered: "You do well. The Council of State have a reason for what they do in this business." Ibid. The alias writ was issued. Ibid.

415. Ibid., p. 391.

416. Ibid., p. 396.

417. Ibid., p. 402.

418. *Anon.*, 82 Eng. Rep. 827, 827 (U. B. 1654).

419. Ibid.

420. Ibid.

421. For an account of *Cony's Case, see* "Administration of Justice during the Usurpation of the Government," 5 State Trials 935-38.

422. Ibid., p. 936.

423. Ibid.

424. Ibid., p. 937.

425. Ibid., p. 938.

426. Ibid.

427. Ibid.

428. Ibid.

429. Ibid.

430. Ibid.

431. Ibid., pp. 936, 938.

432. Ibid., p. 936.

433. Ibid.

434. Ibid., pp. 935-37.

435. Ibid., p. 937.

436. Ibid.

437. Ibid.

438. Ibid.

439. Ibid. For additional examples of abuse of the judicial machinery during this period, *see* ibid., pp. 938-48.

440. Ibid., p. 941.

441. Ibid.

442. Ibid.

443. Ibid.

444. Ibid.

445. 31 Car. 2, c. 2 (1679).

446. For the political background of this period, *see* Wilbur C. Abbott, "The Long Parliament of Charles II," 21 Eng. Hist. Rev. 21 pt. 1, 254 pt. 2, (1906).

447. *Proceedings in Parliament against Edward Earl of Clarendon, Lord High Chancellor of England*, [1663-1667] 6 State Trials 291.

448. Ibid., p. 330.

449. Ibid., p. 351.

450. Ibid. Clarendon's defense against the Article IV, *quoted in* text accompanying note 448 *supra*, was: "I have never taken upon me to commit any man to prison, but such who, by the course of the Chancery for matters of contempt, are justly committed." Ibid., p. 414.

451. 9 H. C. Jour. 78 (1668).

452. Ibid., p. 142 (1669).

453. *See* Anchitell Grey, *Debates of the House of Commons* (London, 1763) vol. 1, pp. 236-37 (remark of Finch).

454. Ibid., p. 237.

455. 9 H. C. Jour. 142 (1669). For the provisions of the bill and the vote tally, *see The Royal Commission on Historical Manuscripts*, 8th Report app., pt. 1, no. 276, at 142 (1881).

456. 12 H. L. Jour. 325 (1670).

457. 124 Eng. Rep. 1006 (C. P. 1670); *Case of the Imprisonment of Edward Bushell for alleged Misconduct as a Juryman*, [1670] 6 State Trials 999.

458. *The Trial of William Penn and William Mead, at the Old Bailey, for a Tumultuous Assembly*, [1670] 6 State Trials 951.

459. Ibid., p. 955.

460. Ibid.

461. *See* ibid., pp. 955-61.

462. Ibid., p. 962.

463. Ibid.

464. Ibid.

465. Ibid., p. 963.

466. Ibid., pp. 964-68.

467. 124 Eng. Rep. 1018.

468. *See generally, The Examination of the Jury who tried and acquitted Lieutenant Colonel John Lilburne*, [1653] 5 State Trials 445; *The Trial of Sir Nicholas Throckmorton*, [1554] 1 State Trials 869, 897-902.

469. 124 Eng. Rep. 1007.

470. *See* 2 Grey, *Debates*, pp. 338, 349, 364-67, 389-90.

471. William Cobbett, *Parliamentary History of England* (London, 1808), vol. 8, p. 665; 2 Grey, *Debates*, p. 390.

472. 12 H. L. Jour. 631 (1673).

473. Ibid., pp. 648-49; 4 Cobbett, *Debates*, p. 666.

474. 3 Grey, *Debates*, p. 239.

475. *The Royal Commission on Historical Manuscripts*, 9th Report app., pt. 2, no. 279, p. 65 (1884).

476. 3 Grey, *Debates*, p. 239.

477. 9 H. C. Jour. 349-50 (1675).

478. Ibid., p. 350.

479. Ibid.

480. Ibid.

481. 3 Grey, *Debates*, p. 239.

482. Ibid., pp. 239-40.

483. Ibid., p. 240.

484. Ibid., p. 243.

485. Ibid., p. 276.

486. Ibid., p. 282.

487. 9 H. C. Jour. 356 (1675); 3 Grey, *Debates*, p. 282.

488. 9 H. C. Jour. 357 (1675).

489. Ibid.

490. 3 Grey, *Debates*, p. 281.

491. Ibid., p. 289.

492. *Proceedings against Mr. Francis Jenkes*, |1676| 6 State Trials 1190.

493. For a copy of the warrant, *see* ibid., p. 1195. Soon after his commitment, Jenkes demanded that the keeper deliver the warrant to him as required. Ibid., pp. 1194-95. Two days passed and no copy of the warrant was delivered. Ibid., p. 1195. Some time later, the keeper voluntarily sent him a copy of the warrant, explaining that earlier he had had a positive order to deny Jenkes access to the warrant. Ibid.

494. Ibid., pp. 1195-96.

495. Coke, *Second Part of the Institutes*, p. 53.

496. *Jenkes Proceedings*, 6 State Trials 1196.

497. D. E. C. Yale ed., *Lord Nottingham's Chancery Cases* (Seldon Society, 1957), p. 424.

498. Ibid., p. 424.

499. Ibid.

500. Ibid.; *see* ibid., pp. 429-34.

501. *Jenkes Proceedings*, 6 State Trials 1207-08. Jenkes attempted to secure release by bail a second time (this time before a lower court), ibid., p. 1196, but again failed, ibid., p. 1200. The court first gave as its reason the fact that the case was not one listed on its calendar. Ibid., p. 1196. Counsel argued that according to 3 Hen. 7, c. 3 (1468), every keeper of a prison was required to certify the names of his prisoners at the next gaol-delivery, insuring that prisoners might be delivered according to law. Ibid., p. 1197. He insisted, therefore, that the court command the jailer to calendar Jenkes immediately. Ibid. The court implicitly acknowledged the correctness of counsel's argument, but would not record the jailer's fault. Ibid. Further, the court said, it was not a general gaol-delivery. Ibid. Finally, the court admitted the true reason for its refusal to act, explaining that it would not bail one who had been denied habeas corpus by the Lord Chief Justice and Lord Chancellor. Ibid., pp. 1198-99.

The attempt at release via bail being thoroughly frustrated, Jenkes' friends sought remedy by means of a writ of mainprise to Lord Chancellor Finch. Ibid., p. 1201. Finch attempted to comfort them by saying that he agreed with their cause, but suggested that since the councilboard imprisoned Jenkes, they should be petitioned. Ibid.

On August 11, 1676, a month and a half after his first imprisonment, Jenkes remained in confinement, denied bail on a charge that warranted it. On that day, he addressed a letter to the Lord Privy-Seal, president of the Council:

> My Lord, I have been imprisoned since the 28th of June, to my great loss, charge, and prejudice of my health. I have hitherto been denied bail, Habeas Corpus and the Writ of Main-Prize . . . And this only for moving in a lawful court, and in a quiet and peaceable manner, that which I did believe to be for his majesty's service, and the

good of the city and kingdom . . . and which I conceive I can make
appear to be according to the laws and statutes of this realm, if I am
publicly called thereto. Wherefore I do not bet a discharge, for I desire
nothing more than to clear my innocence by a public trial. . . .

Ibid., p. 1205.

502. 13 H. L. Jour. 87 (1677). *See* ibid., pp. 88, 89, 91.

503. Ibid., p. 100.

504. *Royal Commission on Historical Manuscripts* 9th Report, note 475,
pt. 2, no. 388, p. 88 *supra*.

505. *Proceedings in the Case of Anthony Earl of Shaftsbury*, [1677] 6
State Trials 1269, 1270-73.

506. Ibid., pp. 1269-70.

507. Ibid., pp. 1277-78.

508. Ibid., pp. 1278-79.

509. Ibid., p. 1296.

510. Ibid., p. 1306.

511. 31 Car. 2, c. 2 (1679).

512. 22 Calendar of State Papers 675, 677 (Domestic 1680-1681).

Lord Grey and Lord Norris were named to be the tellers. Lord
Norris, being a man subject to vapours, was not at all times attentive
to what he was doing; so a very fat lord coming in, Lord Grey counted
him for ten, as a jest at first; but, seeing Lord Norris had not observed
it, he went on with the misreckoning of ten. . . .

Tanner, *English Constitutional Conflicts*, p. 244 n.3. The vote was reported
as being in favor of passage, though in fact, it went against the bill. Ibid.

513. *See* 9 Holdsworth 119; Maxwell Cohen, "Habeas Corpus Cum Causa
—The Emergence of the Modern Writ—II," 18 Can. B. Rev. 172, 185-96
(1940).

514. *See* William F. Duker, "The President's Power to Pardon: A Constitutional History," 18 Wm. and M. L. Rev. 475, 487-95 (1977).

515. Ibid., p. 488. For the Articles of Impeachment presented against
Danby, *see* 4 Cobbett, *Debates*, pp. 1067-69.

516. Duker, "Power to Pardon," 18 Wm. and M. L. Rev. 475, 489.

517. Ibid., p. 495.

518. Ibid.

519. *Proceedings in the King's-Bench, upon the Earl of Danby's Motion
for Bail*, [K. B. 1682] 11 State Trials 831.

520. Ibid., pp. 835-36.

521. Ibid., pp. 853-54.

522. Ibid., p. 854. The Court released Danby to bail in 1683. Ibid., p. 871.

523. 8 Grey, *Debates*, pp. 220-22, 229-33.

524. Ibid., p. 220.

525. Ibid., pp. 230-31 (remarks of Winnington).

526. 91 Eng. Rep. 431 (K. B. 1704).

527. Ibid., p. 431.

528. Ibid.

529. Ibid.

530. Ibid.

531. *See Case of the Sheriff of Middlesex*, 113 Eng. Rep. 419, 424 (Q. B.

1840); *Burdett v. Abbot*, 104 Eng. Rep. 501, 553-54, 561-63 (K. B. 1811); *Case of Brass Crosby*, 95 Eng. Rep. 1005, 1011-14 (C. P. 1771); *Murray's Case*, 95 Eng. Rep. 629, 629 (K. B. 1751); Thomas Erskine May, *A Treatise On the Law, Privileges, Proceedings, and Usages of Parliament* (Shannon, Ireland: Irish University Press, 1971, 1st ed. 1844), p. 56.

532. 31 Car. 2, c. 2, sect. 3 (1679).

533. 1 W. and M., c. 36, sect. 10 (1688).

534. 9 Grey, *Debates*, pp. 129-30.

535. Ibid., p. 131 (remarks of Boscawen).

536. Ibid., pp. 131-32.

537. Ibid., p. 135.

538. Ibid., p. 262.

539. Ibid., p. 263.

540. Ibid., pp. 266-67.

541. Ibid., p. 276 (vote of 126-83).

542. *The Spirit of the Laws* (Dublin, 1751, 1st French ed. Geneva, 1748), vol. 1, p. 104.

543. United States Constitution, Art. I, sect. 9, clause 2.

The British Colonies in North America: Extension of theWrit of Habeas Corpus

2

To prepare for an examination of the habeas clause of the Constitution, it is necessary to consider the question of whether the Englishmen who settled in the eastern seaboard of North America shared the benefit of the writ of habeas corpus.[2] Before an examination of the actual case histories of each colony, which is required in dealing with this issue, it is useful to set forth the theory of extension.

In the same year that the first British colony in America was founded,[3] the Exchequer Chamber decided the *Case of Robert Calvin*.[4] The issue before the Court was whether Calvin, the plaintiff, having been born in Scotland after the English Crown had descended to King James I, was an alien and consequently unable to bring any real or personal action for any lands within the realm of England. Following extensive arguments before the bench by the most able lawyers of the day, the Court held for the plaintiff. In dicta, the Court, *per* Coke, noted a distinction between the conquest of a Christian kingdom and the conquest of the kingdom of an infidel. In the former case, the king could alter and change the laws of the conquered land at his pleasure; but until he did effect an alteration, the established laws of the land remained in force.[5] Once the king extended the laws of England to the conquered Christian kingdom, no succeeding monarch could alter those laws without the cooperation of Parliament. In the case of the conquest of the kingdom of an infidel, the indigenous laws were instantly abrogated; until the adoption of a new code, the king, by himself, and such judges as he should appoint, were to adjudicate any matters that might arise there by the standard of "natural equity."[6]

Later in the century, this doctrine was extended in the *Earl of Derby's Case*,[7] where it was held that an English statute was not binding on the inhabitants of the Isle of Man, a conquered province, unless the statute specifically mentioned that it extended to the region. In *Blankard v. Galdy* (1694),[8] Mr. Chief Justice Holt, in deciding the issue of whether a certain English statute applied to Jamaica, further supplemented the *Calvin* doctrine by holding:

> . . . In [the] case of an uninhabited country, newly found out by English subjects, all laws in force in England are in force there. . . .
>
> . . . Jamaica being conquered, and not pleaded to be parcel of the kingdom of England, but part of the possessions and revenue of the Crown, the laws of England did not take place there, until declared so by the conqueror or his successor.[9]

In applying the doctrine of the just-noted cases to the American colonies, Blackstone, in his *Commentaries*,[10] was of the opinion that the colonies fell into the category of "conquered or ceded countries," and as such the common law of England had no allowance or authority there *per se*: "they being no part of the mother country, but distinct (though dependent) dominions." Nevertheless, observed Blackstone, the colonies were subject to the control of Parliament though not bound by any acts of Parliament, unless particularly named.

A century later, Joseph Story took exception to the theory espoused by Blackstone. The American legal commentator suggested that the American colonies were of a class of territory "acquired by discovery," a class that he equated with "an uninhabited country." He noted that "the title of the Indians was not treated as a right of propriety and dominion, but as a mere right of occupancy. As infidels, heathens, and savages, they were not allowed to possess the prerogatives belonging to absolute, sovereign, and independent nations."[11]

Although there is some precedent for Story's position,[12] the colonies were generally considered conquered infidel kingdoms (with the exception, perhaps, of New Netherlands).[13] Nevertheless, the harsh *Calvin* doctrine was ameliorated by the *Privy Council Memo-*

randum of 9 August 1722.[14] While continuing the established rule of extension in the instance of new and uninhabited countries and conquered Christian countries, the Privy Council held that in countries governed by laws "contrary to our own religion" or in cases where the laws were "malum in se" or were silent, the laws of the conquering country would prevail. As the Indians could scarcely be said to have had any laws within the sense of the English jurists, the laws of England might be regarded as having extended *in toto* to the colonies.

Story's analysis continued by noting that in each of the charters under which the colonies were settled:

> there is . . . an express declaration, that all subjects and their children inhabiting therein shall be deemed natural-born subjects, and shall enjoy all the privileges and immunities thereof. There is also in all of them an express restriction that no laws be made repugnant to those of England, or that as near as . . . [is convenient], shall be consonant with and conformable thereto; and that either expressly or by necessary implication it is provided that the laws of England so far as applicable shall be in force there. Now this declaration, even if the crown previously possessed a right to establish what laws it pleased over the territory, as a conquent from the natives, being a fundamental rule of the original settlement of the colonies, and before the emigrations thither, was conclusive, and could not afterwards be abrogated by the Crown. It was an irrevocable annexation of the colonies to the mother country, as dependencies governed by the same laws, and entitled to the same rights.[15]

Corollary to this argument was another frequently employed by the colonists,[16] that those who came from England and settled in an area formerly peopled only by Indians were the conquerors. The laws that were abolished were those of the vanquished. Those of the conqueror, which were their birthright, were carried, so far as they were "applicable to their own situation and the condition of an infant colony,"[17] with them.[18]

Several of the most distinguished lawyers in the English government supported the position that the common law and certain acts of Parliament[19] should be regarded as applicable in the colonies. In 1702, Attorney General Edward Northey, examining the right of presentation of benefices in Virginia, implicitly accepted the view that the laws of England in question were in effect in Virginia unless limited by act of assembly.[20] The following year, Solicitor General Harcourt, in passing on some Bermuda acts, stated that it was unnecessary to enact certain acts of Henry III and Edward III because they were "declaratory of the common law."[21] In 1720, Mr. West, counsel to the Board of Trade, noted that

> The common law of England, is the common law of the plantations, and all statutes in affirmance of the common law, passed in England, antecedent to the settlement of a colony, are in force in that colony, unless there is some private act to the contrary. . . . Let an Englishman go where he will, he carries as much of law and liberty with him, as the nature of things will bear.[22]

Endorsement for this position was forthcoming in 1729 from Attorney General Philip Yorke,[23] and shortly thereafter from a later attorney general, Charles Pratt, and Solicitor General Charles York.[24] In 1757, Attorney General Henley and Solicitor General York rendered an opinion, in concurrence with those just cited, in a Nova Scotia counterfeiting case concerning the applicability of an English statute, and emphasized that only so much of the law as was applicable to the colony extended: "the proposition . . . that the inhabitants of the colonies carry with them *the statute laws* of this realm, is not true, as a general proposition, but depends upon circumstances, the effect of their charter, usage, and acts of their legislature. . . ."[25] In sum, the general rule was that the Englishmen who came to settle in the American colonies, by conquering the former inhabitants, brought with them as much of the common law and affirming statutory law,[26] existing at the time of their settlement, as was applicable to colonial life.

The common-law writ of habeas corpus was a well-established judicial writ as early as the formulation of the first colonial charter.[27]

Which of the seventeenth-century statutes that sought to remedy the deficiencies in the procedure for obtaining the benefit of the writ were extended depended upon: (1) whether they were declared to extend by the act itself[28] or (2) were extended subsequently by the conqueror or his successor,[29] (3) whether they were introduced and declared to be law by some act of the assembly of the province (subject, of course, to veto),[30] or (4) whether the statute was received in a colony by "long uninterrupted usage, or practice."[31]

In general, the problem of extension was a difficult one for the colonists themselves. Total extension would have seriously damaged the liberty of the colonial legislatures, and in any event was not practical. However, the colonists did desire the extension of those laws that limited the royal prerogative. From the perspective of the colonists, the primary tenet of English law was "liberty, and the Freedom of a Man from [unlawful] Imprisonment. . . ."[32] and it was well known that the "great and efficacious"[33] remedy in cases of illegal imprisonment was the writ of habeas corpus.[34] Whether the colonists actually had the benefit of this writ is a question which requires the examination of each individual colony.

English law and liberty had a great history in the first English settlement in the New World, Virginia.[35] A decade after its settlement by the Virginia Company, the colony welcomed a governor, Sir George Yeardly, who had instructions from the Company ordering him to introduce English common law and the orderly processes thereof, and to summon a representative assembly for the purpose of enacting by-laws. Although the Company was soon dissolved in favor of royal control, the colony's affection for the common law was unaltered. In 1651, the assembly enacted a provision that held that

> It is agreed and constituted that the plantation of Virginia and all the inhabitants thereof, shall be and remain in due obedience and subjection to the Commonwealth of England according to the laws there established, and that this submission and subscription be acknowledged a voluntary act not forced nor constrained by a conquest upon the country, and that they shall have and enjoy such freedoms and privileges as belong

to the free borne people of England, and that the former government by the commissioners and instructions be void and
null.[36]

Not only does the enactment provide an affirmation of the laws of
the mother country, but it displays a recognition and sets forth an
opinion as to its own case, of the extension principle laid down in
the *Case of Robert Calvin*.[37] A decade later, in the preamble to
the revision of the statutes of 1660-1661, it was declared that "We
have endeavored in all things (as near as the capacity and construction of this country would admit) to adhere to these excellent
and often refined laws of England to which we profess and acknowledge all our obedience and reverence."[38] Illustrative of the fact that
one of those institutions was the writ of habeas corpus was the *Case
of Robert Beverley*.

Robert Beverley, clerk of the House of Burgesses, had incurred
the displeasure of Governor Chicheley for refusing to supply him
and the executive council with copies of the House's journal without the permission of that body.[39] The council's opportunity for
revenge came when the tobacco-cutting riots of 1682 began.[40] Beverley was arrested on May seventh[41] on a mere suspicion[42] and kept
a close prisoner.[43] On the twenty-seventh of September, he applied
for a writ of habeas corpus,[44] which was rejected by order of council on the ground that the case had been referred to England.[45] The
case resembled those from the early seventeenth century in England,
prior to the successful limitation of the executive department's arbitrary power of imprisonment, and showed the circumscribed effectiveness of the common-law writ of habeas corpus, unaided by the
remedial statutes, against a powerful executive.[46] This situation was
corrected in 1710 when the Habeas Corpus Act was extended to
Virginia by proclamation of Governor Spotswood, pursuant to instructions given him in 1707 by Queen Anne.[47]

A. H. Carpenter, in a brief article published in 1902 entitled
"Habeas Corpus in the American Colonies"[48] (written basically to
publish Spotswood's proclamation) questioned the validity of the
extension by arguing that the instructions were in the nature of a
legislative act whereby the Crown extended an act of Parliament to
the colonies, which was a "doubtful" power of the Crown.[49] Car-

penter's doubts were legitimate. Although the Crown possessed prerogatives over the colonies far in excess of those exercised at home during the same period,[50] under the *Calvin* doctrine, once the laws of England were activated in a conquered Christian kingdom, the authority of the king *and Parliament* was required to effect an alteration.[51] Although the colonies (excepting New Netherlands) were considered conquered infidel kingdoms, the same principle might apply.[52] The essential question then is: did the provisions in the charters declaring that the colonists and their heirs and successors were entitled to the same privileges and immunities as subjects born in England and that no law repugnant to the laws of England shall be passed, intend to extend the laws of England? The provisions were more likely intended to insure loyalty to England.[53]

In 1736, Virginia extended the benefits of the writ of *habeas corpus cum causa* to civil cases.[54] This provision was reenacted, with slight modification, two years after independence was declared.[55] Late in the Revolution, the legislature empowered the governor, with the advice of the council, "to apprehend or cause to be apprehended and committed to close confinement, any person or persons whatsoever, whom they may have just cause to suspect disaffection to the independence of the United States or of attachment to their enemies, and such person or persons shall not be set at liberty by bail, mainprise or habeas corpus."[56] The Virginia Constitution did not contain a clause pertaining to the writ of habeas corpus until 1830, when the policy allowing suspension was reversed. Article III, section 9 of the new Constitution provided: "The privilege of the writ of habeas corpus shall not in any case be suspended."[57]

Shortly after the passage of the Habeas Corpus Act (1679), Cotton Mather recommended that Massachusetts' agents in London attempt to secure for the citizens of the colony the benefits of the 1679 statute. Without the Act, Mather wrote, "We are slaves. . . ."[58] Unfortunately, the agents were unsuccessful, and Mather's appeal was shown to be all too prophetic.

During the administration of Governor Andros, the executive council began to exercise the right of levying and assessing taxes upon several towns without the consent of the legislature.[59] The town of Ipswich, in which the Reverend Mr. Wise was the minister, regarded the levies as arbitrary and illegal impositions, and at a town meeting in 1689, it was resolved not to submit to the tax. For this "contempt," six prominent residents of the town, including the Reverend Mr. Wise, were arrested and confined in the prison at Boston. Wise petitioned for a writ of habeas corpus, but the request was denied by Mr. Chief Judge Dudley. The case, resembling the *Darnel Case* of 1627 in England,[60] once more displayed the awesomeness of the executive power *vis à vis* the precarious state of the subject's liberty unprotected by the Habeas Corpus Act.

Three years after the *Case of Wise*, the Massachusetts assembly adopted a provision including a declaration that no tax should be imposed without the consent of the general court and an act, which was virtually the same as the English Habeas Corpus Act, entitled, "An Act for the Better Securing the Liberty of the Subject and for the Prevention of Illegal Imprisonments."[61] Both provisions were vetoed by the Privy Council. The Council explained:

> Whereas . . . the writt of Habeas Corpus is required to be granted in like manner as is appointed by the Statute 31 Car. II in England, which privilege has not as yet been granted to any of His Majesty's Plantations, It was not thought fitt in His Majesty's absence that the said Act should continue in force and therefore the same was repealed.[62]

The *Wise Case* is a typical example of the situation in which the Habeas Corpus Act was needed in order for the subject to receive the benefit of the writ of habeas corpus. However, in those cases where there was no executive interference—in "non-political" cases —the citizens of Massachusetts did know the writ through acts establishing and regulating the judicial system. An act of 29 December 1687 gave defendants the right of removal from inferior courts to the Supreme Court of Judicature by habeas corpus or certiorari.[63] In 1701, the "Act for Establishing a Superior Court of Judicature, Court of Assize, and General Gaol Delivery" empowered those courts to deal with all matters "as fully and amply, to all Intents and Purposes whatsoever, as the Courts of King's Bench, Common Pleas, and Exchequer, within His Majesty's Kingdom of England, have or ought to have. . . ."[64] Thus, although the remedial statutes were not in operation, the common-law writ was available.[65] This state of affairs persisted throughout the colonial period in Massachusetts. After independence, the designers of the 1780 *Frame of Government* included a clause in the document outlining the new governmental structure providing that the privileges of habeas corpus were not to be suspended, except in times of emergency.[66]

In the Carolinas, the writ, reinforced by the statutory remedies, seems to have operated de jure or de facto, with minor interruptions, from a very early date.[67] A 1692 enactment empowered magistrates to "execute and put in force an Act made in the Kingdom of England, Anno 31, Caroli 2, Regis, commonly called the Habeas Corpus Act."[68] The proprietors, assuming that all the laws of England applied to the colony, disallowed the act on the grounds that it was unnecessary to reenact the famous statute: "[I]t is expressed in our grant from the crown," argued the proprietors, "that the inhabitants of Carolina shall be of the King's allegiance; which makes them subject to the laws of England."[69] Despite the veto of the proprietors, whose opinion was incongruent with case law,[70] the colonists seem to have regarded their enactment as having full force. For example, in 1712 a statute repealing the 1692 enactment was passed. This statute went on to provide that

> all and every person which now is or hereafter shall be within any part of this Province, shall have to all intents, constructions and purposes whatsoever, and in all things whatsoever, as large ample and effectual right to and benefit of the said act, commonly called the Habeas Corpus Act, as if he were personally in the said Kingdom of England.

Any two of the proprietors, or the Chief Justice of the province, or any of the local proprietors' deputies and one justice of the peace, or any two justices of the peace could put the act into execution.[71] The act remained in force until the first quarter of the nineteenth century.[72]

In 1730 the Royal Governors of South Carolina and North Carolina were given instructions similar to those given to Governor Spotswood of Virginia.[73] A case arose in South Carolina shortly after these instructions were issued illustrating the facility with which the writ operated in that colony. Early in 1732, Governor Johnson issued the King's instructions, which, to prevent the inconvenience of granting excessive quantities of land to people not likely to cultivate and improve them, provided that no grants were to be made to any person, except in proportion to his ability to cultivate the lands granted.[74] Soon after the announcement of the proclamation, settlers on the frontier, having been driven from their homes by Indians, returned to find that most of the land in the east was in the hands of speculators. They sought to get a case into court to test the validity of the speculators' title. Among those seeking the test case was Dr. Thomas Cooper. Instead of submitting their case to the courts, Cooper *et al.* presented a petition to the Commons' House of Assembly against one of the large landholders, Job Rothmaller. The Assembly examined the matter and ordered Cooper into the custody of the House messenger. Cooper petitioned for a writ of habeas corpus, which was allowed without question by Mr. Chief Justice Robert Wright. The legislators were infuriated by what they regarded as a breach of the House's privileges. They directed the House messenger not to obey the writ. Then they ordered Cooper's attorneys to be taken into custody. Finally the House passed a series of resolutions in support of its privileges similar to those passed by the House of Commons in England during the Dalmahoy affair in 1675.[75] Those committed thereupon petitioned the Governor and Council, but no support from the executive department was forthcoming. Mr. Chief Justice Wright, a member of the Council, observed that the resolutions of the Assembly were "of a most extraordinary nature, tending to the subversion of all government by disallowing his Majesty's undoubted prerogative, removing all obedience to his writ of habeas corpus and assuming to themselves power to abrogate and make void the known laws of the land by arbitrarily imprisoning their fellow subjects." The majority of the Council, however, resolved that the Commons' House of Assembly had a right to commit persons for breach of privilege and notorious grievances that might affect the people of the province, and that in cases of contempt or breach of privilege of any court, no writ of habeas corpus would be or ought to be granted. A short time later, upon their submission to the House's authority, Cooper and his attorneys were released.

In order to shield themselves and their messenger against civil action for their disregard of the writ of habeas corpus, the Assembly passed "An Act for the prevention of suits and disturbances to His Majesty's Judges and Magistrates in this Province on Account of the Habeas Corpus Act."[76] The indemnity act provided that no public official should be liable to any suit or penalty for refusing to issue or obey a writ of habeas corpus petitioned for by anyone committed by the legislature in violation of its privilege. Wright denounced the Act, calling the writ of habeas corpus "the strongest barrier that the wisdom of our ancestors could devise to preserve the liberty of the subject and secure the people from arbitrary violance and oppression."[77] Governor Johnson supported the measure, and transmitted this approval to the Council of Trade and Plantations.[78] Cooper and his attorneys forwarded a brief in opposition to the Act.[79] On 19 June 1734, Mr. Fane, advisor to the Council, recommended the repeal of the Act:

[The Act is, in effect,] a suspension of the Habeas Corpus Act in this Colony, and an indemnification . . . to persons who have acted in an illegal and arbitrary manner, and in violation of the liberty of the subject. The Habeas Corpus Act has always been considered as the great barrier of the liberty of the subject in this Kingdom. For by that Law if any Person is committed to prison for an offense that's bailable by law, he has a right to pray His Majesty's Writt of Habeas Corpus. . . . This law has sometimes been suspended in this country, but it has been in the time of open rebellion or the certain apprehension of it or when the Government itself has been in the most imminent danger; what necessity there was of suspending it in this Colony do's not appear to me. . . . But I apprehend the design of the suspension is to oppress and injure His Majesty's subjects without any cause . . . and skreen themselves from the resentment of the injured. . . .[80]

The Council accepted Fane's recommendation, and the Act was repealed.

Less than ten years after the Cooper affair, the Habeas Corpus Act in South Carolina was supplemented by a statute, which, in order to prevent excessive exactions that might be made upon prisoners, provided, *inter alia*, "that no Baron or Justice shall receive for himself or Clerks for granting a Writ of Habeas Corpus more than two Shillings and six Pence. . . ."[81]

A North Carolina act of 1749 entitled "An Act to put in Force in this Province the several Statutes of the Kingdom of England, or South-Britain, therein particularly mentioned,"[82] provided for the extension of, among other English statutes, chapter twenty-nine of the Magna Carta, the Petition of Right, and the Habeas Corpus Act of 1679. In the same year as the Declaration of Independence was published, North Carolina adopted a new constitution which provided, *inter alia*, "That every freeman restrained of his liberty, is entitled to a remedy, to enquire into the lawfulness thereof, and to remove the same, if unlawful; and that such remedy ought not to be denied or delayed."[83]

The situation in Georgia was similar to that in Virginia and the Carolinas: both the common-law writ of habeas corpus and its statutory safeguards extended. In 1754 the Governor of Georgia was given instructions similar to those earlier given to the Governors of the other southern plantations.[84] The 1777 constitution of Georgia declared "The principles of the habeas-corpus act" to be part of the fundamental order.[85] The constitution adopted two years after the framing of the United States Constitution did not follow the federal provision, which allowed for suspension in "Cases of Rebellion or Invasion,"[86] but instead provided without qualification that "All persons shall be entitled to the benefit of the writ of *habeas corpus*."[87]

From the founding of Maryland in 1634, the colonists embraced the common law of the mother country. In 1642, the Assembly enacted rules for the judiciary which provided that criminal cases were to be "judged and determined according to the laws of that Province, or in defect of certain laws then they may be determined according to the best discretion of the judge or judges, judging as near as conveniently may be to the laudable laws of usage of England in the same or like offenses."[88] Eighteen years later, it was enacted that when the laws of the province were silent, justice was to be administered according to the laws of England *if*, in the judgment of the court, the laws of England were consistent with the good of the province.[89] The reservation was incorporated to satisfy the objection of the upper house that it would be inconvenient to extend all English laws to the colony.[90]

Later in the century, a minor conflict developed between the proprietors and the upper house on the one hand, and the lower house on the other, over the Speaker's right to issue warrants for election to vacancies.[91] In support of their position, the proprietors at one point claimed that "the King had power to dispose of his conquests as he pleases." The lower house found such a claim appalling and responded with an assertion of their English birthright. The upper body immediately replied that the argument was in no way intended to link the freemen of Maryland to a conquered people.

A more serious conflict arose forty years later when the Governor of Maryland insisted, in the face of the lower house's argument to the contrary, that the Habeas Corpus Act of 1679 did not extend to that colony since the Act had "often been adjudged by all the judges not to extend either to Ireland or to the plantations, which is as strong a case as can be mentioned. . . ."[92] For the lower house, Daniel Dulany responded first by admitting that the Act, by express words, was limited to a specified area, but he then maintained that as Englishmen, the colonists of Maryland were entitled to the same liberties, franchises, and privileges as Englishmen dwelling within the mother country.[93] Dulany, under the pseudonym Cato, reiterated his argument in a 1728 pamphlet entitled, "The Right of Inhabitants of Maryland to the Benefit of English Laws."[94] He wrote:

> Can a thing be more evident, than that all the Subjects, of the same Prince, living within his Dominions, adhering to their allegiance, and in a Word, behaving themselves, as dutiful and loyal Subjects ought, and promiscuously born under the same Obligation of Allegiance, Obedience, and loyalty to their Prince, and to the same Right of Protection, should also be entitled to the same Right, and Liberties, with the rest of the Subjects, of the same Prince, of their Degree, and Condition. Or can anything be more clear, than that the Subject,

having equal Right to Privileges, must also have an equal
Right to Laws, made to create or preserve such Privileges?[95]

In other words, Dulany was arguing that since the common-law
guarantee of "liberty," including its procedural safeguard, the common-law writ of habeas corpus, had been transplanted to the American soil, any deprivation of the statutes that remedied the flaws in
the procedure for insuring the benefit of English liberties was unjust, because those without the relief of the positive law were help-
less against the same abuse that in times past had shown the common law to be insufficient.[96] But neither Dulany's arguments in the
House, nor those in his 1728 publication were accepted, and Maryland, like Massachusetts, experienced only the benefits of the common-law writ of habeas corpus.

In the year that the Habeas Corpus Act was passed in England,
the common-law writ of habeas corpus could be observed operating
in the New York case of *Fransa*.[97] Fransa had been committed to
a New York jail by virtue of a *mittimus* for breach of peace against
an "Act of Parliament made in the Fifteenth Year of King Charles
the second." In fact, the act he was accused of violating was enacted
in the fifteenth year of King Richard the second. Upon a habeas
corpus challenging the confinement under the wrong act, the prisoner was remanded. The court ruled that the mistake was "a Bare
Error in the Clerkship which by the Clerke might be supplied, [or]
Amended. . . ."

Four years later, *The Charter of Liberties and Privileges of New
York* was framed.[98] It contained many of the provisions found in
the Magna Carta and the Habeas Corpus Act; however, after examining the document, the Committee of Trade and Plantations
vetoed it on the ground that the privileges of the Habeas Corpus Act
had not been extended to any of the plantations.[99] The common-
law writ, however, continued to issue (perhaps leading later gen-
erations of colonial New Yorkers into believing that the 1679 statute
extended to the colony[100]), as illustrated by three early cases.[101]

The first case resulted from the Leisler Rebellion. On 12 December 1689, Jacob Leisler, in possession of the office of Lieutenant
Governor, gave notice of a continuation of certain customs and

excise taxes.[102] This was viewed as an arbitrary imposition because it violated the maxim

> That no aid, Tax, Tollage, Assessment, Custom, Loan, Benevolence or imposition whatsoever shall be laid, assessed, imposed or levied on any of His Majesty's Subjects within this Province, or their Estates upon any manner or colour of pretence, but by act and consent of the Governor, Council, and representatives of the People in General Assembly met and assembled,[103]

or, as a later generation would say, "no taxation without representation." Eleven days later, two young men, Jacob De Key Jr. and Cornelius Depeyster, and an Indian slave belonging to Philip French were arrested without legal process for their part in protesting the imposition of the taxes. After complaining of the incident, French was arrested and held close prisoner. His counsel requested the gaoler to supply him with a copy of the *mittimus*. After some delay, the request was granted. The *mittimus* stated that French had "in a most insolent manner condemned this Government, threatening to take off the Proclamation for continuing his Majesty's Customs and Excise. . . ." Counsel then sought to have his client released on bail since he was held for a charge that, by the laws of England and New York, was bailable. The petition was denied. On the fourth of January, French's lawyer applied for and was granted a writ of habeas corpus from the Mayor's Court. The writ was delivered to French and by him conveyed to his keeper, who forthwith acquainted Leisler with the judicial writ. Leisler immediately ordered that the windows where French was confined be nailed closed and that a strict watch be kept over the prisoner. On the return day, his client not having been produced, French's attorney queried, "is a writ granted in the subject's favour to prevent the illegal detainure of any of the King's Subjects falsely Imprisoned, so that a violation of this kind was a crime of the deepest dye, and every subject was nearly concerned therein," no one knowing whose turn it might be next to have their liberties subjected to the arbitrary will and pleasure of Leisler? Milborne, one of Leisler's lieutenants, answered: "Mr. French is none of the King's Subjects." To this return, many in the courtroom hissed. As if it had not been shown often enough, the executive power was once more displayed. French was released after submitting to the proud Leisler by petitioning him by the title of Lieutenant Governor.[104]

Another interesting case demonstrating the use of the common-law writ of habeas corpus, which also highlights the distinction between the extension of statutory and common law, was adjudicated in 1707.[105] The case concerned two Presbyterian ministers who were arraigned for preaching in New York without a license, in violation of the codes of that state. They pointed to an act of Parliament and argued that "If the law for Liberty . . . had directed us to any particular persons in Authority for License, we would have observed the same; but we cannot find any directions in said Act of Parliament, therefore could not take notice thereof." Lord Cornbury responded, however, by noting that "That Law does not extend to the American Plantations, but only to England," and remanded the two to await trial. Later, they petitioned for and were granted a writ of habeas corpus by Mr. Chief Justice Roger Mompesson.

A politically and legally more salient case was the *Trial of John Peter Zenger* in 1734.[106] Zenger was committed "for printing several Seditious Libels, dispersed throughout his Journals . . . [which have tended] to raise Factions and Tumults, among the People of this Province, inflaming their Minds with Contempt of His Majesty's Government, and greatly disturbing the Peace thereof. . . ." Upon this commitment, friends of Zenger petitioned for a writ of habeas corpus. The writ was granted by the colony's Chief Justice and on the return day, James Alexander and William Smith, for Zenger, argued that the return was insufficient and requested that bail be allowed. In support of their application for bail they cited the Magna Carta, the Petition of Right, the Habeas Corpus Act, and the Bill of Rights. They further submitted an affidavit estimating Zenger's worth at forty pounds over and above his debts, wearing apparel, and tools of trade. Nevertheless, bail was set at four hundred pounds. Although the Court did not speak to the arguments based upon English statutes, its failure to set bail at a nonexcessive amount would seem to indicate either that it regarded the crime charged to be extraordinarily serious, or that it looked upon the extension of the excessive bail clause of the Bill of Rights, at least, with disfavor.

Thirty years later, a writ of habeas corpus was granted explicitly on the basis of 31 Car. II c. 2 in *Cunningham's Case*.[107] Although the *Cunningham* and *Zenger* cases are far from conclusive proof of the extension of the 1679 Habeas Corpus Act, supporting authority exists. In 1756, William Smith, an eminent lawyer, expressing his opinion on the extension of English laws to the colonies (which was influenced, perhaps, by his role in the *Zenger Case*), wrote: "The Common Law of *England* is generally received, together with such Statutes as were enacted before we had a Legislature of our own."[108] Although most discussions of the "settled colony" principle set the date of reception at the date of actual settlement or at the date of the charter grant, the rule in New York established the reception date at the assembly of the first legislature, set by Smith at 1691[109] (a date that allowed extension of the Bill of Rights as well as the Habeas Corpus Act). Smith's opinion was endorsed by Mr. Chief Justice Horsmanden in 1764,[110] by Thomas Pownall in his famous work on the administration of the colonies,[111] and by Governor Tryon in his 1774 report on the constitution of New York.[112] According to this rule, the Habeas Corpus Act should have been effective in New York. Nevertheless, as noted, the Committee on Trade and Plantations vetoed the Charter of Liberties specifically because the Habeas Corpus Act had not been extended to the plantations. Although the Committee would probably have refused to permit the prerogatives of the Crown to be curtailed anyway, Smith's rule seems faulty. There had been no legislative vacuum in the colony as the rule implies, except for a brief period following the conquest before the Nicolls Code (1665).[113] Until 1789, when the State of New York enacted a statute modeled after the English Act of 1679,[114] the benefits of the Habeas Corpus Act would seem to have had no application in New York.

In the remaining northern colonies of Connecticut, Rhode Island, New Jersey, New Hampshire, Pennsylvania and Delaware, the situation was similar to that in Massachusetts, Maryland, and probably New York. The citizens of Connecticut, though in many respects extremely independent of the common law,[115] were naturally receptive to English liberties. The colony's Superior Court was given cognizance of all pleas of the Crown,[116] and therefore able to issue writs of habeas corpus. It was not until 1818 that a constitutional provision pertaining to the writ of habeas corpus was enshrined. Article I, section 14 of the Connecticut Constitution of 1818 was similar to, though less ambiguous than, the federal constitutional clause pertaining to habeas corpus in that it affixed to the non-suspension-except-in-emergency clause the phrase: "nor in any case, but by the legislature."[117]

The citizens of Rhode Island, likewise, were familiar only with the common-law writ, which was introduced to them by acts establishing and regulating the judicial department. A 1666 statute provided for the formation of two general courts of trial and a general gaol-delivery, which were to have cognizance

> of all Pleas, Real and Personal and Mixt, and also Pleas of the Crown, and Causes Criminal, and Matters relating to the Conservation of the Peace, and Punishment of Offenders, and generally of all Matters as fully and amply, to all Intents and Purposes whatsoever; as the Courts of Common Pleas, King's Bench, or Exchequer, in His Majesty's Kingdom of England, Have or ought to Have. . . .[118]

A 1729 act provided for the holding of two superior courts, courts of assize, and general gaol-delivery, which were given the same authority as that given the courts established by the 1666 act.[119]

In the same year that Governor Spotswood arrived in Virginia with the Queen's proclamation extending the Habeas Corpus Act to that colony, the circumscribed effect of the common-law writ was evident in the colony of New Jersey. Differences between the Council and Assembly during Lieutenant Governor Cornbury's administration resulted in the arrest of Thomas Gordon, Speaker of the Assembly. His office notwithstanding, he was kept prisoner and arbitrarily denied benefit of the writ of habeas corpus by Judge William Pinhorne of the Supreme Court. He was later let to bail owing to the unique position of his lawyer, Pinhorne's son. In a letter to Governor Robert Hunter, the Assembly criticized Pinhorne's judgment and Cornbury's administration, claiming that it was evident "that the said Pinhorne would not stick to join with the lord Cornbury in the most daring and violent measures, to subvert the liberties of this country. . . ."[120] With Hunter's support, the Assembly was successful in attempting to have all of the members of Council removed. Although New Jersey did not incorporate a habeas corpus provision into its fundamental law until 1844,[121] in 1795 it enacted a statute incorporating the principles of the Habeas Corpus Act of 1679.[122]

In New Hampshire, the first judicial system was organized in 1682. Lieutenant-Governor Cranfield asserted full authority to establish the courts, which were run more in his interest than in the interests of the public. His capricious conduct with regard to the administration of justice was naturally the source of much unrest. If judges and other officers did not do his bidding, they were threatened and removed. It was also a matter of complaint that persons who offended the lieutenant-governor were imprisoned and/or compelled to give heavy bail, even when no crime was charged against them.[123] In 1687, under Governor Edmund Andros, the judiciary was reformed and reorganized. Following the pattern set by Rhode Island, New Hampshire's Supreme Court was given cognizance of all manner of pleas, criminal, civil, and mixed, "to all intents and purposes" as the English courts of King's Bench, Common Pleas, and Exchequer.[124] When the government of Andros was overthrown in 1689, each town was left to administer justice by itself. In 1699, "An Act for the Establishing Courts of Public Justice" was passed. It reestablished the Supreme Court and endowed it with the same powers it had possessed under Andros.[125] This situation persisted throughout the colonial period. In 1794, a new constitution was adopted providing that "The privilege and benefit of the habeas corpus shall be enjoyed in this State in the most free, easy, cheap, expeditious, and ample manner, and shall not be suspended by the legislature, except upon the most urgent and pressing occasions, and for a time not exceeding three months."[126] This provision was renewed in the constitution of 1792.[127]

Like the residents of the colonies to the north, the citizens of Pennsylvania did not enjoy the benefit of the Habeas Corpus Act, though they did know the common-law writ. A 1682 provision, however, provided that "all persons wrongfully imprisoned or prosecuted at law, shall have double damages against the informer or prosecutor."[128] This provision was supplemented by a 1705 enactment that required that there be a general gaol-delivery every six months in every county, where causes of imprisonment should be examined, and if a person were held without cause he was to have double damages against the informer or prosecutor, to be recovered by an action at common law.[129] The writ of habeas corpus was a remedy recognized by the "Act for the establishing of courts of Judicature" of 1722,[130] which allowed Supreme Court justices power "to issue forth writs of *habeas corpus*, *certiorari*, and writs of error, and all remedial and other writs and process. . . ."[131] During the confederation period, the common-law writ of habeas corpus was buttressed by "an Act for the better securing personal liberty, and preventing wrongful imprisonments."[132] The act was quite similar to the English act of the preceding century. Pennsylvania's 1790 constitution forbade suspension of the privileges of the writ of habeas corpus "unless when, in cases of rebellion or invasion, the public safety may require it."[133]

The territory now known as the state of Delaware had been regulated at various times during the seventeenth century by the charters and laws of Virginia, Maryland, and Pennsylvania. In their 1701 charter from William Penn, the citizens of the colony were guaranteed the liberties, privileges and benefits granted by the charter and known by usage and custom.[134] This undoubtedly included the common-law writ of habeas corpus, though not the English statutes supplementing it, as the preamble to a 1719 statute admitted: "Whereas the common law is justly esteemed to be the birthright of English subjects, and ought to be regarded in this government as the safest rule of our conduct; and whereas acts of Parliament have been adjudged not to extend to these plantations, except when they are particularly named in the body of such acts. . . ."[135] The act, which went on to set forth the guidelines for criminal procedure, was explicit recognition of the extension theory set forth earlier.[136] In 1719, the Supreme Court was established in Delaware and its justices were given authority to issue writs of habeas corpus, certiorari, error, and other remedial writs.[137] The power was reaffirmed by a 1760 enactment.[138] The state's 1792 constitution prohibited suspension of the privileges of the writ of habeas corpus "unless when, in cases of rebellion or invasion, the public safety may require it."[139] The provision was fortified the following year by a statute similar to the English Habeas Corpus Act.[140]

Thus, one finds that the common-law writ of habeas corpus was in operation in all thirteen of the British colonies that rebelled in 1776.[141] In addition, by the time of the Declaration of Independence, the benefits of the principles of the Habeas Corpus Act were known in Virginia, North Carolina, South Carolina, and Georgia. The disparity between the northern and southern colonies raises an interesting question: why were the latter and not the former colonies given benefit of the Habeas Corpus Act? Were the southern colonies perceived by the English authorities as more stable than their northern counterparts? An even more perplexing question raised by the evidence is: why during the confederation period did so few former colonies adopt provisions embodying the principles of the Habeas Corpus Act? Had they lost sight of the difference between extension of common and statutory writ and did they regard the Habeas Corpus Act as applicable? Instances of the writ, granted on the basis of the Habeas Corpus Act, issuing in New Hampshire[142] and New York[143] were noted above. In attempting to secure the loyalty of Quebec to their cause, the American Congress on 21 October 1774 addressed a letter to Great Britain decrying the failure of the bill in Parliament for the extension of the Habeas Corpus Act to Quebec:

> . . . [W]e cannot help deploring the unhappy condition to which it has reduced the many British settlers, who, encouraged by the royal proclamation, promising the enjoyment of all their rights, have purchased estates in that country. —They are now the subjects of an arbitrary government, deprived of trial by jury, and when imprisoned, cannot claim the benefit of the *habeas corpus* act, that great bulwark and palladium of English liberty.[144]

Such a statement might lead one to believe that the Habeas Corpus Act was in effect in America generally, though an inference based upon such propaganda is obviously weak. Alternatively, and more simply, perhaps the reason so few colonies enacted habeas statutes was because the passage of the Habeas Corpus Act was no longer viewed as urgent. Development of the writ in the seventeenth century was in response to arbitrary executive power. It was that power, too, which was the source of colonial grievances. That power was now gone. More important for present purposes are the questions posed for the standard interpretation of the habeas clause of the federal Constitution, which holds that the clause guaranteed a federal writ. With the writ provided for in some form in every state, was there a need to provide for a federal writ? Could the framers of the federal Constitution have been concerned only about Congressional interference with the established writ? Those questions are the subject of the following chapter.

NOTES

1. There have been two previous articles on the extension of the writ of habeas corpus. A. H. Carpenter, "Habeas Corpus in the American Colonies," 8 American Hist. Rev. 18 (1902); Robert S. Walker, "The American Reception of the Writ of Habeas Corpus," Political Science Research Reports, Department of Political Science, Oklahoma State University, 1961. An article by Milton Cantor, "The Writ of Habeas Corpus: Early American Origins and Development," *Freedom and Reform: Essays in Honor of Henry Steele Commager*, Harold M. Hyman and Leonard W. Levy ed. (New York: Harper and Row, 1967), p. 55 provides a brief and general survey of the writ's history from its English origins until 1806, focusing on the colonial period.

2. For a general discussion of the extension of English law, *see* George L. Haskins, *Law and Authority in Early Massachusetts* (New York: Macmillan Co., 1960), pp. 1-8; George Althan Billias, *Law and Authority in Colonial America* (Barre, Mass.: Barre Publications, 1965); Joseph H. Smith, "The English Criminal Law in Early America," in *The English Legal System: Carryover to the Colonies* (Los Angeles: William Andrews Clark Library, 1975).

For contemporary expressions of the difficulty of identifying which laws were in force in the colonies *see Calendar of State Papers* (Colonial) 1701, p. 576, no. 945; ibid., 1702, pp. 272-73, no. 388; ibid., 1704-05, pp. 457-58, nos. 975-76; unknown Author, *An Essay Upon the Continent of America*, L. B. Wright ed. (San Marino, Calif.: Huntington Library, 1945), pp. 23-24; and authorities cited at note 19 *infra*.

3. Virginia, 1607.

4. 77 Eng. Rep. 377.

5. Cf. a 1766 opinion on the extension of the Acts of Trade by the Lord President of the Privy Council, Northington. Joseph H. Smith, *Appeals to the Privy Council from the American Plantations* (New York: Columbia University Press, 1950), pp. 496-99 [King's prerogative constrained by fundamental principles of government].

6. Ibid., pp. 397-98. *See* 2 State Trials 559, 575, 659 for arguments of Bacon and Ellesmore in the Exchequer, setting forth the notion that an Englishman carried the laws of England with him as his birthright.

7. 123 Eng. Rep. 575 (1665).

8. 91 Eng. Rep. 356.

9. *See also Campbell v. Hall*, 20 State Trials 239, 98 Eng. Rep. 1045 (1774) [For a contemporary critique of *Campbell*, *see* Francis Maseres, *The Canadian Freeholder: In Three Dialogues Between An Englishman and a Frenchman* . . . (London, 1779), vol. 2]; *Dutton v. Howell*, 1 Eng. Rep. 17 (1693).

10. Vol. 1, pp. 106-08.

11. Joseph Story, *Commentaries on the Constitution of the United States* (Boston: Little and Brown, 1851), sect. 152, pp. 101-02.

12. *See Craw v. Ramsey*, 124 Eng. Rep. 1072 (1670) and "Concerning Process Out of the Courts at Westminster into Wales of Late Times and How Anciently," 124 Eng. Rep. 1130.

13. *See Smith v. Brown and Cooper*, 97 Eng. Rep. 566 (1702).

14. 29 Eng. Rep. 646.

15. Story, *Commentaries*, sect. 156, p. 104. *See* Francis N. Thorpe ed., *American Charters, Constitutions, and Organic Laws of the States, Territories, and Colonies* (Washington, D.C.: Government Printing Office, 1909), vol. 1, p. 533 (Conn.); ibid., p. 599 (Del.); ibid., vol. 2, p. 773 (Ga.); ibid., vol. 3, pp. 1635, 1638 (Maine [p. 1638 referring to grant of 1664 covering N.Y. as well]); ibid., p. 1681 (Md.); ibid., pp. 1832, 1839, 1853, 1857, 1881 (Mass.); ibid., vol. 4, p. 2442 (N.H.); ibid., p. 3220 (R.I.); ibid., vol. 5, pp. 2538, 2591-2592 (N.J.); ibid., pp. 2746, 2755, 2758, 2765 (Car.); ibid., p. 3038 (Pa.); ibid., vol. 7, pp. 3788, 3800, 3806 (Va.). Cf. however, Smith, "English Criminal Law," p. 8 (The provisions declaring that the colonists shall enjoy the privileges and immunities of natural born citizens were intended only to insure that the colonists and their heirs and successors remained British subjects.) *See* note 53 *infra*.

16. Note especially the early eighteenth century conflict in Maryland. 34 Archives of Maryland 441-42, 487, 493, 601-03, 616-17, 661-79, 692-98; 35 ibid. 196-200, 296-301, 309-11, 412-26, 496. *See generally*, St. George L. Sioussat, "English Statutes in Maryland," 21 Johns Hopkins Studies in Historical and Political Science 465 (1903).

17. Blackstone, *Commentaries*, vol. 1, p. 107.

18. *See* arguments of counsel in *Blankard v. Galdy*, 91 Eng. Rep. 356 (1694). *See* note 6 *supra*.

19. Sir William Keith, a former governor of Pennsylvania, reported to the Board of Trade in 1728 that:

> It is generally acknowledged in the Plantations, that the subject is entitled by birthright unto the benefit of the Common Law of England; But then as the Common Law has been altered from time to time and restricted by Statute, it is still a question in many of the American Courts of Judicature, whether any of the English Statutes, which do not particularly mention the Plantations, can be of force there untill they be brought over by some Act of Assembly in that Colony where they are pleaded. . . .

Calendar of State Papers (Colonial), 1728-1729, p. 266, no. 513ii. *See also* ibid., 1701, pp. 604-07, no. 997ii; ibid., 1706-1708, pp. 67-68, no. 160; ibid., 1708-1709, pp. 433-35, no. 662. *See also* Smith, *Appeals to the Privy Council,* pp. 486-92; William Smith, Jr., *The History of the Province of New York* Michael Kammen ed. (Cambridge, Mass.: Belknap Press, 1972) vol. 1, pp. 266-67 note [opinion of John Randolph].

20. George Chalmers ed., *Opinions of Eminent Lawyers . . . (Great Britain)* (London: Reed and Hunter, 1814), vol. 1, pp. 18-22.

21. *Calendar of State Papers* (Colonial), 1702-1703, p. 858, no. 1356.

22. Chalmers, *Opinions of Eminent Lawyers . . . (Great Britain),* vol. 1, p. 194.

23. Ibid., p. 197.

24. Ibid., p. 195.

25. Ibid., p. 198.

26. *See,* however, Smith, *Appeals to the Privy Council,* pp. 487-92 (The colonists sometimes had difficulty applying statutes enacted prior to settlement).

27. Virginia's first charter, 1606.

28. Opinion of Attorney General of England William Jones, 2 Va. Col. Dec. B1-B2 (1681).

29. *See* text accompanying notes 3-11 *supra.*

30. William Forsyth ed., *Cases and Opinions on Constitutional Law, and Various Points of English Jurisprudence* (London: Stevens and Haynes, 1869), pp. 421-22 [Opinion of Sir William Jones on the extension of the Statute of Monopolies, 21 James I c. 3 (1623) to Barbadoes].

31. Quote from Attorney General Yorke's 1729 opinion, note 24 *supra. See also* item VI of the Declaration of the Continental Congress (1774), which insisted that the Americans were entitled to the benefit of the common law and such of the English statutes as existed at the time of their colonization, and such as they have found to be applicable to their several local and other circumstances. Cf., however, Elizabeth Gaspar Brown, *British Statutes in American Law 1776-1836* (Ann Arbor: University of Michigan Law School, 1964), p. 10. (Statements such as those in the Declaration did not automatically extend the laws of England.)

32. Wood, *Institution,* 1772, p. 16.

33. Blackstone, *Commentaries,* vol. 4, p. 131.

34. Charles Warren, in his brilliant *History of the American Bar* (Cambridge: Cambridge University Press, 1912), noted the invaluable influence of the English-bred lawyers in the colonies. "The training which they received in the Inns, confined almost exclusively to the Common law, based as it was on historical precedent and customary law, the habits which they formed there of solving all legal questions by the standards of English liberties and of rights of the English subject," observed Warren, "proved of immense value . . ." Ibid., p. 188. *See* also ibid., p. 211. In addition, even those who were not trained in England were steeped in the teachings of Coke [Roscoe Pound, *The Development of the Constitutional Guarantees of Liberty* (New Haven, Connecticut: Yale University Press, 1957), p. 57]; teachings that were in no small measure influenced by his involvement in the conflicts of the seventeenth century. *See* ch. 1, text accompanying notes, 345-97 *supra.* In 1647, the governor of Massachusetts ordered the importation of two copies each of Coke's *First* and *Second Institutes* "to the end that we may have

better light for making and proceeding about the law." Pound, *Constitutional Guarantees of Liberty*, p. 60. Of equal importance was the legal material printed in the colonies for the nonprofessional lawyer. The laymen in America were avid readers of law. As a result of the acute shortage of lawyers, in the hundred-year period between William Penn's gleaning from Coke in 1687 until Buller's *Nisi Prius* and Gilbert's *Evidence* in 1788, there were no books published in America for the professional lawyer. Eldon Revare James, "Legal Treatises Printed in the British Colonies and American States Before 1801," *Harvard Legal Essays* (presented to J. H. Beale and S. Williston) (Cambridge, Mass.: Harvard University Press, 1934), p. 159. The legal material that was published was intended for the layman.

In 1687, William Penn's *The Excellent Privilege of Liberty and Property Being the Birthright of Free-Born Subjects of England* was published in Philadelphia (printed by William Bradford). The title aptly describes the tone of its contents, which included a copy of the *Magna Carta* and commentary. In 1721, Henry Care's fifth edition of *English Liberties, or the Free-Born Subject's Inheritance* was published in Boston. It contained, *inter alia*, copies of the *Magna Carta*, the Petition of Right, and the Habeas Corpus Act. Seven years later, Daniel Dulany, Sr., under the pseudonym Cato, wrote *The Rights of the Inhabitants of Maryland, to the Benefits of English Laws* (Annapolis, printed by William Parks). The treatise, which was inspired directly by a conflict over whether the Habeas Corpus Act extended to Maryland, *see* text accompanying notes 92-96 *infra.*, argued eloquently that the citizens of Maryland were entitled to the benefits of English laws and liberties because they were British subjects, and as such adhered to their allegiance to the Crown. In 1768, the very popular *Every Man His Own Lawyer: or, A Summary of the Laws of England*, by Lord Raymond, was published in New York, and the following year in Philadelphia (New York edition printed by Hugh Gaine; Philadelphia edition printed by John Dunlap). It contained a section on writs, including process, arrest, and bail, and a section entitled "Of the Liberty of the Subject," which cited the *Magna Carta* and the habeas corpus acts. Finally, in 1771-1772, the first American edition of Blackstone's *Commentaries* vols. 1 and 2 in 1771, 3 and 4 in 1772; second American edition in 1774 was published in the colonies. The first English edition in 1765 had sold 1,000 copies in America, which exceeded the number sold in England, and before the Declaration of Independence, 25,000 copies of the *Commentaries* had been sold in the colonies. Roscoe Pound, *Criminal Justice in America* (New York: Da Capo Press, 1972), p. 82. These treatises, and the more professionally oriented works that were imported, such as Coke's *Institutes*, Hale's *Pleas*, *Historia Plactorum*, *Analysis of the Law*, and *History of the Common Law*, Thomas Wood's *An Institution of the Laws of England*, Hawkins' *Pleas*, the works of Bracton, Glanvil and Britton, and the printed reports, depicted English law as the bulwark between the prerogative of the Crown and the liberty of the subject.

35. *See generally*, Samuel Eliot Morison and Henry Steele Commager, *The Growth of the American Republic* (New York: Oxford University Press, 1954) pp. 37-46; Oliver P. Chitwood, "Justice in Colonial Virginia," 23 Johns Hopkins Studies in Historical and Political Science Nos. 7-8 (1905).

36. William Hening ed., *Virginia Statutes at Large* (New York: 1823), vol. 1, pp. 363-64.

37. *See* text accompanying notes 3-6 *supra.*

38. Cited in Warren, *History of the American Bar*, p. 39.

39. Arthur P. Scott, *Criminal Law in Colonial Virginia* (Chicago: Chicago University Press, 1930), p. 59; Author Unknown, "Writ of Habeas Corpus," 3 William and Mary Quarterly 147 (1895).

40. See *Calendar of State Papers* (Colonial), 1681-1685, p. 229, no. 495.

41. Ibid., p. 227, no. 492; p. 223, no. 507 (1); p. 241, no. 532.

42. Ibid., pp. 237-38, no. 524.

43. Ibid., p. 275, no. 649.

44. Ibid., p. 299, no. 704.

45. H. R. McIlwaine ed., *Executive Journals of the Council of Colonial Virginia* (Richmond, Va.: 1925), p. 27.

46. In nonpolitical criminal cases, however, the writ alone could prove an effective instrument for securing an individual's liberty. *See e.g., George Mason's Case* (1690), *Calendar of State Papers* (Colonial), 1689-1692, p. 254, no. 858.

47. Leonard Woods Labaree, ed., *Royal Instructions to British Governors 1670-1776* (New York: D. Appleton-Century Co., 1935), pp. 334-36, no. 464. *See* also ibid., pp. 336-37, no. 466 [During the period of Confederation, Virginia enacted a statute directing the mode of suing out and prosecuting writs of habeas corpus which reaffirmed some of the safeguards of the Habeas Corpus Act. Virginia Statutes at Large, vol. 11, p. 408].

48. 8 American Hist. Rev. 18.

49. Ibid., at p. 24.

50. Indeed, the vetoing of habeas corpus acts, passed by various colonial assemblies, was motivated by a policy of the executive department not to lessen its power in the colonies. For example, a bill passed by the Barbados Assembly on May 17, 1681, which was substantially the same as the Habeas Corpus Act of 1679, *Calendar of State Papers* (Colonial), 1681-1685, p. 53, no. 111, was vetoed by Governor Sir Richard Dutton. Ibid., p. 61, no. 123. In communicating their approval of the veto, the Board of Trade and Plantations wrote the Governor: "The Bill of Habeas Corpus was timely prevented, nor had we any reason to apprehend that you would even have permitted it to pass." Ibid., p. 116, no. 231. Dutton, acknowledging the receipt of their message, replied: "As to the Habeas Corpus Bill, the Bill declaring when the laws of England shall come into force, and other Bills of the Kind, I shall always refuse them whatever the pressure put on me . . . I shall preserve the royal prerogative and do my duty without thanks in spite of the temptations of the Assembly." Ibid., p. 180, no. 357. Virginia, a politically stable and legally mature royal province, provided an ideal colony to test a change in the executive policy of nonextension of the principles of the Habeas Corpus Act.

51. *See* text accompanying notes 3-6 *supra*.

52. Smith, "The English Criminal Law," p. 7.

53. *See* note 15 *supra*. [argument of Joseph Smith]. Even if "privileges and immunities" is not broad enough to cover the criminal law, it would be difficult to exclude a cherished remedy such as habeas relief. Moreover, note text accompanying notes 10-11 *supra*. and *Campbell v. Hall*, 98 Eng. Rep. 1045 (1774). Although decided quite late in the colonial period, *Campbell* established the principle that once the powers of legislation had been granted to a conquered colony by means of a provision in the governor's commission,

the king could no longer give laws to such a country. Ibid., pp. 1049-50. *See* text accompanying notes 108-09 *infra*. Under the *Campbell* doctrine, admittedly formulated well after 1710, Queen Anne's instructions went beyond the realm of executive power.

54. Virginia Statutes at Large, vol. 4, p. 489.

55. Ibid., vol. 9, p. 414.

56. Ibid., vol. 10, p. 414.

57. Thorpe, *American Charters*, vol. 7, p. 3824. Thomas Jefferson had long advocated such a provision for Virginia. *See* Julian P. Boyd ed., *The Papers of Thomas Jefferson* (Princeton, N.J.: Princeton University Press, 1955), vol. 6, pp. 304, 315-16; vol. 12, pp. 558, 571. Cf. Jefferson's actions during the *Burr* affair. *See* ch. 3, text accompanying notes 71-76 *infra*.

58. *Massachusetts Historical Society Collections*, ser. 4, vol. 8, p. 390.

59. Emory Washburn, *Sketches of the Judicial History of Massachusetts* (Boston: Little and Brown, 1840), pp. 105-06.

60. *See* ch. 1, text accompanying notes 345-55 *supra*.

61. The Charter and General Laws of the Colony and Province of Massachusetts Bay (Boston: 1814 edition), p. 224.

62. Cited by Carpenter, "Habeas Corpus in the American Colonies," 8 American Hist. Rev. 18, 21. *See also* Edward Channing, *A History of the United States* (New York: Macmillan Co., 1905) vol. 2, pp. 223, 235-36; George Chalmers, *Political Annals of the Present United Colonies* (New York: New York Historical Society (Collections, 1868), pp. 112-13. The veto was of sufficient importance to be communicated to other colonies, *see* note 99 *infra*.

63. Cited by Joseph H. Smith, *Colonial Justice in Western Massachusetts, 1639-1702* (Cambridge, Mass.: Harvard University Press, 1961), p. 81.

64. Acts and Laws Passed by the Great and General Court of Assembly of the Province of Massachusetts-Bay, 1692-1719 (London: 1724 edition), p. 147.

65. *See e.g., Massachusetts Historical Society Collections*, ser. 5, vol. 6, p. 147; Acts and Resolutions of the Province of Massachusetts Bay, vol. 4, p. 32 (act of 1757).

66. Thorpe, *American Charters*, vol. 3, p. 1910. In 1777, the legislature had empowered the Council to issue, under seal, a warrant to apprehend persons dangerous to the state. Anyone so apprehended was to be "continued in imprisonment, without bail or mainprise, until he shall be discharged by order of council or of the general court." The act expired after one year. Acts and Resolutions of the Province of Massachusetts-Bay, vol. 5, p. 641. Again, during Shay's Rebellion, the privilege of habeas corpus was suspended. Massachusetts Laws 1786 c. 42.

67. *See*, however, the *Case of Samuel Pricklove* (1680), Mattie Erma Edwards Parker ed., *North Carolina Higher-Court Records 1670-1696* (Raleigh, N.C.: State Department of Archives and History, 1968), p. 9, which demonstrates that the act was not in effect on 27 March 1680.

68. Edward McCrady, *The History of South Carolina Under the Proprietary Government* (New York: Macmillan Co., 1897), p. 247. *See also* Thomas Cooper ed., Statutes of South Carolina, vol. 2, p. 74.

69. McCrady, *South Carolina*, p. 248.

70. *See* text accompanying notes 3-9 *supra*.

71. Statutes of South Carolina, vol. 2, p. 399. *See also* A. H. Carpenter, "Habeas Corpus in the American Colonies," 8 American Hist. Rev. 18, 23.

72. Richard Everard, who was commissioned governor of North Carolina in 1724, had by 1726 so alienated the popular house of the provincial government that the representatives issued "The Exclamations of the Injured and Oppress'd." *See generally*, A. E. Howard, *The Road from Runnymede: Magna Carta and Constitutionalism in America* (Charlottesville, Va.: University of Virginia Press, 1968), pp. 68-69. The remonstrances particularly complained of the governor's arbitrary and illegal imprisonment of members of the House and his refusal to show cause for their imprisonment. The Assembly declared this to be "a great Infringement of [their] Libertys as . . . Freemen Brittains, to be Contrary to the Great Charter and to that Invaluable Act of Parliament commonly called the Habeas Corpus Act." William L. Sanders and Walter Clark eds., *Colonial Records of North Carolina* (Raleigh, North Carolina: 1886-1914), vol. 2, pp. 613-14. The governor's critics were severely dealt with. Ibid., pp. 687-89. Shortly afterwards, however, North Carolina became a royal colony and Everard was replaced by George Burrington. *See* ibid., vol. 3, pp. 202-03, 224, 231-32.

73. Labaree, *Royal Instructions*, pp. 334-36, no. 464; 336-37, no. 466.

74. *See* Edward McCrady, *The History of South Carolina Under the Royal Government* (New York: Macmillan Co., 1899), pp. 151-63; W. Roy Smith, *South Carolina as a Province* (New York: Macmillan Co., 1903), pp. 43-45.

75. *See* ch. 1, text accompanying notes 477-91 *supra*.

76. Statutes of South Carolina, vol. 3, p. 347.

77. Cited in Smith, *South Carolina*, p. 45.

78. *Calendar of State Papers* (Colonial), 1733, p. 91, no. 140.

79. Ibid., pp. 250-51, no. 427i.

80. Ibid., 1734-1735, p. 9, no. 15.

81. J. H. Easterley ed., *The Journal of the Commons' House of Assembly* (*The Colonial Records of South Carolina*), (1954), pp. 340-42.

82. *See* Brown, *British Statutes*, app.

83. Thorpe, *American Charters*, vol. 5, p. 2788.

84. Labaree, *Royal Instructions*, pp. 334-36, no. 464; 336-37, no. 466.

85. Thorpe, *American Charters*, vol. 2, p. 785.

86. United States Constitution, Article I, section 9, clause 2.

87. Thorpe, *American Charters*, vol. 2, p. 789.

88. Cited in Warren, *History of the American Bar*, p. 49.

89. Ibid., pp. 49-50.

90. Sioussat, "English Statutes in Maryland," 21 Johns Hopkins Studies in Historical and Political Science 465.

91. St. George Leakin Sioussat, "The Theory of the Extension of English Statute," 1 *Select Essays in Anglo-American Legal History* 416, 424 (1907).

92. The controversy had been brewing for a generation, beginning after the Provincial Court of Maryland's decision in *Loyd's Lessee v. Helmsley*, 1 Harris and McHenry 28 (1712), which denied the extension of an English statute of limitations, 21 James I c. 16 (1623). Ten years later, the Assembly passed an act adopting 21 James I c. 16.

93. Sioussat, "English Statutes in Maryland," 21 Johns Hopkins Studies in Historical and Political Science 465, 511.

94. *See* note 34 *supra*.

95. Cato, *The Rights of the Inhabitants of Maryland*, p. 10. *See* also Richard Beale Davis ed., *William Fitzhugh and His Chesapeake World 1676-1701: The Fitzhugh Letters and Other Documents* (Chapel Hill: University of North Carolina Press, for the Virginia Historical Society, 1963), pp. 152-59, a 1683 opinion of Fitzhugh, a prominent Virginia lawyer, in favor of the extension of English laws.

96. *See* Cato, *The Rights of the Inhabitants of Maryland*, pp. 10-14.

97. Cited in Julius Goebel Jr. and T. Raymond Naughton, *Law Enforcement in Colonial New York* (New York: Commonwealth Fund, 1944), pp. 503-04.

98. Colonial Laws of New York (Albany, 1894-1896), vol. 1, p. 114.

99. John Romeyn Brodhead ed., *Documents Relative to the Colonial History of the State of New York* (Albany, N.Y.: Weld, Parsons and Co., 1853), vol. 3, pp. 354, 357. In 1699, Governor Bellomont forwarded to the legislature the ruling of the home authorities against the Massachusetts "Act for the Better Securing the Liberty of the Subject," *see* text accompanying note 61 *supra*.

100. *See* text accompanying notes 104-14 *infra*.

101. *See also* authorities cited at Paul M. Hamlin and Charles E. Baker, *Supreme Court of Judicature of the Province of New York 1691-1704* (New York: New York Historical Society, 1959), vol. 1, p. 390, fn. 208; pp. 394-96; and at Goebel and Naughton, *Colonial New York*, p. 504, fn. 78.

102. Case recorded by an unnamed author, "A Modest and Impartial Narrative of Several Grievances and Great Oppressions," (New York, 1690) (contained in Brodhead, *Documents*, vol. 3, p. 676).

103. Ibid.

104. Leisler warned that if French did not refer to him as Lieutenant Governor, he would put the prisoner where "he should never see the face of Man more." French was released on a £500 recognizance for good behavior for one year.

105. Author unknown except by pseudonym, Learner of Law, and Lover of Liberty, "A Narrative of a New and Unusual American Imprisonment," (New York, 1707) [contained in Peter Force ed., *Four Tracts and Other Papers Relating Principally to the Origin, Settlement, and Progress of the Colonies of North America* (New York: Peter Smith, 1947)].

106. Reprinted in Livingston Rutherford, *John Peter Zenger, His Press, His Trial* (New York: Dodd, Mead and Co., 1906), app.

107. Goebel and Naughton, *Colonial New York*, pp. 504-05, *Case of Waddell Cunningham. See also McCullock v. Murphy* (undated), in *Select Cases of the Mayor's Court of New York City (1674-1787)*,Richard B. Morris ed. (Washington, D.C.: American Historical Association, 1935), p. 132.

108. *The History of the Province of New York*, Michael Kammen ed. (Cambridge, Mass.: Belknap Press, 1972), vol. 1, p. 259.

109. Hamlin and Baker, *Supreme Court of Judicature of New York*, vol. 1, pp. 378-85.

110. Ibid., p. 378.

111. *The Administration of the Colonies* (London: fourth edition, 1768), pp. 127-128.

112. Brodhead, *Documents*, vol. 8, pp. 434, 444.

113. Hamlin and Baker, *Supreme Court of Judicature of New York*, vol. 1, pp. 381-83.

114. Thomas Greenleaf ed., *Laws of New York*, vol. 1, p. 369.

115. *See* Charles McLean Andrews, "The Influence of Colonial Conditions as Illustrated in the Connecticut Intestacy Law," *Select Essays in Anglo-American Legal History*, vol. 1, p. 431; Warren, *History of the American Bar*, p. 12.

116. Acts and Laws of Connecticut (New-London, 1750 edition), p. 30.

117. Thorpe, *American Charters*, vol. 1, p. 538.

118. The Charter [and Laws] . . . of Rhode Island (Newport, 1730 edition), p. 8.

119. Ibid., p. 191.

120. *See* Samuel Smith, *The History of the Colony of Nova-Caesaria or New Jersey* (New Jersey: J. Parker, 1765), p. 391.

121. Thorpe, *American Charters*, vol. 5, p. 2600.

122. Laws of the State of New Jersey (Newark, New Jersey: William Paterson, 1800 edition), p. 168.

123. William Henry Fry, *New Hampshire as a Province*, Ph.D. thesis, Columbia University, 1908, pp. 442-44. *See* Nathaniel Bouton ed., *Documents and Records Relating to the Province of New-Hampshire* (Concord, 1867), vol. 1, p. 557. *See also Case of William Vaughan* (1684), ibid., pp. 477, 478-502, 518, 519, 534, 538, 539, 542-43 (note, habeas petition based on 1679 Act), 546, 561, 563, 565, 571, 573, 577.

124. Fry, *New Hampshire as a Province*, p. 446.

125. Acts and Laws Passed by the General Court or Assembly of New Hampshire (Portsmouth, 1729 edition), p. 5.

126. Thorpe, *American Charters*, vol. 4, p. 2469.

127. Ibid., p. 2488.

128. "The Frame of Government of the Province of Pennsylvania together with certain laws of England," *Minutes of the Provincial Council of Pennsylvania* (Philadelphia, 1851 edition), vol. 1, p. 38.

129. Laws of the Commonwealth of Pennsylvania (Philadelphia, 1810 edition), vol. 1, p. 56.

130. Ibid., p. 139.

131. *See e.g., Minutes of the Provincial Council*, vol. 3, p. 162; vol. 4, pp. 391-92. Cf. Cantor, "The Writ of Habeas Corpus," *Freedom and Reform*, pp. 71-72 (habeas corpus denied in a case involving the privilege of the legislature).

132. Laws of the Commonwealth of Pennsylvania, vol. 2, p. 275.

133. Thorpe, *American Charters*, vol. 5, p. 3101. During the Revolution, the legislature authorized the Executive Council of the Commonwealth to suspend the writ. *See* Sidney George Fisher, *The Trial of the Constitution* (Philadelphia: J. B. Lippincott and Co., 1862), pp. 223-26.

134. Thorpe, *American Charters*, vol. 1, pp. 557-62.

135. Laws of the State of Delaware (New-Castle, 1797 edition), vol. 1, p. 64.

136. *See* text accompanying note 26 *supra*.

137. Laws of the State of Delaware, vol. 1, p. 126, sect. 6. Sect. 14, vol. 1, p. 128 went on to provide "That nothing herein contained, shall obligate the Judges of the Supreme Court, nor any of them, to go on their circuit, or

hold a court in any county of this government, but when there shall be some cause removed from some inferior court by Writ of Error, *Habeas Corpus, Certiorari*, or Appeal, or some other matter or case cognizable by them, which shall require their coming. . ."

138. Ibid., vol. 1, p. 375.

139. Thorpe, *American Charters*, vol. 1, p. 569.

140. Laws of the State of Delaware, vol. 2, p. 1056.

141. In 1787, the "benefits of the writ of habeas corpus" were extended to the Northwest Territory. Thorpe, *American Charters*, vol. 2, pp. 960-61.

142. *See* note 123 *supra*.

143. *See* text accompanying note 107 *supra*.

144. *Journals of the American Congress, 1774-1788* (Washington, D.C., 1823 edition), vol. 1, p. 30.

The Writ of Habeas Corpus, the Constitution, and State Habeas for Federal Prisoners

3

INTRODUCTION

The habeas clause of the Constitution provides that "[t]he Privilege of the Writ of Habeas Corpus shall not be suspended, unless when in Cases of Rebellion or Invasion the public Safety may require it."[1] Since *Ex parte Bollman*,[2] it has generally been accepted that the intent of the habeas clause was somehow to guarantee a federal writ of habeas corpus.[3] Variations on this interpretation have suggested that the clause imposed an obligation on Congress to provide for the writ;[4] that the clause itself guaranteed federal habeas;[5] that the clause created a privilege;[6] and that the clause directed the judiciary to make the writ routinely available.[7]

This chapter will argue that the framers intended the clause only to restrict Congressional power to suspend state habeas for federal prisoners. This theory is supported not only by the context within which the Constitution was formulated, but by the relevant history, the location of the provision in the Constitution, the contemporary commentary, and the records of the state constitutional conventions.

Following an examination of the historical evidence, the question of how the transformation in the meaning occurred will be considered. As in the case of the development of the writ in early England, the "invisible hand" of constitutional law plays a large part in effecting the metamorphosis. Jurisdictional conflicts among the departments of the federal government during the Bollman Affair and during the Civil War, and between the state and federal judiciaries over the Fugitive Slave Act and the power of state courts to issue habeas to release federal prisoners, preempted the intent of the framers.

THE FORMULATION OF THE HABEAS CLAUSE

THE FEDERAL CONVENTION

In response to the apparent failure of the government established by the Articles of Confederation, a convention assembled in Philadelphia in 1787 for the purpose of "form[ing] a more perfect Union."[8] To rectify the inefficiencies of the confederation, the delegates designed an instrument that would superimpose a federal government upon the thirteen existing state governments. The federal government was to be one of limited powers. The states would continue to possess the totality of governmental authority excepting that authority ceded to the federal government.

The first mention of the writ of habeas corpus was in Charles Pinckney's "Draught of a Federal Government" submitted on 29 May 1787, four days after the Philadelphia Convention was called to order.[9] Article XVIII provided, among other things, for trial by jury and for the privilege of the writ of habeas corpus.[10] The next mention of the writ was again made by Pinckney. On August twentieth, he proposed the following:[11]

> The privileges and benefits of the writ of habeas corpus shall be enjoyed in this government in the most expeditious and ample manner: and shall not be suspended by the Legislature except upon the most urgent and pressing occasion and for a time period not exceeding .... months.[12]

The first part of the proposal implicitly declares that the privileges and benefits of the writ be made available to federal prisoners. Note that by August twentieth, the Convention had already firmly fixed upon the idea that the lower federal courts were to be at the option of Congress.[13] In its final form, the Constitution provided for only a Supreme Court "and such inferior-courts as the Congress *may* from time to time ordain and establish." Further, the Supreme Court had original jurisdiction only in cases affecting ambassadors, other public ministers and consuls and those in which a state shall be a party—cases where habeas power would not often be employed.[15] The Court's appellate jurisdiction was left open to the discretion of Congress. Thus if Congress allowed the Supreme Court to retain broad appellate powers, the Court, in addition to limited original jurisdiction, would have habeas jurisdiction only where imprisonment was by *judicial* command. Where imprisonment was without process—an area where supervision was even more important—the Court would lack jurisdiction. However, as shall be argued at length below, even after the establishment of the federal judiciary, the state courts—in theory and in practice until the mid-nineteenth century—retained power to issue habeas corpus for federal prisoners.[16] The first part of the clause therefore, is most naturally viewed as an affirmation of already existing power as a new field of law opens. The second member of the clause goes on to restrict Congress from suspending that power as to persons committed by federal authority except in certain cases, and then for a limited time.

Debate on Pinckney's proposal took place eight days later, during the consideration of Article XI, section 4 of the plan presented by the Committee on Detail.[17] Article XI dealt with the judiciary, and it was as an amendment to the section requiring trial by jury that Pinckney raised the writ of habeas corpus.[18] According to the above analysis of the August twentieth proposal, this was the natural place for Pinckney to raise the habeas issue. Like his proposal, the jury guarantee provision of the Committee on Detail's plan concerned a highly esteemed English judicial tradition, already in operation in the several states, which was being secured against interference by Congress.[19]

Madison's complete entry for August twenty-eighth pertaining to the writ of habeas corpus follows:

> Mr. Pinckney, urging the propriety of securing the benefit of the Habeas corpus in the most ample manner, moved "that it should not be suspended but on the most urgent occasions, and then for a limited time not exceeding twelve months."
>
> Mr. Rutledge was for declaring the Habeas Corpus inviolate —He did (not) conceive that a suspension could ever be necessary at the same time through all the States—
>
> Mr. Govr Morris moved that "The privilege of the writ of Habeas Corpus shall not be suspended, unless where in cases of Rebellion or invasion the public Safety may require it."

Mr. Wilson doubted whether in any case (a suspension) could be necessary, as the discretion now exists with Judges, in most important cases to keep in Gaol or admit to Bail.

The first part of Govr. Morris' (motion,) to the word "unless" was agreed to nem: con: on the remaining part; N. H. ay. Mas. ay. Ct. ay. Pa. ay. Del. ay. Md. ay. Va. ay. N.C. no. S.C. no. Goe. no. [Ayes—7; noes—3.][20]

Unlike his original motion, Pinckney's proposal of August twenty-eighth did not begin with an affirmative clause. He did, however, introduce his proposal by "urging the propriety of securing the benefit of the Habeas Corpus in the most ample manner. . . ." Clearly, therefore, to Pinckney, the absence of the affirmative clause was insignificant.[21] It changed nothing. Every state, either by common, statutory, or constitutional law, secured the writ.[22] The chief concern for Pinckney and for the other members who spoke to the issue, was over the power to suspend. In the area of personal rights, it was the new government that concerned the delegates. The states were thought to be competent to pass laws to protect individual liberty.[23] As the precious remedy was already supplied in various forms in the several states, the worry now was about interference from the federal government. Similarly, jury trial in criminal cases was the practice in each state; the restraint in that clause was meant to shield that practice from the powers of Congress to regulate the trials of federal prisoners.[24] The jury provision was later amended.[25] The clause directing Congress to prescribe the manner of proceeding was removed—the provisions in Article I, section 8 empowering Congress to constitute inferior tribunals[26] and to make all laws necessary and proper to execute that power[27] being an equivalent power in the federal domain if Congress decided to create federal courts—thus leaving the proceeding to the state except that it must at least be by jury. The clause, therefore, prescribed only the location of the trial and a minimum standard for the procedures under which a federal prisoner was tried, whether in state or federal court. The habeas clause was, of course, later dissociated from the jury clause, removed from the judicial article, and placed in the section of the legislative article prescribing limits on Congress.

Pinckney's proposed limitation on Congress was not strict enough for Rutledge. He could not conceive that a suspension throughout all the states would ever be necessary, and therefore suggested that no federal legislative power to suspend be allowed. In other words, the states already had the power to suspend (witness the cases of Massachusetts, Pennsylvania and Virginia);[28] if the situation arose they were completely capable of dealing with the matter. This reasoning influenced the votes of the delegations from North Carolina, South Carolina and Georgia, who, although voting for the first member of the clause, refused to give Congress even a qualified power to suspend. By voting for the first part of the clause, and against the second, the three states were voting in effect for a provision that would completely deny Congress the power to suspend.[29] Rutledge's argument influenced others as well. Although Maryland voted for both members of the provision, there was dissent within the delegation. Luther Martin opposed the "unless" clause, because, as he explained to the Maryland legislature:

> As the State governments have a power of suspending the *habeas corpus* act in those cases, it was said, there could be no occasion for giving such a power to the general government; since whenever the State which is invaded, or in which an insurrection takes place, finds its safety requires, it will make use of that power. And it was urged, that if we gave this power to the general government, it would be an engine of oppression in its hands; since whenever the State should oppose its views, however arbitrary and unconstitutional, and refuse submission to them, the general government may declare it to be *an act of rebellion*, and, suspending the habeas corpus act, may *seize* upon the persons of those *advocates of freedom*, who have had *virtue* and *resolution* enough to excite the opposition, and may *imprison* them during its pleasure, in the *remotest* part of the Union; so that a citizen of Georgia might be bastiled in the furthest past of New Hampshire, or a citizen of New Hampshire in the furthest extreme to the south, cut off from their family, their friends, and their every connexion.[30]

Not only does Martin's explanation shed light on the form of the argument presented by Rutledge,[31] it also supports the proposition that the clause was meant only as a restriction on the federal legis-lature *vis à vis* state habeas. Since the state governments have power to suspend the "habeas corpus act,"[32] it was unnecessary (not to mention dangerous) to give "such a power" to the federal govern-ment.

Morris, believing that a power to suspend should exist at the federal level, offered a compromise.[33] He suggested that, because it was true that universal suspension might not be necessary, the privi-lege not be suspended except "where . . . the public Safety may require. . . ." The necessity was defined by the terms whence the power to suspend was derived: as Congress was to be charged with calling forth the militia to suppress insurrection and repel inva-sion[34] (a power which was put in its final form by Morris only five days before[35]), when one of these situations existed—and it was not only necessary and proper, but required by the public safety— the privileges of the writ could be suspended by Congress.[36]

Morris' argument was open to doubt. Judges, observed Wilson, have in most cases discretionary power to deny bail. Since release on bail was usually within the discretionary power of the courts, in cases requiring the pretrial imprisonment of an individual, judges could simply deny release.[37] Further debate was cut off by a call for a vote,[38] and the clause was passed. As noted earlier, the habeas clause was moved to its present position by the Committee on Style and Arrangement whose office did not include changing the mean-ing of any provision.[39]

LOCATION OF THE CLAUSE

The location of the clause chosen by the Committee on Style and Arrangement reinforces the conclusion that the provision was de-signed to restrict Congress from suspending state habeas for federal prisoners. The clause is found in the legislative Article, following the section enumerating legislative powers. The enumerated powers include the power to suppress insurrection and repel invasion, and concludes with the "necessary and proper" clause. Section 9 is fol-lowed by the final section of the Article, which limits the powers of the states *vis à vis* the federal government and the people. Section 9 itself, with the possible exception of the final clause, is a series of limitations on Congressional power *vis à vis* the states and the people. The final clause forbids the granting of titles of nobility—a power that was thought incongruent with republican government, but one which if exercised would presumably require legislative action. (Regular legislative measure or consent of the Senate?) In addition it prohibits any person holding federal office from accepting any "present, Emolument, or Title, of any kind whatever, from any King, Prince, or foreign State" without the consent of Congress. The second part of the clause was inserted as an amendment to the first and probably placed there for lack of a more suitable place. Its purpose, of course, was to check corruption.[40] Nevertheless, both parts concerned the Congress—the first part limiting its power—and protected the people. It has also been suggested that clause 7 of section 9 indicates that the position of the habeas clause is irrelevant.[41] The clause prohibits money from being drawn from the Treasury, "but in Consequence of an Appropriation made by Law" and requires that a regular statement and account of receipts and expenditures of all public money be published. It is said that since this clause undoubtedly pertains to the executive, there is no reason why the habeas clause could not apply as well. The writer of an 1861 article observed: "To say that Congress shall not draw money from the Treasury without an appropriation, would be to say that Congress shall not make an appropriation without an appropriation. . . ."[42] The clause, however, does apply to the legislature. It was a matter of public complaint during the colonial period that the legislatures appropriated money without due course.[43] This provision, as the debates clearly show, required Congress to appropriate money only by the procedure sanctioned by the Constitution.[44] The requirement of producing a statement and account was the public check on Congressional appropriations. The remaining clauses clearly limit only legislative power.[45]

CONTEMPORARY COMMENTARY

The contemporary commentary on the habeas clause likewise supports this interpretation of its meaning. Alexander Hamilton, addressing the people of New York State under the pseudonym *Publius*, argued that the proposed Constitution was not defective for want of a bill of rights since many of its provisions acted as such. He noted that "trial by jury in criminal cases, aided by the habeas corpus act . . . [is] provided for, in the most ample manner. . . ."[46] Using words similar to those of Pinckney in introducing the proposal of August twenty-eighth, Hamilton referred explicitly to the "habeas corpus act." In a later paper, Hamilton referred to the "establishment of the writ of habeas corpus."[47] It has been contended that this indicates Hamilton's belief that the clause itself provided for the writ, and that it directed the courts to make the writ available.[48] But here as well, Hamilton directed his comments to the "habeas corpus act." New York had, only three months before the convention met, enacted "An Act for better securing the Liberty of the Citizens of this State, and for Prevention of Imprisonment,"[49] which was almost identical to the famous Habeas Corpus Act of 1679.[50] More likely, it was to this act which Hamilton was referring.[51]

Similarly, Jefferson, corresponding with Madison on the Constitution, wrote that the first defect of the document was its lack of a bill of rights, providing, among other things, for "the eternal and unremitting force of the habeas corpus laws. . . . "[52] It would seem that what Jefferson was objecting to was the Constitution's limited sanction of power to suspend "the habeas corpus laws" of the several states.[53]

THE STATE RATIFYING CONVENTIONS

How the state conventions interpreted the various clauses of the document they ratified is, in many respects, just as important as what the framers intended the clauses to denote. In Pennsylvania, James Wilson told the state constitutional convention that "the right of habeas corpus was secured by a particular declaration in its favor."[54] The statement could very well have been made with studied ambiguity. In any event, it is far from a declaration that "the Constitution itself had provided for habeas corpus without any necessary resort to legislation."[55] Rather, this is one thing that the statement seems not to be saying.

The statements made in the Massachusetts convention are easier to understand. In response to an inquiry by the Honorable Mr. Taylor, Adams explained that the power given to the "general government"[56] to suspend "did not take away the power of the several states to suspend, if they saw fit."[57] Taylor then expressed his concern for the absence of a time limitation on the federal power. But Judge Dana pointed out that there was no benefit in such a limitation since the suspension could be renewed. "The safest and best restriction," argued Dana, "arises from the nature of the cases in which Congress are authorized to exercise that power at all, namely, in those of rebellion or invasion. These are clear and certain times, facts of public notoriety, and whenever these shall cease to exist, the suspension of the writ must cease also."[58] Judge Sumner had the final word on the subject and he used it to explain the operation of the writ and the need for suspension in certain cases to the other members of the State Convention. This suspension power needed to be restricted, however, because the privilege was "essential to freedom." He stated further that the clause was a "restriction on Congress" and affected only federal prisoners. Even if the privilege were suspended by Congress, explained Sumner, a person committed under authority of the state government would still be entitled to the writ.[59]

Patrick Henry, in the debates in Virginia, expressed his dislike for the notion of implied powers, finding it in complete conflict with the doctrine of limited government. He pointed to the habeas clause and observed:

> It results clearly that, if it had not said so, they could suspend [the privilege] in all cases whatsoever. . . . It does not speak affirmatively, and say that it shall be suspended in those cases; but that it shall not be suspended but in certain cases, going on a supposition that every thing which is not negatived shall remain with Congress.[60]

Governor Randolph explained that only those powers that were necessary and proper for the execution of those powers enumerated were implied.[61] The convention endorsed an amendment that provided: "That every freeman restrained of his liberty is entitled to a remedy, to enquire into the lawfulness thereof, and to remove the same if unlawful, and that such remedy ought not to be denied or delayed."[62] Similar recommendations were endorsed by the conventions of Rhode Island[63] and North Carolina.[64] The amendment was a rejection of the implied power theory in general, and the suspension power in particular. Implied power to suspend was also criticized in the New York convention. One delegate queried, "Why is it said that the privilege of the writ of *habeas corpus* shall not be suspended, unless, in cases of rebellion or invasion, the public safety may require it? What clause in the Constitution, except this very clause itself, gives the general government a power to deprive us of that great privilege, so sacredly secured us *by our state constitutions*?"[65] But even that delegate was in favor of a federal suspending power,[66] and the convention recommended an amendment that put the clause in the affirmative.[67]

In sum, the debates in the federal and state conventions, the location of the habeas clause, and the contemporary commentary support the thesis that the habeas clause was designed to restrict Congressional power to suspend state habeas for federal prisoners.

THE BOLLMAN AFFAIR AND THE ESTABLISHMENT OF THE OBLIGATION THEORY

The Supreme Court's first effort to define the habeas clause of the Constitution was in the 1807 case of *Ex parte Bollman*.[68] Eric Bollman and his copetitioner, Samuel Swartwout, were arrested in New Orleans for their part in the "Burr conspiracy."[69] General James Wilkinson, military commander in the territory of New Orleans, declared martial law, and refused to regard a writ of habeas corpus issued by the Supreme Court of New Orleans. The prisoners were sent under military guard to Charleston, and from there, in defiance of another writ of habeas corpus issued by a federal district court, were sent to Washington. They arrived in Washington on the evening of 22 January 1807, and without the benefit of warrant, were kept under military arrest.[70]

The following day, while the government was taking steps for the commitment of Bollman and Swartwout on a charge of treason, and counsel for the prisoners was petitioning the circuit court for a writ of habeas corpus, the administration, fearing release of the prisoners by the courts, requested Congress to authorize the suspension of the writ of habeas corpus.[71] The request was presented in a closed session of the Senate by Senator William B. Giles of Virginia, "Jefferson's personal representative in that body."[72] A

committee was immediately appointed, and on the same day, Giles
reported out a bill to suspend the writ of habeas corpus.[73] The bill
provided:

> . . . That in all cases, where any person or persons, charged
> with treason, misprison of treason, or other high crime or
> misdemeanor, endangering the peace, safety, or neutrality of
> the United States, having been or shall be arrested or impris-
> oned, by virtue of any warrant or authority of the President of
> the United States, or from the Chief Executive Magistrate of
> any State or Territorial Government, or from any person act-
> ing under the direction or authority of the President of the
> United States, the privilege of the writ of *habeas corpus* shall
> be, and the same hereby is suspended, for and during the term
> three months from and after the passage of his act, and no
> longer.

Note, the suspension bill did not seek to delegate power to suspend
to the President, but provided directly for that suspension. Professor
Pascal[74] has observed that the draftsmen of this proposal did not
seek to limit its effect to federal courts only and that they must have
thought that a state prisoner ("one held by the authority of a state's
'Chief Executive Magistrate' ") would have habeas protection in
the absence of the proposed statute. The proposal, however, was
referring to persons charged with offenses against the United States,
not state prisoners. It did seek to go beyond the federal courts: it
sought to suspend the privilege secured through state habeas to
those charged with the commission of the named crimes. In other
words, far from supporting Pascal's theory that the habeas clause
was a directive to all superior courts of record, state and federal,
to make the writ routinely available, the bill further supports the
thesis argued herein. It would have suspended federal habeas simply because it was secured by federal legislative enactment and to
undo it would have required a subsequent enactment. Following
the form of the constitutional provision, it would have suspended
state habeas, which was secured against interference from Congress
except in certain cases.

With only one dissenting vote (Senator James A. Bayard, Delaware), the Senate bill was passed and sent to the House with a request that it be considered in secret session.[75] Instead, the House threw open its doors and on the first reading rejected the bill 113-19.[76]

Meanwhile, the circuit court issued a habeas corpus returnable 26 January. A prompt return was not forthcoming, but the court refused to issue an attachment because the three days allowed by common law had not passed. The following day, on the motion of the Government, the circuit court, finding probable cause, issued a bench warrant for Bollman and Swartwout. After hearings on the twenty-ninth and thirtieth to determine whether there was sufficient evidence, the circuit court committed the two defendants.[77] On February second, counsel for the prisoners orally moved the Supreme Court for habeas corpus.[78] Although the Court had twice before exercised habeas jurisdiction,[79] Justices Chase and Johnson doubted the Court's jurisdiction to issue the writ.[80] Marshall then stated that the whole subject would be taken up *"de novo*, without reference to precedents."[81]

The decision of the Court, written by Marshall, was in favor of the motion.[82] In spite of the categorical language of the clause, which is set in limiting terms, and the location of the clause in the Constitution, the Chief Justice, who undoubtedly enjoyed embarrassing the President, stated that the habeas clause placed Congress under an "obligation" to provide an efficient means by which the privilege should be activated.[83] He reasoned that "if the means be not in existence, the privilege itself would be lost, although no law for its suspension be enacted."[84] In support of this thesis, Marshall pointed confidently to section 14 of the Judiciary Act of 1789.[85] Marshall held that by section 14, Congress granted the Supreme Court independent appellate jurisdiction to issue the writ of *habeas corpus ad subjiciendum*. None of Marshall's reasons for the holding were compelling. First, the Chief Justice observed that the second sentence clearly empowered individual justices and judges to issue the writ of *habeas corpus ad subjiciendum*. A construction that would deny *ad subjiciendum* jurisdiction to the Supreme Court would deny it to every federal court. To Marshall's mind, it would be "strange" if the judge in chambers were to have greater power than the judge sitting in open court.[86] (However, legislation extending federal habeas jurisdiction in 1833[87] and 1842[88] applied only to individual justices and judges.)[89] Next Marshall struggled to demonstrate the absurdity of construing the habeas jurisdiction authorized by section 14, sentence 1, as merely ancillary. According to Marshall's analysis, if section 14 conferred only ancillary power on the courts, then the only power given would be *ad testificandum*. Since the proviso of section 14 excepted *ad testificandum* from its general qualification, Marshall reasoned that the whole power would not be the subject of an exception.[90] However, Marshall's analysis was faulty in failing to recognize ancillary forms of habeas corpus other than *ad testificandum*. For example, he stated that *ad satisfaciendum* was inapplicable to the American judicial system because one court never awards execution on the judgment of another,[91] when in fact such an award had been provided for in an act of 1799.[92] Finally, the Chief Justice observed that section 33 of the Judiciary Act included the Supreme Court among those endowed with discretionary power to bail in capital cases.[93] Since habeas corpus was the usual means of procuring bail, Marshall construed section 33 as proceeding upon the supposition that habeas jurisdiction was given to the Court. However, as Mr. Justice Johnson observed, the clause, far from giving power to revise and correct, "vests in the district judge the same latitude of discretion by the same words that it communicates to this court."[94] The power vested in the district judge was obviously original. That by the same words it vested appellate jurisdiction in the Supreme Court is more than the words can bear. The Supreme Court therefore was given power to bail only in the exercise of its original jurisdiction, that is, in criminal proceedings involving ambassadors.[95]

The most that can be said of the independent power given by the clause is that it allowed the Supreme Court power to issue *ad subjiciendum* in the exercise of its original jurisdiction. This same power was of course extended equally to the other courts, which had far wider original jurisdiction. Although Marshall, following *Hamilton* and *Burford*, found this exercise of habeas to be an exercise of appellate jurisdiction,[96] the office of habeas corpus was not to review the erroneous judgments of a lower court;[97] rather, it was limited to an inquiry into the competency of jurisdiction. Further, district courts had habeas jurisdiction and they were not in any sense appellate. One habeas court did not technically "revise" the judgment of another. Its habeas inquiry was independent. Habeas corpus decisions were not *res judicata.*

The grammatical construction of the clause indicates that more than merely ancillary forms of habeas corpus was intended in the grant of power to the courts. The section employs the term "habeas corpus" on three occasions. On the second occasion it was explicitly limited to the *ad subjiciendum* form. It was used without modification on the other two occasions. On the third occasion it referred to the use of the writ by individual judges as well as courts.[98] Surely, if on the final and all-inclusive occasion of its use, the term was used to refer to *ad subjiciendum* as well as to forms of habeas corpus excluding *ad subjiciendum,* a more limiting term would have been used on the first occasion if merely ancillary jurisdiction were conferred there.

It might be argued that irrespective of whether the limiting words "which may be necessary for the exercise of their respective jurisdictions" modified the term habeas corpus (which grammatically seems untenable), the form *ad subjiciendum* would not be excepted; that that form was not only necessary for the exercise of the Supreme Court's appellate jurisdiction, but essential to it. The Judiciary Act gave no appellate jurisdiction in criminal matters to the Court, unless the jurisdiction could be found in section 14. As the Constitution provided that the "Supreme Court *shall have appellate Jurisdiction,* both as to Law and Fact, *with such Exceptions,* and under such Regulations *as Congress* shall make,"[99] it was incumbent upon Congress to provide a means for the exercise of that appellate jurisdiction, which the Court had unless specifically deprived of it.[100] However, could the framers of the Judiciary Act have failed to take account of this clause? The Act was not hailed by its framers as the most satisfying act ever passed. Senator James A. Bayard said of it that while it "displays great ability, it is no disparagement of its authors to say its plan is not perfect. . . ."[101] James Brown, Congressman from the Kentucky district of Virginia wrote that he feared the "great embarrassment and clashing" between the courts of the United States and several states; however, it was "absolutely necessary to pass a Judiciary Law at this session. . . ."[102] The act, of course, must be understood as a compromise resulting from a political battle between those who worked to confine federal judicial power within narrow limits and those who wished to extend it to the full letter of the Constitution.[103] Nevertheless, no account of the clause need have been taken. Since the appellate jurisdiction of the Court was given by the Constitution, a statute was not needed to confirm it, and the means of exercising that jurisdiction need not have been by habeas corpus, since the statute specifically provided for "all other writs . . . which may be necessary for the exercise of . . . jurisdiction." Although habeas corpus may not have been an appropriate means of exercising appellate jurisdiction, the writ of certiorari was. Here was a means for the exercise of appellate criminal jurisdiction and a means for the exercise of habeas jurisdiction in cases such as Bollman's. *Ad subjiciendum* could have been issued after the case had been brought up by the certiorari. *Ad subjiciendum* was another form of the writ of habeas corpus that Marshall failed to see as an appropriate ancillary writ. Habeas corpus *ad subjiciendum* and certiorari had, after all, a long association.[104]

Beyond the problems caused by using section 14 as support, Marshall's thesis conflicted with both the history and clear wording of the clause, both of which indicate that the framers categorically assumed that the privilege was already in existence, as in fact it was —secured by state constitutional, statutory and common law. In addition, the creation of the lower federal courts was optional,[105] and the Supreme Court, at most, could be endowed with power to issue the writ in the exercise of its extremely narrow original jurisdiction and in the exercise of its appellate jurisdiction.[106] Even accepting the broad definition of appellate jurisdiction expounded by Marshall in *Bollman*,[107] if Congress did not opt to create lower federal courts, the privilege would be available only if imprisonment were the result of judicial process.[108] It would be unavailable for those who required it most. However, if state habeas is considered as well, the privilege was secured in all cases of illegal imprisonment even without the creation of lower federal courts. Because state habeas was in most cases secured only by state statute or common law and was therefore subject to the volitions of the state legislature, it does not follow that the writ was not secured in the "most ample manner." To have secured the writ in the "*most* ample manner" would have been to insulate it against the possibility of suspension in any case and to raise it above the Constitution (that is, the amendment procedure) itself. But moreover, it should be recalled that the framers had no concern that the privilege would be threatened by the state legislatures. If they had, it would have been likely that they would have included a restriction on suspension in Article I, section 10, where limitations, similar to those imposed upon the Congress, were imposed upon the states. Although the framers were a little shortsighted in this regard, their concern for habeas corpus was only that it not be interfered with by the federal legislature.

AUTHORITY TO SUSPEND

The thesis herein argued would also resolve the unresolved question of which branch of the federal government was meant to have the authority to suspend the privilege of the writ. The thesis that the habeas clause was a restriction on the power of Congress *vis à vis* state habeas implies that the Congress was meant to have the power to suspend the writ "when in Cases of Rebellion or Invasion the public safety may require it."[109] Obviously, there would have been no need to restrict a power nowhere granted. On 25 April 1861, the President of the United States, Abraham Lincoln, claimed that the power was vested in the executive branch.[110] An independent search of the precedents and commentary prior to the Civil War raises questions about Lincoln's claim.

Like the writ itself, the notion that the benefit of the writ of habeas corpus might be suspended for the public good in times of urgent political necessary[111] was derived from English practice.[112] In their quest for more responsible government, Parliament refused to accept an executive claim to emergency power of arrest and detention,[113] and forced the Crown to acknowledge a Petition of Right[114] denying such power.[115] Parliamentary efforts to secure the benefits and privileges of the writ from arbitrary executive power climaxed in the Habeas Corpus Act of 1679.[116] As the benefits of the writ were secured by legislative enactment, Parliament could by subsequent act suspend them.[117] A suspension usually meant that the Crown was empowered by an act with a specified expiration date to detain one suspected of High Treason or treasonable practices (or other specified offenses) without bail or mainprise, or trial (unless the sanction of usually six members of the Privy Council was obtained). After the date specified for the expiration of the suspension act, the "Benefit and Advantage" of the Habeas Corpus Act of 1679 and all other acts providing for the liberty of the subject were, by command of the suspension act, to go back into force.[118] The enactment was not so much a suspension of the writ itself as a suspension of the rights secured by the act, namely, discharge, bail or speedy trial.[119] A prisoner charged with a specified offense could still apply for habeas corpus to determine whether he had been committed on a sufficient warrant.[120] However, since the writ was not a writ of course, if it appeared that the warrant was sufficient, the petition would be denied.[121]

Not only was power to suspend a legislative office in England, but it was the practice in the several states during the confederation period for the legislature to authorize suspension. This procedure was followed on four occasions: twice in Massachusetts,[122] once in Pennsylvania[123] and once in Virginia.[124] Surely, if this practice were meant to be abandoned by the framers, they would have been more careful.[125]

After the adoption of the federal Constitution, that suspension was to be by the legislature exclusively was assumed by the President, the Congress, the Judiciary, and commentators alike. During the *Bollman* Affair, both Jefferson and the Congress operated under this assumption. Similarly, the Court in *Bollman's Case* specifically held that the power to suspend was vested in Congress.[126] The Supreme Court of Louisiana in *Johnson v. Duncan*[127]—a case arising from General Andrew Jackson's declaration of martial law in New Orleans during the War of 1812[128]—citing *Bollman*, declared that the Constitution had exclusively vested in Congress the right of suspending the privilege of the writ of habeas corpus, and that that body was the sole judge of the necessity that called for the suspension.[129] Further, Joseph Story, commenting on the habeas clause of the Constitution, wrote: "It would seem, as the power is given to Congress to suspend the writ of habeas corpus in cases of rebellion or invasion, that the right to judge, whether exigency had arisen, must exclusively belong to that body."[130] And finally, the author of the most exhaustive study of habeas corpus prior to the Civil War, Rollin C. Hurd, placed the power to suspend in the legislative branch.[131]

In the face of overwhelming precedent and authoritative commentary, how did Lincoln justify his claim of executive cognizance to suspend? In his special message delivered to the Congress on the first day of the special session (4 July 1861) called by Lincoln two days after the firing on Fort Sumter, the President provided two justifications for his actions.[132] First, he noted that the laws that he was required to execute faithfully were being resisted in nearly one-third of the states. He asked:

> Must they be allowed to finally fail of execution, even had it been perfectly clear that by the use of the means necessary to their execution some single law, made in such extreme tenderness of the citizens' liberty that practically it relieves more of the guilty than of the innocent, should to a very limited extent be violated? To state the question more directly, Are all the laws *but one* to go unexecuted, and the Government itself go to pieces lest one law be violated? Even in such a case, would not the official oath be broken if the Government should be overthrown when it was believed that disregarding the single law would tend to preserve it?[133]

The purported justification warrants little comment: the Constitution prescribes the means as well as the end of government. It is law "for rulers and people, equally in war and in peace, and covers with the shield of its protection all classes of men, at all times, under all circumstances."[134] Lincoln's interrogatories distorted the issue. If the means to preserve the Constitution was given to Congress, and they were to judge the necessity of invoking that means, could the President's particular evaluation of the situation justify a usurpation?[135] Finally, an oath to execute faithfully all the laws was indeed a strange place to locate a grant of power that conflicted with other parts of the Constitution.

Lincoln did not, however, rest his case on this ground. He denied any violation of the Constitution and observed that the habeas clause was silent as to which branch of government the power to suspend was confined. As the provision was formulated for cases of extreme emergency, Lincoln found it inconceivable that the framers intended in every case to allow the danger to run its course until Congress could be convened.[136] If by this, Lincoln was saying that in case of a "sudden attack," before Congress could be consulted, the President as "First General"[137] had the duty to repel such attack and if in the exercise of that authority it was "absolutely and indispensably necessary"[138] to exercise the power of suspension, there was authority for such a claim. By endowing Congress with power to "declare" war rather than to "make" war, it was the explicit intention of the framers to leave "to the Executive the power to repel sudden attacks."[139] The words "sudden attack" imply conditions where there is no time for consultation with Congress and where the *attack* is upon the American soil.[140] Where these conditions exist, the President might employ the means "absolutely and indispensably necessary" for repulsion.[141] As the firing on Fort Sumter could be construed as a "sudden attack" on American soil, the question was the *absolute and indispensable necessity* of suspension for the purpose of repulsion. As soon as Congress was able to be consulted, they would become the policy makers and the President would become the obedient "first general."[142] As the courts are the ultimate judges of the Constitution[143] and therefore determine whether Congress has remained within the bounds of the authority delegated it by the "necessary and proper" clause[144]— although Congress is of course the primary judge of what laws are necessary and proper[145]—so too are the courts the ultimate judges of whether the actions taken by the President are consistent with the Constitution.[146]

Would suspension ever fall within the purview of the President's duty to suppress sudden attacks? Note first that the habeas clause meant to restrict Congressional exercise of a "necessary and proper" power. The power was restricted to suppressing insurrections and repelling invasions *only* where the public safety may *require*. In other words, the power was to be exercised by Congress only where essential in cases of insurrection and rebellion. Since the framers had foreseen that the power might be essential in those cases, they might also have foreseen that it would be particularly essential where those cases arose suddenly. Since the word "attack" is broad enough to cover both cases of insurrection and invasion, the President would have power identical to that of Congress when faced with a sudden attack.[147]

The question arises, if the Pinckney and Morris proposals were designed to limit Congressional power, how does one explain the votes of three states against any power at all in Congress to suspend? Why vote to eliminate the power of Congress to suspend, if the President was to have that power? The answer is simple: by voting for the entire clause, the framers were recognizing that not only was the power "necessary and proper," but it was essential under certain conditions. By restricting the power but yet allowing it in certain cases, they were conceding that it was absolutely and indispensably necessary in those cases. If the vote had been to eliminate totally, by the same reasoning, the framers would have been denying that the power was ever essential.[148]

It seems unlikely that Lincoln viewed his power as so restricted. In response to certain resolutions of the Ohio Democratic State Convention,[149] Lincoln claimed that since suspension was reserved for cases of rebellion or invasion, by "necessary implication," "the man whom, for the time, the people have, under the constitution, made the commander-in-chief, of their Army and Navy is the man who holds the power, and bears the responsibility of making [the decision to suspend]."[150] Lincoln thus believed that as Commander-in-chief he had implied power to execute the habeas clause.[151]

It has been shown that the habeas clause was meant as a restriction on Congressional power. Further, unlike Congress, the President was not invested with broad auxiliary power.[152] At the outset of the Convention, Madison emphasized that it was essential "to fix the extent of the Executive authority. . . ."[153] He explained that the executive powers should be "confined and defined."[154] This design was not disregarded. Charles Pinckney told the South Carolina ratifying convention that "we have defined his powers, and bound him to such limits, as will effectively prevent his usurping authority. . . ."[155] As Commander-in-chief, the President was to be no more than the "first General and Admiral."[156] As such, his office was to command the troops in the execution of the policies set by Congress.[157] Of course, like any officer presented with an emergency, the Commander-in-chief would have the duty to do what he perceived to be essential until the agency charged with power to suppress insurrections and repel invasions could be consulted. If the power to suspend were not intended to remain with Congress, the power to repel *sudden* attacks seems superfluous.[158]

In the interval between the events of spring, 1861 (the attack on Fort Sumter on 13 April, Lincoln's call two days later for the special convening of Congress to begin 4 July, and his suspensions beginning on 25 April) and the special session of Congress in the summer of 1861, the issue of who had power to suspend came before the courts. Less than a week after Lincoln had authorized General Scott himself, or any of his officers in command at the point where resistance should occur, between Washington and Philadelphia, to suspend the writ,[159] a writ issued by Judge William F. Giles of the United States district court in Baltimore to release a minor who had enlisted without parental consent was ignored by the Commanding Officer at Fort McHenry, Major W. W. Morris.[160] Giles immediately issued an order directing Morris to show cause why an attachment should not issue against him. The order was drafted in the form of a denunciation of military disobedience to the writ, and before delivery to Morris, it was given to the press. The order suggested that there had been no suspension by a competent authority.

In so acting Judge Giles failed to confront the question the above reasoning would suggest, that is, whether the limited conditions under which the President could suspend the privileges of the writ were fulfilled. It was a very good question whether the President's authority, and indeed the words of his proclamation,[161] extended to the case of an illegally enlisted minor.[162] In his reply, Morris spoke directly to this question: first, he stated that he had no knowledge of the Presidential order and that his actions were taken "entirely on [his] own responsibility without instruction from, or consultation with any person whatsoever." In addition, he justified his action on the ground that the writ might be used by an unfriendly power to depopulate the fortification and place it at the mercy of the "Baltimore Mob." Giles responded in turn by stating that the power to suspend resided exclusively in Congress. Morris refused receipt of further court orders, and subsequent action by Giles was therefore futile. The judge forwarded copies of his communications with Morris to the district attorney with a suggestion that they be sent to the attorney general. They were sent to Attorney General Bates and, reportedly, the matter became an issue at the Cabinet meeting the following day, even as the minor was being quietly released.

A fortnight after this incident, troops under the command of Captain Samuel Yoke, who was charged with the protection of the railroad between Baltimore and Harrisburg, entered the home of John Merryman and arrested him for his part in the destruction of railroad bridges after the Baltimore riot of 19 April 1861.[163] The following day a petition for habeas corpus was made to Mr. Chief Justice Taney, whose sympathies for the South and opposition to the administration were well known. The writ issued to General Cadwalader, commander at Fort McHenry, where Merryman was held in close confinement.[164] Cadwalader refused obedience to the writ, informing Taney *via* an aide-de-camp that Merryman was "charged with various acts of treason, and with being publicly associated with, and holding a commission as lieutenant in a company having possession of arms belonging to the United States, and avowing his purpose of armed hostility against the Government."[165] Further, Cadwalader took the position that he had been "duly authorized by the President of the United States, in such cases, to suspend the writ of *Habeas Corpus*, for the public safety."[166]

Taney, refusing to debate the issue with the General's assistant, simply asked whether Merryman had been brought in response to the writ. When he was told that Merryman was not brought, he issued an attachment against Cadwalader. As in the earlier case, delivery of the attachment was not permitted.[167] In explaining the attachment, Taney said that "the president, under the constitution of the United States, cannot suspend the privilege of the writ of habeas corpus, nor authorize a military officer to do it."[168] Because an oral statement might be misunderstood, Taney did not immediately elaborate upon his holding, but stated that he would file a written opinion and have it laid before the President "in order that he might perform his constitutional duty, to enforce the laws, by securing obedience to the process of the United States."[169]

In his written opinion, Taney based his holding on the precedent established by Jefferson during the *Bollman* affair[170] and on the dicta in the *Bollman Case*.[171] Further, Taney noted the commentaries of Blackstone, which pointed to Parliament as the proper authority to suspend,[172] and the commentaries of Story, which placed the power to suspend in Congress.[173] He also explored the suspect nature of executive power[174] and the sacrosanct position of habeas corpus.[175] He disputed the notion that the President derived any authority from the clause commanding him to take care that the laws be faithfully executed,[176] and denied the existence of an "emergency power."[177] Taney could not believe that the framers of the Constitution would have conferred upon the President "more regal and absolute power over the liberty of the citizen, than the people of England have thought it safe to entrust to the crown. . . ."[178] Having rendered his opinion, Taney, convinced that Lincoln was establishing a military tyranny, once more reminded the President of his oath to execute faithfully the laws.[179]

Although Taney's analysis was faulty in failing to acknowledge a presidential power to suspend where essential to repel sudden invasion and in questioning whether Merryman's case fell within the purview of the President's authority, Lincoln thereafter was, of course, acting contrary to the law as expounded by the branch entrusted with the interpretation of the laws. This was the first issue to which Attorney General Bates spoke in his opinion of 24 June 1861.[180] Rejecting the principle of *Marbury v. Madison*,[181] Bates argued that "if we allow one of the three [branches of government] to determine the extent of its own powers, and also the extent of the powers of the other two, that one can control the whole government, and has in fact achieved the sovereignty."[182] (Taney, himself, had expressed a similar view thirty years earlier when he occupied the office of the attorney general.[183]) Having attempted to throw off the effect of judicial decisions to the contrary, Bates began his affirmative case by assuming the very question at issue: he claimed that the President had power to suspend because he had "lawful discretionary power to arrest and hold in custody persons known to have criminal intercourse with the insurgents, or persons against whom there is probable cause for suspicions of such criminal complicity."[184] Further, Bates argued that because the subject matter was "purely political," the judicial department could not interfere by means of a writ of habeas corpus.[185] This was peculiar reasoning: history had taught the framers that *habeas corpus ad subjiciendum* was the most efficacious remedy to check the political arrests of a ruler.[186]

The debate concerning who had power to suspend continued until 1865, when the suspension orders began to be revoked.[187] The courts generally followed *Merryman*,[188] though pamphleteers were to be found on both sides of the issue.[189] As all suspensions subsequent to the Civil War have been performed by the executive pursuant to authority delegated by Congress,[190] the question has not again arisen,[191] and hence remains unanswered.

STATE HABEAS FOR FEDERAL PRISONERS

ABLEMAN v. BOOTH

In the mid-nineteenth century, questions were raised not only with regard to which branch of the national government could suspend the privilege of the writ but also with regard to which courts in the federal system had authority to issue the writ of habeas corpus in federal cases. Until that time, the well-settled rule applied by the courts[192] and recognized by commentators[193] was that a state, as well as a federal, court had authority to issue a writ of habeas corpus to inquire into the imprisonment of a federal prisoner held within its jurisdiction.

In 1853, Attorney General Caleb Cushing was asked for his opinion as to the legality of the proceedings of a state judge who had issued a writ of habeas corpus in the case of an individual indicted for embezzlement by a federal grand jury, arrested by warrant of a United States district judge, and held pending extradition to another state. The state judge had released the party on bail pending a hearing on the return of the writ.[194] The attorney general found the habeas jurisdiction of state courts in cases of federal prisoners held without civil process by agents of the United States "definitely settled" in favor of the prisoner.[195] Where a federal prisoner was held pursuant to civil process, the attorney general was of the opinion that the state court could issue the writ on application of any party showing probable cause. If the confinement were "in obedience to any constitutional law," the state court should neither discharge nor bail a party whose commitment was regularly made with a view toward prosecution in the United States court, for an offense alleged "which is cognizable therein." "[I]n such case, although the State courts have concurrent jurisdiction with those of the United States in all cases of illegal confinement under the color of the authority of the United States, yet the State court will not look beyond the warrant of commitment, issued by a competent court of the United States."[196] Up to this point, the attorney general's opinion was in complete conformance with the English common law.[197] However, he went on to assert that "[t]he courts of the United States are the constitutional judges of their own jurisdiction."[198] To allow state courts to question the jurisdiction of the courts of the United States would bring the judicial powers of the two systems into direct conflict and contradiction in the same case. Such a power would result in the destruction of the Constitution: "As well might a state judge sustain a writ of error to review and revise a decision to the Supreme Court of the United States."[199]

The attorney general's reasoning was erroneous: in England, the jurisdiction of any court could be inquired into (although the presumption *omnia praesumntur rite essa acta* was applied to instruments issued by a superior court).[200] In the United States, one exception was requisite: because the Supreme Court was specifically designated and designed as the *supreme* court, its determination of its own jurisdiction was necessarily final. This designation also demonstrates the error in the suggestion that a state judge might review and revise a decision of the Supreme Court. Further the office of habeas corpus at this time was precisely that of inquiry into the jurisdictional competency of the committing agent.[201] It would be meaningless to allow state courts to issue the writ involving federal prisoners held in obedience to civil process if the jurisdiction of the United States court could not be inquired into. American case law had acknowledged the rule that "the jurisdiction of any court exercising authority over a subject may be inquired into in every other court, when the proceedings in the former are relied upon, and brought before the latter, by a party claiming the benefit of such proceedings."[202] Finally, the argument based upon the federal system might be persuasive if there were no federal appellate jurisdiction over state courts.

The following year, Franklin Pierce's attorney general saw an opportunity to resolve this issue in a Wisconsin case[203] involving one of the most controversial issues of the day: the constitutionality of the Fugitive Slave Act.[204] Although the election of Pierce in 1852 was taken by many to signal an end to the slavery issue,[205] it soon became apparent that the militant minority would not accept the solution of 1850 (that is, the Compromise of 1850) and would resist the Fugitive Slave Act at every opportunity. Pierce and Cushing could have none of that. Nor could James Buchanan and Jeremiah Black who continued the case with equal enthusiasm.

After being convicted by a federal court of "aiding and abetting, and assisting" the escape of a slave, Sherman M. Booth petitioned the Supreme Court of Wisconsin for a writ of habeas corpus, alleging that his imprisonment was illegal because the act under which he was convicted was unconstitutional and void.[206] The Wisconsin Supreme Court found Booth's detention illegal, and in the exercise of its habeas jurisdiction, ordered him discharged.[207] The attorney general petitioned the Chief Justice of the United States for a writ of error, alleging that the state court had acted beyond its jurisdiction. The writ issued, but the state court had directed its clerk to make no return, thereby insulting the Supreme Court and insuring that the issue would be decided by the United States Supreme Court without benefit of argument from counsel for the defendant in error.[208]

Mr. Chief Justice Taney, who wrote the majority opinion for the Court in *Dred Scott* and who saw that decision being resisted through interference with the Fugitive Slave Act, wrote for the Court and reversed the decision of the Wisconsin Supreme Court.[209] He stated that the state court had claimed and exercised power to set aside and annul the proceedings of a United States commissioner and District Court. If this power were reserved to the states, "no offense against the laws of the United States could be punished by their courts without the assent of the courts of the state where the party is held."[210] It was also held that the state courts lacked jurisdiction in this matter because it had never been conferred upon them by the United States, and because the state could not confer such jurisdiction upon itself.[211] Taney did not question the authority of a state court or judge, properly empowered by state law, to issue a habeas corpus to inquire into the imprisonment of anyone held within the jurisdiction of the state court or judge. However, Taney observed,

> after the return is made, and the state judge or court judicially apprised that the party is in custody under the authority of the United States, they can proceed no further. They then know that the prisoner is within the dominion and jurisdiction of another government, and that neither the writ of habeas corpus, nor any other process issued under the state authority, can pass over the line of division between the two sovereignties. He is then within the dominion and exclusive jurisdiction of the United States. If he has committed an offense against their laws, their tribunals alone can punish him. If he is wrongfully imprisoned, their tribunals can release him and afford him redress.[212]

Taney exaggerated the situation—whether intentionally or not can not be said with certainty; the Wisconsin court's action insulted the authority of the Court, but there can be no mistake about Taney's partisanship on the slavery question[213] and his desire to extend national protection to slavery. Whatever his motives, Taney conflated the decision of the Wisconsin Supreme Court with its subsequent actions. Its failure to obey the writ of the Supreme Court of the United States was certainly an error, and an action which, if allowed, would be destructive to the federal system. Its decision in the case of *Booth*, however, did not undermine the authority of the Constitution. The fact that the case was before the Supreme Court for review demonstrated Taney's error in thinking that the power of a state court to issue a writ of habeas corpus, and upon inquiry to remand or release, would deny to the federal government power to enforce its laws. Indeed, state courts too are charged with the duty to enforce the Constitution and laws.

Taney was also in error when he reasoned that the state courts lacked jurisdiction since the federal Constitution did not confer it upon them, and it was not within the power of the states to confer. This was a remarkable shift of the burden of proof. In fact, it was the federal government that was superimposed upon the states. It was the government of limited, delegated powers. All powers not delegated to the federal government were reserved to the states or people.[214] The habeas jurisdiction of the state courts in all cases of detention without competent authority was not ceded to the federal government. In fact, as argued, the federal Constitution meant to provide specifically for the securement of state habeas for federal prisoners. Finally, Taney did not explain what use state habeas was to federal prisoners if the state courts were denied the power to release one wrongfully imprisoned. When it is said that state habeas for federal prisoners was secured by the Constitution, recall that it was the *privileges* of the writ that were secured, not simply the process.

Underlying the assertion of power by the state habeas court was the finding that the federal statute under which Booth was held was unconstitutional and therefore the federal court under whose command Booth was held was found to lack jurisdiction. The power of a federal habeas court to release an individual imprisoned by order of a court lacking jurisdiction due to a finding that the statute under which the prisoner was held was unconstitutional, was not claimed until *Ex parte Siebold*.[215] The rule eventually established in *Siebold*[216] was mentioned by no one in *Booth*.

Ironically, Taney's opinion placed Southerners, who were, at this time, speaking of conditional Unionism but urging national protection of slavery in the territories,[217] in a position of support for strong central government. The conflicting nature of the opinion may explain the absence of measures by Republicans in Congress to curb the Court's power[218]—a means of attack used in the following decade.[219] The next time a case of this sort came before the Supreme Court it would reveal no conflicting character, for it would come on the heels of a civil war that settled the supremacy question.[220]

U.S. v. TARBLE

After the opinion of the Court in *Booth*, lower courts generally distinguished it from the case of a federal prisoner held without judicial process.[221] In one such case, emanating from the same court whence *Booth's* case arose, this distinction was explicitly rejected, as was the decision of the Supreme Court in *Booth*.[222] *In re Tarble* was commenced by the father of a minor who had enlisted in the army without parental consent. Finding that United States law prohibited such an enlistment, the court ordered the minor released. The court made use of the case to bolster its reasoning in *Booth* and boldly asserted that the 1858 Supreme Court failed to properly decide that case because slavery was at issue.[223]

The United States Supreme Court responded by also denying the distinction between cases of detention under an order of a judicial tribunal and those under the power of mere ministerial officers.[224] The Court held that *Booth* disposed of the claim of jurisdiction by a state court or judge to interfere with the authority of the United States irrespective of whether that authority was exercised by a federal tribunal or federal officer.[225] The opinion was based upon the notion of the supremacy of the Constitution. Since the national government was exclusively charged with raising and supporting armies and providing for the government and regulation of the land and naval forces, allowing state courts to issue habeas corpus to question the validity of enlistments would subject military commanders to "constant annoyance and embarrassment," and might often "be used to the great detriment of the public service."[226] The Court therefore held that state judges and courts authorized to issue habeas corpus undoubtedly have a right to issue the writ in any case when a party is alleged to be illegally confined within their limits, unless it appears from the application that the prisoner is detained "under the authority, or claim and color of the authority" of the federal government by an officer of that government. If it did not appear from the application that the detention was under the authority or claim or color of the authority of the federal government, the writ could issue to inquire into the cause of imprisonment. However, the court could proceed no further once the writ was returned by the custodian, who was required to show that the imprisonment was under the authority or claim or color of the authority of the United States.[227]

The Court's reasoning in *Tarble* falls upon grounds similar to those that were raised in response to the Opinion of the Attorney General and the case of *Ableman v. Booth*. Moreover, here the Court failed to explain how the doctrine of supremacy of the Constitution required that state habeas for federal prisoners be denied.

State, as well as federal, judges are required to support the Constitution.[228] Further, while state habeas might be an annoyance and embarrassment, the writ also serves a legitimate function. Moreover, the Constitution was not meant to be interpreted to suit the dictates of convenience. Should the federal courts also have been deprived of the power to issue habeas corpus for federal prisoners because the writ can be an annoyance and embarrassment to military commanders?

The exposition given by the Court in *Booth* and *Tarble* is now the accepted view.[229] In recent years it has gone unquestioned. Perhaps it is a question already reserved for the antiquarian. The question of federal habeas for state prisoners has of late required far more attention.

SUMMARY

The thesis herein argued is that the habeas clause was meant to restrict Congress from suspending state habeas for federal prisoners except in certain cases where essential for public safety. This thesis is in direct discord with Marshall's "obligation theory," and with the notion that state courts are without authority to issue the writ to question the custody of federal prisoners, and if improperly held, to release them. Implicit also in this thesis is the proposition that Congress was the department invested by the framers with power to suspend, although in the case of "sudden attack," the President, under the conditions implied by that situation, likewise was to have power to suspend.

The framers of the Constitution did not intend to guarantee a right to a federal writ. Under the intent of the framers any right to federal habeas would be purely statutory.[230] An argument that certain congressional measures restrict or even deny the writ would, accordingly, be without substance.[231] Moreover, although the federal Constitution was to secure the privilege of the writ from congressional interference, it did not provide security against state interference, nor did it require a state to provide for the writ.[232] Thus under the design of the framers, the privileges of the writ of habeas corpus were poorly secured. That that design has not been followed can be explained by the propensity of habeas corpus to find itself as the context in which a more general dialogue takes place, that is, a dialogue of political power. In early England, as shown above, habeas corpus was the ground upon which the battle between the local and superior courts was fought; followed by the battle among the superior courts; followed by the battle between the legislative and executive departments of government. These battles transformed habeas corpus from a writ compelling appearance to the "Great Writ" of liberty it is today. Throughout this century in the United States, habeas corpus has been the medium of the dialogue of federalism between the federal and state courts. So a history of the transformation of the Constitution from a document that provided for a restriction on the power of Congress from interfering with state habeas for federal prisoners to one that prohibits a state court from issuing habeas corpus for federal prisoners is not anomalous. One of the most important factors in the interpretation of habeas corpus then, has been the distribution of political power.

NOTES

1. United States Constitution Art. 1, sect. 9, clause 2.

2. 4 Cranch 75 (1807).

3. *Fay v. Noia*, 372 U.S. 391 (1963).

4. *Ex parte Bollman*, 4 Cranch 75 (1807). See also, *Eisentrager v. Forrestal*, 174 F.2d 961 (1949), rev'd on other grounds, 339 U.S. 763 (1950).

5. Zechariah Chafee, Jr., *How Human Rights Got Into the Constitution* (Boston: Boston University Press, 1952), pp. 51-74.

6. *Ex parte Billings*, 46 F. Supp. 663 (1942), aff'd 135 F.2d 505 (1943), rev'd on other grounds, 321 U.S. 542 (1944); *Robertson v. Cameron*, 224 F. Supp. 60 (1963); *Brooks v. State of Texas*, 256 F. Supp 806 (1966), rev'd on other grounds, 381 F.2d 619 (1967).

7. Francis Pascal, "Habeas Corpus and the Constitution," 1970 Duke L. J. 605 (1969).

8. United States Constitution, Preamble.

9. Max Farrand ed., *The Records of the Federal Convention of 1787* (New Haven: Yale University Press, 1966), vol. 3, pp. 604-09.

10. Ibid., vol. 3, p. 609. The exact wording is unknown. Madison reported that the clause read:

> The United States shall not grant any title of Nobility—The Legislature of the United States shall pass no Law on the subject of Religion, nor touching or abridging the Liberty of the Press nor shall the Privilege of the Writ of Habeas Corpus ever be suspended except in case of Rebellion or Invasion.

Ibid., vol. 3, p. 599. The judgment of a number of writers is that the Pinckney Plan reported in Madison's notes is inaccurate. Ibid., vol. 3, pp. 601-04. Madison himself was skeptical as to whether this was the actual plan submitted by Pinckney on May twenty-ninth, as was Rufus King (delegate from Massachusetts, and when Madison published his notes in 1819, one of the few members of the Convention still living). The draft that Madison recorded, however, may well represent Pinckney's perception of the significant difference between the proposal he advocated and the one that was adopted. Note, the habeas clause here clearly appeared as a restriction on the power of the legislature. It was separated from the first member of the clause restricting the powers of the United States generally by a hyphen. *See* John J. Montgomery, *The Writ of Habeas Corpus and Mr. Binney* (Philadelphia, second edition, 1862), p. 8 where the wording of this clause is analyzed.

11. The proposal was one of a set introduced by Pinckney. It fell after an enumeration of procedural-type powers of the legislature, and before a limitation of the legislative power. 2 Farrand 340-42.

12. Ibid., p. 341.

13. This idea was embraced as early as 5 July, affirmed 18 July, and reaffirmed 6 August. Jonathan Elliot ed., *Debates of the State Conventions on the Adoption of the Federal Constitution* (Philadelphia, 1861), vol. 5, pp. 159-60, 331-32, 376-81. *See also* 1 Farrand 119, 124-25, 352, 2 Ibid. 638. The notion demonstrates that the "obligation theory" espoused by Marshall in *Ex parte Bollman*, 4 Cranch 75 (1807) is questionable, since Congress was without power to impose jurisdiction on the state courts. *Houston v. Moore*, 5 Wheat. 1, 27 (1820).

14. Art. 3, sect. 1 (emphasis added).

15. *See* Dallin H. Oaks, "The 'Original' Writ of Habeas Corpus in the Supreme Court," 1962 S. Ct. Rev. 153, 156-58.

16. *See* text accompanying notes 192-229 *infra*.

17. 5 Elliot 376-81.

18. It has been suggested that by submitting his proposal as an amendment to the judicial article, Pinckney meant it to be a directive to the courts to make the writ routinely available. Pascal, "Habeas Corpus and the Constitution," 1970 Duke L. J. 605, 609-10. (*See also* Horace Binney, *The Privilege of the Writ of Habeas Corpus Under the Constitution* (Philadelphia, vol. 1, 1862; 2, 1862; 3, 1865), vol. 1, p. 31). The argument is self-defeating: Why then was the clause moved to the legislative article? *See* J. C. Bullitt, *A Review of Mr. Binney's Pamphlet on the Privilege of Habeas Corpus Under the Constitution* (Philadelphia, 1862), pp. 17-18; Montgomery, *Habeas Corpus and Mr. Binney*, p. 9.

19. Article 11, sect. 4, on August twenty-seventh, provided:

> The trial of all crimes except in cases of impeachment shall be in the Superior Court of that State where the offence shall have been committed in such manner as the Congress shall by law direct except that the trial shall be by a jury. But when the crime shall not have been committed within any one of the United States the trial shall be at such place and in such manner as Congress shall by law direct, except that such trial shall also be by a jury.

2 Farrand 433. The clause "except that the trial shall be by jury" was to restrict Congressional power. The provision, as far as the states were concerned, required the state superior court to follow the procedure set out by Congress. (Of course that procedure must be constitutional and therefore mini-

mally require jury trial). In fine, the clause was meant as a grant of power to Congress to define the jurisdiction of state courts in cases of federal prisoners, and a limitation on that power.

20. Ibid., p. 438.

21. *See also* note 12 *supra.*

22. *See* ch. 20 *supra.*

23. *See* ch. 4, text accompanying notes 22-24 *infra.*

24. *See* note 19 *supra.*

25. 2 Farrand 434, 576.

26. Art. 1, sect. 8, clause 9.

27. Ibid., clause 18.

28. *See* ch. 2, note 67 (Ma.); note 133 (Pa.); text accompanying note 56 (Va.) *supra.* Note also situation in South Carolina, ch. 2, text accompanying notes 73-80 *supra.*

29. Pascal, "Habeas Corpus and the Constitution," 1970 Duke L. J. 605, 612, found that the vote of the three states against any power to suspend lost all meaning unless the habeas clause was regarded as a grant of power to suspend. He asked, "Why vote against the suspension member of the clause if suspensions were to be permitted by some other provision of the Constitution irrespective of the outcome of the vote?" *See also* Binney 1, pp. 1-38. The answer is that this clause was meant to restrict power elsewhere granted. If the suspension member of the clause were defeated, no suspension would be allowed. The question, therefore, is why vote for a clause that would state merely that "The Privilege of the Writ of Habeas Corpus shall not be suspended" and therefore eliminate suspensions, if power to suspend did not elsewhere exist? *See* Samuel Smith Nicolas, *Habeas Corpus—A Response to Mr. Binney* (Louisville, 1862), p. 10.

30. 3 Farrand 213. *See also* ibid., p. 157.

31. I presume it was Rutledge's arguments Martin was repeating since, from the record, he would seem to have been the only one likely to have voiced those arguments.

32. *See* text accompanying notes 46-53 *infra.*

33. Pascal, "Habeas Corpus and the Constitution," 1970 Duke L. J. 605, 613, argued that the change in phrasing from "most urgent and pressing occasion" to "unless where in cases of Rebellion or invasion the public safety may require it" in conjunction with the absence of explicit reference to Congress, indicated that the Convention contemplated no role for Congress. *See also* Binney 1, p. 31. Whereas Pascal argued that the clause did all that Congress could do, and left to the courts the discretion to judge whether the situation called for the automatic suspension of the writ, Binney recognized that the clause called for a political organ of the government in recognition of the urgency of the situation to act accordingly. Finding suspension an executive function, Binney pointed to the Presidency as the organ of government with power to suspend. He reasoned that all of the conditions under which suspension takes place are of executive cognizance: "The power to imprison, and to deny or delay a discharge from imprisonment, is an executive function." 1, p. 7. Further, "[t]he power to suspend the privilege of the Writ, is moreover inseparably connected with rebellion or invasion. . . . The direction of such a war is necessarily with the Executive. . . . It is the duty of the Executive office . . . to suppress insurrection. . . . The power to sus-

pend the privilege, is supplementary to the military power to suppress or repel." Ibid., p. 8. *See also* remarks of Howard, *Congressional Globe,* (1863) 37th Cong., 3rd Sess., p. 544. In contrast, it was argued that since the writ was instituted by law, it required a law to suspend. David Boyer Brown, *Reply to Horace Binney on the Privilege of the Writ of Habeas Corpus Under the Constitution* (Philadelphia, 1862), p. 11. None of the arguments are persuasive. Brown's arguments were faulty because at the time the habeas clause was enacted there was no habeas corpus statute. The clause referred to state habeas and therefore there was no Congressional right to suspend that was incident to the power to enact. Binney's argument is representative of his basic view of the question as "political rather than legal . . ." (1, preface). What matter is it that the conditions under which suspension takes place are of executive cognizance? What was best in Mr. Binney's view was not necessarily equivalent to what was constitutional. His argument rested solely upon the nature of the act. But the framers were not only concerned with the necessity of an act of Congress, but with the nature of suspension *and* the desirability of securing the writ against suspension. Direction of war is necessarily an executive function, but the President was to be no more than a "first General." *Federalist,* no. 69 (Hamilton). It was the duty of Congress to make laws "necessary and proper" to "suppress Insurrection and repel Invasions." United States Constitution, Article I, section 8, clauses 18 and 15. (*See* qualification, text accompanying notes 137-48 *infra.*) Finally, Pascal acknowledged that Pinckney's "most urgent and pressing occasions" formula required legislative elaboration and therefore Congress was brought into the picture; however, Morris' alteration made the function of Congress superfluous. The true question, however, is not whether the legislature is *necessary* but whether the Convention intended that the legislature should determine the conditions. Morris gave us no hint that he intended to alter Pinckney's design for congressional suspension. Morris' proposal was in response to a plea to make the writ inviolate. He was simply further limiting the power of Congress to suspend.

34. Art. 1, sect. 8, clause 15.

35. 2 Farrand 390.

36. The notion that the actual power to suspend was an implied power was supported by cryptic, yet noteworthy dicta of the Supreme Court, *per* Story, in *Prigg v. Pennsylvania,* 41 U.S. 539, 619-20 (1842):

> The Constitution . . . declares that the privilege of the writ of habeas corpus shall not be suspended, unless, when in cases of rebellion or invasion, the public safety may require it. No express power is given to Congress to secure this invaluable right in the nonenumerated cases, or to suspend the writ in cases of rebellion or invasion. And yet it would be difficult to say, since this great writ of liberty is usually provided for by the ordinary functions of legislation, and can be effectually provided for only in this way, that it ought not to be deemed by necessary implication within the scope of the legislative power of Congress.

37. *See generally*, Duker, "The Right to Bail," 42 Alb. L. Rev. 33.

38. 3 Farrand 157.

39. James F. Johnson, *The Suspending Power and the Writ of Habeas Corpus* (Philadelphia, 1862), noted that the word "where" was originally

used by Morris to convey the idea that suspension was limited to a certain area, but a little reflection convinced him that the words "the public Safety may require it" would limit the suspension to the place where the public safety might require it. *See In re Spurlock*, 66 F. Supp. 997, 1004 (1944). (It might be suggested that the word "when" limited the suspension as to time, while the latter clause limited it to location, though no such conscious design can be located.)

40. 2 Farrand 389; 3 ibid. 150, and especially, 327.

41. Pascal, "Habeas Corpus and the Constitution," 1970 Duke L. J. 605, 613 fn. 26.

42. Henry Dutton, "Writ of Habeas Corpus," 9 Am. L. Reg. 705, 710 (1862).

43. J. R. Pole, paper delivered to the American Studies seminar at Churchill College, Cambridge, May, 1977.

44. The proposal read:

> That all bills for raising or appropriating money, and for fixing salaries of the officers of the government of the United States, shall originate in the first branch of the legislature, and shall not be altered or amended by the second branch; and that no money shall be drawn from the public treasury, but in pursuance of appropriations to be originated in the first branch.

1 Farrand 523. The two parts of the above provision were separated by the Committee on Style and Arrangement. *See* 2 Farrand 568, 593, 596. *See also* 1 ibid. 524, 526, 538; 2 ibid. 14, 16, 154, 164, 178, 280, 509; 3 ibid. 149-150, 311, 326. *Accord*, Charles Ingersoll, *An Undelivered Speech on Executive Arrests* (Philadelphia, 1862), pp. 15-16.

45. The remaining five clauses provide:

> Clause 1—"The Migration or Importation of such Persons as any State now existing shall think proper to admit, shall not be prohibited by Congress prior to the Year one thousand eight hundred and eight, but a Tax or duty may be imposed on such Importation, not exceeding ten dollars for each Person."

> Clause 3—"No Bill of Attainder or ex post facto Law shall be passed."

> Clause 4—"No Capitation, or other direct, Tax shall be laid, unless in Proportion to the Census or Enumeration herein before directed to be taken."

> Clause 5—"No Tax or Duty shall be laid on Articles exported from any State."

> Clause 6—"No Preference shall be given by any Regulation of Commerce or Revenue to the Port of one State over those of another: nor shall Vessels bound to, or from, one State, be obliged to enter, clear, or pay duties in another."

All of these clauses set out in section 8 were clearly designed as limitations on the powers of Congress and were to the benefit of the state and people.

46. *Federalist*, no. 83.

47. Ibid., no. 84.

48. Pascal, "Habeas Corpus and the Constitution," 1970 Duke L. J. 605, 611, fn. 23.

49. Greenleaf ed., Laws of the State of New York, vol. 1, p. 369.

50. 31 Car. 2 c. 2 (1679).

51. *See* text accompanying note 65 *infra*.

52. Julian P. Boyd ed., *The Papers of Thomas Jefferson* (Princeton: Princeton University Press, 1955), vol. 12, p. 440 (emphasis added). Moreover, upon examining Madison's proposed Bill of Rights, Jefferson wrote Madison: "I like it as far as it goes; but I should have been for going further." He suggested the inclusion of a habeas corpus amendment. P. L. Ford ed., *Writings of Thomas Jefferson* (New York: Putnam, 1904), vol. 5, p. 493:

> No person shall be held in confinement more than .... days after they have demanded and have been refused a writ of Habeas corpus by the judge appointed by law nor more than .... days after such a writ shall Have been served on the person holding him in confinement and no order given on due examination for his remandment or discharge, nor more than .... hours in any place at a greater distance than .... miles from the usual residence of some judge authorized to issue Habeas corpus, nor more than .... miles distance from the station or encampment of enemies or insurgents.

53. *See* text accompanying notes 71-76 *infra*.

54. 2 Elliot 455.

55. Pascal, "Habeas Corpus and the Constitution," 1970 Duke L. J. 605, 611, n. 23.

56. Others might suggest such words meant that Congress was not understood to have power, but the phrase probably was merely a more general means of locating the power. Note, although the other speakers explicitly mentioned Congress as the agency with power to suspend, no one took issue with the phrase used by Adams. 2 Elliot 108-09.

57. Ibid., p. 108.

58. Ibid.

59. Ibid., pp. 108-09.

60. 3 ibid. 461. *See also* ibid., p. 449.

61. Ibid., p. 464. Randolph viewed the power to suspend as incident to the power of Congress to regulate the Courts. The power to "constitute" inferior tribunals, or "ordain and establish" such courts, and the authority to regulate the appellate jurisdiction of the Supreme Court seem unlikely sources for a power to "suspend." Of course, since Congress was empowered to establish courts, it could empower them to issue the writ of habeas corpus, or command them to proceed according to a habeas corpus act, and therefore Congress could, by a corollary power, revoke power to issue the writ, or amend, suspend, or revoke the act. But, as already noted, the establishment of lower federal courts was optional and the appellate power of the Supreme Court existed at the discretion of Congress. By withholding the Supreme Court's habeas jurisdiction and refusing to create lower federal courts, the Congress could, without suspending the privilege of the writ, effectively withhold it at the federal level. Although such action by Congress could frustrate a federal writ, the power of Congress to suspend, implied in the clause empowering Congress to constitute, ordain and establish federal courts, applied

only to the federal judiciary, whereas an effective suspension would have to take account of the state judiciaries, which retained a power to issue habeas for federal prisoners. *See* text accompanying notes 192-229 *infra*. Note also that the clause does not speak of the writ of habeas corpus, nor a habeas corpus act, but of the privilege of habeas corpus, which, according to the clause, seems to be in existence.

Randolph's view was elaborated on in *Warren v. Paul*, 22 Ind. 287 (1864). The court there argued that art. 1, sect. 8 empowered Congress to organize courts and therein delegated power to authorize and to suspend issuance of the writ of habeas corpus, because habeas corpus is a judicial writ, and the power to organize courts includes the power of determining which writs they may issue, or not issue, from time to time. Therefore, according to this argument, it was necessary to place the restriction upon the power thus delegated to Congress to legislate for the courts. Art. 1, sect. 9 demanded that Congress should not, in so legislating, withhold from the courts the right to issue the writ of habeas corpus except when in cases of invasion or rebellion, the public safety may require. Although the initial premise is fine, and—following the analogy of suspensions by the English Parliament—the idea that whatever writs are enacted by the legislature may be destroyed by the legislature is clear, the remaining line of argument fails, as did the Randolph view, to take account of state habeas and, moreover, then becomes merely a variation of the "obligation theory" and falls on the shortcomings of that theory as well. That the Virginia convention did not accept Randolph's view can be inferred from the amendment endorsed. *See* text accompanying note 62 *infra*.

62. 3 Elliot 658.

63. 1 ibid. 334.

64. Ibid., p. 243.

65. 2 ibid. 399 (emphasis added). *See* text accompanying notes 49-53 *supra*.

66. Ibid., pp. 403, 407.

67. 1 ibid. 328. The recommendation provided: "That every person restrained of his liberty is entitled to an inquiry into the lawfulness of such restraint, and to a removal thereof if unlawful: and that such inquiry or removal ought not to be denied or delayed, except when, on account of public danger, the Congress shall suspend the privilege of the writ of habeas corpus."

68. 4 Cranch 75 (1807).

69. Albert J. Beveridge, *The Life of John Marshall* (Boston: Houghton Mifflin Co., 1919), vol. 3, pp. 274-397; Nathan Schachner, *Aaron Burr* (New York: Frederick A. Stokes Co., 1937); Charles Warren, *The Supreme Court in United States History* (Boston: Little, Brown and Co., 1935), vol. 1, pp. 301-08; Joseph Alston (Agrestis [pseud.]), *A Short Review of the Late Proceedings at New Orleans* (South Carolina, 1807).

70. While the prisoners were on their way from New Orleans, they became objects of great public excitement, deliberately aroused by the Administration. To prime Congress for the request to suspend habeas corpus, which was presented the following day, Jefferson, on the twenty-second of January, sent a message to Congress informing them that one of the principal emmissaries of Burr had been liberated by means of the writ of habeas corpus, and the other two were about to arrive. *Annals*, 9th Congress, 2d sess., pp. 39-43.

71. The request seems to have been at the urging of Navy Secretary Smith. Irving Brant, *James Madison, Secretary of State 1800-1809* (Indianapolis: The Bobbs-Merrill Co., Inc., 1953), p. 349.

72. Beveridge, *John Marshall*, vol. 3, p. 346.

73. *Annals*, 9th Congress, 2nd sess., p. 44. Since the Senate was proceeding behind closed doors, a copy of the bill does not appear on its journal. Almost twenty years later, John Randolph moved the Senate to send to the House of Representatives for a copy of the bill. *Congressional Debates*, 1825-1826, vol. 2, pt. 1, p. 137. Apparently realizing the futility of the motion, Randolph later withdrew the motion. Ibid., p. 142. A copy of the bill is found on the House's journals, *Annals*, 9th Congress, 2nd sess., p. 402.

74. Pascal, "Habeas Corpus and the Constitution," 1970 Duke L. J. 605, 624, n. 70.

75. *Annals*, 9th Congress, 2nd sess., p. 44.

76. Ibid., p. 402 *et seq.* It is interesting to note that no one during the debate over this bill even suggested that the power to suspend might reside in the executive branch. Although most were willing to agree that there was an invasion, they did not agree that the public safety required the suspension. Mr. Eppes' remarks at ibid., pp. 409-10 are particularly worthy of citation:

> By this bill, we are called upon to exercise one of the most important powers vested in Congress by the Constitution of the United States. . . . It is not in every case of invasion, nor in every case of rebellion, that the exercise of this power by Congress can be justified under the words of the Constitution. The words of the Constitution confine the exercise of this power exclusively to cases of rebellion or invasion, where the public safety requires it. . . . The Constitution, however, having vested this power in Congress, and a branch of the Legislature having thought its exercise necessary, it remains for us to inquire whether the present situation of our country authorizes, on our part, a resort to this extraordinary measure.

Even those in favor of suspension suggested that the constitutional provision applied to Congress. *See especially* Varnum's remarks, ibid., pp. 411-13. This position was evident after rejection of the Senate bill and during the consideration of a proposal of Representative Broom from Delaware. Ibid., pp. 502-90. In response to what he perceived as Wilkinson's violation of constitutional rights in New Orleans, Broom moved "That it is expedient to make further provision, by law, for securing the privilege of the writ of habeas corpus, to persons in custody, under, or by color of, the authority of the United States." The motion was later amended by Representative Burwell who sought to limit the Supreme Court's power to issue the writ. For this reason, and because many felt that the states were competent to protect individual rights, and because the *Bollman* case was now under consideration, and because of the nearness of the end of the session, the motion was indefinitely postponed. Ibid., p. 589.

77. In both the decision to issue the bench warrant and the finding of probable cause, the two Jeffersonian appointments (Nicholas Fitzhugh and Allen Bowie Duckett) constituted the majority (William Cranch, C. J., dissenting).

78. *Ex parte Bollman*, 4 Cranch 75.

79. On the two previous occasions, habeas corpus had issued with little or no discussion. *United States v. Hamilton*, 3 Dall. 17 (1795); *Ex parte Burford*, 3 Cranch 448 (1806). In *Hamilton* the Court released to bail a prisoner committed on the warrant of a federal district judge, charged with the crime of high treason. Under sect. 33 of the Judiciary Act, 1 U.S. Statutes at Large 91-92, treason— being an offense punishable by death—was a case in which bail was within the discretion of the Supreme or circuit court, or a justice or judge thereof, or a judge of the district court. The district judge, in the exercise of his discretionary power, denied bail. Before the Supreme Court, the attorney for the United States made no argument denying the Supreme Court's habeas jurisdiction, but contended that the Court's power to bail was "concurrent" with the power of the district judge, and that the bail decision should be "revised" only if a new matter were adduced or if there were a charge of misconduct. The Court rejected the argument and reversed the bail decision of the district judge. In *Burford*, the Court granted habeas corpus and discharged an individual imprisoned on the warrant of a justice of the peace, which failed to show good cause certain. Burford had previously been granted habeas corpus by a circuit court, but was remanded. Pointing to sect. 14, the attorney for the petitioner noted, "if this is an exercise of [the Court's] appellate jurisdiction, the mode by *habeas corpus* is especially provided by statute for that purpose." Marshall reported that the Court found "some obscurity in the act of Congress, and some doubts were entertained by the court as to the construction of the constitution." However, "in favor of liberty" and on the basis of *Hamilton*, the writ issued.

The Court was not the only branch having difficulty with the act of Congress. Both houses of Congress themselves during the *Bollman* affair expressed puzzlement over the meaning of the act. *See* Burwell's remarks in the House on 19 February 1807. *Annals*, 9th Congress, 2nd Sess., p. 555; and Senator Giles' resolution of 16 February 1808. *Annals*, 10th Congress, 1st sess., pp. 130, 131.

80. *Ex parte Bollman*, 4 Cranch 75.

81. Ibid.

82. Ibid., p. 93 *et seq.*

83. *Ex parte Bollman*, 4 Cranch 75, 95. Marshall also disclaimed all jurisdiction not given by the Constitution and laws of the United States. [He observed, however, that for the meaning of the term "habeas corpus," resort could be had to common law. Ibid., p. 94]. No authority was cited for this assertion. Marshall stated that "Courts which originate in the common law possess a jurisdiction which must be regulated by common law, until some statute shall change their established principles; but courts which are created by written law, and those whose jurisdiction is defined by written law, cannot transcend that jurisdiction." He felt it unnecessary to elaborate upon the principle since "it has been repeatedly given by this Court . . ." In support, *see* Chase, J. (individual remark), *Turner v. Bank of North America*, 4 Dall. 8, 10, fn. a (1799); *Marbury v. Madison*, 1 Cranch 137, 174 (1803) (cited by Johnson, J., dissenting opinion). For a historical explanation of this interpretation, *see* Morton J. Horwitz, *The Transformation of American Law, 1780-1860* (Cambridge, Massachusetts: Harvard University Press, 1977), pp.

4-16. *See also* James Kent's introductory lecture at Columbia (17 November 1794), published in 3 Columbia Law Review 330 (1903), pp. 335-37. This principle, although it arguably might not apply to courts created by written law in all governments (*see In re Bryan*, 60 N.C. 1 (1863), but note ch. 2, text accompanying notes 82-83 *supra*.) it arguably could be said to be required by the notion permeating every instrument of the federal system, i.e. that the federal government was designed as one of limited, delegated powers. Cf. William Winslow Crosskey, *Politics and the Constitution in the History of the United States* (Chicago: University of Chicago Press, 1953), vol. 1, pp. 610-20; *Eisentrager v. Forrestal*, 174 F.2d 961 (1949).

84. *Ex parte Bollman*, 4 Cranch 75, 95. *See also* ibid., p. 101, where, following his thesis, Marshall stated:

> If at any time the public safety shall require the suspension of the power vested by this act in the courts of the United States, it is for the legislature to say so.
>
> That question depends on political considerations, on which the legislature is to decide. Until the legislative will be expressed, the courts can only see its duty, and must obey the law.

The significance of the statement on the question of which branch has the power to suspend is treated at note 126 *infra*.

85. For a copy of the sect. *see* ch. 4, text accompanying note 4 *infra*.

86. *Ex parte Bollman*, 4 Cranch 75, 96.

87. 4 U.S. Statutes at Large 632 (*see* ch. 4, text accompanying notes 28-43) *infra*.

88. 5 U.S. Statutes at Large 539 (*see* ch. 4, text accompanying notes 44-52) *infra*.

89. Moreover, sect. 33 of the Judiciary Act, 1 U.S. Statutes at Large 91-92, empowered only the Supreme and circuit courts and justices and judges thereof and district judges with discretionary power to bail in capital cases. No mention was made of district courts. An argument can perhaps be made that by endowing district judges with power the Congress assumed that district courts would be endowed with similar power. The judge in open court was, after all, the same judge in chambers. A similar argument could not be made with respect to the individual justices *vis à vis* the Supreme Court as the Constitution specifically limits the original jurisdiction of the Court, though the individual justice in chambers or on circuit is subject to no such limit.

90. *Ex parte Bollman*, 4 Cranch 75, 97-99. Pascal, "Habeas Corpus and the Constitution," 1970 Duke L. J. 605, 630-32 misinterprets *Bollman* on this point. *See* ch. 4, text accompanying note 7 *infra*. (Pascal reads Marshall to suggest that *habeas corpus ad testificandum* was only useful to court. In fact, Marshall was saying that *ad testificandum* jurisdiction was limited by statute to courts and could not be exercised by individual judges.)

91. *Ex parte Bollman*, 4 Cranch 75, 98.

92. 1 U. S. Statutes at Large 727.

93. *Ex parte Bollman*, 4 Cranch 75, 99-100.

94. Ibid., p. 106.

95. *See* ibid., pp. 106-07.

96. Ibid., p. 106.

97. *See* ch. 5, text accompanying notes 1-30 *infra*.

98. This statement is supported in ch. 4, text accompanying notes 10-11 *infra*.

99. Art. 3, sect. 2, clause 2 (emphasis added).

100. *Martin v. Hunter's Lessee*, 1 Wheat. 304 (1816). *See generally*, Cross-key, *Politics and the Constitution*, vol. 1, pp. 610-20.

101. Quoted by Charles Warren, "New Light on the History of the Federal Judiciary Act of 1789," 37 Harv. L. Rev. 49, 52.

102. Ibid., p. 53.

103. Ibid., pp. 53, 62. Note, as early as 1789 limits on the Constitution were suggested. (*Independent Gazetteer* (Philadelphia), 25 February 1789). Among other things, it was suggested that the federal appellate power be confined to questions of law and not fact, that federal courts of first instance be eliminated or that a very limited original jurisdiction be restricted to the Supreme Court alone, and that all jurisdiction based on diversity of citizenship and status as a foreigner be eliminated. *See also* Randolph's suggestions. Ch. 4, note 13 *infra*. (Especially note proposal specifically authorizing the exercise of appellate jurisdiction by the Supreme Court.)

104. *See* ch. 1, text accompanying notes 170-93 *supra*.

105. United States Constitution, Art. III, sect. 1.

106. *Marbury v. Madison*, 1 Cranch 137 (1803).

107. 4 Cranch 75, 101; ch. 5, text accompanying notes 32-40 *infra*.

108. *Ex parte Watkins*, 7 Peters 568 (1833).

109. Realizing the harm this theory would do to their claim, those who contended that Lincoln's exercise of power to suspend without Congressional authorization was proper argued that the clause was a grant of power. *See* Binney 1, pp. 9, 11, 40; William Kennedy, *The Privilege of the Writ of Habeas Corpus Under the Constitution of the United States* (Philadelphia, 1862), pp. 6, 13. The clause was said to be elliptical. When the ellipse was supplied the clause read: "The privilege of the Writ of Habeas Corpus shall not be suspended, unless, when in case of rebellion or invasion, the public safety may require it; and then it may be suspended." It was then said that this was equivalent to the following: "The privilege of the Writ of Habeas Corpus may be suspended in cases of rebellion or invasion, when the public safety may require it; and it shall not be suspended in any other case." Read this way, the clause itself announced the law and permitted the President to treat the clause as suspended in the named circumstances. In contrast, it was argued that the clause was restrictive. Nicolas, *Habeas Corpus—A Response to Mr. Binney*, pp. 14-41 argued that the power to suspend was implicit in Congressional authority to regulate the judiciary. However, this failed to take account of Binney's argument that the clause did not speak of the writ of habeas corpus or the habeas corpus act. Binney acknowledged that if these were spoken of there might be some ground for the argument that the power to suspend was legislative. [Of course the argument that the habeas clause was referring to state habeas amply satisfies Binney's argument.] Binney 2, pp. 8-27, made a separate response to this argument and pointed out that the federal courts were optional with Congress. George M. Wharton, *Remarks on Mr. Binney's Treatise on the Writ of Habeas Corpus* (Philadelphia, 1862) argued that the grant was to be found in the enumerated powers of Congress. *See also* Ingersoll, *Executive Arrests*, pp. 25-26. To this argument Binney responded:

It is impossible to treat this argument seriously. The writer has tran-
scribed nearly half the express powers of Congress, and left his readers
a perfectly uncontrolled liberty to select one or another, or half a dozen,
without the least influence from himself, or an intimation of the slightest
preference on his part for one more than another, Nay, he does not
give the least hint of the nature or mode of application of the incidental
or implied power, which, according to his notion, arises from any one
of these express powers, to suspend the Writ of Habeas Corpus. He
names eight express powers, and there are but eighteen in the Eighth
Section; and it is true to the very letter, that the member of the Philadelphia Bar neither makes a choice himself, nor writes a word to influence the choice, of one rather than another of them. He contents himself with saying, "that there are such grants of power, in language amply
sufficient to vest discretion on the subject-matter in Congress, we think
may be safely asserted by any one reading the clause conferring legislative power in the several particulars we have recited above." This is
not argument, but dogmatism.

Binney 2, p. 35. But Binney was unable to answer the argument when the
specific power to suppress insurrection and repel invasion was pointed to.
George M. Wharton, *Answer to Mr. Binney's Reply to "Remarks" on his
Treatise on the Habeas Corpus* (Philadelphia, 1862); Bullitt, *A Review of
Mr. Binney's Pamphlet*, p. 10. Nor could Binney sufficiently answer the argument that if the Constitution itself suspended the writ upon the occurrence
of particular circumstances, it would have plainly said so by adding a clause
to that effect. As it stands, the clause gave permission to suspend, not to treat
the privilege as suspended. Samuel Smith Nicholas, *The Law of War and
Confiscation* (Louisville, 1862), pp. 6-7. Finally, it was asked if clause 2 of
Article 9 was to be read with an ellipse, should not clauses 4, 5 and 6? Surely
these clauses were not self-executing, merely awaiting presidential action carrying them into execution. Brown, *Reply to Horace Binney*, pp. 22-23.

110. The claim was asserted in the form of an order to General Winfield
Scott informing him that the Maryland legislature was about to assemble to
consider the issue of whether to break with the Union. Lincoln ordered Scott
to "watch, and wait their action, which, if it shall be to arm their people
against the United States, he is to adopt the most prompt, and efficient means
to countervail, even, if necessary, to a bombardment of their cities—and in
the extreme necessity, the suspension of the writ of habeas corpus." James P.
Richardson ed., *A Compilation of the Messages and Papers of the Presidents
(1789-1897)* (Washington, D.C.: Government Printing Office, 1896), vol. 6,
pp. 17-18. It is interesting that Lincoln viewed suspension as a step to be
taken only if absolutely and indispensably necessary; a step even more extreme than bombardment.

Two days after this message, Lincoln authorized Scott (or other commanding officer) to suspend the writ "[i]f at any point on or in the vicinity
of the [any] military line, which is now [or which shall be] used between
the City of Philadelphia and Washington, *via* Perryville, Annapolis City, and
Annapolis Junction, [he found] resistance which [should render] it necessary
to suspend the writ of Habeas Corpus for the public safety. . . ." Ibid., p. 18.

On 10 May 1861, the writ was suspended in Florida. Ibid., pp. 16-17. On 20 June 1861 (in what amounted to a bill of attainder) Lincoln authorized Scott to suspend the writ of habeas corpus so far as it related to Major Chase, who was accused of treason. Ibid., p. 19. On 2 July 1861 suspension between the cities of Washington and New York, where any resistance should occur, was authorized. Roy P. Basler ed., *The Collected Words of Abraham Lincoln* (New Brunswick, N.J.: Rutgers University Press, 1955), vol. 4, p. 419. On 14 October 1861 suspension was extended as far North as Bangor, Maine. Ibid., p. 554. Lincoln authorized suspension in Missouri on 2 December 1861. Ibid., vol. 5, p. 35. On 24 September 1862 Lincoln proclaimed that "the writ of *habeas corpus* is suspended in respect to all persons arrested, or who are now or hereafter during the rebellion shall be imprisoned in any fort, camp, arsenal, military prison, or other place of confinement by any military authority or by the sentence of any court-martial or military commission." 6 Richardson, *Messages* 98-99. An 8 August 1862 suspension applied to all draft evaders. Ibid., p. 121.

The above suspensions were without explicit Congressional sanction. It might be claimed that the Act of 6 August 1861, 12 U.S. Statutes at Large 326 [passed during the special session which Lincoln called 15 April 1861 (two days after the firing on Ft. Sumter) to meet on 4 July 1861, 12 U.S. Statutes at Large 1258] authorized the suspensions proclaimed earlier. Arthur E. Sutherland, *Constitutionalism in America: Origin and Evolution of Its Fundamental Ideas* (New York: Blarsdell Publishing Co., 1965), p. 411. It provided, *inter alia*, that

> . . . All the acts, proclamations, and orders of the President of United States after the fourth of March, eighteen hundred and sixty-one, respecting the army and navy of the United States, and calling out or relating to the militia or volunteers from the State, are hereby approved and in all respects legalized and made valid, to the same intent and with the same effect as if they had been issued and done under the previous express authority and direction of the Congress of the United States.

The provision was the third and final section of "An Act to increase the Pay of the Privates in the Regular Army and in the Volunteers in the Service of the United States, and other Purposes." It is likely that the provision meant only to apply to the subject of pay and raising an army. In light of the fact that Lincoln, in his 4 July 1861 message, 6 Richardson, *Messages* 24, pointedly called the matter of suspension to Congressional attention, some more specific statute would have been enacted if Congress intended to "validate" the presidential suspensions. The question whether such validation for past suspensions was necessary will be explored herein. (It could not be suggested that the provision authorized future suspensions. The wording of the provision could not bear that interpretation). But, even if suspension could be found to have been authorized by this provision, the question arises, was Congress authorized to validate an illegal executive act? This is not to suggest that Lincoln's pre-summer 1861 suspensions were illegal. *See* text accompanying notes 137-48 *infra*.

Finally, on 3 March 1863, 12 U.S. Statutes at Large 755, Congress enacted a suspension law. It provided:

That during the present rebellion the President of the United States whenever in his judgment the public safety may require it is authorized to suspend the privilege of the writ of *habeas corpus* in any case throughout the United States or any part thereof. And whenever and wherever the said privileges shall be suspended as aforesaid no military or other officer shall be compelled in answer to any writ of *habeas corpus* to return the body of any person or persons detained by him by authority of the President; but upon a certificate oath of the officer having charge of any one detained that such person is detained by him as a prisoner under the authority of the President further proceedings under the writ of *habeas corpus* shall be suspended by the judge or court having issued the writ so long as said suspension of the President shall remain in force and said rebellion continues.

The phraseology of the act is peculiar. It stated that the President "is authorized" rather than "is hereby authorized." The ambiguity as to whether Congress intended the act to be an investiture or a validation was designed. Stevens, who introduced the bill in the House (*Congressional Globe*, 37th Congress, 3rd Sess., pp. 14, 20), was of the opinion that the power to suspend was exclusively vested in Congress. However, in response to an argument by Representative Olin, who asserted that the bill was unnecessary because "the President had the authority by law, and was the proper tribunal, to exercise all the powers that he has exercised in suspending the writ of habeas corpus . . ." (ibid., pp. 20-21), Stevens noted that his bill did not confess the illegality of the President's suspension: "if the President of the United States has the power, then this bill confers nothing additional, and can do no harm. If the President does not have the power, then it seems to me proper that he should receive it. . . ." Ibid., p. 22. In the Senate, Doolittle said of the clause (The clause was not only contained in Stevens' bill— H.R. 591—but was inserted as an amendment to H.R. 362 by Senator Trumbull. It is to the clause as contained in the latter bill that Doolittle's remarks are addressed.):

> It does not assume to say that "the President is hereby authorized to do it"; and therefore those persons who conscientiously maintain that under the Constitution the President is clothed with power without any legislation of Congress, can vote for this sanction upon the ground that this section is merely declaratory of a power which inheres in him under the Constitution itself; and those who maintain that it is to be derived from an act of Congress can sustain this section upon the ground that it is an enacting clause which gives him the power.

Congressional Globe, 37th Congress, 3rd Sess., p. 1092. *See generally,* George Clarke Sellery, "Lincoln's Suspension of Habeas Corpus As Viewed by Congress," Bulletin of the University of Wisconsin, History Series, vol. 1, no. 3, p. 213 at 249-50; Homer Carey Hockett, *Constitutional History of the United States 1826-1876* (New York: Macmillan Co., 1939), pp. 283-84; John D. Sharer, "Power, Idealism, and Compromise: The Coordinate Branches and the Writ of Habeas Corpus," 26 Emory L. J. 149, 168-75 (1977). Sect. 2 of the 1863 statute placed regulations on the suspension proclamation. *See generally,* James G. Randall, *Constitutional Problems Under Lincoln* (New York: D. Appleton and Co., 1926), pp. 165-67. Lincoln's assent, therefore, might be interpreted as an acknowledgment of at least Congressional power to regulate suspension. And of course, the power to regulate is the power to destroy. *McCullock v. Maryland,* 4 Wheat. 316 (1819). But, legal and constitutional issues probably did not interest Lincoln, who viewed the power to suspend as essential for the Union's survival. Whether it was given to him by Congress or whether he had to take it was insignificant.

A substantial minority protested the constitutionality of the congressional delegation. A protest by thirty-six members of the House submitted in the form of a resolution by Pendleton on 22 December 1862, challenging the legality of the delegation [however, *see Martin v. Mott,* 12 Wheat. 19, 28-29 (1827); *Luther v. Borden,* 7 How. 1, 42-45 (1849)], was tabled 75-41. *Congressional Globe,* 37th Congress, 3rd Sess., pp. 165-66.

Lincoln's suspension policy continued on the same course after the Act of 1863. On 15 September 1863 Lincoln, citing both the habeas clause of the Constitution and the Congressional statute, issued a general suspension to continue for the duration of the rebellion, or until modified or revoked by subsequent proclamation, for any persons held "by the authority of the President of the United States, military, naval, and civil officers of the United States, or any of them" who are in custody

> either as prisoners of war, spies, or aiders or abetters of the enemy, or officers, soldiers, or seamen enrolled or drafted or mustered or enlisted in or belonging to the land or naval forces of the United States, or as deserters therefrom, or otherwise amenable to the military laws or the rules and articles of war or the rules and regulations prescribed for the military or naval services by authority of the President of the United States, or for resisting a draft, or for any other offense against the military or naval service.

6 Richardson, *Messages* 170-71. Two days later, Lincoln ordered all military officers to refuse to produce the body of a prisoner before a court if directed by habeas corpus. Basler, *Lincoln,* vol. 6, p. 460. Finally, on 5 July 1864, the suspension was extended to Kentucky. 6 Richardson, *Messages* 219-21.

111. *See* Unknown Author, *Thoughts on the Suspension of the Writ of Habeas Corpus* (London, 1794); Lord John Russell, *An Essay on the History of English Government and Constitution* (London, 1823). *See also* Glanville Sharp, "An address to the People of England Being a Protest of a Private Person Against every Suspension of Law that is liable to injure or endanger Personal Security," London, 1778; R. S. Sheridan, "Liberty and Peace," speech in House of Commons, 5 January 1795. *See also* Basler, *Lincoln,* vol. 6, p. 264; *Ex parte Milligan,* 71 U.S. 2, 125-26 (1866); *McCall v. McDowell,* 15 Fed. Cas. 1235 (1867); Binney, 1, p. 18; and, especially, remarks of Judge Sumner in Massachusetts convention, text accompanying note 59 *supra.*

112. It is admitted that an argument based solely upon an analogy between the practice of the British Parliament and the United States Congress would be fatal. It is one thing to draw analogies when private and individual

rights are concerned, or when one is searching for the meaning of a term; but in the distribution of political powers between the departments of government there is such a wide difference between the English and American governments that it is unsafe to reason from any supposed resemblance between them. The Constitution is the basic guide. However, when questions concerning the practice established by the framers arise, it is useful to attempt to reconstruct what the framers knew.

113. *Darnel's Case*, 3 State Trials 1 (1627) and debates following.

114. 5 Car. I c. 1 (1627).

115. *See* ch. 1, text accompanying notes 356-64 *supra*.

116. 31 Car. 2 c. 2 (1679).

117. *See* 1 Wm. and M. I c. 2, 7, 19 (1688); 7 and 8 Wm. III c. 11 (1694); 6 Ann I c. 15 (1707); 1 Geo. I s. 2 c. 8, 30 (1714); 9 Geo. I c. 1 (1722); 17 Geo. II c. 6 (1744); 17 Geo. III c. 9 (1777); 18 Geo. III c. 1 (1778); 19 Geo. III c. 1, 17 (1779); 20 Geo. III c. 5 (1780); 21 Geo. III c. 2 (1781); 22 Geo. III c. 1 (1782). Suspension occasionally amounted to a bill of attainder and specifically named the individual it was directed towards, 7 and 8 Wm. III c. 11 (1696) [continued by 8 and 9 Wm. III c. 5 (1696); 9 Wm. III c. 4 (1697); 10 and 11 Wm. III c. 13 (1698); 1 Ann I s. 1 c. 29 (1702); 1 Geo. I s. 2 c. 7 (1704); 1 Geo. II s. 1 c. 4 (1727)].

118. It should be noted that suspension did not legalize arrest and detention. Isaac Myer, *Presidential Power Over Personal Liberty* (1862), p. 28. It merely suspended the benefit of a particular remedy in the specified cases. The suspension statute was usually accompanied by an act of indemnity.

119. *Rex v. Despard*, 101 Eng. Rep. 1226 (1798) (Grose, J.).

120. *Rex. v. Earl of Orrery et al.*, 88 Eng. Rep. 75 (1722).

121. *See* intro., text accompanying note 24 *supra*. The operation and effect of suspension in the United States is similar to that in England. By the habeas clause, it is the *privilege* of the writ that is suspended and not the writ of habeas corpus nor any habeas corpus act. In *Ex parte Milligan*, 71 U.S. 2, 130-31 (1866) the Court, in *dicta*, stated:

> The suspension of the privilege of the writ of habeas corpus does not suspend the writ itself. The writ issues as a matter of course; and on the return made to it the court decides whether the party applying is denied the right of proceeding any further with it.

[Those interested in exploring this case should consult Samuel Klaus (ed.), *The Milligan Case* (London: George Routledge and Sons Ltd., 1929); Charles Fairman, *History of the Supreme Court: Reconstruction and Reunion, 1864-1888* (New York: Macmillan Co., 1971), pt. 1, pp. 185-237; Warren, *Supreme Court*, vol. 2, pp. 418-54.] This is not to say that habeas corpus is a writ of course. *See* intro., text accompanying note 24 *supra*; *Ex parte Vallandigham*, 28 Fed. Cas. 874 (1863). In *Ex parte Zimmerman*, 132 F.2d 422 (1942), the court found the *Milligan* dicta of little use because the petition itself disclosed the futility of further inquiry. On the face of the petition it was apparent that the prisoner had been subject to detention by the military authorities after an inquiry related in some way to the public safety, in an area where martial law was in force and the privilege of the writ had been lawfully suspended. The rejection of the petition for habeas relief in *Zimmerman* was therefore not commanded directly by the suspension; rather, the nature of the writ itself led the court to refuse the petitioner. The suspension composed part of the factual context within which the court considered the petition. Thus, if for any reason it appears on the face of the petition that the prisoner is rightfully detained, the writ will be denied. In the case of suspension, if it does not appear that the petitioner falls within the class excluded from the privilege of the writ, or if there is an irregularity in the suspension, the court may issue the writ. Very simply, the writ is only the means. The ends are discharge, bail, or a speedy trial. Suspension of the privilege is suspension of those ends as secured by means of the writ. *See* William S. Church, *A Treatise on Habeas Corpus* (San Francisco: Bancroft-Whitney Co., second edition, 1893), p. 42; Charles Fairman, *The Law of Martial Rule* (Chicago: Callaghan and Co., 1930), pp. 44 and 45 and cases cited at note 61; *McCall v. McDowell*, 15 Fed. Cas. 1235 (1867); *People v. Gaul*, 44 Barb. (N.Y.) 98, 105 (1865).

122. *See* Ch. 2, text accompanying note 66 *supra*.

123. *See* Ch. 2, text accompanying note 133 *supra*.

124. *See* Ch. 2, text accompanying note 56 *supra*.

125. Marshall in *United States v. Burr*, 25 Fed. Cas. 55, 165 (1807) stated: "[It would] be expected that an opinion which is to override all former precedents, and to establish a practice never before recognized, should be expressed in plain and explicit terms. A mere implication ought not to prostrate a principle which seems to have been well established."

126. Attorney General Bates pointed out that Marshall, in *Bollman*, was referring to the power vested by the Judiciary Act of 1789. *The War of Rebellion: A Compilation of the Official Records of the Union and Confederate Armies* (Washington: Government Printing Office, 1880-1901), series 2, vol. 2, p. 28. This point was later embraced by Randall, *Constitutional Problems Under Lincoln*, p. 133 and Sherrill Halbert, "Suspension of the Writ of Habeas Corpus by President Lincoln," 2 Am. J. Leg. Hist. 95, 109 (1958). However, according to Marshall's thesis, the habeas clause imposed an obligation on Congress to empower the courts with habeas jurisdiction, the privilege of the writ could only be activated by legislation. In the absence of legislation, the privilege did not exist, and only Congress could suspend the act, therefore only Congress could suspend the privilege.

127. 3 Martin 530, 6 Am. Dec. 675 (1815).

128. *See generally*, Joseph Alston (pseud. Agrestis), *A Short Review of the Late Rebellion at New Orleans* (South Carolina, 1815); John Spenser Bassett, *The Life of Andrew Jackson* (Archon Books, 1967; reprint of 1937 ed.), pp. 208-32. Jackson not only disregarded the writ during his declaration of martial law, but when in the case of Louailler (a member of the Assembly) United States District Judge Dominick A. Hall issued the writ, the judge was arrested. When the federal district attorney applied to a state judge for Hall's release on habeas corpus, both the district attorney and the state judge were arrested. Louailler's case was dismissed for want of jurisdiction by a court-martial, but Jackson set aside the court's decision. After receiving official word of the treaty of peace between England and the United States, Jackson revoked martial law and released his prisoners. Hall, determined to vindicate the authority of the civil government, held Jackson in contempt for refusing obedience to the writ of habeas corpus and fined him $1,000. Jackson paid the fine, which on 16 February 1844 was remitted by Congress with interest.

The reason for the remission seems to have been simply a desire to pay honor to a national hero on the verge of death. Ibid., pp. 224-32, 745. Perhaps in response to Jackson's actions, a motion was introduced in the House by Wilde on 13 December 1815 requesting the Judiciary Committee to inquire whether any, and if any what additional, provisions were necessary for the more effectual awarding, granting, issuing, and returning writs of habeas corpus. *Annals*, 14th Cong., 1st Sess., p. 385. Nothing seems to have come of the inquiry. Interestingly, an unsuccessful bill to more firmly secure the benefits of the writ was reported from Senate Judiciary Committee less than a year after Jackson's refund.

129. 6 Am. Dec. 675, 676. *See also* Derbigney, J. (concurring) at ibid., p. 685:

> "[C]onscience of the necessity of removing all impediments to the exercise of the executive power in cases of rebellion or invasion, [the framers] have permitted congress to suspend the privilege of the writ of *habeas corpus* in those circumstances [i.e. rebellion or invasion], if the public safety should require it. Thus far, and no further, goes the constitution. Congress has not hitherto thought it necessary to authorize that suspension. Should the case ever happen, it is to be supposed that it would be accomplished with such restrictions as would permit any wanton abuse of power."

130. *Commentaries*, vol. 2, section 1342, pp. 196-97.

131. *A Treatise on the Right of Personal Liberty and on the Writ of Habeas Corpus* (Albany, New York: W. C. Little and Co., 1876; first ed. 1858), p. 116. For additional sources supporting exclusive legislative power to suspend, *see* Tatlow Jackson, *Authorities Cited Antagonistic to Mr. Horace Binney's Conclusion on the Writ of Habeas Corpus* (Philadelphia, 1862). Further, it is also interesting to note the difference between Lincoln's view and the view of Davis on the suspension member of the habeas clause. (Art. I, sect. 9, cl. 2 of the United States Constitution was reenacted verbatim in the Constitution of the Confederate States, Art. I, sect. 9, cl. 3). Unlike Lincoln, Davis refrained from suspension until he was authorized by Congress. Act of 27 February 1862, 1st Sess., c. 2. The act was passed without debate in the upper house and with only slight maneuvering in the lower. Journal of Confederate Congress, vol. 2, pp. 28-29; 5, p. 34 (extended, Act of 13 October 1862, 1st Congress, 2nd Sess., c. 51). *See generally,* Frank Lawrence Owsley, *State Rights in the Confederacy* (Chicago: University of Chicago Press, 1925), p. 151; William M. Robinson, Jr., *Justice In Grey* (Cambridge, Mass.: Harvard University Press, 1941), chapter 27; Clarence D. Douglas, "Conscription and the Writ of Habeas Corpus in North Carolina during the Civil War," Trinity College Historical Papers (Durham, N.C.: 1922), series 14, pp. 34-39.

132. 6 Richardson, *Messages* 24-25.

133. Concurring in this view was the author of an 1861 article entitled "Writ of Habeas Corpus," Henry Dutton (9 Am. L. Reg. 705, 716), who stated:

> It would be a strange way of preserving the privilege of the writ of habeas corpus, to so construe the Constitution as to cause its loss. If the Constitution is destroyed, what use is the privilege.

What right has any one to the privilege but a legal citizen? Why should any one trouble himself to secure a rebel a franchise under a Constitution he is endeavoring to destroy?

See also Kennedy, *Habeas Corpus*, p. 9:

The President, as Executive, executes, and takes care that the laws are faithfully executed. As President, presiding over the laws, he employs the authority of the constitution and laws, and the means furnished under them, *with such others as the exigences of the occasion require* . . . The cause that justifies, is the law that orders the act. . . .

134. *Ex parte Milligan*, 71 U.S. 2, 120-21 (1866). (Obviously, the case is cited not for its authority but for its reasoning.)

135. *See Youngstown Sheet and Tube Co. v. Sawyer*, 343 U.S. 579 (1952).

136. This argument was first suggested by Theophilus Parsons in an article written for the *Boston Daily Advertiser* (5 June 1861), reprinted in Edward McPherson, *The Political History of the United States of America during the Great Rebellion* (Washington: Phillip and Solomons, 1864), p. 162.

137. *Federalist*, no. 69 (Hamilton).

138. I suggest that the action be "absolutely and indispensably necessary" because the President by the Constitution was not invested with auxiliary power—unlike Congress, which was given power "To make all Laws which shall be necessary and proper for carrying into Execution the foregoing Powers, and all other Powers vested by this Constitution in the Government of the United States, or in any Department or Officer thereof." Art. I, sect. 8, cl. 18. By this clause, Congress is said to be not limited to such measures as are absolutely and indispensably necessary, but is empowered to take all appropriate means that are conducive or adapted to the end to be accomplished. *Legal Tender Case*, 110 U.S. 440 (1884). The corollary is that without a "necessary and proper" power, only those actions that are absolutely and indispensably necessary to the office are permissible. Sydney G. Fisher, "The Suspension of Habeas Corpus During the War of Rebellion," 3 Political Science Quarterly 454, 466 asserted that "If it can be shown that the [habeas] clause is a restriction without a grant, it is at once fatal to Binney's whole chain of reasoning. For if the power to suspend could exist without the clause it would be an unlimited power, and no one would think of arguing that the convention would have given it to the President." In fact, the clause was only restrictive and restrictive of only Congressional power, yet it is possible to argue that the President was empowered to suspend in a certain situation, and it is no argument to say that if this were so, the President had been given a greater power than he, the Senate and the House—limited by the habeas clause—had jointly [*Johnson v. Duncan*, 6 Am. Dec. 675, 677 (1815)], for his power would be limited to a very certain case.

139. 2 Farrand 318.

140. Hamilton (*Federalist* no. 70), explained that an energetic executive was "essential to protect the community against foreign attacks . . ."

141. *See* Bernard Schwartz, *Law and the Executive in Britain: A Comparative Study* (New York: New York University Press, 1949), p. 343.

142. Cf. Joel Parker, *Habeas Corpus and Martial Law: A Review of the Opinion of Chief Justice Taney in the Case of John Merryman* (Cambridge, Mass.: Welch, Bigelow and Co., 1861). He argued that "in time of actual war, whether foreign or domestic, there may be justifiable refusals to obey

the command of the writ, without any act of Congress, or any other authority of the President, or any State legislature for that purpose; and that principle upon which such cases are based, is that the existence of martial law, so far as the operation of that law extends, is, *ipso facto*, a suspension of the writ," ibid., pp. 28-29. (Note, *Luther v. Borden*, 12 L. ed. 581, 582-83 note: "The suspension of the writ of habeas corpus is not, in itself, a declaration of martial law; it is simply an incident, though a very important incident, to such declaration. But practically, in England and the United States, the essence of martial law is the suspension of the writ of *habeas corpus*, and a declaration of martial law would be utterly useless unless accompanied by the suspension of the privilege of such a writ. Hence, in the United States the two, martial law and the suspension of the writ is [sic] regarded as one and the same thing.") *See also* Fairman, *The Law of Martial Rule*, p. 165 and *contra*, Samuel Smith Nicholas, *Martial Law* (Philadelphia, 1842); Tatlow Jackson, *Martial Law: What Is It? and Who Can Declare It?* (Philadelphia, 1862); Robert L. Breck, *The Habeas Corpus and Martial Law* (Cincinnati, 1862), who argued that the power to declare martial law resides in Congress. Since Congress was principally charged by the Constitution with power to suspend, if after consultation it refused to sanction the suspension issued by the President in pursuance of his duty to repel a sudden attack, the writ would, under this view, continue in force. This view is strongly supported by *Youngstown Sheet and Tube Co. v. Sawyer*, 343 U.S. 579 (1952).

143. *Marbury v. Madison*, 1 Cranch 137 (1803).

144. *McCollock v. Maryland*, 4 Wheat. 316 (1819).

145. *Hoffman v. Lynch*, 28 F.2d 518 (1928).

146. *See Ex Parte Quirin*, 317 U.S. 1 (1942) and Note, "Habeas Corpus—Suspension of the Writ by Executive or Military Order," 43 Colum. L. R. 408 (1943); and *Ex parte Zimmerman*, 132 F.2d 442 (1942) and Note, "Habeas Corpus—Power of Courts to determine That the Danger Requiring Suspension of the Writ has Passed," 92 U. Pa. L. Rev. 107 (1943).

147. Again it is important to emphasize that the presidential power is activated only when the conditions aforementioned exist.

148. An argument in concurrence with the one set forth here was presented in 1862 by Fisher, *The Trial of the Constitution*, pp. 206-35.

149. Basler, *Lincoln*, vol. 6, 301 note.

150. Ibid., pp. 302-03. Although this statement was made well after the 1861 special session, this was no doubt the position Lincoln had taken even before that session. Note, 10 Opinion Attorney General 71 (24 June 1861).

151. *See also* Dutton, "Writ of Habeas Corpus," 9 Am. L. Reg. 705, 707.

152. *See* remarks of Senator Davis, *Congressional Globe*, 37th Congress, 3rd Sess., p. 530.

153. 1 Farrand 66.

154. Ibid., p. 70.

155. 4 Elliot 329.

156. *Federalist*, no. 69 (Hamilton).

157. Louis Henkin, *Foreign Affairs and the Constitution* (Mineola, New York: Foundation Press, 1972), pp. 50-51; James Wilson, *Works*, R. G. McCloskey ed. (Cambridge, Mass.: Harvard University Press, 1967), vol. 1, p. 440, wrote: "The power of declaring war, *and the other powers naturally connected with it*, are vested in Congress." Emphasis added. *See also* remarks of Senator Davis, *Congressional Globe*, 37th Congress, 3rd Sess., p. 531.

158. Raoul Berger, *Executive Privilege: A Constitutional Myth* (Cambridge, Mass.: Harvard University Press, 1974), p. 67.

159. 6 Richardson, *Messages* 18.

160. Carl Brent Swisher, *Roger B. Taney* (New York: Macmillan Co., 1935), pp. 548-50; Carl Brent Swisher, *The Taney Period 1836-1864* (New York: Macmillan Co., 1974), pp. 843-44.

161. The proclamation itself was couched in terms of resistance to the enemy.

162. What did the case of an illegally enlisted minor have to do with repelling a sudden attack?

163. Full accounts of this incident are to be found at Swisher, *Taney*, pp. 550-56; Swisher, *Taney Period*, pp. 844-54.

164. *Ex parte Merryman*, 17 Fed. Cas. 144 (1861).

165. Ibid., p. 146.

166. Ibid.

167. Similarly, *see In re Winder*, 30 Fed. Cas. 288, 294 (1862). *See* also cases cited by Sharer, "The Coordinate Branches and the Writ of Habeas Corpus," 26 Emory L. J. 149, 162-67.

168. *Ex parte Merryman*, 17 Fed. Cas. 144, 147.

169. Ibid.

170. Ibid., p. 148.

171. Ibid., p. 151.

172. Ibid., pp. 150-51 (referring to Blackstone, *Commentaries*, vol. 1, p. 136).

173. Ibid., pp. 151-52.

174. Ibid., p. 149.

175. Ibid., p. 148.

176. Ibid., p. 149.

177. Ibid., pp. 149-50.

178. Ibid., p. 151.

179. Ibid., p. 153.

180. 10 Opinion of the Attorney General 71 (1861). Lincoln's 4th of July message referred to this opinion for support for his authority, and on 12 July 1861, the House ordered a copy of the opinion to be delivered. *War on Rebellion Records*, series 2, vol. 2, p. 18.

181. 1 Cranch 137 (1803). *See generally*, Edwin S. Corwin, *The Doctrine of Judicial Review: Its Legal and Historical Basis* (Gloucester, Mass.: Peter Smith, 1963).

182. 10 Opinion of the Attorney General 71, 76. Binney 1, p. 36, also perceiving the need to deny the authority of the judicial department to determine the extent of constitutional powers, maintained:

> Chief Justice Taney's opinion in Merryman's case is not an authority. This of course is said in the judicial sense. But it is not even an argument, in the full sense. He does not argue the question from the language of the clause, nor from the history of the clause, nor from the principles of the Constitution. . . . The opinion, moreover, has a tone, not to say a ring, of disaffection to the President and to the Northern and Western side of his house. . . .

See also ibid., p. 5, where Binney, too, asserted that all three branches have co-equal authority to interpret the Constitution.

183. Swisher, *Taney*, pp. 155-57; 196-97.

184. 10 Opinion of the Attorney General 71, 81. Cf. with Myers, *Presidential Power*, p. 28.

185. Ibid., p. 86.

186. *See* A. V. Dicey, *Introduction to the Study of the Laws of the Constitution* (London: Macmillan and Co., 1959), pp. 222-28. *See also* Myers, *Presidential Power*, pp. 76-81. Binney 1, p. 36 argued that the executive branch was in fact the safest place to locate the power. Cf. Myers, *Presidential Power*, pp. 74-81; G. H. Gross, *A Reply to Horace Binney's Pamphlet on the Habeas Corpus* (Philadelphia, 1862), pp. 9-10, 32-34. Unlike the Crown, the American executive is severely limited.

Two comments are perhaps obvious: (1) by resting the power to suspend in limited cases in Congress and allowing the executive such power only when essential to repel sudden attacks, the framers secured the writ from the branch that would exercise powers of arrest and detention. Except in the case where suspension was absolutely necessary to repel a sudden attack, suspension can be effected only by the cooperation of the House of Representatives, the Senate and the Executive; (2) the fact that the executive was limited was a response to the fear of broad executive power—this provides no evidence of broad executive power.

187. 6 Richardson, *Messages* 331-32; 333. *See also Congressional Globe*, 39th Congress, 1st Sess., p. 23. By the Habeas Corpus Act of 1863, suspensions were to cease on 17 February 1865.

188. *In re McDonald*, 16 Fed. Cas. 17 (1861) *See* Swisher, *Taney*, p. 554 for discussion. *See also United States ex rel. Murphy v. Porter*, 27 Fed. Cas. 599 (1861). The writ here issued at the requisition of the parent of a minor who had enlisted without parental consent. Judge William M. Merrick who issued the writ, and the attorney who served it, were placed under arrest. The two remaining circuit judges could do nothing but protest the action and request the President to fulfill his constitutional duty to execute the law. *Ex parte Bender*, 3 Fed. Cas. 159 (1862); *Ex parte Benedict*, 3 Fed. Cas. 159 (1862); *In re Dunn*, 8 Fed. Cas. 93 (1863); *In re Fagan*, 8 Fed. Cas. 947 (1863). The state courts likewise followed *Merryman*: *Jones v. Seward*, 40 Barb. (N.Y.) 563 (1863); *Griffin v. Wilcox*, 21 Ind. 383 (1863); *In re Kemp*, 16 Wisc. 359 (1863). For cases decided after this period, *see McCall v. McDowell*, 15 Fed. Cas. 1235 (1867). The Supreme Court has never dealt directly with the issue; however, in *Ex parte Milligan*, 71 U.S. 2 (1866), in examining the Habeas Corpus Suspension Act of 1863, it stated that "[t]he President was authorized *by it* to suspend the privilege of the writ of *habeas corpus*. . . ." Ibid., at 115 [emphasis added]. Note, the statement was made directly in the face of the government's claim to the contrary, at 18 L. ed. 282.

Contra: *In re Dugan*, 6 D.C. 131 (1865) The case involved two police officers charged with complicity in the robbery of an army paymaster. The prisoners were held in contravention of sect. 2 of the Act of 3 March 1863, 12 U.S. Statutes at Large 755, which provided that if when the federal grand jury met it failed to indict, the prisoners would be entitled to release upon taking an oath of allegiance. It was alleged that two grand juries had come and gone since the arrest. The district court, however, held that the power to suspend was by the Constitution vested exclusively in the President, and therefore the statute was unconstitutional. Counsel for the prisoners filed a petition for habeas corpus and certiorari in the Supreme Court, but before the case could be brought to a decision, the administration, alarmed because many prisoners of high and low degree were held in contravention to the 1863 statute, arranged for Dugan to be released and thus the issue became moot. *See,* however, *Ex parte Milligan,* 71 U.S. 2 (1866) upholding the act; also for a good analogy *see In re Boyle,* 6 Ida. 609, 57P. 706 (1899).

189. Compare Binney, note 18 *supra.*; McParsons, note 136 *supra.*; Kennedy, note 109 *supra.*; Dutton, note 133 *supra.*; Parker, note 142 *supra.*; with Montgomery, note 10 *supra.*; Wharton, note 109(2) *supra.*; Nicholas, notes 29, 109, 142 *supra.*; Myers, note 118 *supra.*; Jackson, note 142 *supra.*; Bullitt, note 18 *supra.*; Brown, note 33 *supra.*; Breck, note 142 *supra.*; Gross, note 186 *supra.*; Ingersoll, note 44 *supra.*; Johnson, note 39 *supra.*; George Ticknor Curtis, *Constitutional History of the United States* (New York, Harper and Brothers, 1896), vol. 2, p. 675. For a survey of many of these pamphlets *see* Sydney G. Fisher, "The Suspension of Habeas Corpus During the War of Rebellion," 3 Political Science Quarterly 454 (1888). For a critique of Binney's work put to lyrics *see* Richard Vaux, *The Habeas Corpus: Its Death and How it Came By It* (Philadelphia, 1862).

190. Congress empowered President Grant to suspend the privilege of the writ of habeas corpus in order to combat the activities of the Klu Klux Klan (17 U.S. Statutes at Large 14-15, 20 April 1871) [exercised on 17 October 1871 in nine counties of North Carolina (Spantenburg, York, Marion, Chester, Laurens, Newberry, Fairfield, Lancester, Chesterfield; revoked in Marion on 3 November 1871; extended to Union county on 10 November 1871). 7 Richardson, *Messages* 136, 138-39, 139-41]. The act carefully limited the duration of the delegation of power to suspend, and the permissible scope and duration of any suspensions under it. It also specified detailed conditions that would justify its exercise. The privilege of the writ was suspended by Theodore Roosevelt in the Philippines in 1905 pursuant to an act of 1 July 1902, 32 U.S. Statutes at Large 692. *See Fisher v. Baker,* 203 U.S. 174 (1906). Suspension in Hawaii during World War II was pursuant to the Hawaiian Organic Act, 31 U.S. Statutes at Large 153 (1900). *See Duncan v. Kahanamoku,* 327 U.S. 304 (1946); J. Garner Anthony, *Hawaii Under Army Rule* (Stanford, Calif.: Stanford University Press, 1955). Cf. however, "Brief in Support of Petitions for Writ of Habeas Corpus," p. 38; *Ex parte Quirin,* text accompanying note 146 *supra.* The issue was raised by counsel but avoided by the Court.

191. The generally accepted view now seems to be that Taney was correct in his contention that the power to suspend was vested in the legislative branch, but that the President might be authorized by Congress to execute an act of suspension. *See* John Mabry Mathews, *The American Constitutional System* (New York: McGraw-Hill Book Co., second edition, 1940), p. 373.

192. *Commonwealth v. Murphy,* 4 Binney 487, 5 Am. Dec. 412 (1812); *In re Stacy,* 10 Johns. (N.Y.) 327 (1813); *Commonwealth v. Cushing,* 11 Massachusetts 67, 6 Am. Dec. 156 (1814); *State v. Dimick,* 12 New Hampshire 197 (1841) and cases therein cited at p. 198. *See also* cases cited by Fairman, *Martial Law,* p. 163 notes; *In re Reynolds,* 20 Fed. Cas. 592 (1867) gives the most extensive list of authorities on this issue; *See In re Bryan,* 60 N.C. 1 (1863) for a case arising in North Carolina during the Civil War.

193. Hurd, *A Treatise on the Right of Personal Liberty and on the Writ of Habeas Corpus,* p. 166, stated: "It may be considered that state courts may

grant the writ in all cases of illegal confinement under the authority of the United States." *See also* Kent, *Commentaries* (Boston: Little, Brown and Co., 1873, 12th ed. by O. W. Holmes; first edition, 1826), pp. 400-10.

194. 6 Opinion of the Attorney General 103 (1853).

195. Ibid., pp. 105-06.

196. Ibid., pp. 107-08.

197. *See* Ch. 5, text accompanying notes 1-30 *infra*.

198. 6 Opinion of the Attorney General 103, 111.

199. Ibid.

200. *See* ch. 5, text accompanying note 12 *infra*.

201. *See* ch. 5, text accompanying notes 1-30 *infra*.

202. *Williamson et al. v. Berry*, 8 How. 495, 540 (1850). *See also Elliot et al. v. Persol et al.*, 1 Peters 328, 340 (1828).

203. 6 Opinion of the Attorney General 713 (1854).

204. 9 U.S. Statutes at Large 462 (1850). On passage of the Act, *see* Don E. Fehrenbacher, *The Dred Scott Case: Its Significance in American Law and Politics* (N.Y.: Oxford University Press, 1978), pp. 160, 161, 162-3.

205. Ibid., p. 177.

206. *In re Booth*, 3 Wisc. 144 (1854).

207. *See also Bagnall v. Ableman*, 4 Wisc. 163 (1855). Cf. 7 Opinions of the Attorney General 482 (1855).

208. The situation now began to resemble the jurisdictional battles which took place in England. *See* ch. 1, text accompanying notes 211-308 *supra*.

209. *Ableman v. Booth*, 62 U.S. 503 (1858).

210. Ibid., pp. 514-15.

211. Ibid., pp. 515-16.

212. Ibid., p. 523.

213. *See* Fehrenbacher, *Dred Scott*, pp. 234, 341.

214. United States Constitution, Amendment 10. This argument may have seemed less compelling to a judge watching more and more states being added to the federal system.

215. 100 U.S. 371 (1879).

216. *See* ch. 5, text accompanying notes 59-63 *infra*.

217. *See* Arthur Bestor, "State Sovereignty and Slavery: A Reinterpretation of Proslavery Constitutional Doctrine, 1846-1861," 54 Journal of the Illinois State Historical Society 117-80 (1961).

218. *See generally*, Stanley I. Kutler, *Judicial Power and Reconstruction Politics* (Chicago: University of Chicago Press, 1968), Ch. 2.

219. *See* ch. 4, text accompanying notes 88-108 *infra*.

220. *See* sources cited at ch. 4, text accompanying note 67 *infra*.

221. *Ex parte Anderson*, 16 Iowa 595 (1864); *People v. Gaul*, 44 Barb. (N.Y.) 98 (1865); *Ex parte McCarey*, 2 American Law Review (Me.) 347 (1867); *In re Reynolds*, 20 Fed. Cas. 592 (1867) and cases therein cited at p. 596, col. 2, first full paragraph. *See also* cases cited at 37 Am. Dec. 203.

This use of the writ was not enthusiastically supported by the federal government. 7 Opinions of the Attorney General 123, 132 (1855).

222. *In re Tarble*, 25 Wisc. 390, 3 Am. Rep. 85 (1870).

223. 3 Am. Rep. 95-96.

224. *United States v. Tarble*, 80 U.S. 397 (1871).

225. Ibid., pp. 403-04.

226. Ibid., pp. 408-09. This reasoning was inspired no doubt by Civil War.

227. Ibid., pp. 409-10.

228. United States Constitution, Article VI, clause 3. *See Robb v. Connolly,* 111 U.S. 624, 637 (1883): "Upon the State courts generally with the courts of the Union, rests the obligation to guard, enforce, and protect every right granted or secured by the Constitution of the United States and the laws made in pursuance thereof, whenever those rights are involved in any suit or proceeding before them. . . ." Note the difficulty the Court in *Ex parte Royall,* 117 U.S. 241, 248-49 (1885), had with bringing the *Connolly* and *Booth-Tarble* principles into line. *See also Cook v. Hart,* 146 U.S. 183 (1892); *Eisentrager v. Forrestal,* 174 F.2d 961, 966 (1949).

229. *See* Thomas Carl Spelling, *A Treatise on Extraordinary Relief In Equity and At Law* (Boston: Little, Brown and Co., 1893), pp. 947-51.

230. *See* Elizabeth Zoline, *Federal Appellate Jurisdiction and Procedure* (New York: Clark Boardman Ltd., 1928), p. 214; Rex A. Collings, "Habeas Corpus for Convicts—Constitutional Right or Legal Grace?" 40 Calif. L. Rev. 335, 346-61; Oaks, "The Original Writ of Habeas Corpus," 1962 S. Ct. Rev. 153, 154-55. *See also Ex parte Bollman,* 4 Cranch 75, 93-94; *United States v. Hudson,* 7 Cranch 32 (1812); *In re Burrus,* 136 U.S. 586 (1890); *Carbo v. United States,* 364 U.S. 611, 614 (1961).

Two attempts were made in 1864 to amend the Constitution and secure the privileges of habeas corpus. *See* Herman Ames, *The Proposed Amendments of the Constitution of the United States During the First Century of its History* (1896, New York: Burt Franklin, 1970) pp. 190-92.

231. Cf. *Zakonaite v. Wolf,* 226 U.S. 272 (1912); *United States v. Hayman,* 342 U.S. 205 (1951); *United States v. Anselmi,* 207 F.2d 312 (1953), *cert. den.* 347 U.S. 902, *reh. den.* 347 U.S. 940 (1954); *Tanfara v. Esperdy,* 347 F.2d 149 (1965). Cf. also *Fay v. Noia,* 372 U.S. 391, 406 (1963) and Abraham D. Sofaer, "Federal Habeas Corpus for State Prisoners: The Isolation Principle," 39 N.Y.U. L. Rev. 78, 79, fn. 6; Louis H. Pollack, "Proposals to Curtail Federal Habeas Corpus for State Prisoners: Collateral Attack on the Great Writ," 66 Yale L. J. 50, 63.

232. *Gasquet v. Lapeyre,* 242 U.S. 367 (1916); *Geach v. Olsen,* 211 F.2d 682 (1954). Cf. *Alcorcha v. State of California,* 86 S. Ct. 1359 (1966), where Mr. Justice Douglas suggested that Art. I, sect. 9 applies to the state government as well as to the federal government. Support for Douglas' assertion may be found in Attorney General Randolph's brief for the government in *Chisolm v. State of Georgia,* 2 Dall. 418, 421 (1793). Randolph seems to have inadvertently included the restriction in the habeas clause among the restrictions on the states contained in Art. I, sect. 10.

Federal Habeas for State Prisoners   -4-

INTRODUCTION

The preceding chapter presented only part of the story of the impact of political conflict between the state and federal governments upon the law of habeas corpus. As dramatic as, and more significant today than, the impact of that political conflict on the habeas clause was its impact on the availability of federal habeas for state prisoners.

The states were conceived of as the primary protectors of individual liberty and therefore, shortly after adoption of the Constitution, which secured state habeas for federal prisoners, Congress denied federal courts habeas jurisdiction in state cases. In time, however, that jurisdiction was gradually extended by Congress to effectuate federal policy. The "new federalism" symbolized by the Civil War should not be exaggerated. The federal policy which Congress sought to further by habeas legislation enacted after the Civil War seemed to be threatened by that legislation and adjustments were made. The adjustments themselves caused an unwelcome change in the established view of federalism and Congress moved to restore state courts as the primary protectors of individual liberty. The Supreme Court responded with the doctrine of exhaustion. That doctrine was strengthened during the first half of the twentieth century. The more progressive idea of criminal justice articulated by the Warren Court, however, demanded that the exhaustion doctrine be recognized as a more flexible concept so that the Court could communicate more effectively its more progressive idea to the states. Once again, habeas corpus became the medium for broadcasting federal policy.

The writ, therefore, has not merely been a legal process used to effect an individual's release. The Great Writ has been a means of announcing federal policy. When Mr. Justice Powell, in a recent case to be considered in the following chapter,[1] accused the Court of a lack of "historical perspective"[2] by allowing habeas corpus to serve as a "*general* writ meant to promote the social good" rather than "to serve a precise and particular *purpose*,"[3] it was he who had lost perspective.

THE ACT OF 1789

Section 14 of the Act of 1789 provided:

> . . . That all the before-mentioned courts of the United States, shall have power to issue writs of *scire facias*, *habeas corpus*, and all other writs not specifically provided for by statute, which may be necessary for the exercise of their respective jurisdictions, and agreeable to the principles and usages of law. And that either of the justices of the supreme court, as well as judges of the district courts, shall have power to grant writs of *habeas corpus* for the purpose of an inquiry into the cause of commitment.—Provided, That writs of *habeas corpus* shall in no case extend to prisoners in gaol, unless where they are in custody, under or by colour of the authority of the United States, or are committed for trial before some court of the same, or are necessary to be brought into court to testify.[4]

For present purposes, attention is directed to the proviso with which the section concludes. The grammatical construction of the section creates a problem: does the proviso refer to the second clause only and therefore leave unrestricted the habeas power of federal *courts* in cases of state prisoners, or does the proviso apply to the entire preceding part?[5] Mr. Chief Justice Marshall read the proviso as applicable to the entire section: "It limits the power previously granted the courts, because it specifies a case in which it is particularly applicable to the use of the power by courts—where the person is necessary to be brought into court to testify."[6] If by "particularly applicable," Marshall meant that *habeas corpus ad testi-*

ficandum was "only useful" to the courts,[7] his reasoning gives no support to his conclusion. The writ of habeas corpus was, in the words of the preamble of a British statute enacted four years before Bollman, "frequently awarded by *Judges* of his Majesty's Courts of Record at *Westminster*, for bringing Persons detained in Custody under civil or criminal Process before Magistrates or Courts of Record, as well for Trial for Examination touching Matters depending before such Magistrates or Courts. . . ."[8] There can be little doubt that the power was useful to a judge in chambers as he planned the term's agenda.

Marshall employed the argument to refute the contention that by the first sentence of section 14 Congress meant to give the courts no more than ancillary power. If the section were only ancillary, then according to Marshall's analysis,[9] the only power given by the section was authority to issue *ad testificandum*. This construction was to Marshall's mind clearly erroneous: "That construction cannot be a fair one which would make the legislature except from the operation of a proviso, limiting the express grant of a power, the whole power intended to be granted." That is, the whole power would not be the object of an exception. If at this point Marshall, by the phrase "particularly applicable," was saying that *ad testificandum* was limited to the courts because *by statute* individual judges were not empowered to issue *ad testificandum*, then the argument follows.

If one examines the constituent elements of the section individually, this final reading of *Bollman* would seem correct. The section consists of two distinct affirmative sentences and a qualifying proviso. The first sentence confers the power to issue writs of habeas corpus on the courts generally.[10] No particular form of the writ is specified—the phrase being "generic," it "includes every species of the writ."[11] The second sentence confers power on both justices of the Supreme Court and judges of the district courts to grant the writ for the purpose of inquiring into the cause of commitment. The phrase is no longer used in its generic sense; it is qualified. The individual justices and judges are empowered to issue *only* writs of *habeas corpus ad subjiciendum*. The proviso limits the power of exercising jurisdiction by means of the writ in the case of prisoners in jail unless they are in custody under or by color of the authority of the federal government. The general scope of the proviso is also qualified by the last clause, which allows *habeas corpus ad testificandum* to issue in order that prisoners in jail may be brought up to act as witnesses, irrespective of the authority, state or federal, under which they are confined. Since only the courts have this power, the qualifying section of the proviso necessarily applied solely to the courts.

The short-lived Judiciary Act of 1801[12] does not detract from this reading.[13] Although the second sentence, along with the proviso,[14] was separated from the first sentence,[15] the proviso was amended to read: "that no writ of habeas corpus, *to be granted under this act*,[16] shall extend to any prisoner or prisoners in gaol, unless such prisoner or prisoners be in custody, under or by colour of the authority of the United States, or be committed for trial before some court of the same; or be necessary to be brought into court to give testimony." The separated first clause was thereby united with the proviso.

It has been argued that the final clause of the proviso is not a limitation of power at all, but rather a grant of power to allow *habeas corpus ad subjiciendum* to issue regardless of the character of a prisoner's custody if he is needed to testify. This rather tortuous reading was suggested by counsel for the respondent in *Bennett v. Bennett* in 1867.[17] The court there noted that "this construction rests the power upon the proviso alone, and simply ignores all the rest of the section." If the proviso had stood alone, or perhaps if the section had begun with the proviso, this suggestion might seem valid. But, the proviso was placed in a position to qualify those powers already delegated. In addition, if Congress had meant to give individual justices and judges this power, a more artful means would have been available. Further, if this were their intention, why specifically limit the power of the individual justice or judge to issue the *ad subjiciendum* form of the writ? Why utilize an *ad subjiciendum* to perform the function of an *ad testificandum*? In no way does this argument rise to even a *prima facie* case.

The reading of the provision endorsed here is consonant with the intellectual predisposition of those who framed the "first habeas corpus act" of the United States. Naturally, one of the first thoughts men considering such legislation would have would be of the famous Habeas Corpus Act of 1679. The *Commentaries* by Blackstone,[18] the most popular legal text of the day, pointed to the *Case of Jenkes*[19] as the impetus for the Act, [20] and of course, the problem for Jenkes was obtaining habeas corpus in vacation. The Habeas Corpus Act of 1679 solved problems such as those of Jenkes by empowering "the lord chancellor or lord keeper, or any one of his majesty's justices, either of one bench or of the other, or the barons of the exchequer of the degree of coif" to issue the writ of *habeas corpus ad subjiciendum* in vacation.[21] Likewise, the American "habeas corpus act" of 1789 sought to eliminate such a problem by empowering the justices of the Supreme Court and judges of the district courts to issue the writ in chambers, as well as when assembled as a court.

Another of the first thoughts probably occurring to the men of the first Congress as they sought to enact the grand design for the judiciary's operation was the fact that they were not only members of the United States Congress, but representatives of their various states; that is, the dictates of federalism were working their influences in the writing of the act. There was strong opposition even to the establishment of inferior federal tribunals during the Convention and during the first Congress. Mason, for one, was not happy with the final form of Article III. He wrote:

> The Judiciary of the United States is so constructed and extended, as to absorb and destroy the judiciaries of the several States; thereby rendering law as tedious, intricate and expensive, and justice as unattainable, by a great part of the community, as in England, and enabling the rich to oppress and ruin the poor.[22]

This view remained strong after ratification of the Constitution. During the *Bollman* affair, Mr. Broom introduced a resolution in the House "That it is expedient to make further provision by law, for securing the privilege of the writ of habeas corpus. . . ."[23] He noted that "[t]he violations of our Constitutional provisions at New

Orleans, have shown clearly the insufficiency of existing laws. . . ."
One of the objections raised against the resolution was that

> Each State is competent, it is presumed, to pass laws for the
> protection of the rights and liberties of its citizens; for the
> regulation of its internal and domestic concerns—and in this
> consists the independence of the respective States. The means
> of obtaining the benefit of the writ of habeas corpus, and the
> mode of prosecuting the same, are evidently domestic regu-
> lations, essential to every free government, and constitute an
> important part of the laws of the several States—and the right
> to the privileges of this writ is secured to the citizens by the
> Constitution of every State in the Union. This will not be
> denied, nor will it be pretended that the States have not laws
> to enforce obedience to the writ. If, therefore, you pass a law
> on this subject, it will, if it has any effect, control the laws of
> the several States; and, in Proportion as it has this effect, it
> weakens the respective State authorities, and tends to consoli-
> date their powers in the General Government.[24]

Marshall's reading of the proviso was endorsed by a later Court
in *Ex parte Dorr*.[25] There, Thomas W. Dorr, who had been sentenced to life imprisonment by a state court for his part in the Rhode
Island rebellion, was before the Supreme Court on a writ of *habeas
corpus ad testificandum*. However, Dorr's petition for an *ad subjiciendum* was denied, the Court finding that

> Neither this nor any other court of the United States, or
> judge thereof, can issue a habeas corpus to bring up a prisoner,
> who is in custody under a sentence or execution of a State
> court, for any other purpose than to be used as a witness. And
> it is immaterial whether the imprisonment be under civil or
> criminal process.[26]

As may be inferred from the citations above, and as stated explicitly by the judiciary, the purpose of the proviso was to prevent conflict between the tribunals of the state and federal governments.[27]

THE ACTS OF 1833 AND 1842

In the first half of the nineteenth century, federal habeas corpus was extended to two classes of state prisoners. The first act extending federal habeas relief was passed in 1833 [28] during the nullification controversy in South Carolina.[29] South Carolina was particularly affected by the tariffs established during the first third of the nineteenth century, and in the fall of 1828, the South Carolina legislature passed the "Exposition and Protests," setting forth the theory of nullification.[30] In response to the tariff of 1832, a convention of the "People of South Carolina" was assembled and the tariffs of 1828 and 1832 were declared unconstitutional and therefore null and void in South Carolina.[31] To enforce the tariff, Jackson consented to the idea of using South Carolinians loyal to the federal government as *posse comitatus* to aid the federal marshals attempting to enforce the tariff.[32] This approach was not successful. Unionists could supply neither customs inspectors nor a marshal's posse because the loyalists feared that they would render themselves amenable to state laws.[33] On 16 January 1833, Jackson sent a special message to Congress on the South Carolina situation.[34] Congress responded with "An Act to further provide for the collection of duties on imports," or as it is more commonly called, the Force Bill.[35] Section 7 of the Force Bill provided:

> . . . That either of the justices of the Supreme Court, or a judge of any district court of the United States, in addition to the authority already conferred by law, shall have power to grant writs of habeas corpus in all cases of a prisoner or prisoners, in jail or confinement, where he or they shall be committed or confined on, or by any authority or law, for any act done, or omitted to be done, in pursuance of a law of the United States, or any order, process, or decree, of any judge or court thereof. . . .

At about the same time as the Force Bill was going through Congress, an act modifying the tariffs was also being debated. A reduction in the tariff was worked out and South Carolina repealed its nullification ordinance less than two weeks after the Force Bill went into operation.[36]

Section 7 of the Force Bill remains in effect.[37] Following the South Carolina controversy, the act was used, ironically, to release officers acting under the Fugitive Slave Act [38] imprisoned in northern state jails [39] as well as to release federal officers in southern states following the Civil War.[40] In 1873, section 7 of the 1833 Act was consolidated into section 753 of the Revised Statutes. After formulation of the "exhaustion" rule[41] in 1885, those held "in custody for an act done or omitted in pursuance of a law of the United States, or of an order, process, or decree of a court or judge thereof" were placed in the category of "exceptional circumstances," thus relieving them from the requirement of exhausting state remedies before applying for federal habeas corpus. As shall be seen when some of the cases involving this category are analyzed,[42] the courts that exercised the power to issue the writ were not acting under this provision alone. The provision did not endow the courts with any power to issue the writ. It was addressed to justices of the Supreme Court and judges of the district courts. This distinction was disguised by the Revised Statutes. Any question was avoided by courts issuing the writ because the individual was acting in pursuance of a law of the United States, and his detention therefore was said to be, in the words of the Habeas Corpus Act of 1867, "in violation of the constitution, or any treaty or law of the United States."[43]

The second extension of federal habeas corpus was in response to the case of Alexander McLeod.[44] McLeod, a British citizen, had been indicted in a United States court for his part in the destruction of the American-owned steamboat, the Carolina—which was lending support to the rebellious forces in Canada during the revolt of the winter of 1837-1838. McLeod had been indicted in 1838, and upon entering New York State two years later, was arrested and imprisoned. The British immediately called upon the government of the United States "to take prompt and effectual steps for McLeod's release."[45] The United States responded that since the alleged offense was committed within the jurisdiction of the state of New York, it did not "present an occasion where under the constitution and laws of the Union, the interposition called for would be proper. . . ."[46] McLeod was acquitted.[47] In the opinion of the editor of *American Decisions*,[48] "the conviction of McLeod would doubtless have been followed by an immediate declaration of war [by England] against the United States."

In order to avoid such a situation in the future, Congress enacted a statute that empowered justices of the Supreme Court and judges of the district courts to grant writs of habeas corpus

> in all cases of any prisoner or prisoners in jail or confinement, where he, she, or they, being subjects or citizens of a foreign State, and domicile therein, shall be committed or confined, or [be] in custody, under or by authority or law, or process founded thereon, of the United States or any one of them; for or on account of any act done or omitted under any alleged right, title, authority, privilege, protection, or exemption, set up or claimed under the commission, or order, or sanction, of any foreign State or Sovereignty, the validity and effect whereof depend upon the law of nations, or under color therof.

From the decision of a federal justice or judge, an appeal could be taken to the circuit court, and from the circuit court to the Supreme Court.[49] The Act was passed on a strict party vote[50] after a heated debate—the Democrats[51] arguing that the Act was destructive of state sovereignty in the enforcement of their criminal codes.[52]

THE HABEAS CORPUS ACT OF 1867

The habeas corpus acts considered above were to have a relatively minor impact upon state prisoners in comparison with the act that became law on 5 February 1867.[53] The Act empowered the federal courts and judges, acting "within their respective jurisdictions" with power, "in addition to the authority already conferred by law," to issue writs of habeas corpus "in all cases where any person may be restrained of his or her liberty in violation of the constitution, or of any treaty or law of the United States. . . ."

The words of the statute are unambiguous: that a state, as well as a federal, prisoner may avail himself of the protection of the Act seems all too obvious. However, when one ventures beyond the text of the statute, the meaning of the Act and the intent of its framers are not easy to determine.[54]

There was very little discussion of the Act in Congress. Representative Lawrence, after reading his bill[55] and the Judiciary Committee's amendments thereto, was asked "whether in a case of a person who is not bound to perform service in the Army or Navy is taken possession of by the Government, he is cut off from the benefits of the writ of habeas corpus under this bill."[56] Lawrence answered:

> On the 19th of December last, my colleague [Mr. Shellabarger] introduced a resolution instructing the Judiciary Committee to inquire and report to the House as soon as practicable, by bill or otherwise, what legislation is necessary to enable the courts of the United States to enforce the freedom of the wife [sic] and children of soldiers of the United States, and also to enforce the liberty of all persons.[57] Judge Ballard, of the district court of Kentucky, decided that there was no act of Congress giving courts of the United States jurisdiction to enforce the rights and liberties of such persons.[58] In pursuance of that resolution of my colleagues this bill has been introduced, the effect of which is to enlarge the privilege of the writ of hobeas [sic] corpus, and make the jurisdiction of the courts and judges of the United States coextensive with all the powers that can be conferred upon them. It is a bill of the largest liberty, and does not interfere with persons in military custody, or restrain the writ of habeas corpus at all. I am satisfied there will not be a solitary objection to this bill if it is understood by the House.[59]

The questioner remained confused: "I confess that it is exceedingly difficult for us to determine the scope of this bill." On that comment, discussion ended and the bill was passed.

If the bill were only "[i]n pursuance of" the resolution of 19 December 1865, it would be clear that the Act of 1867 was designed for the class of citizens who continued to be held in slavery or involuntary servitude in contravention of the Thirteenth Amendment and the Joint Resolution of 3 March 1865.[60] In fact, the Lawrence bill was preceded by another habeas bill,[61] introduced by Representative Wilson, chairman of the House Judiciary Committee, which referred specifically to persons "held in slavery or involuntary servitude contrary to the constitution of the United States."[62] Curiously enough, Wilson's proposal was referred to his own committee and died there.

It is reasonable to question the significance of the broader wording of the Lawrence bill. Was it, as Professor Mayers suggested, a change that was effected because those "restrained"[63] under state vagrancy and contract labor statutes might find the broader phrase "more serviceable?"[64] Or did it represent a deliberate attempt to give "all persons" benefit of federal habeas corpus? Was there no thought of the returning Southerners who fought on the side of the Union?[65] Is one to believe that just because the Habeas Corpus Act was considered by the Judiciary Committee and the Reconstruction Acts were considered in the Committee on Reconstruction, and because there was no cross-reference in the discussion of the respective acts,[66] that it did not occur to the framers or legislators who voted for the bill that its provisions would give some benefit to those executing the reconstruction program? If the benefits of the Act were to be extended to some, why not to all? Had not the earlier view that the state courts were the best forums for the preservation of liberty been shaken momentarily by the Civil War? Did not the Act reflect the stronger federal attitude?[67]

In addition, Lawrence's closing statement to his colleagues might be read to carry the intention of the bill beyond the resolution referred to. In explaining the scope of the bill, Lawrence stated that it would enlarge the privilege of the writ, and "make the jurisdiction of the courts and judges . . . coextensive with all the powers that can be conferred upon them." Professor Bator found the clause "largely meaningless."[68] Professor Mayers, reading it in conjunction with the preceding reference to Judge Ballard's decision, suggested that it might indicate an intention "to convey only that lack of jurisdiction. . . ."[69] When Lawrence said that the bill was intended to extend the jurisdiction of the courts and judges to their constitutional limit, were the earlier habeas statutes absent from his mind? There was perhaps still lingering doubt about the power of the courts under the 1789 statute, and the enactments of 1833 and

1842 clearly pertained only to individual judges. Only this can explain the reference in the statute to restraint in violation of the "constitution, or any treaty or laws of the United States. . . ."[70] What application did the second member of that triad have to the case of a freedman? In addition, with the exception of the Civil Rights Act of 1866[71], which adequately provided for removal to the federal courts in cases of freedmen restrained under state vagrancy and contract labor statutes, there were no federal laws that protected the state criminal defendant unless he had been acting under federal authority.[72] Mayers pointed to the statutes of 1863 and 1866,[73] which he contended provided ample protection to state criminal defendants acting under federal authority. But these statutes pertained only to "acts done or omitted to be done during the . . . rebellion. . . ." Acts done or omitted to be done during Reconstruction were not protected by those statutes. And what is the relationship of the phrase extending jurisdiction to the subsequent one? Was it "a bill of the largest liberty" because it extended its benefits to both state and federal prisoners without altering the courts' and judges' existing habeas jurisdiction in the case of military prisoners? This would make Lawrence's answer relevant to the question. One must indeed confess that it is not only difficult to understand the statute, but Lawrence's explanation of it as well.

After the bill was read in the Senate,[74] Senator Davis also expressed difficulty understanding the bill.[75] The chairman of the Judiciary Committee, Senator Lyman Trumbull, explained:

> [T]he *habeas corpus* act of 1789, to which this bill is an amendment, confines the jurisdiction of the United States courts in using writs of habeas corpus to persons who are held under United States laws. Now, a person might be held under a State law in violation of the Constitution and laws of the United States, and he ought to have in such a case the benefit of the writ, and we agree that he ought to have recourse to the United States courts to show that he is illegally imprisoned in violation of the Constitution or laws of the United States. . . .
>
> It is a bill in aid of the rights of the people.[76]

Trumbull's explanation seems clearly to mean that the bill was not limited to freedmen; that it was designed for all those imprisoned for violation of a state statute repugnant to the Constitution and laws of the United States—as distinct from federal prisoners.[77] The chairman, however, confessed his less than complete understanding of the bill. He said that "it was a House bill, not prepared by the Senate," and that he was "sorry that the Senator from Maryland [Mr. Johnson] is not here; he examined it in committee and is in favor of its passage."[78] However, for an understanding of legislative intent, *even if* Trumbull's comprehension were faulty, would his faulty analysis be relevant? Was not Trumbull's vote, as well as the votes of those who listened to his explanation, influenced by his understanding?

When the Act of 1867 is compared with the earlier provisions regulating federal habeas corpus, differences are obvious. The 1867 Act substituted the phrase "any person restrained of his or her liberty" for the word "prisoner." It contained a unique provision for fact determination.[79] Undoubtedly the provisions were well designed as remedies for the situation of the freedman faced with a new system, backed by state law, no better than the "peculiar institution" from which he had been released. But these provisions were not uniquely useful to the case of the freedman—in fact, the provisions were not unique at all. They were all parts of comprehensive habeas corpus acts passed earlier, for other cases. The English habeas corpus acts—long models for state habeas corpus statutes[80] —were the sources of these provisions. The phrase "any person" committed, detained, or in custody, was used interchangeably with the word "prisoner" in the English Acts of 1679[81] and 1816.[82] The time limitation was taken directly from the famous Habeas Corpus Act of 1679,[83] and the fact-determination clause is similar to that in the 1816 statute.[84] Could the provisions of the first comprehensive United States habeas statute have been designed for the federal judiciary as it went about its new assignment dealing with foreign jurisdictions?

In summary, the legislative history of the Act of 1867 adds little to an effort to understand the legislative intent. From the statute itself, a reasonable man would be forced to conclude that any state prisoner was covered by it. Under the reasoning of *Yick Wo v. Hopkins*,[85] a citizen of China, as well as a freedman or a white newspaper reporter from Mississippi, held in violation of federal law, could not be deprived of the protection of the Act, given its broad wording.

SUSPENSION AND RESTORATION OF THE SUPREME COURT'S POWER UNDER THE ACT OF 1867

The year after the passage of the Act of 1867, the case of *Ex parte McCardle*[86] came before the Supreme Court. For the first time, the Court was being called upon to exercise jurisdiction under the new habeas corpus legislation. The case was not that of a freedman, nor even of a state prisoner. It involved, rather, a Mississippi newspaper editor arrested under the Reconstruction Acts and held for trial before a military commission. McCardle petitioned for a writ of habeas corpus in a federal circuit court, challenging the validity of the Reconstruction Act authorizing the military detention and trial of citizens. The circuit court denied the writ and an appeal was taken to the Supreme Court under the 1867 statute, which authorized appeals from the circuit courts.

The government argued that since the Act of 1867 conferred jurisdiction "in addition to" that already conferred, and since under the Judiciary Act of 1789 the courts of the United States already had power to issue the writ in the case of persons in custody under or by color of the authority of the United States, and that the 1867 Act did not overlap the 1789 Act, therefore, the federal courts were given no authority by the later Act in the case of a federal prisoner. The reasoning was rejected. The Court held unanimously that it had jurisdiction to hear McCardle's appeal:

> This legislation is of the most comprehensive character. It brings within the habeas corpus jurisdiction of every court and of every judge every possible case of privation of liberty contrary to the National Constitution, treaties, or laws. It is impossible to widen this jurisdiction.[87]

Under the 1789 measure, in cases such as McCardle's, no review as of right was available; under the 1867 statute, it was. Thus the Court was holding that the benefits of the new act extended to all persons restrained in violation of the Constitution, or of any treaty or law of the United States, irrespective of the authority—state, federal, or otherwise—so restraining.

A few weeks later, the case of *McCardle* was argued on the merits. The Court allowed six hours of oral argument to each side—three times the normal amount.[88] It appeared to observers that the Court would rule on the whole of the reconstruction program.[89] Three days after argument, James F. Wilson, chairman of the House Judiciary Committee, introduced an amendment repealing the appellate jurisdiction of the Court under the 1867 Act.[90] In a sharp parliamentary maneuver, with the opposition caught off guard, the bill was swept through both houses of Congress.[91] Although impeachment proceedings against him were in progress, President Andrew Johnson vetoed the bill, saying that it would establish a precedent, which, if followed, might "eventually sweep away every check on arbitrary and unconstitutional legislation."[92]

The veto, though in the end unsuccessful, allowed debate on the measure. Senator Trumbull, who had been responsible for the passage of the 1867 Act in the Senate, but who was also counsel for the government in *McCardle*, attempted to argue (while the decision in *McCardle* was pending before the Supreme Court) that there was at present no case before the Supreme Court under the Act of 1867:

> The act of 1867 authorized the issuing of all such [habeas corpus] writs in cases where persons were deprived of their liberty under authority or color of authority of the United States. Why, then, was the act of 1867 passed? It was passed to authorize writs of *habeas corpus* to issue in cases where the persons were deprived of their liberty under State laws or pretended State laws. It was the object of the act of 1867 to confer jurisdiction on the United States courts in cases not before provided for, and it was to meet a class of cases, which were arising in the rebel States, where, under pretense of certain state laws, men made free by the Constitution of the United States were virtually being enslaved, and it was also

applicable to cases in the State of Maryland where, under the apprentice laws, freedmen were being subjected to a species of bondage. The object was to authorize *habeas corpus* in those cases to issue from United States courts. . . .[93]

Trumbull, as counsel for the government in *McCardle*, obviously knew that the Court in *McCardle* had held that its jurisdiction under the 1867 statute had attached. Perhaps the chairman of the Senate Judiciary Committee was simply saying the Court's view of its jurisdiction was erroneous. His statement in support of the repealing measure was, after all, completely consistent with his explanation of the habeas corpus proposal when it was before the Senate the previous year.[94]

The bill was repassed over Johnson's veto.[95] The Court, which had postponed a decision on the merits in McCardle's case while its jurisdiction was being reconsidered,[96] held the repealing act valid and dismissed *McCardle* for want of jurisdiction.[97] But the Court noted that the repealing act did not deprive it of all appellate jurisdiction in cases of habeas corpus: "The act of 1868 does not exempt from that jurisdiction any cases but appeals from Circuit Courts under the act of 1867."[98] McCardle therefore could have[99] petitioned the Court for an original writ of habeas corpus and a writ of certiorari. The following year in *Ex parte Yerger*,[100] the Court was asked to exercise its jurisdiction under the Act of 1789.[101]

Yerger had been brought to trial for the murder of Joseph G. Crane, an army officer assigned to act as mayor for the city of Jackson, Mississippi. While on trial before a military commission, Yerger petitioned for, but was denied, a writ of habeas corpus by Circuit Justice Swayne. A later application was granted by Mr. Chief Justice Chase; however, it was superseded by an agreement between the attorney general and counsel for Yerger. Thereafter, an application was addressed to the circuit court. The circuit court found the imprisonment lawful and remanded the applicant. Yerger then sought writs of habeas corpus and certiorari from the Supreme Court. The Court could find nothing in any act of Congress "except the Act of 1868, which indicate[d] any intention to withhold [from it] appellate jurisdiction in habeas corpus cases. . . ."[102] The

Court's jurisdiction was upheld, the writs were granted, and once more a means of reviewing the Reconstruction Acts was open. Again, there was a reaction in Congress: Senator Drake introduced a bill denying the Court's power to review congressional enactments;[103] Senator Sumner introduced a bill that set forth a long philosophical declaration that all three branches of government, "each in its appropriate sphere is authorized to pronounce officially the conclusions of the Government in the matters on which it is required to act" and that such conclusions could not be declared null by another branch;[104] and most important for present purposes was another proposal by Sumner that sought to abolish the Supreme Court's appellate jurisdiction in habeas corpus cases.[105] The Judiciary Committee amended this proposal and recommended a bill that declared the Reconstruction Acts political in character and therefore not open to question by the courts, and further, that until the reconstruction program was complete, the Supreme Court's appellate jurisdiction in habeas corpus cases would be suspended.[106] The Judiciary Committee, *per* Trumbull, further suggested an amendment that declared that no justice or judge could grant a writ of habeas corpus outside his respective circuit or district.[107] In the end, none of these measures succeeded: the Fourteenth Amendment had been adopted; the reconstruction program was drawing to an end; and Yerger's case was not being pressed.[108] The remaining program was more important, and the Republicans must have felt no need to fight the Democrats on this seemingly moot point.

The significance of these events for state prisoners was that the Act of 1868 allowed the lower federal courts and judges to proceed without the aid of the Supreme Court in interpreting the Habeas Corpus Act of 1867. The district and circuit courts exercised jurisdiction under the 1867 statute immediately following trial court convictions,[109] as well as before trial,[110] without regard for the availability of state remedies. In the early 1880s, for example, the federal courts, in a number of cases involving discrimination by the Pacific states and municipalities against immigrant Chinese, released such applicants on habeas corpus prior to trial[111] or immediately following summary convictions,[112] on the ground that the statute or ordinance under which the applicants were being held was unconstitutional under the Fourteenth Amendment. These holdings were not well received by the legal profession. Seymour D. Thompson, editor of the *American Law Review*, at the convention of the American Bar Association in 1883 criticized the lower federal courts' utilization of the writ "to annul the criminal process of the states, to reverse and set aside . . . the criminal judgments of the State courts, and to pass finally and conclusively upon the validity of the criminal codes, the political regulations, and even the constitutions of the states." He argued that although the Congress intended by the 1867 statute that persons arrested upon state process might be enlarged by the federal courts by means of the writ, it was not intended "that it should become a means in the hands of the Federal district and circuit judges of reviewing and reversing the judgments of the States without regard to their rank or dignity."[113] He suggested, therefore, that a method be established whereby "the judgments of the Federal District and Circuit Courts, where such judgments result in annulling the laws or constitutional ordinances of the States, might be brought before the Supreme Court of the United States for revision."[114] Congress was called upon to correct what was perceived as a threat to the federal system. On 3 March 1885, the Supreme Court's jurisdiction under the Act of 1867 was restored.[115] The House Judiciary Committee reported that "[w]ith this right of appeal restored, the true extent of the Act of 1867, and the true limits of the Federal courts and judges under it, will become defined, and it can be seen whether further legislation is necessary."[116] The Court apparently read this as a mandate.

Shortly after the passage of the 1885 statute, the case of *Ex parte Royall*[117] came before the Supreme Court. Royall had been indicted before a Virginia court for selling a tax receivable coupon without a license in violation of a state law. Royall argued that the law was repugnant to Article I, section 10 of the federal Constitution, and therefore null and void. Believing that it lacked jurisdiction, the circuit court denied Royall's petition for a writ of habeas corpus. Royall then appealed to the Supreme Court. The Court was thus asked to determine whether the circuit courts had jurisdiction on habeas corpus to discharge from custody one who was restrained of his liberty in violation of the federal Constitution, but who, at the time, was held under state process for trial on an indictment charging an offense against the laws of the state. Although the Court noted that an unconstitutional statute robbed the state court of jurisdiction[118] and that therefore the circuit courts have power to issue the writ of habeas corpus and discharge an accused in advance of his trial if he were held in violation of the Constitution, it held that the circuit courts were not bound in every case to exercise such power:

> We cannot suppose that Congress intended to compel those courts . . . to draw to themselves, in the first instance, the control of all criminal prosecutions commenced in state courts exercising authority within the same territorial limits, where the accused claims that he is held in custody in violation of the Constitution of the United States. The injunction to hear the case summarily, and thereupon to "dispose of the party as law and justice require," does not deprive the court of discretion as to the time and mode in which it will exert the power conferred upon it. That discretion should be exercised in light of the relations existing, under our system of government, between the judicial tribunals of the Union and of the State, and in recognition of the fact that the public good requires that those relations be not disturbed by unnecessary conflict between courts equally bound to guard and protect rights secured by the Constitution.[119]

This discretionary power, guided by the principle of comity,[120] was, however, to be subordinate to any "special circumstances" that required immediate federal intervention. No such "special circumstances" were discovered in Royall's case, and the circuit court's ruling therefore was affirmed.

THE PRINCIPLE OF EX PARTE ROYALL

The Court in *Royall* did not address itself to the problem of delineating which questions were properly cognizable. It merely suggested that the exercise of the circuit court's discretionary power to issue the writ be guided by the principle of comity and that this principle was to be subordinate to "special circumstances." The excepted class was also left undefined.

It soon became apparent that the discretionary nature of the power was rather illusory. Shortly after *Royall*, the Court denied a writ of habeas corpus to an applicant convicted in a lower state court for embezzlement from a national bank.[121] The Court observed that no reason had been suggested why the supreme court of the state could not review the judgment of the lower state tribunal, nor why it should not be permitted to do so without interference by the courts of the United States. The Court found no "special circumstances" demanding immediate federal intervention. Following this case, the doctrine requiring exhaustion of state remedies came to be applied with increasing rigidity. Where the lower federal court rejected the habeas application because state remedies were not exhausted, the Supreme Court affirmed.[122] But where the lower federal court in its discretion allowed the writ to issue in cases where state remedies were unexhausted, and in the absence of what the Supreme Court viewed as a "special circumstance," the lower court was reversed.[123] Although *Royall* spoke of the *circuit courts' discretion*, and the early opinions affirming the circuit courts' dismissal of habeas applications affirmed *the circuit courts' discretion* to deny the writ,[124] in the cases reversing the circuit courts' allowance of the writ where they saw special circumstances,[125] it became clear that the discretion of the lower courts was, in fact, discretion in the Supreme Court.[126]

The Supreme Court's "special circumstances" category began to take shape the year after the *Royall* case. In *Mali and Wildenhus et al. v. Keeper of the Common Jail*,[127] *reversing the decision of a circuit court*, the Supreme Court allowed a writ for a Belgian sailor charged in a state court with the murder of another member of his crew while their ship was docked in a New Jersey port. The petitioner contended that his confinement was contrary to a treaty between Belgium and the United States. The Supreme Court agreed, and on the authority of sections 751 and 753 of the Revised Statutes, which empowered the courts of the United States to issue writs of habeas corpus to persons held in custody "in violation of the Constitution or a law or treaty of the United States . . . ," discharged the applicant. In *Thomas v. Loney*,[128] the Court affirmed the decision of the circuit court and released from custody a petitioner held under warrant of arrest issued by a justice of the peace of the city of Richmond upon a complaint charging him with perjury in giving false testimony in his deposition as a witness before a notary public of the city in a case of a contested election of a member of the United States House of Representatives.

The classic case illustrating the "exceptional circumstances" category is *Cunningham v. Neagle*.[129] The case came to the Supreme Court on appeal[130] from the judgment of the United States Circuit Court for the northern district of California discharging David Neagle from the custody of the sheriff of San Joaquin. Neagle had been assigned by President Harrison to protect United States Supreme Court Justice Stephen Field from David S. Terry, a former Chief Justice of the California Supreme Court.[131] Terry encountered Field in a dining room and there struck the Justice twice before Neagle intervened by shouting "Stop! Stop! I am an officer!" Terry then put his hand on his bosom and Neagle, thinking Terry was reaching for his knife—which he had unsuccessfully attempted (having been wrested down by Neagle and others) to use in an earlier incident[132]—shot and killed him.[133] The Court was of the opinion that even though Neagle was acting under no statute of the United States, his assignment to protect Field, who was engaged in the discharge of his duties as circuit judge, was sufficient to bring him within the meaning of section 753 of the Revised Statutes, and therefore he was in custody "for an act done or omitted in pursuance of a law of the United States or of an order, process or decree of a court or judge thereof, or is in custody in violation of the Constitution or of a law or treaty of the United States." Mr. Justice Lamar dissented, along with Mr. Chief Justice Fuller, finding that the Court had placed "a wholly inadmissible construction . . . on the word 'law.' "[134] He argued that the President's power was that of executing the laws; the Congress alone had the duty to make the laws. The wording of the provision would seem to lend strength to the position of the dissenters. Since an order, process or decree of a court or judge would be just as much a "law" as an executive order, the second clause of the provision would have been superfluous under the majority's definition of the word "law" as used in the first clause. The majority's willingness to take such a broad reading, in conjunction with the earlier "special circumstances" cases, helps clarify the special category the Court was establishing: the Court was willing to allow an exception from the exhaustion rule if the case involved the authority and operation of the general government. That is, a "special circumstance" was present in those cases where it was thought undesirable to have a particular matter litigated in the courts of the several states, specifically, cases involving: the obligation of the country to foreign governments; the election of members of the federal legislature; and an officer or agent of the United States arrested under state process for acts done under authority of the federal government. To summarize still further, the Court seemed to be equating "special circumstances" with the presence of a substantial federal aspect or a federal aspect raising a presumption of supremacy.

Shortly afterwards, the *Neagle* exception was applied in the case of a deputy marshal who, acting in pursuance of an Internal Revenue statute, killed an individual, and for such action was indicted in a state court for murder.[135] The Court stated that what was involved here was "the supremacy of the Constitution and laws of the United States."[136] Similarly, in *State of Ohio v. Thomas*,[137] the Court allowed federal habeas relief to a governor of a United States soldiers' home who had been arrested for not complying with a state law regulating the use of oleomargarine. The Court explicitly stated that the slow process of exhaustion would obstruct the operations of the federal government. Likewise in *Boske v. Cunningham*,[138] the Supreme Court affirmed a district court's discharge of an Internal Revenue collector, noting that the officer's "presence at his post was important to the public interest. . . ." and that his detention by state authorities might interfere "with the regular and orderly business of the department to which he belongs."[139] In *Hunter v. Wood*,[140] this category was extended to include a private railroad company's ticket agent acting under and in obedience to an order of a federal circuit court, enjoining, as being repugnant to the United States Constitution, the enforcement of legislation reducing rates by the state corporation commission and the state attorney general. The Court found that the dignity of the federal court had been insulted.[141]

In *State of Minnesota v. Brundage*,[142] the Court reversed a circuit court's holding, discharging on habeas corpus a private individual who had been arrested upon the complaint of an inspector of the State Dairy and Food Department and charged with having violated a state "Act to Prevent Fraud in the Sale of Dairy Products, Their Imitation or Substitutes, and to Prohibit and Prevent the Manufacture or Sale of Unhealthy or Altered Dairy Products,"[143] even though the Court acknowledged that the act in question might in its operation affect the business of many, and in some degree, but indirectly, the rights of the public. The authority and operation of the general government was not involved here. In *United States ex rel. Drury and Dowd v. Lewis*,[144] the Court refused to discharge a federal officer because the evidence did not sufficiently show that the officer was acting within the scope of his federal authority.[145]

EXHAUSTION OF STATE REMEDIES

Royall provided that the federal courts had "discretion"[146] to refuse an application from a state prisoner in advance of his trial.[147] A case decided later the same year held that the rule applied to the case of a prisoner who had appellate processes available to him.[148] The Court also noted that after the final disposition of the case by the highest court of the state, the circuit court *might* "in its discretion" put a party to his writ of error from the Supreme Court.[149] By 1892, this discretionary rule also became a general requirement of the exhaustion doctrine.[150] In requiring the exhaustion of the writ of error from the Supreme Court, the Court reasoned that the habeas corpus proceeding was "a collateral attack of a civil nature to impeach the validity of a judgment or sentence of another court. . . ."[151] and "not a proceeding for the correction of errors."[152] The writ of error was a remedy to which the state prisoner was entitled as of right.[153]

The exhaustion of state remedies principle was extended to include collateral remedies. A motion for leave to file a petition for an original writ of habeas corpus was denied in *Mooney v. Holohan*[154] because the applicant had failed to exhaust the state remedy of habeas corpus. In *Ex parte Davis*,[155] the Court refused to grant leave to file a petition for habeas corpus to a person convicted in a state court where remedies afforded by state appellate procedure had not been fully exhausted, although the petitioner alleged that a pending appeal in the state courts for an order sustaining a demurrer to a petition for a writ of error *coram nobis* would be futile because of his financial inability to provide the state appellate court with a transcript of the *coram nobis* proceeding. The Court would not anticipate the state appellate court. The state court might avail itself of the transcript, or part of it. The Court was holding, therefore, that appellate processes in collateral proceedings likewise were included in the exhaustion requirement.[156]

In *Ex parte Hawk*,[157] the Supreme Court denied a motion to file a petition for an original writ of habeas corpus because the applicant failed to seek remedy by the common-law writ of error *coram nobis*. The Court here provided a concise summary of the exhaustion of state remedies rule: "Ordinarily an application for habeas corpus by one detained under a state court judgment of conviction for crime will be entertained only after all state remedies available, including all appellate remedies in the state courts and in this Court by appeal or writ of certiorari, have been exhausted. . . . And where those remedies have been exhausted this Court will not ordinarily entertain the application for the writ before it has been sought and denied in a district court or denied by a circuit or district judge."[158] The Court noted, however, that where resort to state remedies has failed to afford a full and fair adjudication of the federal contentions raised, either because the state affords no remedy or because in the particular case the remedy afforded by state laws proves in practice unavailable or seriously inadequate, a federal court should entertain a petition for habeas corpus; otherwise a petitioner would be remediless. In such a case the applicant should proceed in the federal district court before resorting to the Supreme Court by petition for habeas corpus.[159]

This summary shows how far the notion of exhaustion of state remedies had been extended. This burdensome procedure was greatly relieved in *Wade v. Mayo*.[160] The petitioner had exhausted only one of two alternative routes—appeal to the state appellate courts from conviction and habeas corpus—open to him in challenging his conviction. After conviction, he attacked by way of the collateral method of habeas corpus and pursued this method through to the state supreme court. This was sufficient to meet the exhaustion requirement in the opinion of the federal district court, but the federal circuit court of appeals reversed. The United States Supreme Court agreed with the district court and reversed the circuit court, holding that "[t]he exhaustion of but one of several available alternatives is all that is necessary."[161] Speaking to the issue of whether it was proper for a federal district court to entertain a habeas corpus petition filed by a state prisoner who, having secured a ruling from the highest state court on his federal constitutional claim, had failed to seek a writ of certiorari in the Supreme Court, Mr. Justice Murphy, for the Court, stated:

> [T]he reasons for this exhaustion principle cease after the highest state court has rendered a decision on the merits of the federal constitutional claim. The state procedure has then ended and there is no longer any danger of a collision between federal and state authority. The problem shifts from the consummation of state remedies to the nature and extent of the federal review of the constitutional issue. The exertion of such review at this point, however, is not in any real sense a part of the state procedure. It is an invocation of federal authority growing out of the supremacy of the Federal Constitution and the necessity of giving effect to that supremacy if the state processes have failed to do so.
>
> After state procedure has been exhausted, the concern is with the appropriate federal forum in which to pursue further the constitutional claim. The choice lies between applying directly to this Court for review of the Constitutional issue by certiorari or instituting an original habeas corpus proceeding in a federal district court. Consideration of prompt and orderly procedure in the federal courts will often dictate that direct review be sought first in this Court. And where a prisoner has neglected to seek that review, such failure may be a relevant consideration for a district court in determining whether to entertain a subsequent habeas corpus petition.
>
> But the factors which make it desirable to present the constitutional issue directly and initially to this Court do not justify a hard and fast rule to that effect. . . . The prevention of

undue restraints on liberty is more important than mechanical and unrealistic administration of the federal courts.[162]

With such affirmative language and compelling reasoning, the issue would seem to have been settled.

In the 1948 revision of the Judicial Code, the principle of exhaustion was codified by Congress.[163] The codified exhaustion rule provided:

> (b) An Application for a writ of habeas corpus on behalf of a person in custody pursuant to the judgment of a State court shall not be granted unless it appears that the applicant has exhausted the remedies available in the courts of the State, or that there is either an absence of available State corrective process or the existence of circumstances rendering such process ineffective to protect the rights of the prisoner.
>
> (c) An Applicant shall not be deemed to have exhausted the remedies available in the courts of the State, within the meaning of this section, if he has the right under the law of the State to raise, by any available procedure, the question presented.

The revisor's note at the end of the section stated that the enactment was "declaratory of the existing law as affirmed by the Supreme Court." In parentheses the case of *Ex parte Hawk* was cited. In *Darr v. Burford*,[164] decided the year after the enactment, the majority of the Court read the provision as a codification of the *Hawk* case. It noted that in *Wade v. Mayo* alone did there appear language departing from the "established rule" that certiorari to the Supreme Court was included in the exhaustion requirement.[165] In attempting to meet the argument in *Wade v. Mayo*, the Court contended that a petition for certiorari should be required from the Supreme Court because "the responsibility to intervene in state criminal matters rests primarily upon this Court."[166]

First, what the majority failed to notice was that the "established rule" dated only from *Hawk*. The authorities cited by the *Hawk* Court did not support its conclusion;[167] they were authority merely for the exhaustion of purely state remedies and the writ of error from the Supreme Court. It seems the Court was confusing the writ of error and the writ of certiorari. As noted earlier, the writ of error is a writ of right, whereas the writ of certiorari is a discretionary writ. Second, the majority's rationale for requiring certiorari conflicted with the principle that a denial of certiorari has no legal significance. Thus, Frankfurter argued in dissent that "if denial of certiorari remains without bearing on the merits of habeas corpus as in other cases, to require the State prisoner to go through the motion of securing a denial is to command a gesture which is meaningless to him and burdensome to this Court." *Darr v. Burford* was consistent, then, with neither policy nor case history. Further, the revisor's note itself spoke of the "existing law," and the statute addresses itself to only *state* remedies. On the other hand, there was the parenthetical citation, which was supported by the legislative history. Judge John J. Parker, chairman of the Judicial Conference Committee recommending the section, has written that "[t]he thing in mind in the drafting of this section was to provide that review of state court action be had so far as possible only by the Supreme Court of the United States, whose review of such action has historical basis, and that review not be had by the lower federal courts, whose exercise of such power is unseemly and likely to breed dangerous conflicts of jurisdiction."[168] Although Parker was wrong on the historical point—again, confusion in the distinction between the writ of error and the writ of certiorari—his statement, however erroneous, lends support to the decision in *Darr v. Burford.*

That *Darr v. Burford* did not completely overrule *Wade v. Mayo*[169] was made clear in *Brown v. Allen.*[170] The Court there noted that the exhaustion rule was not "intended to require repetitious applications to state courts,"[171] and therefore held that once a petitioner had presented his claim to the highest state court on direct appeal, and application had been made for a writ of certiorari to the United States Supreme Court, he was not required to pursue collateral postconviction relief based on the same evidence and issues in the state courts.[172] It was also observed that likewise an applicant, who had once made use of state collateral remedies and possible appeals from them, need not again present his claim to state courts.[173]

In *Friske v. Collins*,[174] decided shortly before *Brown*, the Court reinstated the view that exhaustion was not a "rigid and inflexible" rule, but could be deviated from in "special circumstances." In addition to the class of "special circumstances" developed in the early history of the exhaustion rule, exhaustion was not required where procedural obstacles make theoretically available processes unavailable, where the available state procedure does not offer swift vindication of the petitioner's rights, and where vindication of the federal right requires immediate action.[175]

Fay v. Noia[176] held that the exhaustion doctrine did not cover state remedies no longer available to the petitioner. Noia had been convicted in 1942 of felony murder. The sole evidence against him was his signed confession. The codefendants in the case were released subsequently on findings that their confessions had been coerced. Noia had not appealed his conviction in 1942 because such action would have created a substantial risk of a sentence of electrocution rather than imprisonment for life. Although it was stipulated that the coerced nature of Noia's confession was also established, the United States district court in 1960 denied relief under 28 U.S.C., section 2254, believing that Noia's failure to appeal his conviction— a remedy long since closed to him—made him ineligible for federal habeas relief under the exhaustion rule.[177] The Court of Appeals reversed, questioning whether section 2254 barred relief on federal habeas corpus because the applicant had failed to exhaust state remedies no longer available at the time the habeas proceeding was commenced. The Supreme Court affirmed, holding that the requirement "refers only to a failure to exhaust state remedies still open to the applicant at the time he files his application for habeas corpus in the federal court."[178] In addition, the Court overruled *Darr v. Burford* to the extent that it barred federal habeas relief to a state prisoner who had failed timely to seek certiorari in the Supreme Court from an adverse state decision.[179]

To the extent, however, that *Darr v. Burford* required an applicant for federal habeas corpus to have presented the same claim in the federal system as was presented in the state system, it is still good law.[180] In *Picard v. Connor*,[181] a state grand jury had returned an indictment for murder against a "John Doe." After the defendant was apprehended, the indictment was amended, pursuant to the state fictitious name statute, so as to substitute the defendant's name for "John Doe." The defendant was convicted, and his conviction was affirmed on appeal against the argument that the procedure used to amend the indictment had not complied with the statute. A petition for federal habeas corpus was dismissed by the United States District Court. The Court of Appeals, although acknowledging that the respondent had not attacked his conviction on the grounds of a denial of equal protection in the state court, reversed on those grounds.[182] The Supreme Court, in turn, reversed the decision of the Court of Appeals, emphasizing that in order to prevent conflict between the state and federal courts, "the federal claim must be fairly presented to the state courts."[183] It is not sufficient that the petitioner has been to the state courts; the same ultimate legal question must be presented in both systems. Douglas dissented, finding that the same ultimate question had been raised in both systems since the respondent raised a "due process" claim, which is "not mutually exclusive" of the claim of "equal protection."[184]

Finally, it is necessary to consider the effect of a change in the law—between the time an applicant exhausted his available state remedies and the time he petitioned for federal habeas relief—upon which the state courts had based their denial of relief. The lower federal courts had generally returned such cases to the state courts.[185] In 1974, the Supreme Court in *Francisco v. Gathright*[186] held that in a federal habeas corpus proceeding, the federal courts should not dismiss the petition and require the petitioner to resubmit it to the state courts for reconsideration, in light of a decision by the highest court holding the statute unconstitutional in another case—decided after the affirmance of the petitioner's conviction on direct appeal and before the filing of the federal habeas petition. The Court reasoned that the state courts, upon direct review, had a full opportunity to determine the federal constitutional issue before resort was made to the federal forum. In the Court's view, the policies served by the exhaustion requirement would not be furthered by requiring resubmission of the claim to the state courts. Note that prior to *Francisco v. Gathright*, exhaustion was not required when the state altered its conception of the substantive federal law, on reasoning similar to that in *Francisco v. Gathright*.[187] The case of a change in federal law brought about by an actor in the federal system is arguably quite different. There, the state court can be said to have a valid interest in applying the new principle.

Exhaustion today is a rule rooted in the relationship between the national and state judicial systems. The rule is consistent with the writ's extraordinary character, but it must be balanced by another characteristic of the writ, to wit: its object of providing "a swift and imperative remedy in all cases of illegal restraint upon personal liberty."[188] That is, it "is not [a rule] defining power but one which relates to the appropriate exercise of power."[189] The standard of appropriateness has shifted dramatically since the exhaustion doctrine was fleshed out by the Fuller Court and gradually extended during the first half of the twentieth century. The reason for the shift will be made clear in the following chapter when the legal process under examination here will be seen transmitting substantive changes in the law.

A NOTE ON WAIVER

Before concluding this chapter, it should be noted that both petitioner and individual state can "waive" the rights considered above. The state, in its discretion,[190] may waive its rights, under the doctrine that prior exhaustion of state remedies is a prerequisite to federal habeas relief,[191] and the federal court may, in the interest of justice and expedition, accept a waiver of exhaustion by the state.[192]

A state prisoner may waive his right to a federal forum. A "waiver"—as defined in the celebrated right to counsel case of *Johnson v. Zerbst*[193]—"is ordinarily an intentional relinquishment or abandonment of a known right or privilege."[194] In *Daniels v. Allen*,[195] the companion case to *Brown v. Allen*, a seemingly very different concept of waiver was applied. *Daniels* had followed the same path through the appellate courts as *Brown* until the last day for filing appeal papers in the state supreme court, when Daniels' attorney had the papers ready, but instead of mailing them on the final day (which would have satisfied the time requirement) delivered them by hand the following day (the same day on which they would have arrived by post), technically one day late. The state supreme court therefore refused to consider the appeal, and the United States Supreme Court denied habeas relief because Daniels had waived his right to appeal. The relinquishment could hardly be called "intentional." This inconsistency was for a time resolved by *Fay v. Noia*.[196] The Court there accepted the classic definition of waiver and held that "the federal habeas judge may in his discretion deny relief to an applicant who has deliberately by-passed the orderly procedures of the state courts and in doing so has forfeited his state court remedies." It went on in *dictum* to elaborate upon the definition:

> If a habeas applicant, after consultation with competent counsel or otherwise, understandingly and knowingly forwent the privilege of seeking to vindicate his federal claims in the state courts, whether for strategic, tactical, or any other reason that can fairly be described as a deliberate by-passing of state procedure, then it is open to the federal court on habeas to deny him all relief if the state courts refused to entertain his federal claim on the merits. . . .[197]

Interestingly, *Noia* seemed to come within the test for deliberate bypass. However, the Court noted the substantial risk of electrocution and concluded: "His was a grisly choice whether to sit content with life imprisonment or to travel the uncertain avenue of appeal which, if successful, might well have led to a retrial and death sentence."[198] Thus, even a deliberate bypass would not constitute waiver if the state prisoner has been presented with a "grisly choice."[199]

With respect to procedural defaults occurring during the trial of a criminal defendant, the present Court, more concerned with state criminal process and less concerned with the constitutional rights of "guilty" persons, has rejected the procedural bypass rule and in its place formulated the "cause and prejudice" test, which bars federal habeas review absent a showing of "cause" and "prejudice" attendant to a state procedural waiver.[200] The precise definition of the cause and prejudice standard has been left open.[201]

NOTES

1. *See* ch. 5, text accompanying notes 230-40 *infra*.
2. *Rose v. Mitchell*, 99 S. Ct. 2993 (1979).
3. Ibid., p. 3013.
4. 1 U.S. Statutes at Large 81 (1789).
5. The particular punctuation used (the period followed by the dash) seems to have the same meaning as a colon. The colon was the punctuation used in the Judiciary Act of 1801, sect. 30, 2 U.S. Statutes at Large 98, though there the proviso was preceded by only one clause. Mr. Justice McLean, in *Ex parte Dorr*, 3 How. 103 (1845), inaccurately copied sect. 14 and substituted a colon for the punctuation used by the framers.
6. *Ex parte Bollman*, 4 Cranch 75 (1807).
7. An interpretation of *Bollman* suggested by Pascal, "Habeas Corpus and the Constitution," 1970 Duke L. J. 605, 631.
8. 43 George III c. 140 (1803), "An Act to enable Judges of his Majesty's Courts of Record and Westminster to award Writs of Habeas Corpus for bringing Persons detained in Gaol before Court Martial, and the several Commissions therein mentioned." (Extended the power mentioned in the preamble to court martials). (Emphasis on "Judges" added). *See* also *Rex v. Reddam*, 98 Eng. Rep. 1300 (1777); Matthew Bacon, *A New Abridgement of the Law* (London, 1832), vol. 4, p. 115.
9. *See Ex parte Bollman*, 4 Cranch 75, 97-99.
10. *See* ch. 3, text accompanying notes 68-108 *supra*.
11. *Ex parte Bollman*, 4 Cranch 75, 95. *See also Morgan v. United States*, 380 F.2d 686 (1967), cert. den. 390 U.S. 962, *reh. den.* 390 U.S. 1008 (1968).
12. 2 U.S. Statutes at Large 89 (1801) (repealed after thirteen months).
13. It is appropriate to look upon the Act of 1801 as explanatory of many of the ill-drafted provisions of the Act of 1789. Following the passage of the first judiciary act, Congress almost immediately directed the attorney general to submit "a report of such alterations and improvements in the system as experience may dictate to be necessary or the public good may require"; and as early as 1790, Attorney General Randolph submitted recommendations for changes. *American State Papers, Misc.* no. 17. Among other suggestions, Randolph recommended that both circuit and district courts be given power to issue "such writs, summons, and other processes . . . for the commencement and prosecution of any civil action, suit, or matter therein. . . . Ibid., pp. 28 and 30. Further, judges should have power "to issue writs of habeas corpus, returnable in vacation before himself. . . ." The circuit judge could order the return to be made to any other judge of his circuit, who was in the district.

Following the delineation of the Supreme Court's original jurisdiction, a new paragraph read:

That, in the cases of which the circuit courts aforesaid, and the district courts of Kentucky and Maine, have cognizance, the Supreme Court shall have appellate jurisdiction, under the regulations of appeals and writs of error hereinafter mentioned; that the Supreme Court shall have power to issue writs of mandamus according to law, and writs of certiorari to the circuit and State courts, according to the rules hereinafter mentioned, to direct the writs, summons, processes, forms, and mode of proceeding to be issued, obeyed, and pursued by the said Supreme Court and the district and circuit courts. . . .

Note, the power was generally in the courts. The exceptional case concerned habeas corpus in vacation. *See* text accompanying notes 18-21 *infra*.

14. Sect. 30, 2 U.S. Statutes at Large 98.

15. Sect. 2, ibid., p. 89, provided that the Supreme Court only "shall have power, and is hereby authorized, to issue writs of prohibition, mandamus, scire facias, habeas corpus, certiorari, procendendo, and all writs not specifically provided for by statute, which may be necessary for the exercise of its jurisdiction, and agreeable to the principles and usages of law."

This was the only place, other than sect. 30, where the Act of 1801 specifically mentioned the writ of habeas corpus. However, sect. 10 gave to the circuit courts "all the power heretofore granted by law to the circuit courts of the United States, unless where otherwise provided by this act."

16. Emphasis added.

17. 3 Fed. Cas. 212, 219. Also argued by Pascal, "Habeas Corpus and the Constitution," 1970 Duke L. J. 605, 644.

18. Vol. 3, p. 135.

19. 6 State Trials 1190, 1196 (1676).

20. *See* ch. 1, text accompanying notes 492-540 *supra*.

21. 31 Car. 2, c. 2, sect. 3.

22. 2 Farrand 638. *See also* 1 ibid. 119, 124-25, 341, 352. For opposition during the first Congress, *see Annals*, 1st Cong., 1st Sess., p. 832.

23. *Annals*, 9th Cong., 2nd Sess., p. 502.

24. Ibid., pp. 544-45.

25. 3 How. 103 (1845).

26. Ibid., p. 105. *See also Ex parte McCann*, 15 Fed. Cas. 1251 (1865).

27. *See Ex parte Des Rochers*, 7 Fed. Cas. 537 (1856); *In re McDonald*, 16 Fed. Cas. 17 (1861).

28. 4 U.S. Statutes at Large 632 (1833).

29. *See generally*, William W. Freehling, *Prelude to Civil War: The Nullification Controversy in South Carolina 1816-1836* (New York: Harper and Row, 1966).

30. 1 South Carolina Statutes at Large 244 (1828).

31. 1 ibid. 201.

32. Freehling, *Nullification*, p. 279.

33. Ibid., p. 283.

34. 2 Richardson, *Messages* 1173-95.

35. 4 U.S. Statutes at Large 632.

36. 1 South Carolina Statutes at Large 380 (1833). Shortly afterwards, South Carolina, in a futile gesture, declared the Force Bill null and void. Ibid., p. 400.

37. 28 U.S.C. sect. 2241 (c) (2).

38. 9 U.S. Statutes at Large 462 (1850).

39. *See Ex parte Jenkins*, 13 Fed. Cas. 445 (1853); *Ex parte Sifford*, 22 Fed. Cas. 105 (1857).

40. *See United States ex rel. Roberts v. Jailer*, 26 Fed. Cas. 571 (1867); *Ex parte Turner, Ex parte Mayer*, 24 Fed. Cas. 334 (1879).

41. *See* text accompanying notes 117-20 *infra*.

42. *See* text accompanying notes 117-45 *infra*.

43. *See e.g., Cunningham v. Neagle*, 135 U.S. 1 (1889).

44. *See generally*, Charles Warren, *The Supreme Court in United States History* (Boston: Little, Brown and Co., 1937), vol. 2, pp. 98-100. Compare *McLeod's Case* with *Holmes v. Jennison*, 14 Peters 540 (1840) [the issue there was whether a state chief executive could deliver an alleged criminal fugitive to a foreign power to stand trial] (*see generally*, Charles Grove Haines and Foster H. Sherwood, *The Role of the Supreme Court in American Government and Politics 1835-1864* (Berkeley and Los Angeles: University of Calif. Press, 1957), pp. 206-17.

45. *See* Thomas H. Benton, *Thirty Years View* (New York: D. Appleton and Co., 1856), vol. 2, p. 282.

46. Ibid., vol. 2, p. 283.

47. *People v. Alexander McLeod*, 1 Hill 377 (1841).

48. 37 Am. Dec. 364.

49. 5 U.S. Statutes at Large 539 (1942).

50. *See* John McKean's speech in the House of Representatives on 12 January 1843, Congressional Globe, 27th Congress, 3rd Sess., p. 155.

51. *See* speeches of Buchanan, Walker and Smith in the Senate, ibid., 27th Congress, 2nd Sess., pp. 382-88 (9 May 1842); 611-21 (21 June 1842); 645-47 (July 1842). Also in Senate, *see* debates on 8 July 1842, ibid., pp. 554-58. *See also* Ingersoll's speech in the House on 26 August 1842, ibid., pp. 718-19; 953-57.

52. The Act was consolidated into Revised Statutes, sect. 753 (1873). Now found in 28 U.S.C., sect. 2241 (c) (4).

53. 14 U.S. Statutes at Large 385 (1867).

54. *See* Anthony G. Amsterdam, "Criminal Prosecutions Affecting Federally Guaranteed Civil Rights: Federal Removal and Habeas Corpus Jurisdiction to Abort State Court Trial," 113 U. Pa. L. Rev. 793, 823-25 (1965); Bator, "Finality in Criminal Law," 76 Harv. L. Rev. 441, 474; William J. Brennan, "Federal Habeas Corpus and State Prisoners," 7 Utah L. Rev. 423, 426 (1961); William J. Brennan, "Some Aspects of Federalism," 39 N.Y.U. L. Rev. 945, 957 (1964); Collings, "Habeas Corpus for Convicts—Constitutional Right or Legislative Grace?" 40 Calif. L. Rev. 335, 351; Lewis Mayers, "The Habeas Corpus Act of 1867: The Supreme Court as Legal Historian," 33 U. Chi. L. Rev. 31 (1965); Reitz, "Federal Habeas Corpus: Impact of An Abortive State Proceeding," 74 Harv. L. Rev. 1315; Sofaer, "Federal Habeas Corpus for State Prisoners: The Isolation Principle," 39 N.Y.U. L. Rev. 78, fn. 4; Mark V. Tushnet, "Judicial Revision of the Habeas Corpus Statutes: A Note on *Schneckloth v. Bustamonte*," 1975 Wisc. L. Rev. 484, 487; and Warren, *The Supreme Court in United States History*, p. 465.

55. *Congressional Globe*, 39th Congress, 1st Sess., pp. 4150-51 (25 July 1866).

56. Ibid., p. 4151. One of the amendments recommended by the Judiciary Committee was a provision that was to be affixed to the end of the Act: "This act shall not apply to the case of any person who is or may be held in custody of the military authorities of the United States, charged with any military offense, or with having aided or abetted rebellion against the Government of the United States prior to this act." It is likely that the question was motivated by this clause and the *Milligan* case.

57. Referring to the resolution at *Congressional Globe*, 39th Congress, 1st Sess., p. 87 (19 December 1865):

"*Resolved*, That the Committee on the Judiciary be directed to inquire and report to this House, as soon as practicable, by bill or otherwise, what legislation is needed to enable the courts of the United States to enforce the freedom of the wives and children of soldiers of the United States under the joint resolution of Congress of March 3, 1865 [Joint Resolution 29, 3 March 1865, 13 U.S. Statutes at Large 571], and also to enforce the liberty of all persons under the operation of the constitutional amendment abolishing slavery [Amendment 13 (which took effect from 18 December 1865—one day before the resolution)]."

58. Referring to *Corbin v. Marsh*, 63 Ky. (2 Div.) 193 (1865).

59. *Congressional Globe*, 39th Congress, 1st Sess., p. 4151.

60. *See* text accompanying notes 57-59 *supra*.

61. *Congressional Globe*, 39th Congress, 1st Sess., p. 135 (8 January 1866).

62. Cited by Mayers, "Habeas Corpus Act of 1867," 33 U. Chi. L. Rev. 31, 34.

63. Note, not only was the phrase referring to the subjects of the acts changed from persons "held in slavery or involuntary servitude" in the Wilson version to "any person" in the Lawrence bill, but there was also no reference to "prisoner"—the word used in the habeas corpus acts of 1833 and 1842—in the proposal that eventually became the Habeas Corpus Act of 1867. Further, the verb "restrained" replaced the verbs "committed" or "confined" used in earlier legislation.

64. Mayers, "Habeas Corpus Act of 1867," 33 U. Chi. L. Rev. 31, 44.

65. *See* Amsterdam, "Federal Removal and Habeas Corpus," 113 U. Pa. L. Rev. 793, 823-25.

66. Mayers, "Habeas Corpus Act of 1867," 33 U. Chi. L. Rev. 31, 49.

67. *See generally*, Kutler, *Reconstruction Politics*, ch. 8; William M. Wiecek, "The Reconstruction of Federal Judicial Power, 1863-1876," 13 Am. J. L. Hist. 333 (1969). *See also* Michael Les Benedict, "Contagion and the Constitution: Quarantine Agitation From 1859 to 1866," 25 J. of the Hist. of Medicine and Allied Sciences 177 (1970); Michael Les Benedict, "Preserving Federalism: Reconstruction and the Waite Court," 1978 S. Ct. Rev. 39 (1979); Phillip Paludan, "John Norton Pomeroy, State Rights Nationalists," 12 Am. J. of L. Hist. 292 (1968); Catherine M. Tarrant, "To 'insure domestic Tranquility': Congress and the Law of Seditious Conspiracy, 1859-1861," 15 Am. J. L. Hist. 167 (1971).

68. Bator, "Finality in Criminal Law," 76 Harv. L. Rev. 441, 477, fn. 82.

69. Mayers, "Habeas Corpus Act of 1867," 33 U. Chi. L. Rev. 31, 37.

70. *See* ibid., p. 44.

71. 14 U.S. Statutes at Large 27.

72. 12 U.S. Statutes at Large 755.

73. 14 U.S. Statutes at Large 46.

74. *Congressional Globe*, 39th Congress, 1st. Sess., pp. 4228-29 (27 July 1866).

75. Ibid., p. 4229.

76. Ibid.

77. This being perhaps insignificant since the Judiciary Act of 1789 could

have been thought to cover federal prisoners to as great an extent as the Act of 1867 covered state prisoners.

78. Oddly enough, the following session Johnson found fault with the bill and requested further time to consider it. *See Congressional Globe,* 39th Congress, 2nd Sess., p. 730 (25 January 1867).

79. This provision was not in Lawrence's proposal, but was among the amendments suggested by the committee. It read:

> [T]he person in whose custody the party is detained, . . . shall make return of said writ and bring the party before the judge who granted the writ, and certify the true cause of the detention . . . The petitioner may deny any of the material facts set forth in the return, or may allege any fact to show that the detention is in contravention of the constitution or laws of the United States, which allegations or denials shall be made on oath. The said return may be amended by leave of the court or judge before or after the same is filed, as also may all suggestions made against it, that thereby the material facts may be ascertained. The said court or judge shall proceed in a summary way to determine the facts of the case, by hearing testimony and the arguments of the parties interested.

At common law, the general rule prohibited controverting the facts in the return to the writ of habeas corpus. *Bagg's Case,* 77 Eng. Rep. 1271 (1615); Wilmot, J., "Opinion," 97 Eng. Rep. 29, 42 *et seq.* For the development of the rule in English law *see* Sharpe, *The Law of Habeas Corpus,* pp. 61-88.

Although habeas actions could turn on disputed facts, *Ex parte Columbia George,* 144 Fed. 985 (1906); *Walsh v. Archer,* 73 F.2d 197 (1934), the habeas court's power to hear testimony on controverted facts was initially of little significance since the Supreme Court seemed to sanction deferral to the express decisions of trial courts on jurisdictional facts. *Toy Toy v. Hopkins,* 212 U.S. 542 (1909); *Ex parte Columbia George, supra.* Its significance grew as due process claims were made cognizable on habeas corpus. *See Frank v. Magnum,* 237 U.S. 309, 331 (1915); *Moore v. Dempsey,* 261 U.S. 86, 91 (1923); and especially *Collongsworth v. Mayo,* 173 F.2d 695, 697 (1949). Cf. however, *Ex parte Hawk,* 321 U.S. 114, 118 (1944) (dictum); *Novotny v. Ragen,* 88 F.2d 72 (1937); *Schechtman v. Foster,* 172 F.2d 339, 341-42 (1949), *cert. den.* 339 U.S. 924 (1950); *Collings v. O'Brien,* 188 F.2d 130, 138 (1951). Making all constitutional claims cognizable on habeas corpus, *Brown v. Allen,* 344 U.S. 443 (1953), significantly increased the likelihood that habeas judges would be asked to relitigate factual contentions. Reed, J., noted, however, that "[w]here the record . . . affords an adequate opportunity to weigh the sufficiency of the . . . evidence, and no unusual circumstances calling for a hearing are presented, a repetition of the trial is not required." Ibid., p. 463. Similarly, Frankfurter, J. observed that "[u]nless a vital flaw be found in the process of ascertaining . . . facts in the State court, the District Judge may accept their determination in the state proceeding and deny the application." Ibid., p. 506. Both justices, however, acknowledged that absent unusual circumstances or vital flaws, the district judge still had discretion to hold a *de novo* fact hearing. Ibid., pp. 463-64, 476, 506. Ten years later, the

Court held: "Where the facts are in dispute, the federal court . . . must hold an evidentiary hearing if the habeas applicant did not receive a full and fair evidentiary hearing in state court, either at the time of the trial or in a collateral proceeding. In other words, a federal evidentiary hearing is required unless the state court trier of fact has after a full hearing reliably found the relevant facts." *Townsend v. Sain*, 372 U.S. 293, 312-13 (1963). The habeas court's discretionary power, acknowledged in *Brown, supra.*, was reaffirmed. Moreover, a list of circumstances where a federal evidentiary hearing was essential was developed: in cases where (1) the merits of the factual dispute were not resolved in the state hearing; (2) the state factual determination was not fairly supported by the record as a whole; (3) the fact-finding procedure employed by the state court was not adequate to afford a full and fair hearing; (4) there was a substantial allegation of newly discovered evidence; (5) the material facts were not adequately developed at the state court hearing; or (6) for any reason it appeared that the state trier of fact did not afford the habeas applicant a full and fair fact hearing. Ibid., p. 313. *See also* 28 U.S.C. sect. 2254 (d). *Kaufman v. United States*, 394 U.S. 217 (1969) held that all but the inadequate procedure criterion were appropriate tests in sect. 2255 proceedings.

80. *See* Dallin H. Oaks, "Habeas Corpus in the States, 1776-1865," 32 U. Chi. L. Rev. 243 (1965).

81. 31 Car. 2, c. 2 (1679).

82. 56 George III c. 100 (1816).

83. 31 Car. II c. 2, sect. 2.

84. The English statute of 1816 did not apply, however, to criminal matters.

85. 118 U.S. 356 (1886).

86. 6 Wall. 318 (1868). *See generally*, William W. Van Alstyne, "A Critical Guide to *Ex parte McCardle*," 15 Ariz. L. Rev. 229 (1973).

87. *Ex parte McCardle*, 6 Wall. 318, 325-26.

88. For excerpts of the oral arguments, *see* Charles Fairman, *History of the Supreme Court: Reconstruction and Reunion* (New York: Macmillan Co., 1971), vol. 6, pt. 1, pp. 452-59.

89. *See* however, Kutler, *Reconstruction Politics* 111-13.

90. *See Congressional Globe*, 40th Congress, 2nd Sess., pp. 1859, 1881 *et seq*. This measure was part of a series of legislative proposals to curb the Court's interference with the Radical Republican program. *See* the House Amendment to S. 163, which provided: "That no cause pending before the Supreme Court of the United States which involves the action or effect of any law of the United States shall be decided adversely to the validity of such laws without the concurrence of two-thirds of all the members of said court, in the decision upon the several points in which said law or any part thereof may be deemed invalid." Ibid., p. 478 (passed 116-39, with 33 not voting. Ibid., p. 489). Substitute amendment suggested in the Senate by Williams of Pennsylvania:

> That in all cases of writs of error from and appeals to the Supreme Court of the United States where is drawn in question the validity of a statute of an authority exercised by the United States, or of the Constitutionality of any clause of the Constitution of the United States, or

of the validity of a statute of or an authority exercised under any State on the ground of repugnance to the Constitution or laws of the United States, the hearing shall be had only before a full bench of the judges of said court, and no judgment shall be rendered or decision made against the validity of any statute of any authority exercised by the United States, except with the concurrence of all judges of said court. Ibid., pp. 490, 503. Shortly afterwards (in fact, on the day when the Court held McCardle's appeal to be properly before it) Senator Trumbull, who represented the government before the Court in *McCardle*, introduced a bill (S. 363) declaring the Reconstruction Acts political in nature and therefore outside the jurisdiction of the judiciary. *See* ibid., pp. 1204, 1428, 1621. Neither S. 363 nor S. 163, as amended, passed. *See generally* Kutler, *Reconstruction Politics.*

91. *See* ibid., pp. 1847, 1884, 2060, 2095.

92. Ibid., p. 2094.

93. Ibid., p. 2096.

94. Compare text accompanying note 76 *supra*. Note especially the third sentence of his 1868 remark. Mayers, "Habeas Corpus Act of 1867," 33 U. Chi. L. Rev. 31, 41, found his two statements inconsistent. He read the later statement as proof of the position that the Act of 1867 was meant to apply only to those formerly held in slavery. He read the sentences following the third sentence as modifying it, rather than as species of the class of cases "where persons were deprived of their liberty under State laws or pretended State laws." In support of the reading endorsed here, note the first conjunction used in sentence four.

95. 15 U.S. Statutes at Large 44 (1868).

96. Grier and Field dissenting in the decision to postpone. Howard K. Beale ed., *Diary of Gideon Wells* (Boston: Houghton Mifflin Co., 1911), vol. 3, p. 320.

97. *Ex parte McCardle*, 7 Wall. 506 (1869). In 1962, Mr. Justice Douglas, joined by Mr. Justice Black, in *Glidden v. Zdanok*, 370 U.S. 530, stated: "There is a serious question whether the *McCardle* case could command a majority view today."

98. 7 Wall. 506, 515.

99. *See* 50 A.B.A.J. 500 (1964) for the anticlimax of the *McCardle Case.*

100. 75 U.S. 85 (1869).

101. Both sides acknowledged the Court's power under the 1789 statute. *Yerger* was preceded by another case where the Court was requested to exercise its habeas jurisdiction under the 1789 statute, its power under the 1867 Act having been withdrawn. *Ex parte Martin* (1869) [not reported]. Although the writ was granted, the case was not pressed. Warren, *The Supreme Court*, vol. 2, p. 484.

102. 75 U.S. 85, 102.

103. S. 274, *Congressional Globe*, 41st Congress, 2nd Sess., pp. 86-93 (died in committee).

104. S. 341, ibid., pp. 2895-96 (the Judiciary Committee obtained a discharge from considering this proposal).

105. S. 280, ibid., p. 3.

106. Ibid., pp. 45, 167.

107. Ibid., pp. 167-69 (no doubt motivated by Chase's allowance of the writ for Yerger, who was imprisoned in Swayne's circuit. *See* Fairman, *Supreme Court*, pp. 569-71).

108. The military had turned Yerger over to the civil authorities, and thus the object of the writ was accomplished.

109. *See, e.g. Ex parte Bridges*, 4 Fed. Cas. 98 (1873).

110. *See, e.g. Ex parte McCready*, 15 Fed. Cas. 1345 (1874); *Ex parte Tatem*, 23 Fed. Cas. 708 (1877).

111. *See, e.g. In re Parrott*, 1 Fed. 481 (1800); *In re Quong Woo*, 13 Fed. 229 (1882); *In re Lee Tong*, 18 Fed. 253 (1883); *In re Tie Loy*, 26 Fed. 611 (1886).

112. *See, e.g. In re Wan Yin*, 22 Fed. 701 (1885); *Ex parte Ah Lit*, 26 Fed. 512 (1886).

113. Seymour D. Thompson, "Abuses of the Writ of Habeas Corpus," 18 Am. L. Rev. 1, 16 (1884).

114. Ibid., p. 20. *See also* American Bar Association, *Report of the Seventh Annual Meeting* (1884), pp. 12-44.

115. 23 U.S. Statutes at Large 437 (1885).

116. House of Representatives, Report No. 730, 48th Congress, 1st Sess. (1884), p. 6.

117. 117 U.S. 241 (1885).

118. *See* ch. 5, text accompanying notes 56-63 *infra*.

119. *Ex parte Royall*, 117 U.S. 241, 251.

120. Although it is usually said that the "exhaustion principle" is "rooted in considerations of federal-state comity rather than in the essential nature of the writ" (Developments, "Federal Habeas Corpus," 83 Harvard Law Review 1038, 1094), it should be noted that this rule is in harmony with the "extraordinary nature" of the writ, i.e. that the writ is not to be used where other remedies are available and adequate. *See* ch. 1, text accompanying notes 13-14, 24-26 *supra*.

121. *Ex parte Fonda*, 117 U.S. 516 (1885).

122. *See Duncan v. McCall*, 139 U.S. 449 (1890); *Wood v. Bush*, 140 U.S. 278 (1890); *In re Jugiro*, 140 U.S. 291 (1890); *McElvaine v. Bush*, 142 U.S. 155 (1891); *Cook v. Hart*, 146 U.S. 183 (1892); *Ex parte Frederich*, 149 U.S. 70 (1892); *Pepke v. Cronan*, 155 U.S. 100 (1894); *Andrews v. Swartz*, 156 U.S. 272 (1894); *Bergemann v. Backer*, 157 U.S. 655 (1894); *Whitten v. Tomlinson*, 160 U.S. 231 (1896); *Kohl v. Lehlback*, 160 U.S. 293 (1896); *Tinsley v. Anderson*, 171 U.S. 101 (1897); *Markuson v. Boucher*, 175 U.S. 184 (1899); *Davis v. Burke*, 179 U.S. 399 (1900); *Gusman v. Marrero*, 180 U.S. 81 (1900); *Reid v. Jones*, 187 U.S. 153 (1902); *Howard v. Fleming*, 191 U.S. 126 (1903); *Rogers v. Peck and Lovell*, 199 U.S. 425 (1905); *United States ex rel. Drury and Dowd v. Lewis*, 200 U.S. 1 (1905); *Pettibone v. Nichols*, 203 U.S. 192 (1906); *Johnson v. Hay*, 227 U.S. 245 (1912); *United States ex rel. Kennedy v. Tyler*, 269 U.S. 13 (1925); *Mooney v. Holohan*, 294 U.S. 103 (1934); *Ex parte Abernathy*, 320 U.S. 219 (1943); *Ex parte Hawk*, 321 U.S. 114 (1944); *Darr v. Burford*, 339 U.S. 200 (1949).

123. *See New York v. Eno*, 155 U.S. 89 (1894); *Baker v. Grice*, 169 U.S. 284 (1898); *Fitts v. McGhee*, 172 U.S. 516 (1898); *State of Minnesota v.*

Brundage, 180 U.S. 499 (1900); *Carfer v. Caldwell,* 200 U.S. 293 (1905); *Urguhart v. Brown,* 205 U.S. 179 (1906); *Ashe v. United States ex rel. Valotta,* 270 U.S. 424 (1926).

It should be noted that the exhaustion requirement was also applicable to the case of federal prisoners. *Ex parte Mirzan,* 119 U.S. 584 (1886); *Re Huntington,* 137 U.S. 63 (1890); *Re Lancaster,* 137 U.S. 393 (1890); *Ex parte Belt,* 159 U.S. 95 (1894); *Re Chapman,* 156 U.S. 211 (1894); *Re Schriver,* 156 U.S. 218 (1894); *Re Lincoln,* 202 U.S. 178 (1906); *Henry v. Henkel,* 235 U.S. 219 (1914). An exhaustion requirement is likewise applied to sect. 2255 proceedings. In the absence of extraordinary circumstances the courts, in the interest of the orderly administration of the criminal law, will not entertain a sect. 2255 motion during the pendency of a direct appeal. *See Masters v. Eide,* 353 F.2d 517 (1965); *Womack v. United States,* 395 F.2d 630 (1968).

124. *See especially, Wood v. Bush,* 140 U.S. 278 (1890); *Tinsley v. Anderson,* 171 U.S. 101 (1897); and *United States ex rel. Drury and Dowd v. Lewis,* 200 U.S. 1 (1905).

125. *See* especially, *Baker v. Grice,* 169 U.S. 284 (1898).

126. *See* Amsterdam, "Federal Removal and Habeas Corpus Jurisdiction," 113 U. Pa. L. Rev. 793, 889; Bator, "Finality in Criminal Law," 76 Harv. L. Rev. 441, 478.

127. 120 U.S. 1 (1886).

128. 134 U.S. 372 (1889).

129. 135 U.S. 1 (1889).

130. The Court emphasized that the case was brought on appeal and not writ of error:

> as Congress has always used these words with a clear understanding of what is meant by them, namely, that by a writ of error only questions of law are brought up for review, as in actions at common law, while an appeal, except when specially provided otherwise, the entire case on both law and facts is to be reconsidered, there seems to be little doubt that, so far as it is essential to a proper decision of this case, the appeal requires us to examine into the evidence.

Ibid., p. 41. The opinion of the Court, consequently, sets out the facts in great length.

131. Field was a member of the California Supreme Court while Terry was Chief Justice. Field succeeded Terry in the post of Chief Justice.

132. *See Ex parte Terry,* 128 U.S. 289 (1888).

133. *See* A. Russell Buchanan, *David S. Terry, Dueling Judge* (San Marino, Calif.: Huntington Library, 1956), pp. 191-231.

134. 135 U.S. 1, 76.

135. *Commonwealth of Virginia v. John Paul,* 148 U.S. 107 (1892).

136. Ibid., p. 114.

137. 173 U.S. 276 (1898).

138. 177 U.S. 459 (1900).

139. Ibid., p. 467.

140. 209 U.S. 205 (1907).

141. *See generally,* Duker, "Mr. Justice Rufus W. Peckham and the Case

of Ex parte Young: Lochnerizing Munn v. Illinois," 1980 Brigham Young L. Rev.—(1980). Private citizens acting under federal officers have been held to fall within this category. *Anderson v. Elliot*, 101 Fed. 609 (1900), appeal dismissed 22 S. Ct. 930 (1902); *State of West Virginia v. Laing*, 133 Fed. 887 (1904).

142. 180 U.S. 499 (1900).

143. Minnesota General Laws, 1899, c. 295 (Act of 19 April 1891).

144. 200 U.S. 1 (1905).

145. *See also Ex parte Tilden*, 218 Fed. 920 (1914); *Castle v. Lewis*, 254 Fed. 917 (1918); *Birsch v. Tumbleson*, 31 F.2d 811 (1929).

146. *See* text accompanying notes 119-20 *supra.*

147. *See Johnson v. Hay*, 227 U.S. 245 (1912).

148. *Ex parte Fonda*, 117 U.S. 516 (1885). *See also Duncan v. McCall*, 139 U.S. 449 (1890); *Cook v. Hart*, 146 U.S. 183 (1892); *Pepke v. Cronan*, 155 U.S. 100 (1894); *Re Chapman*, 156 U.S. 211, 216 (1894) (dictum); *Andrews v. Swartz*, 156 U.S. 272 (1894); *Whitten v. Tomlinson*, 160 U.S. 231 (1896); *Tinsley v. Anderson*, 171 U.S. 101 (1897); *Fitts v. McGhee*, 172 U.S. 516 (1898); *State of Minnesota v. Brundage*, 180 U.S. 499 (1900); *Reid v. Jones*, 187 U.S. 152 (1902); *Pettibone v. Nichols*, 203 U.S. 192 (1906).

149. *Wood v. Bush*, 140 U.S. 278 (1890).

150. *See Cook v. Hart*, 146 U.S. 183 (1892); *Ex parte Frederich*, 149 U.S. 70 (1893); *Pepke v. Cronan*, 155 U.S. 100 (1894); *Re Chapman*, 156 U.S. 211, 216 (1894) (dictum); *Andrews v. Swartz*, 156 U.S. 272 (1894); *Bergemann v. Backer*, 157 U.S. 655 (1895); *Whitten v. Tomlinson*, 160 U.S. 231 (1896); *Baker v. Grice*, 169 U.S. 284 (1898); *Fitts v. McGhee*, 172 U.S. 516 (1898); *Tinsley v. Anderson*, 171 U.S. 101 (1897); *Markuson v. Boucher*, 175 U.S. 184 (1899); *Urquhart v. Brown*, 205 U.S. 179 (1907).

151. *Ex parte Frederich*, 149 U.S. 70, 76 (1893).

152. Ibid., p. 75.

153. Revised Statutes, sect. 709 (1874). In 1916, Congress abolished appeal as of right to the Supreme Court from state decisions involving federal questions, and substituted the discretionary writ of certiorari. 39 U.S. Statutes at Large 726. *See also* 43 U.S. Statutes at Large 936, 937 (1925); 45 U.S. Statutes at Large 54 (1928).

154. 294 U.S. 103 (1934).

155. 318 U.S. 412 (1943).

156. Cf. Developments, "Federal Habeas Corpus," 83 Harv. L. Rev. 1038, 1095:

> Generally, the interests which underlie the [exhaustion] rule are compelling only with respect to appellate, not collateral, processes. It is the appellate process which most directly provides the higher state courts an opportunity to supervise trial courts and facilitate uniform application of the law; requiring exhaustion of the appellate remedies will also accomplish the objective of affording the state judicial system opportunities to enforce and develop federal law. Thus requiring the exhaustion only of appellate remedies will fulfill the major functions of the exhaustion requirement. [However, insofar as the exhaustion

rule serves another interest, providing incentives for the development of effective state corrective processes, it is particularly important when applied to collateral remedies.]

157. 321 U.S. 114 (1944).

158. Ibid., pp. 116-17.

159. Ibid., p. 118. *See also Ex parte Abernathy*, 320 U.S. 219 (1943); *White v. Ragen*, 324 U.S. 760 (1945); *Wood v. Niersteimer*, 328 U.S. 211 (1946).

160. 334 U.S. 672 (1947).

161. Ibid., p. 678.

162. Ibid., p. 680.

163. 62 U.S. Statutes at Large 967 (1948). The exhaustion rule, unchanged since its original codification, is now found at 28 U.S.C., sect. 2254 (b) and (c).

164. 339 U.S. 200 (1949).

165. Ibid., p. 208.

166. Ibid., p. 216.

167. The Court in *Hawk* relied on *Tinsley v. Anderson*, 171 U.S. 101 (1897); *Urquhart v. Brown*, 205 U.S. 179 (1906); *United States ex rel. Kennedy v. Tyler*, 269 U.S. 13 (1925); *Mooney v. Holohan*, 294 U.S. 103 (1934); *Ex parte Abernathy*, 320 U.S. 219 (1943).

168. Parker, "Limiting the Abuse of Habeas Corpus," 8 F.R.D. 171, 176.

169. *See* dissent in *Darr v. Burford*.

170. 344 U.S. 443 (1952).

171. Ibid., p. 448, n. 3.

172. Ibid., p. 447.

173. Ibid., p. 448, n. 3. *See also Roberts v. LaVallee*, 389 U.S. 40 (1967); *Wilwording et al. v. Swenson*, 404 U.S. 249 (1971).

174. 342 U.S. 519 (1952).

175. Amsterdam, "Federal Removal and Habeas Corpus Jurisdiction," 113 U. Pa. L. Rev. 793, 893-94; Developments, "Federal Habeas Corpus," 83 Harv. L. Rev. 1038, 1097-107. Cf. *Markuson v. Boucher*, 175 U.S. 189 (1899) with *Roberts v. LaVallee*, 389 U.S. 40 (1967).

176. 372 U.S. 391 (1963).

177. 183 F. Supp. 222 (1960).

178. 372 U.S. 391, 399, 435.

179. Ibid., p. 436:

[T]he Court in *Darr v. Burford* put a gloss upon these words [i.e. those of section 2254] to include petitioning for certiorari in this Court, which is not the court of any State, among the remedies that an applicant must exhaust before proceeding in federal habeas corpus. It is true that before the enactment of section 2254 the Court had spoken of the obligation to seek review in this Court before applying for habeas. . . . But that was at the time when review of state criminal judgments in this Court was by writ of error. Review here was thus a stage of the normal appellate process. The writ of certiorari, which today provides the usual mode of invoking this Court's appellate jurisdiction of state criminal judgments, 'is not a matter of right, but of sound discretion, and will be granted only where are special and important reasons therefor.' . . . Review on certiorari therefore does not provide a normal appellate channel in any sense comparable to the writ of error.

180. *Darr v. Burford*, 339 U.S. 200, 203. *See also Re Spencer*, 228 U.S. 652 (1913). Cf. *Smith v. Digmon*, 434 U.S. 332 (1978) (not essential that state court respond to argument).

181. 404 U.S. 270 (1971).

182. 434 F.2d 673.

183. 404 U.S. 270, 275.

184. Ibid., p. 279. *See* also *Pitchess v. Davis*, 421 U.S. 482 (1975).

185. *See* Developments, "Federal Habeas Corpus," 83 Harv. L. Rev. 1038, 1101-03.

186. 419 U.S. 59 (1974).

187. *Roberts v. LaVallee*, 389 U.S. 40 (1967).

188. *Price v. Johnson*, 334 U.S. 266, 283 (1947).

189. *Bowen v. Johnston*, 306 U.S. 19, 27 (1939). *See* Brennan, "Some Aspects of Federalism," 39 N.Y.U. L. Rev. 945, 957-58; Brennan, "Federal Habeas Corpus and State Prisoners," 7 Utah L. Rev. 423, 426.

190. *Kelly v. State of North Carolina*, 276 F. Supp. 200 (1967).

191. *Tolg v. Grimes*, 355 F.2d 92 (1966), *cert. den.* 384 U.S. 988 (1966); *Howard v. Sigler*, 325 F. Supp. 278 (1971).

192. *Jenkins v. Fitzberger*, 440 F.2d 1188 (1971); *Edwards v. Patterson*, 249 F. Supp. 311 (1965); *Howard v. Sigler*, 325 F. Supp. 278 (1971).

193. 304 U.S. 458 (1937).

194. Ibid., p. 464.

195. 344 U.S. 443 (1953).

196. 372 U.S. 391 (1963). *See* Reitz, "An Abortive State Proceeding," 74 Harv. L. Rev. 1315, 1332-38; Sofaer, "The Isolation Principle," 39 N.Y.U. L. Rev. 78, 83-86; and Hart, "The Time Chart of the Justices," 73 Harv. L. Rev. 84, 115. *See also Irvin v. Dowd*, 359 U.S. 394 (1959).

197. 372 U.S. 391, 438. *See also Lefkowitz v. Newsome*, 420 U.S. 283, 290, n. 6 (1975).

198. *Fay v. Noia*, 372 U.S. 391, 440.

199. Cf. *Murch v. Mattron*, 409 U.S. 41 (1972) (the Supreme Court held that a state prisoner deliberately bypassed state procedure by electing not to comply with a state court's interpretation of a statute and claim).

200. *See Davis v. United States*, 411 U.S. 233 (1973) (a federal prisoner sought federal collateral relief three years after his conviction on the grounds that his constitutional rights had been violated because blacks had been excluded from the grand jury that indicted him. He had, however, apparently failed to raise his objections prior to trial as required by F. R. C. P. 12 (b) (2), which provided that such a failure constituted a waiver of an objection unless cause was shown. Davis argued that a fundamental constitutional right could only be precluded from collateral relief when the defendant "deliberately bypassed" state procedures or he "understandingly and knowingly" waived his claim. The Court acknowledged that *Fay* had interpreted the habeas statutes as affording relief even when the claim had not been raised in a timely manner, but held that those standards were not applicable where

recognition of the claim would nullify an express statutory waiver provision); *Estelle v. Williams*, 425 U.S. 501 (1976) (the Court denied federal habeas to a state defendant who failed to object before or during trial to being tried in prison clothes. Thus, compulsion—which was deemed lacking absent an objection before or during trial—was required to establish a constitutional objection); *Francis v. Henderson*, 425 U.S. 536 (1976) (*Davis* extended to restrict state prisoners' ability to invoke habeas to review claims deemed to have been "waived" under state procedural rules. There, habeas relief was denied a petitioner who claimed that blacks had been excluded from the grand jury that indicted him because Louisiana law required a defendant to assert such a claim before trial or waive the right to make any objections. Habeas review was therefore barred absent a showing of cause and prejudice attendant to a state procedural waiver); *Wainwright v. Sykes*, 433 U.S. 72 (1977) (the rule of *Francis v. Henderson* extended to a waived objection to the admission of a confession at trial. A state prisoner alleged that testimony was admitted at his trial in violation of his *Miranda* rights. The Supreme Court held that the state procedure did, consistently with the Constitution, require that petitioner's confession be challenged at trial or not at all; and thus his failure to timely object to its admission amounted to an independent and adequate state procedural ground which would have prevented review). *See generally*, Ralph S. Spritzer, "Criminal Waiver, Procedural Default and the Burger Court," 126 U. Pa. L. Rev. 473 (1978); Peter W. Tague, "Federal Habeas Corpus and Ineffective Representation of Counsel: The Supreme Court Has Work To Do," 31 Stan. L. Rev. 1 (1978); Alfred Hill, "The Forfeiture of Constitutional Rights in Criminal Cases," 78 Col. L. Rev. 1050 (1978).

This new federalism, which has resulted in decreasing availability of the writ for state prisoners [*See generally*, Robert Cover & T. Alexander Aleinikoff, "Dialectic Federalism: Habeas Corpus and the Court," 86 Yale L. J. 1035, esp. at 1042-44 (1977); Neil McFeeley, "Habeas Corpus and Due Process: From Warren to Burger, 28 Baylor L. Rev. 533 (1976); Richard M. Michael, "The New Federalism and the Burger Court's Deference to State's in Federal Habeas Proceedings," 64 Iowa L. Rev. 233 (1979)], is strikingly similar to the retrenchment that took place in the mid-1880s. As in the earlier period, the Court's reaction was initiated by legislative suggestion. *See especially*, Omnibus Crime Control and Safe Street Bill, S. 917, 90th Cong., 2d Sess., 114 Cong. Rec. 11,189 (1968); Sen. Bill 567 [H.R. 13,722], 93d Cong., 1st Sess., 119 Cong. Rec. 2220 (1972).

201. *Wainwright v. Sykes*, 433 U.S. 72 (1977).

The Scope of Judicial Inquiry -5-

THE CONCEPT OF JURISDICTION

THE EARLY FEDERAL CASES

The writ of habeas corpus developed most rapidly in response to commitments by the executive and by the prerogative courts.[1] It was not an effective remedy where the confinement was by direction of a court of general common-law jurisdiction. Wrongful conviction by the courts of superior common-law jurisdiction was insured against by the common law and the jury trial.[2] Further, the benefits of the Habeas Corpus Act of 1679 were expressly denied to "persons convict or in execution by legal process."[3] By both common and statute law, the general rule was that the writ was not available to one confined for a crime by a court of competent jurisdiction.[4]

Marshall, finding section 14 of the Judiciary Act[5] undefined, observed that "for the meaning of the term habeas corpus, resort may unquestionably be had to the common law. . . ."[6] Did this mean that the principle of jurisdiction was incorporated into American law? Bollman had been committed by the Circuit Court of the District of Columbia on a treason charge.[7] In arguing for Bollman's release by means of the writ, counsel for Bollman, Mr. Harper, questioned whether the power to issue writs of habeas corpus was restricted by the circumstances of the commitment, it having been ordered by the circuit court:

> What stubborn maxim of law, what binding authority, requires the admission of a principle so repugnant to all our

225

feelings and to the spirit of our constitution? On what grounds or reason of law can it be pretended that a commitment by the circuit court stops the course of the writ of habeas corpus?

Is it because the circuit court has competent jurisdiction to commit? This cannot be the reason, for every justice of the peace has competent jurisdiction to commit, and the reason, therefore, if it existed, would destroy the whole effect of the writ of habeas corpus.

Is it because the circuit court has competent jurisdiction to try the offense? This cannot be the reason, for in *Bushell's case*[8] . . . it appears that a commitment by the sessions at the Old Bailey, a criminal court of high authority, and which had jurisdiction over the offense, did not prevent the court of common pleas from relieving by habeas corpus.[9]

Marshall, in a single sentence, dismissed this fundamental question: "the argument from bar has been so conclusive that nothing can be added to it."[10]

Harper's analysis was faulty.[11] The common law drew a sharp distinction between superior common-law courts and the inferior tribunals. The presumption *omnia praesumuntur rite essa acta* was applied to the instruments issued by a superior court. That is, the jurisdictional rule was "that nothing shall be intended to be out of the jurisdiction of a superior court. . . ."[12] Quite a different rule applied to the inferior courts: there, "nothing shall be intended to be within the jurisdiction . . . but that which is so expressly alleged."[13] The decisions and proceedings of the superior common-law courts were accorded respect and treated as final. This was in marked contrast to the decisions and proceedings of the equity and inferior courts: in the struggle for power with these courts,[14] the rule had developed that the cause for the imprisonment must be shown; thereby, arbitrary and illegal imprisonments could not be hidden from the superior common-law courts. When the jurisdiction of the equity and inferior courts was examined by the courts of common law, the question was "has jurisdiction been made manifest?" rather than "did they, in fact, act within their jurisdictional boundaries?"[15] In contempt cases, the rivals of the courts of common law were not only required to show jurisdiction, but sufficient details of the words alleged to be contemptuous had to be shown.[16] The reason was probably because in such cases a jurisdictional review stopping after the vague reason of "contempt" was returned would have been an insufficient device for scrutinizing and dominating the rival courts.

After the jurisdictional battles were ended, the broad reviewing power of the superior courts of common law continued to function. Thus in *Bushell's Case*,[17] the decision to release was simply "because the cause retorn'd of his imprisonment is too general. . . ."[18] Mr. Chief Justice Vaughan reasoned:

> The Court hath no knowledge of this retorn [sic], whether the evidence given were full and manifest, or doubtful, lame, and dark, or indeed evidence at all material to the issue, because it is not retorn'd what evidence in particular, and as it was deliver'd, was given. For it is not possible to judge of that rightly, what is not expos'd to a mans judgment. But here the evidence given to the jury is not expressed at all to this Court, but the judgment of the Court of Sessions upon that evidence is only expos'd to us, who tell us it is full and manifest. But our judgment ought to be grounded upon our own inferences and understandings, and not theirs.[19]

Bushell's Case, then, was completely consistent with the concept of jurisdiction.[20] It concerned the imprisonment of a group of persons by an inferior court, and was therefore a case in which the Court of Common Pleas required that jurisdiction be made manifest. Marshall therefore either rejected the incorporation of this notion into American law, or considered the Circuit Court of the District of Columbia an inferior court, or overlooked—accidentally or otherwise—this aspect of the nature of the writ. It is also possible that Marshall simply saw pretrial decisions as an exception to the rule of jurisdiction, since the habeas corpus was the traditional method for securing release on bail.[21]

In *Ex Parte Kearney*,[22] a proceeding of the Circuit Court of the District of Columbia was once again before the Supreme Court. There, a writ of habeas corpus was sought for a prisoner confined for an alleged contempt by the circuit court. The Supreme Court, *per* Mr. Justice Story, denied the motion, holding that the writ was "not a proper remedy, where a party was committed for contempt by a court of competent jurisdiction, and if granted the Court could not inquire into the sufficiency of the cause of commitment."[23] The Court relied on *Bollman* and found that there it was "expressly decided"[24] that the Supreme Court had authority to issue the writ where a person was in jail under the warrant of another court of the United States. However, it refused to exercise the power where the commitment was made by a court of competent jurisdiction, reasoning:

> If . . . we are to give any relief in this case, it is by a revision of the opinion of the court, given in the course of a criminal trial, and thus asserting a right to control its proceedings, and take from them the conclusive effect which the law intended to give them. If this was an application for a habeas corpus, after judgment on an indictment for an offense within the jurisdiction of the Circuit Court, it could hardly be maintained that this court could revise such a judgment, or the proceedings which led to it, or set it aside, and discharge the prisoner. There is, in principle, no distinction between that case and the present; for when a court commit a party for contempt, their adjudication is a conviction, and their commitment, in consequence, is execution. . . .[25]

Although the Court did not mention *Bushell*, which was cited in argument, its reasoning implied that this case was different, it having involved a commitment pursuant to an order of a superior court of criminal jurisdiction.[26]

The situations in *Bollman* and *Kearney* were similar. The prisoners in both cases were committed by a court of competent jurisdiction—in fact, they were committed by the same court. If *Kearney* is distinguished because it was a case of contempt, it should be recalled that in cases of contempt the judicial scrutiny of the reviewing court was more searching. Moreover, Bollman was committed on a charge of treason—a charge excluded from the benefits of habeas corpus under both English statutory and common law. Thus, had Kearney been discharged and Bollman remanded, the cases would have been easier to reconcile. As they stand, the cases add fuel to the suspicion that political considerations affected Marshall in *Bollman*.[27]

The principle of jurisdiction was engraved into American law eight years later in *Ex parte Watkins*.[28] Watkins had been tried and convicted of certain offenses before the Circuit Court of the District of Columbia. He petitioned the United States Supreme Court for habeas corpus and claimed that since "no offense was charged in the indictments . . . all the proceedings of [the circuit] court were nullities and void."[29] With Mr. Chief Justice Marshall himself pointing to the doctrine of jurisdiction, the Court denied relief. Once again, the power to issue the writ was recognized, but the question was whether this was a case in which it ought to be exercised. After paying homage to the common-law writ and the Habeas Corpus Act of 1679, Marshall concluded:

> The court can undoubtedly inquire into the sufficiency of [the] cause [of imprisonment]; but if it be the judgment of a court of competent jurisdiction, especially a judgment withdrawn by law from the revision of this court, is that judgment itself sufficient cause? Can the court, upon this writ, look beyond the judgment, and re-examine the charges on which it was rendered? A judgment, in its nature, concludes the subject in which it is rendered, and pronounces the law of the case. The judgment of a court of record whose jurisdiction is final, is as conclusive on all the world as the judgment of this court would be. It is as conclusive on this court as it is on other courts. It puts an end to inquiry concerning the fact by deciding it.[30]

By the mid-nineteenth century, the principle was well established: "However erroneous the judgment of the court may be, either in a civil or criminal case, if it had jurisdiction, and the defendant had been duly committed, under execution or sentence, he [could] not be discharged by this writ."[31] Immediately following this period, however, the clear principle of jurisdiction became less than transparent.

First, the rule that habeas corpus issues only where the ordinary legal remedies are unavailable or inadequate[32] was several times overlooked. In *Watkins II*[33] the Court, as in *Bollman*, went to great pains attempting to justify its appellate jurisdiction. In searching for jurisdiction in *Bollman*, the Court observed that since a proceeding to imprison preceded the habeas application, the Court's exercise of jurisdiction was appellate because the writ was for the purpose of revising the decision to commit.[34] In *Watkins II*, while the prisoner was serving a sentence for embezzlement, the attorney general sued out a writ of *capias ad satisfaciendum* against him. No return was made to the writ. However, after serving his sentence for embezzlement the prisoner was not released by the marshal, apparently because the marshal believed him to have been ordered into commitment in connection with the capias. Watkins petitioned for a writ of habeas corpus. The attorney general argued that on the merits, the petitioner was not entitled to release unless he was confined for a period beyond that authorized by the capias. Therefore, Watkins was complaining of imprisonment without process rather than imprisonment under process. The Court, however, observed that since the award of the capias was a judicial act, review of imprisonment under capias would be an exercise of appellate jurisdiction.[35] So obsessed was the Court with finding a lower court proceeding so as to permit it to exercise its jurisdiction in *Watkins*, that it failed to question whether habeas corpus should issue in light of its extraordinary nature. Further, though the writ of error had several times been acknowledged to be available to review habeas decisions of the lower federal courts,[36] the Court in *In re Kaine*,[37] *Ex parte Wells*,[38] and *Ex parte Yerger*[39] did not even mention the writ of error before invoking its appellate habeas jurisdiction. Again, the most important concern for the Court was with justifying the exercise of appellate jurisdiction.[40] Moreover, the Court did not examine the question of the lower courts' jurisdiction, but reviewed the lower courts' decisions for errors.

In addition to the neglect of the common-law habeas principles tangential to the concept of jurisdiction, the Court, inspired by legislative action, consciously began to shake the common-law bonds of the writ of habeas corpus. Congress in 1867 expanded the habeas jurisdiction of the federal courts and judges.[41] Although the actual intent of the legislative enactment is questionable,[42] and the Supreme Court's power under the act was withdrawn the following year,[43] the significance of the statute for present purposes lies in the effect it had on the rhetoric of the Court. Before its jurisdiction under the act of 1867 was withdrawn, the Court indicated how it would have operated under that statute:

> This legislation is one of the most comprehensive character. It brings within the *habeas corpus* jurisdiction of every court and of every judge every possible cause of privation of liberty contrary to the National Constitution, treaties, or laws. It is impossible to widen this jurisdiction.[44]

When its jurisdiction under the act was withdrawn, the Court continued to take a more liberal view of the writ's nature. In *Ex parte Yerger*,[45] though the prisoner's "original" confinement was not under judicial authority, the Court found the case a proper one for the exercise of its appellate jurisdiction, finding Yerger's "immediate" commitment "a custody to which he [had] been remanded [, having been denied habeas corpus by the United States Circuit Court for the Southern District of Mississippi,] by order of an inferior court of the United States."[46] The Court, in justification of its finding, observed that

> The great and leading intent of the Constitution and laws must be kept constantly in view upon the examination of every question of construction.
> That intent, in respect to the writ of habeas corpus is manifest. It is that every citizen may be protected by judicial action from unlawful imprisonment. To this end the Act of 1789 provided that every court of the United States should have power to issue the writ. The jurisdiction thus given in law to the circuit and district courts is appellate. Given in general terms, it must necessarily extend to all cases to which the judicial power of the United States extends, other than those expressly excepted from it.[47]

Looking at the history of the writ from 1789, the Court continued:

> [T]he general spirit and genius of our institution has tended to the widening and enlarging of the habeas corpus jurisdic-

tion of the courts and judges of the United States; and this tendency, except in one recent instance, has been constant and uniform; and it is in light of it that we must determine the true meaning of the Constitution and laws in respect to the appellate jurisdiction of this court.[48]

Thus, the Court was interpreting its habeas jurisdiction in light of the progressive history of *legislative* action respecting that jurisdiction—a liberal method of interpretation indeed for this period in the Court's history. Further, the Court seemed to warn Congress that any further encroachment upon its appellate authority to issue the writ would not be upheld since it would "weaken the efficacy of the writ, deprive the citizen in many cases of its benefit, and seriously hinder the establishment of that uniformity in deciding upon questions of personal rights. . . ."[49] The Court's opinion was, therefore, influenced also by its desire to flex its muscles after an embarrassing political defeat the previous year.

The neglect of the principle that the writ was to issue only where other remedies were unavailable or inadequate and the more liberal rhetoric applied to the writ following the Civil War were the catalysts for the gradual development of the concept of jurisdiction. In *Stout v. Territory of Utah*[50] the Court was evenly divided on the question of whether on habeas corpus it might discharge a prisoner for matters behind the indictment. The petitioner contended that he had been indicted by a grand jury not drawn according to law. Although the prisoner was not discharged, it is significant that four out of eight justices were willing to discharge, for a matter behind the indictment, for a crime that was within the lower court's jurisdiction.

Shortly after *Stout*, the Court in *Ex parte Lange*[51] granted the petition of a prisoner who alleged that he had been illegally sentenced. A lower court had imposed both parts of an alternative sentence—fine and imprisonment. After paying the fine and serving five days of his sentence of imprisonment, Lange challenged his confinement as unlawful. The Supreme Court agreed, finding that once one part of the alternative sentence was satisfied, the power of the court to punish further was gone. The Court stated that the proceedings of the lower court were an "error, because the power to render any further judgment did not exist." It continued:

> It is no answer to this to say that the court had jurisdiction of the person of the prisoner, and of the offense under the statute. It by no means follows that these two facts make valid, however erroneous it may be, any judgment the court may render in such a case. If a justice of the peace, having jurisdiction to fine for misdemeanor, and with the party charged properly before him, should render a judgment that he be hung, it would simply be void. Why void? Because he had no power to render such a judgment. . . .[52]

Just as the Marshall Court in *Bollman* (and the Warren Court in *Fay v. Noia*[53]) failed to distinguish the common-law jurisdictional rule as applied to inferior courts on one hand, and superior common-law courts on the other, the Court in *Lange* erroneously employed the example of a justice of the peace as an analogy to reduce the contrary view to absurdity. The error in *Lange* was not a substantive error going to the conviction, but was an error in sentencing by a court where jurisdiction was final, and according to *Watkins*, whose judgment was to be "as conclusive on all the world as the judgment of [the Supreme Court] would be." The principled distinction, then, was between an error in the judgment and an error in sentencing.

The habeas inquiry in *Lange* did not stop at the petition and return, but went on to consider the record as well. In bringing the record before it, the Supreme Court went much further than Common Pleas in *Bushell* in its dealings with an inferior tribunal. The Court sought to support its decision with precedent, but none of its citations involved both a prisoner under the sentence of a superior court of competent jurisdiction and a record brought before it on certiorari. Many years later, another Court in *Frank v. Mangum*[54] noted that one of the effects of the Habeas Corpus Act of 1867 was that it substituted

for a bare legal review that seems to have been the limit of judicial authority under common-law practice, and under the act of 31 Car. II, c. 2 [1679], a more searching investigation, in which the applicant is put to his oath to set forth the truth of the matter respecting the cause of his detention, and the court, upon determining the actual facts, is to "dispose of the party as law and justice require."[55]

The more progressive view of habeas corpus thus allowed the Court, during the suspension of its powers under the Act of 1867, to conduct a more searching investigation than was permitted under English common and statute law, though less than that permitted by the 1867 enactment.

How far the rule of *Lange* was to extend was answered to an extent in *Ex parte Parks*.[56] The Court there refused relief to one who claimed that the act for which he was convicted was not a crime under the laws of the United States.[57] The Court saw the question presented as one that the lower court was competent to decide and if it erred, jurisdiction was not lost. The Court distinguished this case from one that was not only erroneous, but void. In the latter case, habeas corpus was an appropriate remedy; however, the remedy was a "special" one, "confined to a limited class of cases."[58] The limit was violated when a sentence not called for by the judgment was rendered; the application of a statute to a case was within the jurisdiction of the trial court.

Similar to the situation in *Lange*, but different from that in *Parks*, was the case of one imprisoned under an unconstitutional statute. In *Ex parte Virginia*,[59] it was alleged by the petitioner that his confinement was warranted neither by the Constitution nor by the laws made in pursuance of the Constitution. Relying on *Lange*, the Court stated that while a writ of habeas corpus could not generally be used to subserve the purposes of a writ of error, "when a prisoner is held without any lawful authority, and by an order beyond the jurisdiction of an inferior Federal Court to make, this court will, in favor of liberty, grant the writ, not to review the whole case, but to examine the authority of the court below to act at all." The act, however, was found constitutional and so the writ was denied. Justices Field and Clifford dissented, finding the statute unconstitutional. Both the majority and minority, however, agreed that in the case of a prisoner confined under an unconstitutional statute, habeas corpus was an appropriate remedy. The Court elaborated upon this decision later in the same year in *Ex parte Siebold*.[60] Whereas the prisoner in *Ex parte Virginia* was held under an indictment, Siebold was held under a conviction. He argued that the statute under which he was convicted was unconstitutional and therefore void. The Court acknowledged that the general rule prohibited relief by habeas corpus where one was imprisoned under the conviction of a court of competent jurisdiction. It noted, however, *Bushell's Case* and a passage in Bacon's *Abridgements*, which provided that "if the commitment be against law, as being made by one who has no jurisdiction of the cause, *or for a matter for which by law no man ought to be punished*, the courts are to discharge him."[61] The Court therefore found:

> An unconstitutional law is void, and is no law. An offense created by it is not a crime. A conviction under it is not merely erroneous but illegal and void, and cannot be a legal cause of imprisonment. It is true, if no error lies, the judgment may be final, in the sense that there be no means of reversing it. But personal liberty is of so great moment in the eye of the law that the judgment of an inferior court affecting it is not deemed so conclusive but that, as we have seen, the question of the court's authority to try and imprison the party may be reviewed on habeas corpus by a superior court or judge having authority to award the writ. We are satisfied that the present is one of the cases in which this court is authorized to take such jurisdiction. We think so, and if the laws are unconstitutional and void, the circuit court acquired no jurisdiction of the case.[62]

Upon examination of the acts, the Court found them constitutional and therefore denied habeas corpus. Once again Field and Clifford dissented on the ground that the acts were unconstitutional and therefore habeas corpus should have been granted.

Bushell's Case has already been examined in the American context. It was concluded that in using the case, the courts had failed to note the distinction between the jurisdictional rule applied to superior as opposed to inferior courts. A similar argument applies to the Bacon extract. The rule referred to by Bacon was descriptive of a mode of procedure for superior courts in their exercise of habeas jurisdiction.[63]

The difficulty with ascertaining the "correct" application of the law springs from the fact that the English common-law principles were being applied in a different judicial system. Was *Siebold* decided correctly? Surely Bacon did not contemplate a situation where the facts fell within the prohibition of a legislative enactment, but the statute itself was subject to being declared null and void by the judiciary. An analogy can perhaps be suggested: given that the American courts have the power to pass on the constitutionality of a legislative enactment, confinement under a statute that was a nullity would seem no different than a confinement under a statute prescribing only a financial penalty or confinement under no statute. But how does one explain the difference between *Ex parte Parks* and *Ex parte Virginia*? As it was proper and necessary at each stage of a proceeding to apply a statute to the facts, was it not equally necessary and proper at each stage of a proceeding to question whether a statute was constitutional? The Bacon quotation, in fact, applied to an error in the application of a statute to a factual situation. This was the case in *Parks*. How good was an analogy when the application of the rule to the exact situation was denied? Why trust the lower federal court with the question of the applicability of the statute and not the constitutionality of the statute? Was it because the lower court had a better perspective for weighing the facts? Of course in *Lange* the Court did not hesitate to examine the record. But there, it searched the record not to review the judgment, but rather to examine the appropriateness of the sentence. Further, was not the integrity of the lower court higher in cases such as *Ex parte Virginia* than in *Ex parte Parks*, since the latter case was calling the judgment of the lower court itself into question? Perhaps the Court would have done better if it had acknowledged the difference between the English and American systems. Judicial review was no part of the English system. During this period, the appellate scrutiny of legislation was far more strict than the review of lower court process.

How, after *Siebold*, was the Court to deal with cases such as

Parks? If on habeas corpus, the constitutionality of the statute, which the lower court was acting under, was open to question, but the facts alleged in the indictment were not, the Court, for the purpose of testing the constitutionality of the act, would have to assume that the actions charged in the indictment were forbidden by the statute, even if, in fact, they were not so forbidden. Understandably, however, the lower court was to be trusted with its application of the statute to the facts. Of course this meant that the constitutionality of a statute depended on the unexamined facts determined to be in conflict with it, since the facts said to be illegal were in fact being weighed against the constitutional provision and not the statute itself. This was the case in *Ex parte Yarbrough*.[64] The Court there held:

> Whether the indictment sets forth, in comprehensive terms, the offense which the statute describes and forbids and for which it prescribes a punishment, is in every case a question of law which necessarily be decided by the court in which the case originates and is, therefore clearly, within its jurisdiction.
>
> Its decisions on the conformity of the indictment to the provisions of the statute may be erroneous, but if so it is an error of law made by a court acting within its jurisdiction, which could be corrected on a writ of error. . . .
>
> This, however, leaves for consideration the more important question, . . . whether the law of Congress . . . is warranted by the Constitution or, being without such warrant, is null and void.
>
> If the law which defines the offense and prescribes its punishment is void, the court was without jurisdiction and the prisoners must be discharged.[65]

Although the Court on habeas corpus would not test whether the indictment stated an offense,[66] it would inquire whether the crime charged required presentment or indictment by a grand jury.[67] The reasoning in the latter case was that if a crime were "infamous" within the meaning of the Fifth Amendment, then no court could have jurisdiction without an indictment or presentment by a grand jury. This can be distinguished from the former case in that it involved purely a question of constitutional law whereas the latter case required a factual examination. This rule was supplemented shortly afterwards. In *Ex parte Bain*,[68] the Court held that an indictment that was amended other than by the grand jury after it had been found by the grand jury, but prior to trial, was "no indictment of the grand jury," and therefore the trial court did not have jurisdiction of the offense. However, where an individual claimed that the indictment under which he was presented, tried, and convicted was void, having not been found by a legal grand jury (one of its members having been an alien) and that the act of the legislature allowing such a grand jury was unconstitutional, the Court denied relief.[69] The Supreme Court in *Ex parte Harding* was of the opinion that the lower court had not been deprived of jurisdiction. The Court held that "[t]he objection, if it be one, goes only to the regularity of the proceedings, and not to the jurisdiction."[70] The question would seem to have required the Court merely to weigh the act against the constitutional provision. If an "unconstitutional law is void, and is no law,"[71] then a grand jury constituted in pursuance of the unconstitutional provisions of an act would not have the legal capacity to find a valid indictment, and therefore their indictment would be "no indictment of [a] grand jury,"[72] and the trial court would be without jurisdiction.[73] *Harding* seems to be in conflict with *Bain*. It is possible, however, that the essential difference for the Court was that a deeper inquiry was required in *Harding*. In support of that possibility consider *Ex parte Snow*.[74] There it was held that where a person was unlawfully convicted on each of several indictments for alleged separate offenses, which in fact constitute but one continuous offense, he could be punished only under one of such convictions; and for an attempt to enforce more than one (and this is to be emphasized), if the want of jurisdiction appeared on the face of the judgment, he was entitled to a writ of habeas corpus. The emphasis placed upon the requirement that a multiple conviction for the same offense appear on the face of the judgment was abandoned later in *Ex parte Neilson*,[75] and it was held that if it appeared anywhere on the record it was sufficient. The Court viewed an "unconstitutional conviction and punishment under a valid law" to be equivalent to "a conviction and punishment under an unconstitutional law."[76] This, in the

Court's opinion, followed from the fact that in the latter instance, "the court had no authority to take cognizance of the case"; in the former, "it had no authority to render judgment."[77] However, in *Ex parte Wilson*,[78] the Court denied a petition for habeas corpus to one whose conviction was based upon an indictment by a grand jury deficient in the number prescribed *by statute*. The Court considered such an issue to be a matter "which must necessarily be considered and determined by the trial court, its ruling thereon, however erroneous, would seem . . . to present simply a matter of error, and not be sufficient to oust the jurisdiction."[79] The Court seemed to have been impressed by the fact that the alleged error was not prejudicial to the defendant.[80]

During this period, the Supreme Court further refused to grant habeas relief, based upon the concept of jurisdiction, to one questioning the constitutionality of a federal statute permitting a criminal defendant to waive trial by jury,[81] or to a petitioner contending that he was denied trial by an impartial jury due to selection defects.[82] Also the Court, *per* Mr. Justice Holmes, denied a petition for habeas corpus and certiorari to an applicant who contended that he was compelled to be a witness against himself contrary to the provisions of the Fifth Amendment because he was required to stand up and walk before the jury, and during a recess, the jury was stationed so as to observe his walk and size.[83] In these cases, the trial court's jurisdiction had already attached with regard to the subject matter and person. These cases were unlike the case of *Neilson*, where the trial court lost jurisdiction at the end of the "first" proceeding and therefore had no jurisdiction in the "second" proceeding.

Traditionally, habeas corpus was "not a proper remedy, where a party was committed for a contempt by a court of competent jurisdiction";[84] however, the developed concept of jurisdiction qualified the general rule for contempt proceedings as well.[85] In *Ex parte Terry*,[86] the Court denied an application for habeas corpus to relieve a petitioner from imprisonment under an order of a United States circuit court for contempt committed in its presence. It held that the circuit court had power to proceed upon its own knowledge of the facts and to punish the offender without further proof. The Court reasoned: "Whether the facts justify such punishment was for that court to determine. Its conclusion upon such facts is not open to inquiry or review in proceedings by habeas corpus."[87] However, where the trial court imposes imprisonment under its contempt power in excess of its jurisdiction, the Court would relieve by habeas corpus. For example, the Court granted a petition for habeas corpus to relieve a prisoner confined under an order of a district court for contempt in disobeying the order of that court requiring him to deliver a child to its parent. Since "[t]he whole subject of domestic relations of husband and wife, parent and child, belongs to the laws of the States," the Court held the order null and void and discharged the prisoners.[88] In *Ex parte Hudgings*,[89] the Court granted an original petition for habeas corpus to a prisoner held in custody for contempt because, in the trial court's opinion, the prisoner as a witness "wilfully refused to testify truthfully. . . ." The Court found the commitment void for excess of power since the "essential character" of contemptuous acts was the "obstructive tendency," which is not inherent in false swearing.[90] The Court noted that if a court were allowed to punish, under its contempt power, a witness who in the opinion of the court was testifying untruthfully, "the power would result to impose a punishment for contempt, with the object or purpose of exacting from the witness a character of testimony which the court would deem to be truthful; and thus it would come to pass that a potentiality of oppression and wrong would result, and the freedom of the citizen, when called as a witness in a court, would be gravely imperiled."[91]

In summary, the general rule was that habeas corpus was not an effective remedy for one held under the commitment of a court of competent jurisdiction. From the earliest cases, pretrial commitments were excepted from the general rule. Habeas corpus was the traditional means of securing bail, and since the Supreme Court had power to award bail,[92] it may have felt that the rule was inapplicable to this stage of the proceedings. By far the most difficult problem in dealing with the rule of jurisdiction is to explain why the Court accepted certain claims and rejected others. Professor Paul M. Bator has remarked that "[o]nce the concept of 'jurisdiction' is taken beyond the question of the court's competence to deal with the class of offenses charged and the person of the prisoner, it becomes a less than luminous beacon."[93] In restoring the clarity of the concept, the causes for development must be kept in mind:

(1) The courts' failure to take note of the "extraordinary character" of the writ, that is, the use of the writ of habeas corpus without questioning the availability of other remedies. By the time this neglect had been corrected and the court began (after *Yerger*) to hold firm to the rule that the writ of habeas corpus was not to be used as a writ of error,[94] the "damage" had already been done. (2) After the enactment of the Act of 1867, the Court, even during the period when its power under the Act was suspended, began to emphasize the "progressive nature" of the writ. This emphasis was inspired not only by the 1867 Act, but very probably also by the 1868 revocation and the Court's effort to overcome total defeat. Irrespective of motivation, taking notice of this aspect of the writ's nature always has been followed immediately by further development. (3) Most important in the development of the common-law concept of jurisdiction was the fact that the notion was being employed in a different judicial system. That a statute may be declared unconstitutional and therefore null and void and lend no support to jurisdiction is the most obvious case in point. The development here was simply a matter of the English concept adapting to its new environs. Likewise is the case of the differentiation between the superior common-law courts as opposed to the equity and inferior courts in England. The rules that were well suited to such a system could not easily be taken account of by the judicial system of the United States.[95] However, operating in opposition to these three reasons was the traditional reluctance of the habeas court to deal with factual matters. These four points sufficiently explain the development *and consistency* of the concept of jurisdiction in the early federal cases.

THE EARLY STATE CASES IN THE FEDERAL COURTS (1867-1915)

In 1867, the federal courts and judges were empowered to grant the writ of habeas corpus to any person restrained "in violation of the constitution or any treaty or law of the United States."[96] The Act extended federal habeas corpus to a larger class than had previously been the case.[97] How great a change in the scope of judicial inquiry on habeas corpus was intended by the statute?

If the Act had been passed a century later than it was, the language might have been considered broad enough to empower the United States courts and judges to issue the writ to redetermine all issues of federal law in both federal and state cases. A person held under execution of, or convicted by, the lowest state criminal tribunal could immediately seek the writ in the highest courts of the United States, and be released if the state court erred in the application of, or neglected the application of, federal statutory, as well as constitutional, law. Similarly, a person convicted in the highest court of a state could be released by a single district court judge by means of the writ, if, in the view of the federal district judge, the high state court erred in answering the federal question. Keeping in mind that the exhaustion of state remedies rule is a judicial invention and not compelled by the 1867 enactment,[98] and that such an interpretation would not be restricted by the words of the statute to federal questions in state cases but would extend as well to federal cases,[99] is such an interpretation feasible? Additionally, in its historical context, is the provision susceptible to such a reading? In the brief discussion on the Act in Congress, although an intent to extend the federal writ of habeas corpus to state prisoners may be discovered,[100] there was no hint that the measure was intended to apply to those convicted by a state court of competent jurisdiction. The concept of jurisdiction was, at this time, a well-established rule.[101] On habeas corpus the only question before the court was the jurisdiction of the sentencing court. The writ of habeas corpus was not to be used to perform the office of a writ of error. This concept was valid in state, as well as federal, courts.[102] If the statute meant to abrogate this rule, the absence of express language in the statute and the complete lack of debate in Congress or discussion in the legal periodicals or treatises of the day is difficult to explain. Doubt that Congress intended to transform the writ of habeas corpus into a writ of error increases when section 2 of the 1867 statute is examined. That section expanded the power of the Supreme Court to dispose of cases coming to it from the state courts on writs of error.[103].

Since the language does not restrict the benefits of the Act to only *state* imprisonments, the argument that extends it as far as state prisoners, confined by other than a court of competent jurisdiction, must take account of federal imprisonments as well. In the Senate, the Act was explained as extending only as far as state prisoners.[104]

However, the explanation of the Act's framer, given in the House, is most appropriately interpreted as meaning that the Act extended to federal, as well as state, prisoners. This interpretation alone reasonably takes account of the qualifying clause at the end of the statute, excepting from the coverage of the Act "any person who is or may be held in custody of the military authorities of the United States, charged with any military offense, or with having aided or abetted rebellion against the government of the United States prior to the passage of this act." Why except from the coverage of the Act a species of a genus not meant to be covered by the Act? The Court, the year after enactment of the statute, held it to be applicable to the case of a federal prisoner.[105] But, if no change in the concept of jurisdiction was to be effected by the 1867 statute, what purpose was there in extending its benefits to federal prisoners? The Act of 1789 did not expressly state the ground on which a person in federal custody could be discharged, but clearly he could be released if confinement "in violation of the constitution, or any treaty or law of the United States." However, under the provisions of the Judiciary Act of 1789, no review of right by the Supreme Court was available; under the 1867 statute, it was. That the benefits of the Habeas Corpus Act of 1867 extended to federal prisoners confined by less than competent authority, in turn supports the proposition that the Act extended to state prisoners similarly confined.

In sum, although the Act of 1867 extended federal habeas to a larger class, and provided for an appeal as of right, it did not effect a change in the concept of jurisdiction.[106] This reading was followed by the Supreme Court in its early decisions in the cases of state prisoners applying for federal habeas.

The first indication of how the Court would read the Act of 1867 came in 1884 in *Ex parte Crouch*.[107] The petitioner, detained for trial by a state court, alleged that he was held in violation of the Constitution of the United States, because the state statute for which he was being held violated Article I, section 10, clause 1's prohibition against state laws which impair the obligation of contracts. As the Court's power under the 1867 statute was still under suspension, it clearly lacked jurisdiction in this case. Nevertheless, presumably on the basis of the Habeas Corpus Act of 1867, the Court allowed its appellate jurisdiction to attach, but refused to grant the petition because the state court was one of competent jurisdiction. It viewed the petitioner's request as one based not upon an alleged want of jurisdiction in the state court, but rather as one based upon an allegation that a valid defense to the charge existed. It continued:

> It is elementary learning that, if a prisoner is in the custody of a state court of competent jurisdiction, not illegally asserted, he cannot be taken from that jurisdiction and discharged on *habeas corpus* issued by a court of the United States, simply because he is not guilty of the offense for which he is held. All questions which may arise in the orderly course of the proceedings against him are to be determined by the court to whose jurisdiction he has been subjected, and no other court is authorized to interfere to prevent it. Here the right of the prisoner to a discharge depends alone on the sufficiency of his defense to the information under which he is held. Whether his defense is sufficient or not is for the court which tries him to determine. If in this determination errors are committed, they can only be corrected in an application form of proceeding for that purpose. The office of a writ of *habeas corpus* is neither to correct such errors, nor to take the prisoner away from the court which holds him for trial, for fear, if he remains, they may be committed.[108]

The Court thus refused to review a federal constitutional question because it did not go to the jurisdiction of the state court which committed the prisoner.

Following the official reestablishment of its jurisdiction under the Act of 1867, the Supreme Court consistently held during this period that state prisoners were not entitled to federal habeas if committed by a court of competent jurisdiction.[109] In *Duncan v. McCall*,[110] the Court rejected a request for habeas corpus from a state prisoner who claimed that he was denied equal protection and due process because, due to a number of legislative irregularities, the "Penal Code and Code of Criminal Procedure" of the state, under which his trial was conducted, was not in effect. The Court, however, held that the state court "had jurisdiction and the power to determine the law applicable to the case, and if it committed error in its action, the remedy of petitioner was . . . an appeal to the Court of Appeals of the State."[111] Although not explicitly stated, at the core of this decision was one of the fundamental laws of the concept of jurisdiction, as clearly established in *Ex parte Parks*:[112] the trial court was to be trusted with its interpretation of a statute. This rule likewise was implicitly followed in *Wood v. Bush*.[113] There the Court denied relief to a black petitioner, convicted of murder in a state court, who alleged that he was denied due process and equal protection because of the unlawful exclusion of blacks from grand and petit juries. The Court found that the state laws, which prescribed the method of jury selection, did not discriminate against blacks because of their race, and therefore the question was whether or not the jurors in this case were selected in conformity with the laws of the state—"a question which the trial court was entirely competent to decide and its determination could not be reviewed by the circuit court of the United States upon a writ of habeas corpus without making that writ serve the purposes of a writ of error."[114] Similarly in *Ex parte Frederich*,[115] the Court refused habeas relief to a state prisoner convicted of first degree murder, but, pursuant to a state law, the state supreme court modified the conviction to second degree murder. The petitioner contended that the supreme court of the state was not empowered by statute to render the judgment it did, but could only affirm, reverse, or remand the case. The United States Supreme Court observed that "[t]he writ of habeas corpus is not a proceeding for the correction of errors."[116] It went on to explain that the habeas corpus proceeding was a collateral attack of a civil nature to impeach the validity of a judgment or sentence of another court in a criminal proceeding, and it should, therefore, be limited to cases in which the judgment or sentence attacked is clearly void by reason of its having been rendered without jurisdiction, or by reason of the court's having exceeded its jurisdiction in the premises.[117].

The rule following from the concept of jurisdiction established in federal cases for dealing with questions on the indictment[118] was followed in the state cases involving that subject. In *Bergemann v. Backer*[119] the Court denied habeas relief to a state prisoner convicted of first degree murder, who argued that the indictment found against him amounted to second degree, and not first degree, murder. In *Kohl v. Lehlback*[120] the Supreme Court held that where the state court had jurisdiction of the offense charged, and of the accused, it was not for the federal courts to determine whether the indictment sufficiently charged the crime for which the prisoner was convicted.

Errors committed in the course of a state trial likewise were not subject to review on federal habeas where the trial court had jurisdiction of both the subject matter and the person accused. In the just-cited case of *Kohl v. Lehlback*, the Court held that there was no denial of due process or equal protection simply because one of the jurors in a criminal case was an alien. In *Re Echart*,[121] the Court denied an application for allowance of a writ of habeas corpus from a state prisoner who alleged that since the jury verdict merely found him guilty of murder, without specifying the degree, the trial court was without jurisdiction to pass sentence. The Court was of the opinion that since the trial court had jurisdiction of the offense charged and the person accused, and the verdict clearly did not acquit the accused of the crime charged, but found that he had committed an offense within the accusation, then it was within the jurisdiction of the trial judge to pass upon the sufficiency of the verdict and to construe its legal meaning. If in so doing he erred and held the verdict to be sufficiently certain to authorize the imposition of punishment for the highest grade of the offense charged, it was an error committed in the exercise of jurisdiction, and one that did not present a jurisdictional defect, remediable by the writ of habeas corpus. In *Crossley v. State of California*[122] the Court held that an error in submitting to the jury the question of murder in the first degree, while the evidence was sufficient at most to convict of second-degree murder, did not constitute such a jurisdictional defect in the conviction for murder in the first degree as to sustain the issuing of a habeas corpus by a United States circuit court. In *Felts v. Murphy*, [123] the Supreme Court affirmed a circuit court's denial of an application for a writ of habeas corpus filed on behalf of an almost totally deaf person convicted in a state court of murder, in the face of an allegation that his constitutional rights were violated because he could not hear the testimony presented against him, and the state trial court made no effort to repeat the testimony to him through an ear trumpet that he had with him. The Court found this "at most an error." "[T]he state court had jurisdiction of both the subject matter and of the person upon the trial of the accused, and such jurisdiction was not lost during the trial, but continued to its end, and it had jurisdiction to direct the judgment which was entered, and to have the same executed."[124]

In keeping with the concept of jurisdiction as developed in federal cases,[125] the Court, however, discharged state prisoners held under statutes repugnant to the federal Constitution. Since an unconstitutional statute (or a statute fair on its face, though effectively discriminatory)[126] was a nullity, no jurisdiction could be said to exist.[127] In *Wo Lee v. Hopkins*,[128] the Court discharged a prisoner from state custody on federal habeas corpus because the administration of the ordinance under which he had been convicted was discriminatory and therefore repugnant to the Fourteenth Amendment of the United States Constitution. In *Ex parte Medley*,[129] the Court discharged on habeas corpus a petitioner who was convicted of a murder perpetrated on the thirteenth of May, 1889, and was sentenced under a statute approved 19 April 1889, but which went into effect 19 July 1889. The Court held that the law was not in force prior to the nineteenth of July, and the crime, having been committed in May, was to be governed in all particulars, of trial and punishment, by the laws then in force: "If these were conducted and administered under the Law of 1889, which became a law after the commission of the offense, and its provisions, so far as applied by the Court to the case of the prisoner, were such invasions of his rights as to properly to be called *ex post facto laws*, they were void."[130] The decision was quite consistent with *Ex parte Lange*.[131]

The Act of 1867 did not enlarge the scope of judicial inquiry. The traditional test of jurisdiction, as adopted to the American judicial system, remained law. Errors of federal law, committed by a court of competent jurisdiction, were to be corrected on appeal and not on habeas corpus. Even jurisdictional issues were subject to the exhaustion requirement.[132] Naturally, the Court was not about to expand the concept of jurisdiction in cases of state prisoners and thereby broaden the availability of the federal writ at the same time as it was limiting the writ's availability *via* the exhaustion rule. Both the exhaustion and jurisdiction doctrines of the law of habeas corpus were quite consistent with the nineteenth-century notion of federalism, which placed primary responsibility for individual liberty and criminal justice on the state courts. Although that notion (which was a guiding factor in the formulation of the habeas clause of the Constitution and section 14 of the Judiciary Act of 1789) was interrupted briefly prior to the Civil War in an attempt to provide national protection for the "peculiar institution" and after the Civil War to effectuate reconstruction policy, it was a fundamental tenet of American constitutional law operative throughout the nineteenth century. The potential of the Fourteenth Amendment for alteration of that notion did not materialize. The first case to explore the "privileges and immunities" clause read it to secure only those privileges and immunities of national citizenship.[133] The first case to examine the "due process" clause held that that clause required only that process that was due by state law.[134] The Amendment therefore was interpreted as requiring that everyone be treated equally before the laws. The due process clause required that the process be equal; privileges and immunities required that certain substance be equal; and equal protection required equality in the protection afforded by the law. The emergence of substantive due process, in this context, was quite natural. It essentially provided that legislative measures not favor any particular class. During the Fuller era, challenges to state criminal proceedings were viewed as, at most, "mere errors in procedure," which did not affect the "substantive rights" (equality before the laws) of the accused.[135]

EXPANSION OF THE SCOPE OF JUDICIAL INQUIRY (1915-PRESENT)

THE DOCTRINE OF FRANK v. MAGNUM

As of 1915, the traditional test on habeas corpus was jurisdiction.[136] If a trial court had jurisdiction of the subject matter and of the person of the accused, habeas relief was unavailable. The Act of 1867, as just shown, effected no change in this concept.[137] However, owing to the relatively liberal legal system whereby the executive and military agencies are greatly deterred from exercising an arbitrary power of imprisonment, and to the development of the concept of exhaustion,[138] habeas corpus was increasingly being used as a collateral method of attack. Moreover, the notion of due process was rapidly expanding. By the end of the Fuller era, pressure was mounting against substantive due process. Limiting government by way of concepts such as "liberty of contract" appeared to ignore the rapidly changing economic situation at the turn of the century. In recognition of that situation and the continuing desire to insure limited government, the progressives sought to replace substantive due process with procedural due process, which limited government by way of the process-oriented rights of the Bill of Rights.

In 1915, the case of *Frank v. Magnum*[139] came to the Supreme Court on appeal from a United States district court to review a decree denying a petition for a writ of habeas corpus. Frank had been indicted for murder in Georgia, found guilty by a state court, and sentenced to death. Prior to his application for federal habeas, Frank unsuccessfully had requested a new trial, had challenged the conviction on appeal to the Supreme Court of Georgia (where an extensive independent inquiry into the merits of Frank's claim was conducted), and had sought various postconviction remedies and writ of error to the United States Supreme Court. Frank's claim was that his trial was completely dominated by a mob, making fair and impartial adjudication impossible.

The Court, *per* Mr. Justice Pitney, although denying the application, rendered a decision that greatly expanded the concept of jurisdiction. Pitney began by acknowledging the limited scope of habeas inquiry:

> if [one] is held in custody by reason of his conviction upon a criminal charge before a court having plenary jurisdiction over the subject-matter or offense, the place where it was committed, and the person of the prisoner, it results from the nature of the writ itself that he cannot have relief on habeas corpus.[140]

He next went on to provide a concise summary of the then current view of the Fourteenth Amendment due process rights:

> a criminal prosecution in the courts of a state, based upon

a law not itself repugnant to the Federal Constitution, and conducted according to the settled course of judicial proceedings as established by the law of the state, so long as it includes notice and a hearing, or an opportunity to be heard, before a court of competent jurisdiction, according to the established modes of procedure, is "due process" in the constitutional sense.[141]

The narrow scope of review on habeas corpus, and the now broadened concept of due process were not easily reconciled. Who was to judge whether the criminal prosecution was "conducted according to the settled course of judicial proceedings?" If the course set by the laws of a particular state included notice and hearing or an opportunity to be heard before a court of competent jurisdiction, was a case arising from that state an appropriate one for federal habeas relief? Traditionally, the trial court was to be trusted with the application of a statute to a case. On the other hand, if the laws of the state did not provide for the requisite elements of judicial procedure as dictated by the Fourteenth Amendment to the Constitution, the proceedings, under the principle of *Siebold*,[142] would have been void, and therefore the trial court's jurisdiction would never have attached. But *Siebold* had been repudiated nine years before *Frank*.[143] According to the concept of jurisdiction then, where the trial court was of competent jurisdiction, the trial court judge's decision was final, subject only to appeal, not habeas corpus. Was the question of "due process" in the course of a trial more appropriately asked on appeal? Pitney did not think so. Conceding a point made by appellant's counsel,[144] Pitney acknowledged that even though a trial court's jurisdiction initially attaches, the conditions surrounding the course of the proceedings could work to deprive the trial court of jurisdiction to receive the verdict and pronounce judgment and sentence.[145] In other words, jurisdiction was not only something that a court initially had or did not have, or acted within or exceeded, but something that could be "lost." One can imagine that the conditions surrounding the course of the proceeding depriving the court of jurisdiction easily could depend upon factual matters outside the record, making adequate appellate review difficult. Habeas corpus was, therefore, better suited to considering "due process" claims such as mob domination.[146]

The notion of want of jurisdiction was qualified by an equally novel view of a state's process of law. Pitney asserted that a state's "process of law" included its appellate, as well as its trial, level, and therefore in determining any question of alleged deprivation of life or liberty contrary to the Fourteenth Amendment, the proceedings of the appellate tribunals were to be taken account of: "the question whether a State is depriving a prisoner of his liberty without due process of law, where the offense for which he is prosecuted is based upon a law that does no violence to the Federal Constitution, cannot ordinarily be determined, with fairness to the State, until the conclusion of the course of justice in its courts."[147] Applying these new ideas to the case at bar, the Court held:

> if a trial is in fact dominated by a mob, so that the jury is so intimidated and the trial judge yields, and so that there is an actual interference with the course of justice, there is, in that court, a departure from due process of law in the proper sense of that term. And if the state, supplying no corrective process, carries into execution a judgment of death or imprisonment based upon a verdict thus produced by mob domination, the state deprives the accused of his life or liberty without due process of law.[148]

If a state failed to provide "corrective process," then a habeas court could inquire into the merits in order to determine whether the detention was lawful.[149]

What exactly was meant by "corrective process" was less than clear. A reading of the just-quoted passage illustrates the ambiguity. Even if the idea that jurisdiction could be "lost" in the course of a trial is accepted, if a trial was in fact dominated by a mob, could the jurisdiction of the trial court be restored by the state supreme court? Mr. Justice Holmes was disturbed by this question.[150] But Pitney saw such a question as embodying "more than one error of reasoning." He responded:

> It regards a part only of the judicial proceeding, instead of

considering the entire process of law. It also begs the question of the existence of such disorder as to cause a loss of jurisdiction in the trial court, which should not be assumed in the face of the decision of the reviewing court, without showing some adequate ground for disregarding that decision. And these errors grow out of the initial error of treating applicant's narrative of disorder as the whole matter, instead of reading it in connection with the context. The rule of law that in ordinary cases requires a prisoner to exhaust his remedies within the state before coming to the courts of the United States for redress would lose the greater part of its statutory force if the prisoner's mere allegations were to stand the same in law after as before the state courts had passed judgment upon them.[151]

Stated more simply, "corrective process" did not mean a process whereby lost jurisdiction was restored; rather it signified a trust for a check on the trial court's jurisdiction already applied by the state appellate courts—that is, the concept of jurisdiction once removed: when the proceedings of a trial court, which possessed jurisdiction of the subject matter and of the person of the accused were attacked, its judgment was final if endorsed by a "court of corrective process." This approach can perhaps be justified on the ground that being part of the facts itself, the trial court could not decide conclusively. However, the decision of the "court of corrective process" was to be accorded respect.[152] Corrective process was found in *Frank* where the proceeding included not only motion for a new trial, and appeal, but appellate examination "not confined to the mere record of conviction, but going at large, and upon evidence adduced outside of that record, into the question whether the processes of justice have been interfered with in the trial court."[153] The application was therefore denied.

To summarize the impact of *Frank*: the concept of jurisdiction remained. However, jurisdiction was now something that could be lost in the course of a trial in a court that initially had jurisdiction. This loss could be brought about by a due process violation such as mob domination. However, since due process, according to the *Frank* court, was something that the entire state judicial system provided, federal habeas review was available only in the absence of state corrective process.

Eight years after *Frank*, the case of *Moore et al. v. Dempsey*[154] came before the Supreme Court. The appellants were five black males convicted in an Arkansas court of murder in the first degree. Their contention, similar to the contention in *Frank*, was that the proceedings in the state trial court, although a trial in form, were in form only, and that they were hurried to conviction under the pressure of a mob without any regard for their rights and without according them due process of law. A motion for a new trial was overruled and the state supreme court affirmed the convictions. Contrary to the situation in *Frank*, the state high court did not conduct an extensive independent investigation into the merits of the claim. When the case came before the Supreme Court on appeal from a district court order dismissing a writ of habeas corpus, Mr. Justice Holmes, after acknowledging that under *Frank* "the corrective process supplied by the State may be so adequate that interference by *habeas corpus* ought not to be allowed,"[155] observed that

> if a case is that the whole proceeding is a mask—that counsel, jury and judge were swept to the fatal end by an irresistible wave of public passion, and that the State Court failed to correct the wrong, neither perfection in the machinery for correction nor the possibility that the trial court and counsel saw no other way of avoiding an immediate outbreak if the mob can prevent the Court from securing to the petitioners their constitutional rights.[156]

Finding that "corrective process" was insufficient, Holmes ruled that in such cases, the habeas judge could not escape the duty of examining the facts for himself.

Moore aids in an understanding of what was required by the "corrective process" approach. The case is similar to *Frank* except for the difference in the scope of the state high court's inquiry. This variation, in conjunction with the emphasis placed upon the extensiveness of the state supreme court's review in *Frank*, suggests that adequate corrective process required a sufficient inquiry by the state appellate courts so that its decision on the federal question would merit the respect of the federal court. The Court in *Moore* found that the state appellate court failed to correct the wrong, that is, it failed to supply adequate corrective process even though the state machinery had the potentiality to supply such.[157] *Moore*, therefore, did no more than elaborate upon the decision in *Frank*.[158]

The *Frank* approach was followed in *Mooney v. Holohan*.[159] The Court there decided that the knowing use by a state of perjured testimony was a denial of due process and that under *Frank* and *Mooney*, the state was required to provide corrective process. In the absence of corrective judicial process, federal habeas relief was available. The Court, however, was not satisfied that the state failed to provide such corrective process and denied the petition "without prejudices," because the petitioner had not exhausted the state remedy of habeas corpus.

THE INDEPENDENCE OF THE CONSTITUTIONAL CLAIM

The law following the cases of *Frank*, *Moore* and *Mooney* can be summarized as follows: the question on habeas corpus remained "jurisdiction."[160] However, jurisdiction could be lost in the midst of a trial if due process requirements went unfulfilled.[161] A state appellate court's review, if it were of sufficient depth, was to be accorded respect. If the appellate court providing adequate corrective process determined that due process rights were not infringed, its determination was conclusive, making federal relief unavailable. Nevertheless, certain due process claims, it need be emphasized, were established as elements of the test of jurisdiction.

Select Cases of Federal Prisoners

The due process component of the test of jurisdiction resulted in the reversing and remanding of the decision of a United States circuit court of appeals affirming a judgment of the federal district court dismissing the habeas petition of a federal prisoner tried without benefit of counsel.[162] The Court, in *Johnson v. Zerbst* held that "[t]he Sixth Amendment withholds from the federal courts, in all criminal proceedings, the power and authority to deprive an accused of his life or liberty unless he has or waives the assistance of counsel." For such a violation of due process, the Court observed that

the writ of habeas corpus was the "only effective remedy."[163] The
Court concluded:

> the Sixth Amendment stands as a jurisdictional bar to a valid
> conviction and sentence depriving [one] of his life or his lib-
> erty. A court's jurisdiction at the beginning of trial may be
> lost "in the course of the proceedings" due to failure to com-
> plete the court—as the Sixth Amendment requires—by pro-
> viding counsel for an accused who is unable to obtain coun-
> sel, who has not intelligently waived this constitutional
> guaranty, and whose life or liberty is at stake. If this require-
> ment of the Sixth Amendment is not complied with, the court
> no longer has jurisdiction to proceed. The judgment of con-
> viction pronounced by a court without jurisdiction is void,
> and one imprisoned thereunder may obtain release by habeas
> corpus.[164]

In *Walker v. Johnson*,[165] the Court reversed the conviction of a
federal prisoner, tried without benefit of counsel, who alleged that
he had been coerced into pleading guilty. Without mentioning the
concept of jurisdiction, the Court noted that if his allegation were
true, he would have been "deprived of a constitutional right."[166]
Walker—like *Johnson, Mooney, Moore* and *Frank*—left open the
question of which claims of denial of constitutional right (not involving coerced guilty pleas, deprivation of Sixth Amendment right
to counsel, knowing use by a state of perjured testimony, or mob
domination) could be examined afresh upon a petition for habeas
corpus. The reasoning behind *Walker* was made clear the following
year in *Waley v. Johnson*.[167] Elevating "due process" in certain
cases to an independent test, the Court in *Waley* held:

> the writ in the federal courts to test the constitutional validity
> of a conviction for crime is not restricted to those cases where
> the judgment of conviction is void for want of jurisdiction of
> the trial court to render it. It extends also to those exceptional
> cases where the conviction has been in disregard of the con-
> stitutional rights of the accused, *and where the writ is the
> only effective means of preserving his rights*.[168]

Thus, constitutional, as well as jurisdictional, claims were cognizable on habeas corpus.[169] However, the broader scope of review was qualified by the "extraordinary character"[170] of the writ.

Select Cases of State Prisoners

While the expansion of issues cognizable in cases of federal prisoners was being limited by the principle that habeas review of a constitutional claim was available only where the writ is the only effective means of preserving the constitutional right, the rule of *Frank, Moore* and *Mooney* worked to check federal habeas relief where adequate corrective state judicial process was available. In *Smith v. O'Grady*,[171] the Court reversed the affirmance of a judgment dismissing an application for habeas corpus from a state prisoner, tried without benefit of counsel, who alleged that he had been tricked into a guilty plea. The Court concluded that if the allegation were true, the petitioner was imprisoned under a judgment that was invalid, because it was obtained in violation of procedural guarantees protected against state invasion through the Fourteenth Amendment.[172] Because of the trial court's failure to appoint and the defendant's inability to obtain counsel, the original sentence was not appealed. Adequate corrective process, even though the state machinery might have had the potentiality to supply such, was absent. In *Ex parte Hawk*,[173] the Court refused to grant an applicant's request for leave to file a petition for a writ of habeas corpus because of his failure to exhaust remedies available under state law. It held that federal habeas relief was available for state prisoners only where state review was inadequate or unavailable:

> Where the state courts have considered and adjudicated the merits of his contention, and this Court has either reviewed or declined to review the state court's decision, a federal court will not ordinarily re-examine upon writ of habeas corpus the questions thus adjudicated. . . . But where resort to state court remedies has failed to afford a full and fair adjudication of the federal contentions raised, either because the state affords no remedy . . . or because in the particular case the remedy afforded by state law proves in practice unavailable

or seriously inadequate, . . . a federal court should entertain his petition for habeas corpus, else he would be remediless.[174]

Thus the availability of federal habeas relief for state prisoners turned on the inadequacy of corrective state judicial process.[175]

Brown v. Allen

Before examining the landmark case of *Brown v. Allen*,[176] a brief summary of the expansion of the scope of judicial inquiry during the first half of the twentieth century is useful. At the outset of the century, the common-law concept of jurisdiction, as applied to the American constitutional system, was still guiding the use of the writ of habeas corpus. The test of jurisdiction was rooted in the trust and respect due decisions of courts of competent jurisdiction. With the development of the concept of due process and the formulation of the idea that state process includes appellate—as well as trial—courts, jurisdiction became something that could be "lost"; however, habeas corpus would question this loss only if adequate corrective state judicial process were absent. If adequate corrective process were present, then the decision of the court of corrective process was conclusive.[177] The due process issues that were cognizable on habeas corpus expanded without an explicit rule designating which constitutional claims, beyond those allowed in specific instances, were appropriately reviewable on the writ. Finally, the Court held that in cases of federal prisoners, all constitutional claims could be tested on habeas corpus where the writ was the only effective means of preserving the constitutional right. The underlying reason for the rules in the cases of both federal and state prisoners was the idea of respect and trust for the regular processes of law.

Brown v. Allen came before the Supreme Court in 1952. Brown had been convicted of rape by a North Carolina court and sentenced to death. He appealed to the state supreme court, claiming that his constitutional rights had been infringed by the use of a coerced confession and by racial discrimination in the selection of grand and petit juries. These claims had been fully litigated, with assistance of counsel, in the trial court and rejected there. After a full review by the North Carolina Supreme Court, they were again rejected.[178]

The United States Supreme Court denied certiorari.[179] Habeas relief was denied without a hearing by the federal district court for the eastern district of North Carolina.[180] This denial was affirmed by the Court of Appeals.[181] The United States Supreme Court granted certiorari and denied the writ; however, the Court ruled that Brown was entitled to a full review of his constitutional claims by the federal district court on a petition for a writ of habeas corpus. Although the constitutional claims had been fully litigated in the state system, the Court assumed that in habeas corpus proceedings federal district courts must provide review of the merits of federal constitutional claims. Mr. Justice Frankfurter, speaking for five of the Justices in one of the two opinions of the Court, reasoned: "The State Court cannot have the last say when it, though on fair consideration and what procedurally may be deemed fairness, may have misconceived a federal constitutional right."[182] The reasoning was based upon the Supremacy Clause.[183] Professor Bator has noted that this argument falls short of the mark: "Of course federal law is higher than state law. But this does not *automatically* tell us that it is better for federal judges to pronounce it than state judges. . . ."[184]

Looking back one finds that in the days when the traditional test of jurisdiction was law, a prisoner held by a state court of competent jurisdiction could not avail himself of federal habeas. After *Frank*, where adequate state corrective process was furnished, federal habeas relief was unavailable. Under *Brown*, all constitutional claims, irrespective of the adequacy of the state process or the fact that the state had fully and fairly construed them, could be relitigated on federal habeas corpus.[185] Professor Hart has observed:

> [*Brown*] seems to say that due process of law in the case of state prisoners is not primarily concerned with the adequacy of the state's corrective process or of the prisoner's personal opportunity to avail himself of this process—with the proper operation, in other words, of the rules distributing authority to make decisions—but relates essentially to the avoidance in the end of any underlying constitutional errors—that is, to the correct application of basic federal rules governing the de-

cision to be made. The decision manifestly broke new ground.[186]

Kaufman v. United States

Brown v. Allen seemed to extend the scope of federal habeas review in cases of state prisoners to all constitutional claims. Prior to *Brown*, habeas corpus was available to federal prisoners raising constitutional claims only where the writ was the only available means of preserving the constitutional right; federal habeas for federal prisoners was constricted by the extraordinary character of the writ.

Four years before *Brown*, Congress substituted 28 U.S.C. section 2255 for habeas corpus in cases of federal prisoners in custody under sentence of a court claiming the right to be released upon the ground that the sentence was imposed in violation of the Constitution or laws of the United States, or that the court was without jurisdiction to impose such sentence, or that the sentence was in excess of the maximum authorized by law, or was otherwise subject to collateral attack. Habeas corpus was available to federal prisoners only where the 1948 statutory remedy was "inadequate or ineffective to test the illegality of his detention." The enactment sought to eliminate a number of procedural problems[187] without impinging upon the prisoners' rights of collateral attack upon their convictions.[188] In other words, except for the elimination of a number of procedural flaws, section 2255 was the equivalent of habeas corpus. (Section 2255 directed the habeas applicant to the sentencing court and not the court within the district of confinement, thus the territorial ambit of 2255 was broader than habeas, which could only be granted by the court or judge within their respective jurisdiction; the sentencing court was not required to entertain a second or successive 2255 motion; and the remedies under 2255 where limited to correcting the sentence.) Did this mean that the parallel rule to Brown, that habeas corpus was available to federal prisoners raising constitutional claims *irrespective of whether the writ was not the only available means of preserving the constitutional right*, was effective? Not all lower federal courts answered in the affirmative.[189] Recalling that *Brown* was based upon the *supposed* right to a federal forum,[190] and that a federal prisoner obviously would always have had an opportunity to raise his claim in a federal trial court, and that if there were available an effective procedure in the direct proceeding there would be no imperative reason for collateral review, no reason for the abandonment of the *Waley* rule seemed to exist.[191] The Supreme Court, in *Kaufman v. United States*,[192] rejected this reasoning and held that all constitutional claims were cognizable in a section 2255 proceeding regardless of the availability of a procedure in the regular process for preservation of the constitutional right.[193]

Kaufman had been tried and convicted in a federal district court on charges of armed robbery. At trial, his only defense was insanity. The Court of Appeals affirmed the conviction.[194] He then filed his postconviction proceeding under section 2255 and included a claim that the finding of sanity was based upon the improper admission of unlawfully seized evidence.[195] Section 2255 relief was denied, the district judge stating that the claim "was not assigned as error on Kaufman's appeal from conviction and is not available as a ground for collateral attack on the instant section 2255 motion."[196] The district court and Court of Appeals denied Kaufman's application for leave to appeal. The decision of the Supreme Court to reverse on certiorari thus meant that even though relief in the regular process was available, a federal constitutional claim could be raised in a section 2255 proceeding where, through no fault of the applicant, the claim did not receive consideration in the regular appellate proceeding.

FUNDAMENTAL DEFECT TEST: BEYOND JURISDICTIONAL AND CONSTITUTIONAL CLAIMS

The traditional question on habeas corpus was jurisdiction. The development of the concept of due process opened constitutional questions to habeas corpus. *Brown* and *Kaufman* seemed to establish that all constitutional claims were cognizable in federal postconviction relief proceedings. In *United States v. Davis*,[197] decided in 1974, the Supreme Court allowed the writ to extend to a question of nonconstitutional federal law.

Davis involved the availability of collateral relief from a federal

conviction based upon an intervening change in the law.[198] Davis
was convicted of failing to report for military induction. He appealed to the Court of Appeals for the Ninth Circuit, where his
case was remanded. On remand, his conviction was affirmed. While
his request for a writ of certiorari to the Supreme Court was pending, the Ninth Circuit decided a case in favor of an individual convicted under circumstances virtually identical to his. In light of the
later decision, Davis unsuccessfully sought a rehearing before the
Court of Appeals. He then instituted collateral proceedings under
section 2255. The district court denied relief and the Court of Appeals affirmed. The Supreme Court granted certiorari, reversed the
judgment of the Court of Appeals, and remanded the case, holding
that confinement in violation of a law of the United States was cognizable in a section 2255 proceeding.

The Court first examined the language of section 2255 and stated
that it "permits a federal prisoner to assert a claim that his conviction is 'in violation of the Constitution *or laws* of the United
States.' "[199] In dissent, Mr. Justice Rehnquist noted that the section
did not refer to illegal "confinement" or "conviction," but rather to
illegal "sentences." Further, Rehnquist argued that paragraph one
of section 2255, from which the clause was extracted, pertains to
the availability of motions and not to the Court's power to grant
relief. The power to grant relief, Rehnquist indicated, was governed
by paragraph three of the statute, which provides, *inter alia*, that

> If the Court finds that the judgment was rendered without
> jurisdiction, or that the sentence imposed was not authorized
> by law or otherwise open to collateral attack, or that there has
> been such a denial or infringement of the constitutional rights
> of the prisoner as to render the judgment vulnerable to col-
> lateral attack, the Court shall vacate and set the judgment
> aside and discharge the prisoner or re-sentence him or grant
> a new trial or correct the sentence as may appear appropriate.

This paragraph, observed Rehnquist, "makes no mention of judgments rendered in violation of the *laws* of the United States."[200] It
allows relief only where (1) the judgment rendered was without

jurisdiction; (2) the sentence was not authorized by law or is otherwise open to collateral attack; and (3) there has been such a denial of constitutional rights as to render the judgment vulnerable to collateral attack. The majority retorted by labeling Rehnquist's analysis "microscopic" and suggesting that "the statutory language is somewhat lacking in precision."[201] The Court asserted that section 2255 was intended to mirror section 2254 in operative effect and that section 2254 authorized habeas relief for state prisoners "in custody in violation of the . . . laws . . . of the United States."[202] Of course, the majority failed to recognize that the phrase "laws of the United States" used in sections 2254 and 2255 is a traditional phrase that had been carried through habeas statutes since the Act of 1867. How likely was it that in 1867, Congress, by this term, meant to effect such a revolutionary transformation in the scope of habeas review?[203] As the term had never been so broadly interpreted prior to this case, how likely was it that framers of later habeas statutes understood the term to extend habeas to questions of nonconstitutional federal questions?

In *Kaufman*, there was dicta noting that in the past courts had refused to allow claims of error of law by a trial court to be raised in collateral attack.[204] In support, the *Kaufman* Court cited *Sunal v. Large*[205] and *Hill v. United States*.[206] The majority in *Davis* argued that neither *Sunal* nor *Hill* supported the contention in *Kaufman*, and that there was no authority for the claim that collateral proceedings are absolutely closed to nonconstitutional questions of law. Though the burden for the majority, which as shown above was not satisfied, was to establish that there was authority for the claim that collateral proceedings were open to nonconstitutional questions of law, it is necessary to pursue this secondary point as it helps pinpoint which nonconstitutional questions of law were cognizable in collateral proceedings.[207]

The Court in *Davis* argued that the *Kaufman* Court was wrong in pointing to *Sunal* as authority for the proposition that section 2255 was not designated for collateral review of errors of law committed by the trial court. Although collateral relief was denied Sunal, the Court distinguished his case because of his failure to avail himself of the regular appellate procedure.[208]

The petitioner in *Hill v. United States* was also denied relief on a section 2255 motion. In denying relief, the Court stated:

> It is an error which is neither jurisdictional nor constitutional. It is not a fundamental defect which inherently results in a complete miscarriage of justice, nor an omission inconsistent with the rudimentary demands of fair procedure. It does not present "exceptional circumstances where the need for the remedy afforded by the writ of habeas corpus is apparent."[209]

The question of whether the second and third sentences in the passage further explain the nature of jurisdictional or constitutional errors or establish additional grounds for relief obviously was answered differently by the Court in *Hill* and the minority in *Davis* on one hand, and the majority in *Davis* on the other.[210]

By interpreting the precedent as it did, the *Davis* Court seemed to be saying that nonconstitutional federal questions were cognizable in collateral proceedings except where the questions could have been raised on appeal, but were not; and only if the alleged error constituted "a fundamental defect which inherently results in a complete miscarriage of justice" or if it is "inconsistent with the rudimentary demands of fair procedure."[211]

IS INNOCENCE RELEVANT? — ROSE v. MITCHELL AND ITS PROGENITORS

James E. Mitchell and James Nichols, Jr., respondents, were indicted by the grand jury of Tipton County, Tennessee and charged with two counts of first degree murder in connection with the shooting deaths of patrons during the robbery of a cafe.[212] Prior to trial, the respondents, who were black, sought dismissal of the indictment on the ground that the grand jury array and the foreman had been selected in a racially discriminatory fashion.[213] After an evidentiary hearing, the motion was denied. Respondents were then tried and found guilty of first-degree murder. The Court of Criminal Appeals of Tennessee affirmed the conviction, finding that the facts failed to demonstrate systematic exclusion of blacks on racial grounds. The Tennessee Supreme Court denied certiorari. Habeas relief was then sought in federal district court. The petitions were then referred to a magistrate, who concluded that the respondents had presented an unrebutted *prima facie* case with respect to the selection of the foreman. The district court ordered the state to make further response. On the basis of affidavits submitted, the petitions were dismissed. The Court of Appeals reversed and ordered that respondents be reindicted within sixty days or released.[214] On writ of certiorari,[215] the Supreme Court questioned whether claims of systematic exclusion in the selection of grand jurors ought to be considered a harmless error when followed by a trial before a properly constituted petit jury and whether such claims ought to be cognizable on habeas in light of *Stone v. Powell*, which held that "where the State has provided an opportunity for a full and fair litigation of a Fourth Amendment claim, the Constitution does not require that a state prisoner be granted federal habeas corpus relief on the ground that evidence obtained in an unconstitutional search or seizure was introduced at trial."[216]

Stone v. Powell represented the triumph of those who had been working to block the expansion of federal habeas jurisdiction which the Warren Court had accelerated to insure the transmission of its concept of criminal justice to the state court. Habeas corpus served the Warren Court as the "remedial counterpart to the constitutionalization of criminal procedure. . . ."[217] The rapid expansion of habeas did not fail to arouse the voices of dissent. Employing the forum of the *University of Chicago Law Review*,[218] Judge Henry J. Friendly provided the intellectual content for a thesis that had emerged in lower court opinions[219] but had been rejected by the Supreme Court in *Kaufman v. United States*.[220] The thesis asserted that convictions should be subject to attack only when the prisoner supplements his constitutional plea with a colorable claim of innocence. This position gained important support in 1973 when Mr. Justice Powell, concurring in *Schneckloth v. Bustamonte*,[221] addressed the issue that the majority opinion had avoided and questioned the extent to which federal habeas should be available to a state prisoner seeking to exclude evidence obtained from an unlawful search and seizure. Although the last major habeas case of the Warren Court had extended habeas relief to a federal prisoner asserting an illegal search and seizure claim.[222] Powell observed that, unlike claims impugning the integrity of the fact-finding process or challenging the evidence as inherently unreliable, the exclusionary rule was simply a prophylactic device intended generally to deter Fourth Amendment violations.[223] Although acknowledging the absence of historical support for tying habeas to guilt or innocence,[224] Powell argued that the manipulation was necessary to accommodate the historical respect for finality of the judgment of the committing court with the expanded role of the writ.[225] Powell could find no evidence of Congressional intent to extend habeas or 2255 relief to every allegation of constitutional violation.[226] *Stone v. Powell* provided Powell with an opportunity to elevate his concurring opinion to majority status.

The impact of *Stone* on the availability of federal habeas was difficult to discern. Although *Mapp v. Ohio*[227] held that "all evidence obtained by searches and seizures in violation of the Constitution is, by that same authority, inadmissible in a state court,"[228] the Court in *Stone* labeled the exclusionary rule "a judicially created means of effectuating the rights secured by the Fourth Amendment."[229] Coupled with this finding, the Court discovered that, after balancing the utility of the exclusionary rule against the costs of extending it to collateral review of Fourth Amendment claims, "the contribution of the exclusionary rule, if any, to effectuation of the Fourth Amendment is minimal. . . ."[230] Nevertheless, the Court acknowledged that the Fourth and Fourteenth Amendments "require" exclusion of illegally seized evidence at trial and reversal of conviction upon direct review.[231] While the refusal to overrule *Mapp* suggested a curtailment of the scope of habeas jurisdiction, the definition of the exclusionary rule merely indicated continuing difficulty with implementing the command of the Fourth Amendment.[232] The solution to the puzzle was finally provided in *Rose v. Mitchell*.[233]

Writing for the Court in *Rose*, Mr. Justice Blackmun refused to consider innocence relevant when systematic exclusion of Blacks from a grand jury was claimed.[234] As in the instance of a claim of admission of illegally seized evidence, systematic exclusion from a grand jury is a constitutional violation that safeguards against arbitrary government but has little to do with guarding against the conviction of an innocent person. It is an antecedent constitutional violation that has no impact on the fairness of the trial that resulted in conviction, since grand juries sit to determine probable cause and not innocence or guilt. The conviction of the accused by a representative petit jury breaks the chain of events that preceded it. Observing that systematic exclusion "strikes at the fundamental values of our judicial system and our society as a whole,"[235] Blackmun quoted from *Hill v. Texas*[236] and noted: "Nor is this Court at liberty to grant or withhold the benefits of equal protection . . . merely because we may deem the defendant innocent or guilty.[237]

Powell challenged Blackmun with reasoning from *Stone*, but Blackmun would have none of that.[238] Blackmun reminded Powell that the Court in *Stone* had made it clear that it was confining its ruling to cases involving the judicially created exclusionary rule. Powell frankly admitted that that was done "only in rejecting the suggestion of the dissent [Brennan] that our decision would lead to a 'drastic withdrawal of federal habeas jurisdiction. . . .' Properly understood, therefore the rationale of our decision in *Stone* is not only consistent with denying collateral relief for claims of unfair indictment, but actually presages such a limitation on habeas corpus."[239]

Mindful of the limited extent of the *Stone* decision, Blackmun set out the differences between the present claim and that raised in *Stone*. Since the claim of systematic exclusion impeaches the state judicial system itself, Blackmun doubted whether a full and fair hearing could be provided in the state system.[240] Second, Blackmun drew a distinction between a judicially created remedy and a personal constitutional right.[241] Next Blackmun denied Powell's claim that the decision would further aggravate federal-state relations since the claim concerned the primary evil at which the Fourteenth Amendment was directed and, observed Blackmun, that amendment has always been directly applicable to the states.[242] The influence of federal habeas on insuring the integrity of the state judicial system was found to be greater than the deterrent value of habeas corpus to Fourth Amendment violations.[243] Since a prisoner released on a claim of systematic exclusion could be retried on the same evidence, the costs to and intrusiveness on the state judicial system were found to be less here than in Fourth Amendment cases.[244] Finally, Blackmun stated that the right asserted in *Rose* was more compelling than that asserted in *Stone*.[245]

The Court's analysis of the availability of federal habeas was unnecessary to its decision since respondents had failed to make out a *prima facie* case of discrimination.[246] The opinion, therefore, was merely a signal from the Court that habeas corpus would continue to be used to articulate constitutional values. That is, habeas corpus would not be demoted to an individual remedy, but would continue to be used as the structural reform mechanism of the criminal justice system, functioning to insure the integrity of the process. This explains the inconsistency between the rhetoric used in *Rose* to celebrate the writ and equal justice, and the Court's refusal to remand the case to remedy the defects in the record. Although habeas corpus would remedy institutional defects, it would not solve the individualistic problems of the case, which were caused by the failure to construct a proper record.[247]

Powell's attack on broad federal habeas jurisdiction was founded upon a reading of legal history that finds the writ extending far beyond its historical uses.[248] Powell's understanding of the writ is that it "is not a *general* writ meant to promote the social good or vindicate all societal interests of even the highest priority."[249] Rather, according to Powell, the writ was "developed by the law to serve a precise and particular purpose . . .," that is, release for the "unjustly incarcerated."[250]

Powell's view of legal history is distorted by the necessity of advocacy. He views history as an event rather than as a process. Why a certain development should be seen outside the course of history is unclear. But even if this view were correct, what use does it serve? History is studied to give perspective not legitimacy.

The constitutional history of habeas corpus provides a case study of the "living constitution."[251] Constitutions serve at least two functions: (1) the distribution of governmental power; and (2) the enshrinement of fundamental values. Because constitutions distribute political power, constitutional history is largely a history of the struggles between departments of government. These political struggles alter the original bargain. Ultimately, the legitimacy of these alterations are based upon their congruence with fundamental values. Although somewhat tautological, this is to say that changes in the fundamental law must pass a test—more difficult to articulate than to understand—to determine conformity to fundamental values, which emerge from an interaction of social forces. Therefore, in the instance of habeas corpus, those who attempt to employ constitutional history to effect a reversal of the liberal trend must demonstrate the congruence of the reaction with fundamental values. This is not to suggest that history is irrelevant or that future courts (or for that matter future legislatures or executive agencies) cannot identify new constitutional values and order their priority. The point is that the terms of the debate ought to be, which values are fundamental and how is priority determined.

At the foundation of Powell's attack is a conception of judicial role that gives the judiciary a subordinate function in the debate over constitutional values. The involvement of habeas corpus is incidental. Habeas jurisdiction had been manipulated throughout the nineteenth century by Congress to reorder constitutional values. However, the victory of the progressives in this century was represented by the decline of substantive due process as a means of limiting government and the rise of procedural due process. As long as government was limited by substantive due process, the traditional test of habeas corpus, jurisdiction, could stand alone. Legislation found to deprive substantive due process was declared void and a court proceeding according to the statute was said to lack jurisdiction. Once procedural due process became the standard of constitutional government and the judiciary focused its attention on its own processes, the traditional test of habeas corpus, jurisdiction, had to be supplemented. Courts that had started out with jurisdiction of a case could lose that jurisdiction by the violation of a process-oriented right. To accommodate the spirit of limited government that prevailed in the age of substantive due process and yet appear true to the idea of democracy that brought that age to an end, the courts very gradually began to expand process-oriented rights. As those rights expanded, so did the range of issues cognizable on habeas. Habeas corpus was thereby becoming a means for the articulation of the modern-day substantive due process—a substantive due process that, coincidentally, embraced a new meaning of equality,[252] one that recognized unequal starting points.

The expansion of process-oriented rights climaxed during the second decade of the Warren era.[253] Because of the dramatic expansion of rights, the scope of the habeas inquiry ballooned. The writ provided the courts with a forum for articulating societal values. This was no new role for the writ. What was new was the spokesman using the forum. Throughout the nineteenth century it was generally the legislative department that employed habeas to effect change in constitutional values. The substitution of procedural due process for substantive due process meant the use of more discreet means by the judiciary for announcing constitutional values. Habeas corpus provided one such means. It is this that lies at the root of Powell's critique. The attack is directed not merely at habeas corpus but at the Court's conception of judicial role. It is the counterpart to the tailoring principle formulated by the Burger Court to limit injunctive relief to that remedy following deductively from the violation rather than that remedy or set of remedies that seek to restructure the systematic flaws at which the violation hints.[254]

In addition to rejecting habeas corpus as an appropriate avenue of relief, Powell would not permit claims of discrimination in the selection of grand jurors to survive conviction even for purposes of direct appeal.[255] This is consistent with his view that such discrimination is harmless to the defendant.[256] Powell noted, however, that "it is a crime to discriminate on the basis of race in the selection of jurors, 18 U.S.C. §243, and both Government and private actions may be brought by those improperly excluded from jury service."[257] However, neither government nor private actions will likely find as many enthusiastic challengers as direct appeal and habeas corpus—and enthusiasm is needed. Even in pretailoring principle times, the Court refused to enjoin enforcement of a statute regulating jury selection, which established qualifications that could be used to discriminate, though the Court did enjoin racially discriminatory application of the act,[258] thus requiring a county-by-county attack upon the state jury selection process.[259]

As evidence for the use of private actions to remedy selective exclusion from grand juries, Powell cited *Carter v. Jury Commission of Grier County*.[260] *Carter* was the first case to reach the Supreme Court in which an attack upon alleged racial discrimination in choosing jurors was voiced by a plaintiff seeking affirmative relief rather than by a defendant challenging the judgment of a criminal conviction. Although the relief supplied was limited,[261] the Court acknowledged the power of the federal courts "to fashion detailed and stringent injunctive relief that will remedy any discriminatory application at the hands of the officials empowered to administer it."[262] However, since that decision, the Burger Court, with the support of Mr. Justice Powell, has severely restricted injunctive relief and it is questionable whether a claim of discrimination in jury selection could withstand the rigorous standing and equity standards of *O'Shea v. Littleton*[263] and *Rizzo v. Goode*.[264]

Of course 18 U.S.C. §243 and affirmative action by the Government remain available. Since the Burger Court's decision in *Linda R.S. v. Richard D.*[265] retards private individuals from bringing injunctive actions against public officials who refuse to enforce criminal statutes, the remaining avenues provide limited access: relief is centralized in the government. Of course, a criminal proceeding under 18 U.S.C. §243 would probably be most satisfactory to Powell: the courts would be relieved of responsibility for articulating any constitutional value against systematic exclusion, for they would merely be enforcing the congressionally articulated value.

Powell buttressed his argument against the use of habeas corpus in cases where the guilt of the incarcerated claimant is not at issue with an analysis of the social costs involved. The societal values damaged by collateral attack, according to Powell, are finality and federalism.[266] As a limitation on national power, federalism has grown weak over the years. The establishment of the state courts as both primary protectors of individual liberty and primary agencies of criminal justice, which seemed natural in 1787, seemed paradoxical during the twentieth century. The weakening of federalism was inevitable after the decline of substantive due process, for the two concepts were complementary: substantive due process limited state government; federalism limited the national government. With government limited by the process-oriented rights of the federal bill of rights, the reason for retaining primacy in the state courts over the constitutional rights of criminal defendants is lost. The exercise of federal power to enforce the provisions of the Bill of Rights presents no threat to the liberty of the individual. Indeed, federal process-oriented rights now stand between government and the individual. A nineteenth-century concept of federalism would only weaken that bulwark.

Powell, however, fails to appreciate the benefits of tension between state and federal government. Like the system of checks and balances, the tension between the two governments, caused by the availability of federal habeas for state prisoners, serves not only to check excess but to foster a dialogue.[267] Cover and Aleinikoff observed that the dialogue fostered by the habeas corpus shaped by the Warren Court engaged the state and federal courts in a joint exploration of constitutional values.[268] Since constitutional values are not immutable, it is not enough to note that state judges too pledge to support the Constitution and therefore can protect constitutional rights. In addition, the parity between state and federal courts implied by the argument that state courts must also protect federal constitutional rights has been demonstrated to be a myth.[269] Federal rights are more forcefully vindicated in federal than in state courts.

Not only does Powell fail to make the case for his brand of federalism, he also fails to demonstrate the ability of his thesis to ease the tension and yield the balance he desires. Powell would retain federal habeas jurisdiction in state cases where the state court has failed to provide a full and fair opportunity to litigate the federal claim. But these are the cases that present the most potential for conflict since the state court has not examined the merits of the claim and a contrary federal decision would clearly imply state court inadequacy. Powell's exception defeats his federalism goal.[270]

Because judicial resources are limited, the case for finality is an easy one to make. The nature of the judiciary is incongruent with bureaucratization and therefore the courts have been least able of all units of government to absorb the impact of the demand for increased governmental intervention in American society. The greatest barrier to an individual's ability to harness the coercive powers of the judiciary (and, therefore, the state) is the lawyer. In the instance of *pro se* prisoner's petitions, even that barrier is absent.[271] But regardless of burden, it seems extreme to argue that all state prisoner applications for federal collateral relief, irrespective of their possible merit, ought to be denied where the state has provided an opportunity for a full and fair hearing. Powell has presented no compelling reason for insisting on finality before, rather than after, the habeas inquiry. By drawing the line before the habeas inquiry, Powell would eliminate the writ's role as the structural reform mechanism of the criminal justice system. It is not sufficient to argue that, as the "opportunity test" only cuts off federal habeas relief where the state has provided an opportunity for a full and fair hearing, the writ is unnecessary because the integrity of the process is not in doubt in such cases. That argument fails to comprehend the dynamic nature of the substantive rights and the role of habeas in offering the procedural opportunities for the development of those rights. The "opportunity test" does not acknowledge the intimacy of the relationship between substance and procedure. *Bell v. Wolfish*,[272] which was handed down shortly before *Rose*, indicates that the failure to acknowledge the relationship is due not to failure to perceive—quite the contrary. In *Bell*, the Court denied a due process challenge to the conditions of confinement at the Metropolitan Corrections Center and yet reserved the question of whether habeas corpus was an appropriate remedy for challenging conditions of confinement. Having denied the substance, there was no need to circumscribe the procedural mechanism for asserting the putative substantive value. The "opportunity test," on the other hand, was a *sub rosa* attack on the substance; it attacked the substance from the direction of procedure.

The "opportunity test" can be faulted on its chosen grounds: it is questionable whether an inquiry into whether the petitioner has had an opportunity for a full and fair hearing would take less time than a decision on the merits.[273] A state prisoner denied access to the federal courts when raising substantive questions will simply cast his challenge in procedural terms. Instead of arguing that he was denied equal protection because the indictment against him was found by a grand jury from which members of his race were systematically excluded, the state prisoner would argue that he had been denied an opportunity for a full and fair hearing on his federal claim in the state system.

The effect on finality and federalism is too slight to be persuasive. In addition, federalism and finality are instrumental concepts. Thus, Powell must have some other interest in mind. That other interest would seem to be protection of society from injustice caused by release of guilty persons. Articulation of that interest is certainly within the rightful place of the judiciary but it ought to be viewed not merely as an effort to limit the ability of federal courts to articulate constitutional values but as the articulation of alternate values. Unlike Powell, the majority in *Rose* found systematic exclusion to be more important than the injustice caused by the release of guilty persons.

NOTES

1. *See* ch. 1, text accompanying notes 309-97 *supra.*

2. If appropriate procedural steps were taken before trial, there was a possibility of a new trial. Sir James Fitzjames Stephen, *A History of Criminal Law in England* (London: Macmillan and Co., 1883), vol. 1, pp. 310-11. Moreover, there was the writ of error. Ibid., vol. 1, pp. 308-10; Holdsworth, *A History of English Law*, vol. 1, p. 215. The courts, by the writ of error, were restricted to dealing with the errors appearing on the face of the record. If this remedy were available, no other direct method of attack, such as the writ of certiorari, could be used.

3. 31 Car. 2 c. 2, sect. 3. Professor Paul A. Freund has suggested that the Habeas Corpus Act of 1679 did not purport to deny habeas corpus to convicted persons, but left their rights to be worked out through the common-law form of the writ, and that the contrary view derived from a curious misreading of the Act by early legislators and judges due to a misplaced parenthesis. "Brief for the Respondent," pp. 30-32, *United States v. Hayman*, 342 U.S. 205 (1952) cited by Paul M. Bator, "Finality in Criminal Law and Federal Habeas Corpus for State Prisoners," 76 Harv. L. Rev. 441, 466 (1962). Even if Freund is correct about the misplaced parenthesis, the common law writ would give no satisfaction to one committed pursuant to a conviction in a court of general common-law jurisdiction. Even Lord Coke—champion of liberty and advocate of an efficacious writ of habeas corpus—in his *Institutes* (vol. 2, p. 52), prior to the passage of the Habeas Corpus Act, noted that persons imprisoned for a crime or in execution were excepted from the privileges of the writ. Freund, however, probably mentioned the common law habeas corpus to emphasize the writ's tendency to develop.

4. *See* Collings, "Habeas Corpus for Convicts—Constitutional Right or Legislative Grace?" 40 Calif. L. Rev. 335, 345. *See* text accompanying notes 11-16 *infra.* for qualification.

5. 1 U.S. Statutes at Large 73, 81-82.

6. *Ex parte Bollman*, 4 Cranch 75, 91 (1807).

7. *See also United States v. Hamilton*, 3 Dall. 17 (1795). The petitioner there, too, had been committed on a warrant (of a district judge) for high treason and was released (on bail) by the Supreme Court.

8. *See* ch. 1, text accompanying notes 457-69 *supra.*

9. *Ex parte Bollman*, 4 Cranch 75, 91.

10. Ibid., p. 100.

11. Since the Attorney General had declined to argue the case on behalf of the United States there was no argument presented against Harper's point.

12. *Peacock v. Bell*, 85 Eng. Rep. 84 (1667).

13. Ibid.

14. *See* ch. 1, text accompanying notes 150-308 *supra*.

15. In *Ex parte Burford*, 3 Cranch 448 (1806), the test for inferior courts seems to have been used. The applicant's imprisonment was held illegal "for want of stating some good cause certain, supported by oath."

16. *Codd v. Turbank*, 81 Eng. Rep. 94 (1615); *Hodd v. High Commission Court*, 81 Eng. Rep. 125 (1615). *See* ch. 1, text accompanying notes 276-88 *supra*.

17. 124 Eng. Rep. 1006 (1670).

18. Ibid., p. 1007. Vaughan, in dicta did note that

> . . . the verdict of a jury, and evidence of a witness are very different things, in the truth and falsehood of them: a witness swears but to what he hath heard or seen, generally or more largely, to what hath fallen under his senses. But a jury-man swears to what he can infer and conclude from the testimony of such witnesses, by the act and force of his understanding, to be the fact inquired after, which differs nothing in the reason, though much in the punishment, from what a Judge, out of various cases consider'd by him, infers to be the law in the question before him. . . .

Ibid., p. 1009.

19. Ibid., p. 1007.

20. The Supreme Court in *Fay v. Noia*, 372 U.S. 391, 404 (1963), erroneously pointed to *Bushell* to support the statement that it was not true at common law that "habeas corpus was available only to inquire into the jurisdiction, in a narrow sense, of the committing court." *See* Dallin H. Oaks, "Legal History in the High Court—Habeas Corpus," 64 U. Mich. L. Rev. 451, 463-64 (1966).

21. Compare *Bollman* with *Ex parte Cuddy*, 131 U.S. 280 (1888). The Court in *Cuddy* held:

> The general rule that, unless the contrary appears from the record, a cause is deemed to be without the jurisdiction of a Circuit or District Court of the United States—their jurisdiction being limited by the Constitution and Acts of Congress—has no application where the judgments of such courts are attacked collaterally.
>
> Unless, therefore, the want of jurisdiction, as to the subject matter or parties, appears, in some proper form, every intendment must be made in support of the jurisdiction of a court of that character.

The attack in *Bollman* was not collateral.

22. 7 Wheat. 38 (1822).

23. Ibid., p. 42.

24. Ibid., p. 41.

25. Ibid., pp. 42-43.

26. The Court observed:

It is to be considered, that this court has no appellate jurisdiction confided to it in criminal cases, by the laws of the United States. It cannot entertain a writ of error, to revise the judgment of the Circuit Court, in any case where a party has been convicted of a public offense. And undoubtedly the denial of this authority proceeded upon great principles of public policy and convenience. . . . If, then, this court cannot revise a judgment of the circuit court in a criminal case, what reason is there to suppose that it was intended to vest it with the authority to do it indirectly?"

Ibid., p. 42. In other words, the lower federal court was not inferior to the Supreme Court in this matter in a technical sense, since its judgment was not subject to review by the Supreme Court.

27. *See* ch. 3, text accompanying notes 68-108 *supra*.

28. 3 Peters 193 (1830).

29. Ibid., p. 197.

30. Ibid., pp. 202-03.

31. *In re Metzer*, 5 How. 176, 191 (1847). *See also Johnson v. United States*, 13 Fed. Cas. 867 (1842). *See also* Richard Vaux, *Reports of Some of the Criminal Cases on Primary Hearing . . . together with some Remarks on the Writ of Habeas Corpus and forms of Proceedings in Criminal Cases* (Philadelphia: T. and J. W. Johnson, 1846), pp. 191-222.

32. *Rex v. Cowle*, 97 Eng. Rep. 587, 599 (1759).

33. 7 Peters 568 (1833).

34. *Ex parte Bollman*, 5 Cranch 75, 101.

35. *Ex parte Watkins*, 7 Peters 568, 572.

36. *Lee v. Lee*, 8 Peters 44 (1834); *Holmes v. Jennison*, 14 Peters 540 (1840). Admittedly, the writ of error often was unavailable owing to statutory requirements such as jurisdictional amount. *Holmes v. Jennison*, ibid.; *Barry v. Mercien*, 5 How. 105 (1847).

37. 14 How. 103 (1852).

38. 18 How. 307 (1856).

39. 75 U.S. 85 (1869).

40. *See* dissenting opinion in *Wells* and *Kaine*, and Attorney General Hoar's brief in *Yerger*.

41. 14 U.S. Statutes at Large 385 (1867).

42. *See* ch. 4, text accompanying notes 53-85 *supra*.

43. 15 U.S. Statutes at Large 44 (1868).

44. *Ex parte McCardle*, 6 Wall. 318, 325-26 (1867).

45. 75 U.S. 85 (1868).

46. Ibid., p. 102. *See also Barth et al. v. Clise*, 79 U.S. 400 (1870).

47. *Ex parte Yerger*, 75 U.S. 85, 101. Dallin H. Oaks, "The Original Writ of Habeas Corpus in the Supreme Court," 1962 S. Ct. Rev. 153, 165, noted that such an interpretation is difficult to reconcile with such leading authorities as *Marbury v. Madison*, 1 Cranch 137 (1803) and *Ex parte Barry*, 2 How. 65 (1844), and cannot be sustained upon reason. However, neither case denied that the Court has appellate jurisdiction over all cases over which it does not have original jurisdiction, and the constitutional clause is easier

read as allowing full appellate jurisdiction except as subsequently limited by Congress. *See* Crosskey, *Politics and the Constitution*, vol. 1, pp. 616-20.

48. *Ex parte Yerger*, 75 U.S. 85, 102.

49. *Ibid.*, p. 103.

50. 80 U.S. 513 (1871).

51. 85 U.S. 163 (1873).

52. Ibid., p. 176. In *Ex parte Bigelow*, 113 U.S. 328 (1885), the Court distinguished *Lange* from the case where the alleged error did not turn on the illegality of the sentence. Rather, it involved an error in the course of the proceedings. The prisoner had been indicted on multiple charges, and after the prosecutor had made a statement of his case to the jury, the court recessed. Upon reconvening, the court decided that the indictments could not be tied together well, and dismissed the jurors. The same jurors were later reassembled to act on a single indictment. The Supreme Court rejected habeas relief to the prisoner who contended that he already had been put in jeopardy with regard to the offenses charged in the consolidated indictment.

53. 372 U.S. 391 (1963). *See* Oaks, "Legal History in the High Court," 64 U. Mich. L. Rev. 451.

54. 237 U.S. 309 (1915).

55. Ibid., pp. 330-31.

56. 93 U.S. 18 (1876).

57. *See also Fitzgerald v. Grien*, 134 U.S. 377 (1889).

58. 93 U.S. 18, 21.

59. 100 U.S. 339 (1879).

60. 100 U.S. 371 (1879).

61. Ibid., p. 376 (emphasis added).

62. Ibid., pp. 376-77.

63. *See* Wilmot, C. J., "Opinion on the Writ of Habeas Corpus," 97 Eng. Rep. 29, 43.

64. 110 U.S. 651 (1883).

65. Ibid., p. 654. The provisions in question were sections 5508 and 5520 of the Revised Statutes. The offense charged was conspiracy to intimidate a black citizen in the exercise of his right to vote for a member of Congress. In execution of that conspiracy, the prisoners were charged with having beaten, bruised, wounded and otherwise maltreated their victim. Further, it was charged that this act was perpetrated because of the victim's race, color, and previous condition of servitude by going in disguise and assaulting him on the public highway and on his premises. The statutory provisions were upheld under the necessary and proper clause. *See also Ex parte Coy*, 127 U.S. 731 (1887).

66. *Ex parte Parks*, 93 U.S. 18 (1876); *Wright v. Nicholson*, 134 U.S. 136 (1889).

67. *Ex parte Wilson*, 114 U.S. 417 (1885).

68. 121 U.S. 1 (1886).

69. *Ex parte Harding*, 120 U.S 782 (1885).

70. Ibid., p. 784. Harding also contended that the trial court denied his right to have compulsory process for obtaining witnesses in his favor, against his constitutional right under the Sixth Amendment. The Court held that here as well, such an objection goes only to the regularity of the proceeding,

and not to the court's jurisdiction. This holding would seem to conform to the above: jurisdiction had attached and the error was not in the sentencing.

71. *Ex parte Siebold*, 100 U.S. 371 (1879).

72. *Ex parte Bain*, 121 U.S. 1 (1886).

73. *Ex parte Wilson*, 114 U.S. 417 (1885).

74. 120 U.S. 274 (1886).

75. 131 U.S. 176 (1888).

76. Ibid., p. 183.

77. It has been suggested that *Neilson* overruled *sub silento Ex parte Bigelow*, *see* note 52 *supra.*, Alexander Holtzoff, "Collateral Review of Convictions in Federal Courts," 25 B. U. L. Rev. 26, 31 (1945). However, *Bigelow* can be distinguished from *Neilson* (as well as *Snow* and *Lange*) by the fact that it did not result in a cumulative sentence. The former view springs from the remark attached to the holding. After finding that "a party is entitled to habeas corpus, not merely where the court is without jurisdiction of the cause, but where it has no constitutional authority to condemn the prisoner," the Court noted: "If we have seemed to hold the contrary in any case, it has been from inadvertence." *Ex parte Neilson*, 131 U.S. 176, 184.

78. 140 U.S. 575 (1890).

79. Ibid., p. 584. *See also In re Moran*, 203 U.S. 96 (1906); *Keizo v. Henry*, 211 U.S. 146 (1908).

80. This may also help explain the difference between the *Lange* line of cases and *Bigelow*. *See* note 77 *supra*.

81. *Ex parte Belt*, 159 U.S. 95 (1894).

82. *Re Schnieder*, 148 U.S. 162 (1892).

83. *In re Moran*, 203 U.S. 96 (1906).

84. *Ex parte Kearney*, 7 Wheat. 38 (1822).

85. *See generally, Ex parte Rowland et al.*, 104 U.S. 861 (1881); *Ex parte Tyler*, 149 U.S. 164 (1892); *In re Swan*, 150 U.S. 637, 648 (1893); *Re Chapman,* 156 U.S. 211, 215 (1894).

86. 128 U.S. 289 (1888).

87. Ibid., p. 310. *See also Ex parte Savin*, 131 U.S. 267 (1888); *Craig v. Hecht*, 263 U.S. 255 (1923).

88. *In re Burrus*, 136 U.S. 586, 593-94. Where, however, the court had jurisdiction to issue an injunction or other order, and therefore had power to commit for contempt in violation, the question of whether its findings that certain acts constituted contempt was not subject to habeas corpus. *In re Debs*, 158 U.S. 564 (1894).

89. 249 U.S. 378 (1918).

90. Ibid., pp. 383-84. (The factual situation calls *Bushell's Case* to mind.)

91. Ibid., p. 384. Where the petitioner was committed for contempt in the presence of the court, for an action over which the court had jurisdiction, habeas corpus would not issue to inquire whether the contempt actually had been committed. *Ex parte Savin*, 131 U.S. 267 (1888). However, a different result occurred when an executive pardon was granted. *See Ex parte Grossman*, 267 U.S. 87 (1924) (*see generally*, Duker, "The President's Power to Pardon," 18 William and Mary Law Review 475, 526-31).

92. 1 U.S. Statutes at Large 91 (1789). Compare, *Ex parte Bollman*, 4 Cranch 75 (1806) with note 88 *supra*.

93. "Finality in Criminal Law," 76 Harv. L. Rev. 441, 470.

94. For example, *see Ex parte Yarbrough*, 110 U.S. 651 (1883); *Davis v. Beason*, 133 U.S. 333 (1889); *In re Swan*, 150 U.S. 637 (1893); *Ex parte Belt*, 159 U.S. 95 (1895); *Ex parte Lennon*, 166 U.S. 548 (1896); *Dimmick v. Tompkins*, 194 U.S. 540 (1903); *Riggins v. United States*, 199 U.S. 303 (1905); *Re Lincoln*, 202 U.S. 178 (1906); *Toy Toy v. Hopkins*, 212 U.S. 542 (1908); and especially *Harlan v. McGourin*, 218 U.S. 442 (1910); *Glasgow v. Moyer*, 225 U.S. 420 (1911); *McNamara v. Henkel*, 226 U.S. 520 (1912); *Johnson v. Hoy*, 227 U.S. 245 (1912); and *Henry v. Henkel*, 235 U.S. 219 (1914).

95. With the reestablishment of the notion that habeas corpus could not subserve the function of the writ of error, after appeal in federal criminal cases was authorized [25 U.S. Statutes at Large 656 (1889) (writ of error made available in capital cases); 26 U.S. Statutes at Large 826, 827 (1891) (writ of error made available in all cases involving infamous crimes). *See In re Claasen*, 140 U.S. 200 (1891)], the doctrine of *Siebold* was overruled *sub silento*. *Re Lincoln*, 202 U.S. 178 (1906). *See also Glasgow v. Moyer*, 225 U.S. 420 (1912); *Henry v. Henkel*, 235 U.S. 219 (1914); *Salinger v. Loisel*, 265 U.S. 224 (1924).

96. 14 U.S. Statutes at Large 385 (1867).

97. *See* ch. 4, text accompanying notes 53-85 *supra*.

98. *See* ch. 4, text accompanying notes 121-89 *supra*.

99. Bator, "Finality in Criminal Law," 76 Harv. L. Rev. 441, 474.

100. *See* ch. 4, text accompanying notes 53-85 *supra*.

101. *See* text accompanying notes 1-26 *supra*.

102. *See* ch. 3, text accompanying notes 192-229 *supra*.

103. Section 2 of the Act of 1867 provided:

That a final judgment or decree in any suit in the highest court of a State in which a discussion in the suit could be had, where is drawn in question the validity of a treaty or statute of or an authority exercised under, the United States, and the decision is against the validity, or where is drawn in question the validity of a statute of or authority exercised under any Statute, on the grounds of their being repugnant to the constitution, treaties, or laws of the United States, and the decision is in favor of the validity, or where any title, right, privilege, or immunity is claimed under the constitution, or any treaty or statute or commission held, or exercised under the United States, and the decision is against the title, right, privilege, or immunity specially set up or claimed by either party under such constitution, treaty, statute, commission, or authority, may be re-examined and reversed in the Supreme Court of the United States, upon a writ of error."

Compare with section 25 of the Judiciary Act of 1789.

104. *See* ch. 4, text accompanying note 76 *supra*.

105. *Ex parte McCardle*, 6 Wall. 318 (1868). *See* ch. 4, text accompanying notes 86-101 *supra*.

106. *See In re Bogart*, 3 Fed. Cas. 796 (1873); *Ex parte Bridges*, 4 Fed. Cas. 98 (1875); *Ex parte Parks*, 18 Fed. Cas. 1217 (1876); *Ex parte Joyce*,

13 Fed. Cas. 1175 (1877); *Ex parte Shaffenburg*, 21 Fed. Cas. 1144 (1877).
107. 112 U.S. 177.
108. Ibid., p. 180.
109. *See generally, United States v. Pridgeon*, 153 U.S. 48 (1893); *Storti v. State of Massachusetts*, 183 U.S. 138 (1901); *Rogers v. Peck and Lovell*, 199 U.S. 425, 434 (1905).
110. 139 U.S. 449 (1890).
111. Ibid., p. 454.
112. 93 U.S. 18 (1876). *See* text accompanying notes 56-58 *supra*.
113. 140 U.S. 278 (1890).
114. Ibid., p. 286. *See also Jugiro v. Bush*, 140 U.S. 291 (1890); *Andrews v. Swartz*, 156 U.S. 272 (1894).
115. 149 U.S. 70 (1892).
116. Ibid., p. 75.
117. Ibid., p. 76.
118. *See* text accompanying notes 51-55.
119. 157 U.S. 655 (1894).
120. 160 U.S. 293 (1895).
121. 166 U.S. 481 (1896).
122. 168 U.S. 640 (1898).
123. 201 U.S. 123 (1905).
124. Ibid., p. 129. *See also Valentina v. Mercer*, 201 U.S. 131 (1905).
125. *See Ex parte Siebold*, 100 U.S. 371 (1879). *Contra,* Walter V. Shaefer, "Federalism and State Criminal Procedures," 70 Harv. L. Rev. 1, 20 (1956).
126. *Yick Wo v. Hopkins*, 118 U.S. 356 (1885).
127. *Ex parte Royall*, 117 U.S. 241, 248 (1885).
128. 118 U.S. 356 (1885).
129. 134 U.S. 160 (1890).
130. Ibid., p. 166. *See also Ex parte Savage*, 134 U.S. 176 (1890). Also, compare *Minnesota v. Barber*, 136 U.S. 313 (1890) and *In re Rahrer*, 140 U.S. 545 (1891) with *Crowley v. Christensen*, 137 U.S. 86 (1890) and *McElvaine v. Bush*, 142 U.S. 155 (1891).
131. *See* text accompanying notes 51-55 *supra*.
132. *See* ch. 4, text accompanying notes 146-89 *supra*.
133. *Slaughter-House Cases*, 16 Wall. 36 (1873).
134. *Hurtado v. California*, 110 U.S. 516 (1884).
135. *See e.g., Ex parte Frederich*, 149 U.S. 70 (1893). *See generally,* Duker, "Mr. Justice Rufus W. Peckham: The Police Power and the Individual in a Changing World," 1980 Brigham Young Univ. L. Rev.—(1980); Duker, The Fuller Court and State Criminal Process: Threshold of Modern Limitations on Government, 1980 Brigham Young Univ. L. Rev.—(1980).
136. *See* text accompanying notes 51-132 *supra*.
137. *See* text accompanying notes 96-132 *supra*.
138. *See* ch. 4, text accompanying notes 146-89 *supra*.
139. 237 U.S. 309 (1915).
140. Ibid., p. 326.
141. Ibid.
142. *See* text accompanying notes 60-62 *supra*.

143. *See* note 95 *supra.*

144. 237 U.S. 309, 318.

145. Ibid., p. 327.

146. *See* note 149 *infra.*

147. 237 U.S. 309, 328.

148. Ibid., p. 335.

149. Ibid. This determination procedurally was made possible by the Habeas Corpus Act of 1867, which provided, *inter alia,* that "[t]he . . . court or judge [on habeas corpus] shall proceed in a summary way to determine the facts of the case, by hearing testimony and the arguments of the parties interested, and if it shall appear that the petitioner is deprived of his or her liberty in contravention of the constitution or laws of the United States, he or she shall forthwith be discharged and set at liberty." The Court in *Frank* observed that the effect of this clause was "to substitute for the bare legal review that seems to have been the limit of judicial authority under the common law practice, and under the act of 31 Car. II chapter 2, a more searching investigation, in which the applicant is put upon his oath to set forth the truth of the matter respecting the causes of his detention, and the court, upon determining the actual facts, is to 'dispose of the party as law and justice require.' " Ibid., pp. 330-31.

150. Ibid., p. 347.

151. Ibid., p. 336.

152. *See* ibid., pp. 335-36.

> Owing to considerations already adverted to (arising not out of comity merely, but out of the very right of the matter to be decided, in view of the relations existing between the state and the Federal government), we hold that such a determination of the facts as was thus made by the court of last resort of Georgia respecting the alleged interference with the trial through disorder and manifestations of hostile sentiment cannot, in this collateral inquiry, be treated as a nullity, but must be taken as setting forth the truth of the matter; certainly until some reasonable ground is shown for an inference that the court which rendered it either was wanting in jurisdiction, or at least erred in the exercise of its jurisdiction; and that the mere assertion by the prisoner that the facts of the matter are other than the state court, upon full investigation, determined them to be, will not be deemed sufficient to raise an issue respecting the correctness of that determination.

153. Ibid., p. 335.

154. 261 U.S. 86 (1923).

155. Ibid., p. 91.

156. Ibid.

157. *Contra,* Hart, "The Time Chart of the Justices," 73 Harv. L. Rev. 84, 105 (1959); Curtis R. Reitz, "Federal Habeas Corpus: Impact of An Abortive State Proceeding," 74 Harv. L. Rev. 1315, 1329 (1961). *Accord,* Bator, "Finality in Criminal Law and Federal Habeas Corpus for State Prisoners," 76 Harv. L. Rev. 441, 448-493. *See also* Developments, "Federal Habeas Corpus," 83 Harv. L. Rev. 1038, 1050-55.

158. *Contra,* McReynold's dissent, *Moore et al. v. Dempsey,* 261 U.S. 86,

92 (which suggests that the majority overruled *Frank*); Developments, "Federal Habeas Corpus," 83 Harv. L. Rev. 1038, 1052-53. *See* however, Bator, "Finality in Criminal Law," 76 Harv. L. Rev. 441, 489-91, n. 131.

159. 294 U.S. 103 (1934) (An interesting note to *Mooney* can be found in *Felix Frankfurter Reminisces*, Harlan B. Philips ed. (London: Secker and Warburg, 1960), pp. 130-35). *See also Pyle v. State of Kansas*, 317 U.S. 213 (1942).

160. *See Knewel v. Evan*, 268 U.S. 442, 445 (1925).

161. *See Ashe v. United States ex rel. Valotta*, 270 U.S. 424 (1926); *Bowen v. Johnston*, 306 U.S. 19 (1939). Cf. development of jurisdiction doctrine of *Pennoyer v. Neff*, 95 U.S. 714 (1877) in the early twentieth century. *Smolick v. Philadelphia and Reading Coal Co.*, 222 Fed. 148 (1915), approved *Pennsylvania Fire Insurance Co. v. Cold Issue Mining Co.*, 243 U.S. 93 (1917); *Hess v. Pawloski*, 274 U.S. 352 (1927); *Washington v. Superior Court*, 289 U.S. 361 (1933).

162. *Johnson v. Zerbst*, 304 U.S. 458 (1938).

163. Ibid., p. 467.

164. Ibid., p. 468.

165. 312 U.S. 275 (1941).

166. Ibid., p. 286.

167. 316 U.S. 101 (1942).

168. Ibid., pp. 104-05 (emphasis added). *See also Adams v. United States ex rel. McCann*, 317 U.S. 269 (1942); *United States ex rel. McCann v. Adams*, 320 U.S. 220 (1943); *Sunal v. Large*, 332 U.S. 174, 179 (1947).

169. The English courts continue to use the formula of jurisdiction for review. *See Bushell's Case*, 124 Eng. Rep. 1006 (1670); *In re Dunn*, 136 Eng. Rep. 859 (1847); *Re Featherstone*, 37 Cr. App. Rep. 146 D.C. (1953): "The court does not grant, and cannot grant, writs of *habeas corpus* to persons who are serving sentences passed by courts of competent jurisdiction." However, *see Anisminic Ltd. v. Foreign Compensation Commission* [1969] 2 A.C. 147; and H. W. R. Wade, "Constitutional and Administrative Aspects of the Anisminic Case," 85 L. Q. Rev. 198, 209-11 (1969).

170. *See* Intro., text accompanying note 8 *supra*.

171. 312 U.S. 329 (1941).

172. Ibid., p. 334.

173. 321 U.S. 114 (1944).

174. Ibid., p. 118.

175. *See also House v. Mayo*, 324 U.S. 42 (1945); *White v. Ragan*, 324 U.S. 760 (1945); *Hawk v. Olson*, 326 U.S. 271 (1945); *Woods v. Nierstheimer*, 328 U.S. 211 (1946); *Carter v. State of Illinois*, 329 U.S. 173 (1946).

176. 344 U.S. 443 (1953).

177. *See*, however, *Frisbe v. Collins*, 342 U.S. 519 (1951) providing that deviation from this rule is allowed in "special circumstances."

178. *State of North Carolina v. Brown*, 63 S.E.2d 99 (1951).

179. *Brown v. State of North Carolina*, 341 U.S. 943 (1951).

180. *Brown v. Crawford*, 98 F. Supp. 866 (1951).

181. *Brown v. Allen*, 192 F.2d 477 (1951).

182. *Brown v. Allen*, 344 U.S. 443, 508.

183. Ibid., p. 510.

184. Bator, "Finality in Criminal Law," 76 Harv. L. Rev. 441, 505.

185. Policy considerations are discussed at ibid., pp. 500-28; Hart, "The Time Chart of the Justices," 73 Harv. L. Rev. 84, 106-07; Developments, "Federal Habeas Corpus," 83 Harv. L. Rev. 1038, 1056-63.

186. Hart, "The Time Chart of the Justices," 73 Harv. L. Rev. 84, 106.

187. *See* Parker, "Limiting the Abuse of Habeas Corpus," 8 F.R.D. 171, 175.

188. *United States v. Hayman*, 342 U.S. 205 (1952).

189. *See* e.g. *Warren v. United States*, 311 F.2d 673, 675 (1963). [Unlawful search and seizure "are not proper matters to be presented by motion to vacate sentence under section 2255 but can only be properly presented by appeal from conviction"]. *Accord: United States v. Jenkins*, 281 F.2d 193 (1960); *Williams v. United States*, 307 F.2d 366 (1962); *Peters v. United States*, 312 F.2d 481 (1963); *Armstead v. United States*, 318 F.2d 725 (1963); *Gendron v. United States*, 340 F.2d 601 (1965); *Springler v. United States*, 340 F.2d 950 (1965); *Eisner v. United States*, 351 F.2d 55 (1965); *De Welles v. United States*, 372 F.2d 67 (1967); *United States v. Re*, 372 F.2d 641 (1967). *Contra: Gaitan v. United States*, 317 F.2d 494 (1963); *United States v. Sutton*, 321 F.2d 211 (1963).

190. This supposition conflicts, of course, with the notion that the lower federal courts were at the option of Congress and that the Supreme Court's appellate power was subject to congressional will.

191. *See Stack v. Boyle*, 342 U.S. 1, 6-7 (1951).

192. 394 U.S. 217 (1969).

193. It should be noted that this was different from saying that relief by section 2255 was available after a federal prisoner had obtained direct review in a federal court of appeals. If the same claim, which the federal prisoner seeks to raise in the collateral attack, had been raised and rejected by the appellate court in the normal process, it seems unlikely that the claim raised a second time would have any greater chance of success, since it would be passing through the same courts (except where the original record did not or could not contain evidence bearing on the present claim, e.g. method of jury selection, and cases where a supervising decision of the Supreme Court has been rendered).

194. *Kaufman v. United States*, 350 F.2d 408 (1965).

195. The Court found that Kaufman's case was not one where there was a "deliberate by-pass." *See* ch. 4, text accompanying notes 190-201 *supra*. The Court observed:

> Appointed counsel had objected at trial to the admission of certain evidence on grounds of unlawful search and seizure, but newly appointed counsel did not assign the admission as error either in his brief or on oral argument of the appeal. After oral argument of the appeal, however, petitioner wrote a letter to appellate counsel asking him to submit to the Court of Appeals a claim of illegal search and seizure of items from his automobile. Counsel forwarded petitioner's letter to the Clerk of the Court of Appeals who notified counsel that petitioner's letter had been given to the panel which had heard and was considering the appeal. The opinion of the Court of Appeals affirming petitioner's

conviction does not appear to pass on the search-and-seizure claim. 394 U.S. 217, 220, n. 3.

196. 268 F. Supp. 484, 487 (1967).

197. 417 U.S. 333 (1974).

198. *See* Comment, "Availability of Federal Post-Conviction Relief in Light of a Subsequent Change in the Law," 66 J. of Crim. L. and Criminology 117 (1975).

199. 417 U.S. 333, 342-43 (emphasis added by Court).

200. Ibid., pp. 356-57.

201. Ibid., p. 343.

202. The holding would apply, therefore, to cases of state prisoners.

203. *See* text accompanying notes 96-132 *supra.*; ch. 4, text accompanying notes 53-85 *supra.*

204. 394 U.S. 217, 223.

205. 332 U.S. 174 (1942).

206. 368 U.S. 424 (1962).

207. The Court seems to have been heavily influenced by an argument presented in Developments, "Federal Habeas Corpus," 83 Harv. L. Rev. 1038, 1066-72.

208. The *Davis* Court noted the following passage from *Sunal* in support of its distinction:

> Of course if Sunal and Kulick had pursued the appellate course and failed, their cases would be quite different. But since they chose not to pursue the remedy which they had, we do not think they should be allowed to justify their failure by saying they deemed any appeals futile.

332 U.S. 174, 181.

209. 368 U.S. 424, 428.

210. *See also U.S. v. Timmreck*, 441 U.S. 780 (1979).

211. In support of this interpretation, *see Stone v. Powell*, 428 U.S. 465, n. 10; and especially, *United States ex rel. Soto v. United States*, 504 F. 2d 1339 (1974). *See also, U.S. v. Addonizio*, 442 U.S. 178 (1979).

212. *See* Tenn. Const., Art. I, 14 (indictment by grand jury required). This section originally appeared as part of an article in 23 How. L. J. 279 (1980) and is reprinted with the authority of the Howard Law Journal.

213. *See* Tenn. Code Ann. sects. 22-222 to 22-228 (supp. 1978); sects. 40-1501 and 40-1502.

214. *Mitchell v. Rose*, 570 F. 2d 129 (1978).

215. 439 U.S. 816 (1978) (*cert. granted*).

216. 428 U.S. 465, 482 (1976).

217. Cover and Aleinikoff, "Dialectical Federalism," 86 Yale L. J. 1035, 1041.

218. Henry J. Friendly, "Is Innocence Irrelevant? Collateral Attack on Criminal Judgments," 38 U. Chi. L. Rev. 142 (1970).

219. *See Thornton v. United States*, 368 F. 2d 822 (1966) and cases cited therein at 824 nn. 1-3.

220. 394 U.S. 217 (1969).

221. 412 U.S. 218, 250.

222. *Kaufman v. United States*, 394 U.S. 217 (1969).

223. *Schneckloth v. Bustamonte*, 412 U.S. 218, 251.

224. Ibid., p. 257.

225. Ibid., pp. 257-58.

226. Ibid., p. 272.

227. 367 U.S. 643 (1961).

228. Ibid., p. 655.

229. *Stone v. Powell*, 428 U.S. 465, 482.

230. Ibid., p. 495.

231. Ibid., p. 481.

232. That difficulty continued during the term in which *Rose* was decided. *See e.g., Rakas v. Illinois*, 439 U.S. 178 (1978); *United States v. Caceres*, 440 U.S. 741 (1979); *North Carolina v. Butler*, 441 U.S. 369 (1979); *Michigan v. DeFillippo*, 99 S. Ct. 2627 (1979).

233. 99 S. Ct. 2993 (1979). *See also, Jackson v. Virginia*, 99 S. Ct. 2781 (1979), which asked what standard was to be applied in a federal habeas proceeding when the claim is raised that a person has been convicted in a state court upon sufficient evidence after that claim has been given a full and fair hearing in the state system. Unlike the right in *Stone*, which was held to be a judicially created right, proof beyond a reasonable doubt was held to be a constitutional imperative. The Court rejected respondent's appeal to extend *Stone*. The costs alleged to be involved were found to be exaggerated. The claim involved, observed Mr. Justice Stewart, almost always could be judged on the written record without need for an evidentiary hearing. The effect of habeas relief on finality and federal-state comity was determined to be more than offset by vindication of the constitutional right involved. Finally, *Jackson* was distinguished from *Stone* because "[t]he question whether a defendant has been convicted upon inadequate evidence is central to the basic question of guilt or innocence." Ibid., p. 4888. Nevertheless, as Stevens noted in his concurring opinion, the rule was unnecessary to the decision because the Court rejected petitioner's claim that under the constitutional standard his conviction could not stand.

234. *Rose v. Mitchell*, 99 S. Ct. 2993, 3002.

235. Ibid., p. 3000.

236. 316 U.S. 400, 406 (1942).

237. *Rose v. Mitchell*, 99 S. Ct. 2993, 3000.

238. Ibid., pp. 3002-04.

239. Ibid., p. 3016 n. 10.

240. Ibid., pp. 3003-04.

241. Ibid., p. 3003.

242. Ibid.

243. Ibid.

244. Ibid.

245. Ibid., p. 3004.

246. *See* ibid., pp. 3005-06 (Rehnquist, J., concurring in part).

247. Ibid., pp. 3007-09.

248. Ibid., p. 3013.

249. Ibid., p. 3016.

250. Ibid.

251. *See* Conclusion, *infra.*

252. *See* text accompanying notes 133-35 *supra.*

253. *See Duncan v. Louisiana*, 391 U.S. 145 (1968); *In re Gault*, 387

U.S. 1 (1967); *Miranda v. Arizona*, 384 U.S. 436 (1966); *Brady v. Maryland*, 373 U.S. 83 (1963); *Gideon v. Wainwright*, 372 U.S. 335 (1963); *Robinson v. California*, 370 U.S. 660 (1962); *Mapp v. Ohio*, 367 U.S. 643 (1961).

254. Owen M. Fiss, "Forward: The Forms of Justice," 93 Harv. L. Rev. 1, 46-50 (1979).

255. *Rose v. Mitchell*, 99 S. Ct. 2993, 3016, n. 9. Even if the claim of systematic exclusion in grand jury selection can be said to be a harmless error, the harmless error doctrine should not be applied to the habeas context. Unlike appeal, the function of habeas corpus is not correction of all prejudicial errors, but institutional reform. (However, compare Powell's "opportunity test" with the "corrective process test" used earlier in the century. Note, however, the "corrective process test" was formulated in the formative era of procedural due process.)

256. *Rose v. Mitchell*, 99 S. Ct. 2993, 3016.

257. Ibid., p. 3014, n. 5.

258. *See Carter v. Jury Commission of Grier County*, 396 U.S. 320 (1970).

259. This argument is sufficient to overcome the charge by Cover and Aleinikoff, "Dialectical Federalism," 86 Yale L. J. 1035, 1041-42, n. 46, that habeas corpus is a weak remedy. As long as prisoners remain invisible, habeas corpus is the best remedy available.

260. 396 U.S. 320 (1970).

261. *See* text accompanying notes 258-59 *supra*.

262. *Carter v. Jury Commission of Grier County*, 396 U.S. 320, 336-37.

263. 414 U.S. 488 (1974). *See also* the standing requirement of *Warth v. Seldin*, 422 U.S. 490 (1975), an opinion written by Powell, which incorporated the standing requirement of *O'Shea*:

> As an aspect of justiciability, the standing question is whether the plaintiff has "alleged such a personal stake in the controversy" as to warrant *his* invocation of federal-court jurisdiction and to justify exercise of the court's remedial powers on his behalf. . . . This Art. III judicial power exists only to redress or otherwise to protect against injury to the complaining party, even though the court's judgment may benefit others collaterally. A federal court's jurisdiction therefore can be invoked only when the plaintiff himself has suffered "some threatened or actual injury from the putative illegal action . . ."

422 U.S. 490, 498-99. In addition to the difficulty of determining exactly which member of the class has been the victim of discrimination by being excluded from jury service, the added requirement of causality would be well-nigh impossible to satisfy in a class (or private) action for injunctive relief.

264. 423 U.S. 362 (1976).

265. 410 U.S. 614 (1973).

266. *Rose v. Mitchell*, 99 S. Ct. 2993, 3014.

267. Similar reasoning would suggest that it would not necessarily be a bad idea to rediscover the power of state courts to issue habeas for federal prisoners.

268. *See* Cover and Aleinikoff, "Dialectical Federalism," 86 Yale L. J. 1035, 1046-68.

269. Burt Neuborne, "The Myth of Parity," 90 Harv. L. Rev. 1105 (1977).

270. Tushnet, "Judicial Revision of the Habeas Corpus Statutes," 1975 Wis. L. Rev. 484, 497.

271. *See generally* William Bennett Turner, "When Prisoners Sue: A Study of Prisoner Section 1983 Suits in Federal Courts," 92 Harv. L. Rev. 910 (1979); Donald H. Zeigler and Michele G. Hermann, "The Invisible Litigant: An Inside View of Pro Se Actions in the Federal Courts," 47 N.Y.U. L. Rev. 157 (1972).

272. 99 S. Ct. 1861 (1979).

273. Tushnet, "Judicial Revision of the Habeas Corpus Statutes," 1975 Wis. L. Rev. 484, 496.

Custody

-6-

THE CUSTODY REQUIREMENT

The writ of habeas corpus probably sprang from a judicial order, directed to a person who had or could exert control over the body of another party, whereby the court sought to compel the appearance of a party before it.[1] During the thirteenth century, it was a step in the *mesne* process.[2] In the fourteenth century, the habeas corpus command was united with the judicial inquiry seeking the cause of the prisoner's detention and the writ of *habeas corpus cum causa*,[3] the direct ancestor of the modern *habeas corpus ad subjiciendum*, was formed.[4] At each stage in its development the judicial command was, naturally, directed to the person who could fulfill the directive, that is, the person who could exert control, or secure the appearance when summonses and attachments failed, or certify the cause and produce the prisoner. Thus, the natural dictates of the situation created the procedural requirement that the writ of habeas corpus be directed "to him who hath the custody of the body."[5] The writ directed that the custodian "produce the body, with the day and cause of his caption and detention, *ad faciendum, subjiciendum*, et *recipiendum*, to do, submit to, and receive, whatever the judge or court awarding such writ shall consider in that belief."[6] Implicit in this procedural aspect of the writ was the requirement of custody. Likewise, the custody requisite was intrinsic to the function, nature, and purpose of the writ.[7] Moreover, from the first federal habeas statute, which provided, *inter alia,*

   . . . That writs of habeas corpus shall in no case extend to

> prisoners in gaol, unless where they are *in custody*, under or
> by colour of the authority of the United States. . . .[8]

the federal courts have been guided by statutory specifications that
circumscribe, *via* a custody requirement, the jurisdictional boundaries of federal habeas relief.[9]

The difficulty with the notion of custody arises when this procedural and jurisdictional element is questioned on the substantive
level; that is, when "custody" is at issue, not to question "to whom
shall the writ properly issue," nor to ask whether this be a proper
case for the exercise of federal jurisdiction, but rather to examine
the degree of confinement that will justify the issuance of a writ
of habeas corpus. I do not find that this issue arose in Anglo-
American law before 1789, and the federal habeas statute of
that year did not define "custody," probably because it was not
thought of in substantive terms. Later statutes also left this question open, and it remained then for judicial determination.[10]

In 1885, the substantive question of custody was, for the first
time, squarely before the Supreme Court.[11] The petitioner, Philip
S. Wales, a navy officer, sought a writ of habeas corpus to challenge his confinement to the city of Washington by the Secretary
of the Navy pending the outcome of court-martial proceedings
initiated against him. Judge Cox of the Supreme Court of the
District of Columbia, upon Wales' petition, issued the writ. W. C.
Whitney, secretary of the navy, returned that "Wales was not now,
nor was at the time of issuing the annexed writ, in the custody or
possession of, or confined or restrained of his liberty, by, your respondent . . ." and further "that neither he nor anyone by his authority has exercised any physical restraint over the said Philip S.
Wales before or since the issue of said writ." The petition was dismissed, and Wales appealed to the Supreme Court of the United
States. The United States Supreme Court affirmed the decision of
the lower court, finding that the petitioner was under "no physical
restraint";[12] thus establishing "physical restraint" as a *sine qua non*
of habeas corpus. The Court went on to hold that "Something more
than moral restraint is necessary to make a case for habeas corpus.
There must be actual confinement or the present means of enforc-

ing it."[13] The requirement established by the Court was not found in the instant case:

> If Dr. Wales had chosen to disregard this order, he had nothing to do but take the next or any subsequent train from the city and leave it. There was no one at hand to hinder him. And though it is said that a file of marines or some proper officer could have been sent to arrest and bring him back, this could only be done by another order of the Secretary, and would be another arrest, and a real imprisonment under another and distinct order. Here would be a real restraint of liberty, quite different from the first.[14]

Although acknowledging that there was no "satisfactory definition" of the character of restraint to be found, the Court attempted to back its holding (1) by quoting various provisions of the habeas statute,[15] which showed only that some form of undefined "custody" was required; (2) by citing a note to two 1758 British cases, implying, perhaps, that actual physical custody was an essential element for the issue of the writ of habeas corpus (the author of the note being uncertain—at best *obiter dictum* by Lord Mansfield, more probably an editorial remark[16]); and (3) by noting two state court decisions. The first state case[17] was a reversal of a judgment awarding the writ of habeas corpus to a party committed to jail on execution for debt who, having given bond to pay the debt if he left the bounds of the prison, was admitted to the privileges of those bounds. Mr. Chief Justice Martin held that "[t]he appellee was under no physical restraint, and there was no necessity to recur to a court or judge to cause any moral restraint to cease." If the appellee left the prison bounds he faced only forfeiture of the bond, not imprisonment. The analogy to *Wales v. Whitney* was anything but "striking," to use the word employed by Mr. Justice Miller in calling attention to the resemblance of the two cases. In the second case cited, the Supreme Court of Pennsylvania held that under *its* habeas statute,[18] one on bail would not be allowed a writ to his surety.[19] However, the Court was there dealing with "custody" as defined by the state's habeas statute, which spoke in terms of "imprisonment" and which was addressed to sheriffs, gaolers and other officers in whose custody one is detained.

Despite the fact that *Wales v. Whitney* presented a unique situation,[20] and that the Court, in fact, noted that "the extent and character of the restraint which justifies the writ must vary according to the nature of the control which is asserted,"[21] a more flexible approach was not followed by later courts, and the *Wales'* requirement of tangible physical restraint remained the established rule for almost eighty years.[22]

In 1905, Circuit Judge Grosscup, for the Seventh Circuit, applying the *Wales'* concept of custody to the case of an individual released on bail, found actual custody sufficient to justify the issuance of the writ of habeas corpus.[23] The federal court judge observed: "The purpose of the writ of habeas corpus is to test the right of the court, or other body issuing the writ of arrest, to restrain the party of his right to go without question, or, as stated in the English case, cited in *Taylor v. Taintor*,[24] without a string upon his liberty."[25] Judge Grosscup found that the "exact point" had been decided in *In re Grice*.[26] However, as pointed out by the Third Circuit six years later, the applicant in *Grice* had surrendered himself before petitioning for the writ.[27] The Third Circuit, *per* Circuit Judge Grey, in the case of an alien who had been released on bail bond pending deportation proceedings, held:

> By the giving of bail bond, the relator had, for the time being, waived the right to this writ. She was no longer in the custody of the inspector, nor restrained by him of her liberty. . . . The custody complained of must be actual and not constructive. . . .[28]

The following year, the conflict among the circuits was, for a time,[29] put to rest by the Supreme Court.[30] In *Johnson v. Hoy*, the petitioner sought review of an order by a district court dismissing habeas corpus. He contended that the act upon which he had been indicted was unconstitutional, and that bail was set at an unconstitutionally excessive amount. The Court dismissed the appeal, noting that since the appeal, the defendant had given bond in the district court; therefore,

He is no longer in the custody of the marshal to whom the writ is addressed, and from whose custody he seeks to be discharged. The defendant is now at liberty . . . [—] having secured the very relief which the writ of habeas corpus was intended to afford to those held under warrant issued on indictments. . . .[31]

This opinion was reaffirmed by the Court eight years later:[32] Mr. Justice Brandeis, for the Court, found that the habeas petition of the applicant—who had in fact been produced before the Court in response to a writ of habeas corpus, but the habeas hearing being postponed, the petitioner was admitted to bail[33]—was moot. Brandeis considered it "well settled that, under such circumstances [that is, the applicant being no longer under "actual restraint"], a petitioner is not entitled to be discharged on habeas corpus."[34] Thus, at least until the 1960s, the rule was that release on bail precluded one's right to habeas corpus.[35]

It can be inferred from the just noted bail cases that the writ was also unavailable to test the validity of a petitioner's conviction after he had been released at the end of his sentence, even if the application were filed while the petitioner was in custody. In 1900, the Supreme Court denied a motion for leave to file a petition for writs of habeas corpus and certiorari, ruling that leave will not be granted where it is obvious that before a return to the writ can be made or any other action taken, the restraint of which the prisoner complains will be terminated.[36] Six years later in *Re Lincoln*,[37] the Court denied a petition for habeas corpus on behalf of a person convicted and sentenced to sixty days for bringing intoxicating beverages into an Indian reservation. The Court, *per* Mr. Justice Brewer, noted that the sixty day sentence had expired before the case was submitted, and indeed, had almost expired before application for the writ was made. The Supreme Court in 1942, in a memorandum decision, denied a petition for a writ of certiorari by an applicant for habeas corpus on the ground that the cause was moot—the petitioner having been paroled and being no longer in the warden's custody.[38] In *Parker v. Ellis*,[39] the Court again dismissed as moot a writ of certiorari by an applicant for habeas corpus, who, after making application and before his case was heard by the Supreme Court, was released from a state prison after having served his sentence with time off for good behavior. The Court held that "it is a condition upon this Court's jurisdiction to adjudicate an application for habeas corpus that the petitioner be in custody when that jurisdiction can become effective."[40] Harlan, in a separate opinion, directed no doubt at the strong dissent of Mr. Chief Justice Warren,[41] added: "The 'moral stigma' of a judgment which no longer affects legal rights does not present a case or controversy for appellate review."[42]

The *Wales'* notion of actual custody, as shown in the above-noted case of *Weber v. Squier*,[43] was applied to frustrate petitions from those on parole, as well as those on bail.[44] In *Jones v. Cunningham*,[45] Circuit Judge Haynsworth dismissed a petition for habeas corpus of a petitioner who was, since application, released on parole. Upon his release on parole, petitioner sought to substitute members of the Virginia Parole Board as party defendants. Haynsworth stated:

> In the nature of things, the "Great Writ" of *habeas corpus ad subjiciendum* may issue only when the applicant is in the actual, physical custody of the person to whom the writ is directed. The court may not order one to produce the body of another who is at liberty and whose arrest would be unlawful. The great purpose of the writ is to afford a means for speedily testing the legality of a present, physical detention of a person. It serves no other purpose.[46]

From this dismissal, Jones petitioned for, and was granted, certiorari by the Supreme Court.[47] The Supreme Court reversed the circuit court's decision and "retreated"[48] from the strict custody rule.[49] In a prodigious examination of legal history, the Court denied that physical restraint was ever an absolute necessity for the issue of habeas corpus. Although acknowledging that the "chief use" of the writ in England, as in the United States, "has been to seek the release of persons held in actual physical custody," the Court noted that English courts have long recognized the writ as a proper remedy even though the restraint is something less than "close physical confinement."[50] The Court then pointed to a 1722 case involving guardian and ward;[51] a 1763 case involving master and servant;[52] and two early nineteenth-century cases involving parent and child.[53] Instances of the use of the writ in the United States by aliens seeking entry, individuals testing the legality of an induction or enlistment, and parents disputing the custody of their children, were also noted.[54] The Court concluded: "History, usage, and precedent can leave no doubt that, besides physical imprisonment, there are other restraints on a man's liberty, restraints not shared by the public generally, which have been thought sufficient in the English-speaking world to support the issuance of habeas corpus."[55] The Court thus held that "legal as well as physical restraints could be properly seen as a 'custody.'"[56] In Jones' case, the parole had imposed "conditions which significantly confine[d] and restrain[ed] his freedom,"[57] so as to bring him within the custody requirement.[58]

The Court was criticized for its use of legal history in *Jones*. Professor Dallin H. Oaks, writing in the University of Michigan Law Review, stated: "If there was any single feature that characterized the writ of habeas corpus in both its early statute and common-law forms, it was the requirement that adult persons be subject to an immediate and confining restraint on their liberty."[59] As authority for this statement, Oaks pointed to *Palmer v. Forsyth*,[60] where, according to Oaks, the King's Bench quashed a writ of habeas corpus because the custodian "had no power at all over the body of the defendants."[61] It is interesting to note first of all, that by "custodian," the King's Bench was referring to the bail. Secondly, the particular effect of giving bail here was being singled out: the practice in the Court of Pleas at Berwick at this time was that when the goods were attached and bail was given, the goods were returned to the defendant, and not to the bail. No appearance was entered for the defendant, and on final judgment, execution issued against the goods of the defendant, over which the bail had no power in this instance. When goods were attached, the defendant was not permitted to discharge them by surrendering himself to prison. The Court therefore held that since "the effect of giving bail was to release the goods, and that bail had no power at all over the bodies of the defendants . . . the writ of habeas corpus must be quashed." The case was thus one of an arrest of goods not of a person. Oaks also noted the case of *Mitchell v. Mitchenham*.[62] Habeas corpus was also quashed there. In this case, however, *habeas corpus cum causa* was being sought against a court below to remove the case. Since the defendant had been let to bail, the King's Bench would not issue a writ of habeas corpus to remove the cause, the court below not being in "actual *or virtual*"[63] possession of the body.[64]

It is true that no cases of the use of habeas corpus can be found in pre-1789 English law.[65] The writ had developed into an instrument to test the jurisdiction of the imprisoning agent. If the party were imprisoned for no crime, or by a person without jurisdiction, that party would be discharged by the court or judge issuing the writ. If the jurisdiction of the imprisoning agent were questionable, or it were doubtful whether the act was a crime, or whether the crime were one for which bail was allowed, the party was let to bail. Thus, by common law (and by section III of the Habeas Corpus Act of 1679) the writ did not benefit "persons convict or in execution by legal process."[66] But even for those committed for high treason or felony "plainly and specially expressed on the warrant," the Habeas Corpus Act provided for their speedy trial, or that failing, their discharge on bail.[67] The writ, then, was basically a pretrial device to prevent arbitrary imprisonment, and in that sense, perhaps it was "somewhat misleading to resort to historical usage to define the meaning of 'custody' for the purposes of post conviction review."[68] In addition, parole is a twentieth-century institution,[69] and bail, even though a well-established preconviction device in English law before 1789,[70] never lent itself to question the "custody" requirement, likely because although bail was theoretically a jailer of one's own choosing, the principal never thought of himself "in custody," as his surety was, as a rule, family or friend.[71] This is by way of explaining why the custody requirement was never a problem; it is not, however, to say that physical custody was a *sine qua non* of habeas corpus.

With the weakening of the *Wales* foundation, the walls of custody built upon it began to crumble. Although it remains the general rule that a writ of habeas corpus does not lie to afford relief after the expiration of the sentence imposed,[72] where the conviction underlying the sentence has collateral consequences, the writ may be appropriate.[73] Five years after its decision in *Jones*, the Supreme Court considered the effect of postconviction disabilities flowing from conviction.[74] James P. Carafas applied to a United States district court, after exhausting his state remedies, alleging that illegally seized evidence had been used against him in his trial in a New York state court. The application was denied. Appeal to the United States Court of Appeals was dismissed. Two weeks before the United States Supreme Court issued the writ of certiorari, he was unconditionally released, his state sentence having had expired. The Court, *per* Mr. Justice Fortas, however, in a decision closely following Mr. Chief Justice Warren's dissent in *Parker v. Ellis*,[75] noted:

> It is clear that petitioner's cause is not moot. In consequence of his conviction, he cannot engage in certain business; he cannot serve as an official of a labor union for a specified period of time; he cannot vote in any election held in New York State; he cannot serve as a juror. Because of these "disabilities or burdens [which] may flow from" petitioner's conviction, he has "a substantial stake in the judgment of conviction which survives the satisfaction of the sentence imposed on him." . . . On account of these "collateral consequences," the case is not moot.[76]

The Court, however, in overruling *Parker*, did not rely on the post-conviction disabilities. Instead, it interpreted the habeas statute[77] to allow the custody elements to be judged as of the time of filing for the petition for habeas corpus.[78] Judging from the fact that Harlan[79] and Stewart,[80] who joined the majority in *Parker*, also joined the majority in *Carafas*, and from the strained interpretation of the habeas statute—an interpretation that could have been, but was not, employed in *Jones* under an analogous situation—the Court in *Carafas* probably took the more conservative approach to obtain a unanimous opinion in overruling *Parker*. The fact that civil disabilities were mentioned in the opinion seems, as yet, to have been immaterial;[81] civil disabilities alone have thus far not been judged to be sufficient to support the writ.

Subsequent to the decision in *Jones*, the lower federal courts seem to have been equally divided on the question of whether one released on bail[82] or on one's own recognizance[83] was in custody sufficient to justify issuance of the writ. In *Hensley v. Municipal*

Court, San Jose-Milpitas Judicial District,[84] the Supreme Court found that one released on his own recognizance was in custody within the meaning of the habeas corpus statute. Unlike the decision in *Jones*, the Court did not attempt to align its decision with history; in fact, it frankly stated that in the past it had "consistently rejected interpretations of the habeas corpus statute that would suffocate the writ in stifling formalism or hobble its effectiveness with the manacles of arcane and scholastic procedural requirements."[85]

PREMATURITY AND IMMEDIATE RELEASE

Since the writ of habeas corpus is a device to relieve one from unlawful restraint, the courts have required that some form of restraint, more substantial than civil disabilities, be apparent. If the individual in custody is found to be restrained illegally, the writ functions to secure his immediate release. Does this mean, however, that the release need be immediate? And further, is the sole office of the writ to secure absolute release, thereby being unavailable to an applicant who is not entitled to release from all restraints?

IMMEDIATE RELEASE

The first question was before the Supreme Court in the 1934 case of *McNally v. Hill*.[86] The petitioner there had been convicted on three counts stemming from his part in the theft of automobiles and was sentenced to a term of two years on the first count and to terms of four years each on the second and third counts, the sentence on the first to run concurrently with that of the second, the sentence on the second and third to run consecutively. When McNally's petition came before the Supreme Court, sentence on the second count, less allowance for good behavior, had not yet expired, and service on the third had not yet begun. The petitioner attacked only the third count. It was argued that under the Parole Act of 1910,[87] the applicant would be eligible for parole if not for the outstanding but "void" sentence on the third count. The Court ruled that since the prisoner had not yet begun to serve the challenged count, he was not entitled to a writ of habeas corpus. It noted that "[d]iligent search of the English authorities and digests before 1789 has failed to disclose any case where the writ was sought or used before or after conviction, as a means of securing the judicial decision of any question which, even if determined in the prisoner's favor, could not have resulted in his immediate release."[88] It went on to say that "[a] sentence which the prisoner has not yet begun to serve cannot be the cause of restraint which the statute makes the subject of inquiry."[89] Thus, on the bases of English legal history and on its interpretation of the habeas statute, the Supreme Court affirmed the court of appeals' dismissal of McNally's petition.[90] The Court reaffirmed its decision in *McNally* seven years later in *Holiday v. Johnston*.[91] In that same year, the Court ruled that a state prisoner's petition for habeas corpus would not be premature where he challenged a second conviction, without attacking the first, in a case where parole under the first conviction was revoked solely because of the entry of a subsequent conviction.[92] The decision was completely consistent with the *McNally* requirement of immediate release. That requirement was later extended to frustrate petitioners' challenges to one of the two concurrent sentences[93] and to excessive single sentences prior to the service of the valid part,[94] and even to the first of two consecutive sentences.[95]

In *Walker v. Wainwright*,[96] the Supreme Court rejected a reading of *McNally* that stressed the notion of immediate release and held that a petitioner was entitled to test the legality of his present imprisonment for murder by an application for habeas corpus, even though after serving a sentence for murder he must serve another sentence for aggravated assault. It read *McNally* to hold merely that "a prisoner cannot employ federal habeas corpus to attack a sentence which [he] has not begun to serve."[97] Two months later, *McNally* was overruled. In reexamining *McNally*, Mr. Chief Justice Earl Warren in *Peyton v. Rowe*[98] concluded "that the decision in that case was compelled neither by statute nor by history and that it represents an indefensible barrier to prompt adjudication of constitutional claims in the federal courts."[99] Warren was absolutely correct: the decision was compelled not by the statute, nor by history because neither "substantive custody" nor cumulative punishment situations had a history before 1789. The case of "substantive custody" was made above;[100] with regard to cumulative punishment situations, the Court observed:

To the extent that the Court thought that the absence of eighteenth century English precedent demonstrated that McNally was not entitled to habeas corpus relief, the Court's reliance seems to have been misplaced. In light of the fact that English judges had no power to impose cumulative punishment in felony cases until 1769, it is not at all surprising that research failed to uncover a pre-1789 common-law analogy for McNally's petition for relief.[101]

The Court further criticized *McNally* and its prematurity rule on a number of policy grounds,[102] but the Court also showed that the petitioner in the instant case fit within the prematurity principle: "Practically speaking, Rowe is in custody for 50 years, or for the aggregate of his 30- and 20-year sentences."[103] The prematurity rule, therefore, was not abrogated.[104]

In *Braden v. Thirtieth Circuit Court of Kentucky*,[105] the doctrine of prematurity was finally laid to rest. There, the petitioner, who was serving a sentence in an Alabama prison, was allowed to challenge, by habeas corpus, an indictment found against him in Kentucky. Mr. Justice Blackmun, who concurred in the decision, felt compelled to observe: "we have come a long way from the traditional notions of the Great Writ. The common-law scholars of the past hardly would recognize what the Court has developed . . ., and they would, I suspect, conclude that it is not for the better."[106] Later in the same year, in *Preiser v. Rodriguez et al.*,[107] where the petitioners alleged that the deprivation of their good-conduct time credits was causing or would cause them to be in illegal physical confinement, the Court stated: "Even if the restoration of the respondents' credit would not have resulted in their immediate release, but only in shortening the length of their actual confinement in prison, habeas corpus would have been the appropriate remedy."[108]

In sum, the rule seems to be that the courts will allow habeas relief if an individual is restrained irrespective of the fact that he will not be immediately liberated, as long as the claim is not totally moot. For example, habeas corpus may be refused where a prisoner challenged one of two concurrent sentences where no prejudice is shown to result from the challenged conviction.[109] From a policy point of view, the new doctrine is much more in tune with the function of the writ today: since the writ is now a great postconviction remedy, the new doctrine eliminates the time the ultimately successful applicant need remain in illegal confinement; and in light of the fact that today's writ permits historical inquiry, the modern doctrine serves to mitigate the prejudice to factual reexamination caused by delay.[110]

ABSOLUTE RELEASE

The requirement that one need be "in custody" in order to avail himself of the benefits of the writ of habeas corpus follows from the fact that the traditional function of the writ was relief from unlawful restraint or imprisonment.[111] In *McNally v. Hill*,[112] the Court noted that traditionally, the *sole* relief available on habeas corpus was discharge or bail.[113] In *Jones*, the concept of custody was expanded beyond immediate physical restraint.[114] Applying this new concept of custody, a federal court in 1965 doubted "whether release on parole, even if a right, is within the purview of the relief authorized by the writ of habeas corpus since it has been held by the Supreme Court of the United States that a person on parole is, nevertheless, subject to significant restraints not imposed on the public generally."[115] That is, since parole is custody, habeas corpus would not issue to one seeking parole since total release was not being sought. In marked contrast to this view was that of the Circuit Court of the District of Columbia rendered prior to *McNally's* demise: "[I]n general habeas corpus is available not only to an applicant who claims he is entitled to be freed of all restraints, but also to an applicant who protests his confinement in a certain place, or under certain conditions, that he claims vitiate the justification for confinement."[116] Similarly, after *McNally's* demise, District Judge Samuel P. King, in *Parker v. Thompson*,[117] observed:

> Generally, whatever affects the quantitative or qualitative aspects of an individual's involuntary or nonconsenting confinement may be judicially reviewed in habeas corpus proceedings. Plaintiff's discrimination, equal protection, and due process claims are not put forward solely for philosophical satisfaction but also because, she alleges, the result of the alleged violations, deprivations, and infringement of her rights

is that the conditions and circumstances of her confinement have become more onerous. This is clearly habeas corpus country.[118]

Although the Supreme Court has not yet ruled on this issue,[119] judging from the recent rhetoric of the courts stressing that habeas corpus is not a static, narrow, formalistic remedy[120] to be circumscribed by technical considerations,[121] but rather a flexible device,[122] which has continually developed in order to protect liberty,[123] the later view seems, by today's standards, the correct one.

In *Bell v. Wolfish*,[124] although at oral argument the Supreme Court requested debate on the propriety of habeas corpus as a means of challenging conditions of confinement, the question was reserved because it had apparently never been contested below.[125] The case, however, is important as a reminder of a significant cause for the development of habeas corpus during the twentieth century. The increased availability of federal habeas for state prisoners, the expansion of issues cognizable on habeas, as well as the broadening of the custody concept, were all due to the expansion of process-oriented rights. There would have been no need to develop the process if the substance were not being enhanced. In *Bell v. Wolfish*, the Court held that restrictions imposed on pretrial detainees that were reasonably related to legitimate, nonpunitive government objectives did not deprive the detainees of liberty without due process of law. Having denied the existence of the right, it would have added little to block the avenue for asserting the putative right.

NOTES

1. *See* ch. 1, text accompanying notes 1-56 *supra*.
2. *See* ch. 1, text accompanying notes 48-56 *supra*.
3. *See* ch. 1, text accompanying notes 126-49 *supra*.
4. *See* ch. 1, text accompanying note 150 *supra. et seq.*
5. *Anon.*, 78 Eng. Rep. 27 (1586).
6. Blackstone, *Commentaries*, vol. 3, p. 131.
7. *See* Intro. *supra*.
8. 1 U.S. Statutes at Large 82 (1789) (emphasis added).
9. *See also* 2 U.S. Statutes at Large 98 (1802); 14 ibid., 385 (1867); Revised Statutes, sect. 753 (1873-1874); presently found in 28 U.S.C. 2241 (c) (1), and 2254 (a).
10. Once the issue did present itself before the federal judiciary, Congress must have felt content to allow the judiciary's solution to stand.

11. *Wales v. Whitney*, 114 U.S. 564 (1885). The issue was tangentially before a federal circuit court fifteen years earlier. *See In re Callicot*, 4 Fed. Cas. 1075 (1870), where it was held that a person on whom a sentence (alleged to have been imposed under a statute that was repealed before such sentence was passed) was imposed and subsequently was pardoned unconditionally (notice of the pardon having been given; though the pardon was not accepted) was not "in custody" for the purposes of habeas corpus. Ibid., pp. 1077-79. This, however, seems to have been a misapplication of the rule that in order to be effective, a pardon must be accepted. *United States v. Wilson*, 7 Pet. 150 (1833). (*See* Duker, "The President's Power to Pardon," 18 Wm. and M. L. Rev. 475, 521).

12. *Wales v. Whitney*, 114 U.S. 564, 569.

13. Ibid., pp. 571-72.

14. Ibid., p. 572.

15. Revised Statutes, sect. 754, 755, 757, 758.

16. *Rex v. Dawes* and *Rex v. Kessel*, 97 Eng. Rep. 486 (1758). Moreover, note argument at text accompanying note 19 *infra*.

17. *Dodge's Case*, 6 Martin (La.) 569 (1819).

18. *See* ch. 1, text accompanying note 132 *supra*.

19. *Republica v. Arnold*, 3 Yeates 263 (1801).

20. *See Wales v. Whitney*, 114 U.S. 564, 569, where Mr. Justice Miller observed:

> It is not stated as a fact of record, but it is a fair inference from all that is found in it, that as Medical Director [Wales] was residing in Washington and performing there the duties of his office. It is beyond dispute that the Secretary of the Navy had a right to direct him to reside in the city in performance of these duties. . . . It is not easy to see how he is under any restraint of his personal liberty by order of arrest, which he was not under before.

21. Ibid., p. 571.

22. Overruled by *Jones v. Cunningham*, 371 U.S. 236 (1963).

23. *MacKenzie v. Barrett*, 141 Fed. 964 (1905).

24. 16 Wall. 366 (1873), referring to *Anon.*, 87 Eng. Rep. 982 (1704).

25. 141 Fed. 964, 966.

26. 79 Fed. 627 (1897).

27. *See Sibray v. United States ex rel. Kupples*, 185 Fed. 401 (1911).

28. Ibid., p. 403.

29. *See* text accompanying notes 48-49 *infra*.

30. *Johnson v. Hoy*, 227 U.S. 245 (1912).

31. Ibid., p. 248.

32. *Stallings v. Splain*, 253 U.S. 339 (1920).

33. *See*, however, *Reis v. U.S. Marshal for the United States District Court for the Eastern District of Pennsylvania*, 192 F. Supp. 79 (1961), where the Court, drawing a distinction between the release of a defendant on bail pending the hearing and decision on a writ of habeas corpus, held that in the latter case, contrary to the former, the accused was "in custody."

34. *Stallings v. Splain*, 253 U.S. 339, 343.

35. *See, e.g. United States ex rel. Patts v. Rabb*, 141 F.2d 45 (1944), *cert. den.* 322 U.S. 727 (1944), opin. supp'd, 147 F.2d 225 (1945), *cert. den.*

324 U.S. 870 (1945); *Rowland v. State of Arkansas,* 179 F.2d 709 (1950), *cert. den.* 339 U.S. 952 (1950), *reh. den.* 339 U.S. 991 (1950).

It is not altogether clear whether the English courts will entertain applications for habeas corpus from one at large on bail. *See* Sharpe, *Habeas Corpus,* p. 161, n. 1.

Although bail theoretically constitutes custody (Duker, "The Right to Bail," 42 Alb. L. Rev. 33, 70), custody was transferred from the gaoler to the surety. It is understandable, from an historical point of view, why the writ was not allowed against the jailer once the applicant was released to bail. However, theoretically, the writ might issue to the bail. This idea seems never to have been innovated. (However, note Brandeis' opinion in *Stallings.* Read broadly, it covers this situation.) The English courts have held that the writ may issue not only to a person who has the actual custody, but also to a person who has the constructive custody in the sense of having power and control over the body. [*Barnardo v. Ford, Gossage's Case,* [1892] AC 326 (House of Lords); *Rex v. Secretary of State for Home Affairs, ex parte O'Brien* [1923] 2 K.B. 361 (Court of Appeals); *Ex parte Mwenya* [1960] 1 Q.B. 241 280, [1959] 3 All E.R. 525, 542 (Court of Appeals).] Also, in *French's Case,* 91 Eng. Rep. 308 (1704), a bail brought the principal before the court upon a habeas corpus, in order that the principal might be committed to the marshal in discharge of the bail's obligation. Might not a *habeas corpus ad subjiciendum* issue to a bail to produce the principal so that the court might examine the custody?

36. *Ex parte Baez,* 117 U.S. 378 (1900).

37. 202 U.S. 178 (1906).

38. *Weber v. Squier,* 315 U.S. 810 (1942).

39. 362 U.S. 574 (1960).

40. Ibid., p. 576. *See Garvin v. Cochran,* 371 U.S. 27 (1962) (declared moot by reason of the petitioner's death).

41. 362 U.S. 574, 582.

42. Ibid., p. 576. *See also Avila-Contreras v. McGranery,* 112 F. Supp. 264 (1953).

43. *See* text accompanying note 38 *supra.*

44. Likewise, this rule held in the case of probation. *See Viles v. United States,* 193 F.2d 776 (1952), *cert. den.* 343 U.S. 915 (1952).

45. 294 F.2d 608 (1961). *See* Daniel John Meador, *Preludes to Gideon* (Charlottesville, Va.: Michie Co., 1967), pp. 87-119.

46. 294 F.2d 608, 609 (without notes). The Court noted also that "some restraint upon a person's liberty is not necessarily the equivalent of the physical detention which is a requisite of the writ." Ibid.

47. *Jones v. Cunningham,* 371 U.S. 236 (1963). *See* Meador, *Preludes to Gideon,* pp. 244-81.

48. Developments, "Federal Habeas Corpus," 83 Harv. L. Rev. 1038, 1074.

49. *See also United States ex rel. Green v. Rundle,* 452 F.2d 232 (1971); *Gunsolus v. Gagnon,* 454 F.2d 416 (1971), *aff'd in part, rev'd in part on other grounds,* 411 U.S. 778 (1973); *Angro v. United States,* 505 F.2d 1373 (1975). The same applies in cases of release on furlough from prison. *United States ex rel. Geisler v. Walters,* 510 F.2d 887 (1975).

50. *Jones v. Cunningham*, 371 U.S. 236, 238.

51. *Rex v. Clarkson*, 93 Eng. Rep. 625.

52. *Rex v. Delaval*, 97 Eng. Rep. 913.

53. *Earl of Westmeath v. Countess of Westmeath*, 37 Eng. Rep. 848 (1821) (merely noted); *Ex parte McClellan*, 1 Dowl. 81 (1831).

54. *Jones v. Cunningham*, 371 U.S. 236, 239-40.

55. Ibid., p. 240.

56. Developments, "Federal Habeas Corpus," 83 Harv. L. Rev. 1038, 1074.

57. *Jones v. Cunningham*, 371 U.S. 236, 243.

58. *See* Developments, "Federal Habeas Corpus," 83 Harv. L. Rev. 1038, 1975: "The Court relied on several different factors in finding the necessary degree of restraint, and it is not clear what, short of actual physical confinement, remains essential to a finding of custody. *See* ibid., pp. 1075-76 for a review of these factors.

59. "Legal History in the High Court—Habeas Corpus," 64, 451, 469.

60. 107 Eng. Rep. 1108, 1109 (1825).

61. Oaks, "Legal History," 64 U. Mich. L. Rev. 451, 469, fn. 91.

62. 107 Eng. Rep. 189 (1823).

63. Emphasis added. No doubt referring to this phrase, Oaks acknowledged that in cases where *corpus cum causa* was being sought, "the courts seem to have been less exacting in the custody requirement." 64 U. Mich. L. Rev. 451, 469, n. 91.

64. *See also* Thomas M. Hitch, "Federal Habeas Corpus: The Concept of Custody and Access to Federal Courts," 53 J. of Urban L. 61, 68 (1975); "At common law one was in custody only if he was physically confined. . . . [T]he absence of actual confinement implied that there could be no release, hence the court lacked jurisdiction."

65. In fact, as noted above, it is not clear whether today one at large on bail in England is entitled to the writ. *See* text accompanying note 35 *supra*. Moreover, Sharpe, *Habeas Corpus*, p. 164, also notes that "[t]here has been virtually no consideration of the appropriateness of habeas corpus [in England] to challenge the legality of parole, probation or suspended sentence controls."

66. 31 Car. 2, c. 2, s. 3.

67. 31 Car. 2, c. 2, s. 7.

68. Note, "The Custody Requirement for Habeas Corpus in the Federal Courts," 51 Calif. L. Rev. 228, 230 (1963).

69. The system of parole was used first in conjunction with indeterminate sentences at Elmira Reformatory, New York in 1869. By 1900, twenty states had introduced parole statutes, and by 1922, all but four states had such statutes. *See Attorney General's Survey of Release Procedures* (Washington, D.C.: Government Printing Office, 1939), vol. 4, especially pp. 121-35.

70. Duker, "The Right to Bail," 42 Alb. L. Rev. 33 (1977).

71. Ronald Goldfarb, *Ransom: A Critique of the American Bail System* (New York: Harper and Row, 1965), p. 93.

72. *United States ex rel. Kamsler v. Attorney General of the United States*, 430 F.2d 635 (1970), *cert. den.* 400 U.S. 1014 (1970); *Wade v. Carsley*, 433 F.2d 68 (1970); *United States ex rel. Stuart v. Yeager*, 434 F.2d

1308 (1970); *Diehl v. Wainwright*, 423 F.2d 1108 (1970); *Theriault v. United States ex rel. State of Mississippi*, 433 F.2d 990 (1970); *Brown v. Wainwright*, 447 F.2d 980 (1971); *Lynch v. Henderson*, 469 F.2d 1081 (1972).

73. *See Jackson v. State of Louisiana*, 452 F.2d 451 (1971); *Gareau v. United States*, 474 F.2d 24 (1973); *United States ex rel. Urbano v. Yeager*, 323 F. Supp. 774 (1971); *LaFond v. Quatsoe*, 325 F. Supp. 1010 (1971).

74. *Carafas v. LaVallee*, 391 U.S. 234 (1968).

75. 362 U.S. 574, 582 (1960).

76. *Carafas v. LaVallee*, 391 U.S. 234, 237-38.

77. 28 U.S.C., sect. 2241 (c) (1964).

78. *Carafas v. LaVallee*, 391 U.S. 234, 238-40. *See* also *Marchand v. Director, United States Probation Office*, 421 F.2d 331 (1970); *United States ex rel. Bailey v. United States Commanding Officer of Provost Marshal, United States Army*, 496 F.2d 324 (1974).

79. Note *Parker v. Ellis*, 362 U.S. 574, 576.

80. *See Carafas v. LaValle*, 391 U.S. 234, 242-43.

81. *See*, however, Hitch, "Federal Habeas Corpus," 53 J. of Urban L. 61, 75.

82. Compare: *Burris v. Ryan*, 397 U.S. 553 (1968); *Settler v. Yakema Tribal Court*, 419 F.2d 486 (1969), *cert. den.* 398 U.S. 903 (1970); *Settler v. Lameer*, 419 F.2d 1311 (1969), *cert. den. Settler v. Yakema Tribal Court*, 398 U.S. 903 (1970); *Orito v. Powers*, 479 F.2d 435 (1973); *United States ex rel. Russo v. Superior Court of New Jersey, Law Division, Passaic County*, 483 F.2d 7 ((1973), *cert. den.* 414 U.S. 1023 (1973) (sufficient); with *Matyek v. United States*, 339 F.2d 389, 392 (1964), *cert. den.* 381 U.S. 917 (1964); *Allen v. United States*, 349 F.2d 362 (1965); *United States ex rel. Meyer v. Weil*, 458 F.2d 1068 (1972), *cert. den.* 409 U.S. 1060 (1972); *reh. den.* 412 U.S. 914 (1973); *United States ex rel. Rosenberg v. United States District Court, Eastern District, Pennsylvania*, 460 F.2d 1233 (1972) (insufficient).

83. Compare: *Whittington v. Gaither*, 272 F. Supp. 507 (1967), rev'd on other grounds 391 F.2d 905 (1968) (sufficient); with: *Moss v. State of Maryland*, 272 F. Supp. 371 (1967); *Odell v. Haas*, 280 F. Supp. 208 (1968) (insufficient).

84. 411 U.S. 345 (1973).

85. Ibid., p. 350.

86. 293 U.S. 131.

87. 36 U.S. Statutes at Large 819, as amended, 37 U.S. Statutes at Large 650 (1913).

88. *McNally v. Hill*, 293 U.S. 131, 137-138.

89. Ibid., p. 138.

90. One authority that the Court could have used, by way of analogy, was *In re Swan*, 150 U.S. 637, 653 (1893). The Court there denied an application for habeas corpus by one imprisoned under and by virtue of an order of the Circuit Court of the United States for the District of Columbia, punishing him for contempt of court in seizing goods without warrant, from the custody of a receiver appointed by said court and ordering him committed to the custody of the marshal to be imprisoned, until he returned the goods, and that he be further imprisoned for three months and until he pay the costs of the proceedings for contempt. Among other arguments, it

was contended that the circuit court exceeded its power in that the payment of costs was required, because the costs were in the nature of a fine, and therefore the punishment inflicted was both fine and imprisonment. Mr. Chief Justice Fuller, for the Court, observed:

> As the prisoner had neither restored the goods nor suffered the imprisonment for three months, even if it was not within the power of the court to require payment of costs and its judgment to that extent excluded its authority, yet he cannot be discharged on habeas corpus until he has performed so much of the judgment or served out so much of the sentence as it was within the power of the court to impose.

91. 313 U.S. 342 (1941). *See also Carlson v. Landon*, 342 U.S. 524 (1952).

92. *Ex parte Hull*, 312 U.S. 546 (1941).

93. *E.g. Wilson v. Gray*, 345 F.2d 282 (1965), *cert. den.* 382 U.S. 919 (1965).

94. *E.g. Carpenter v. Crouse*, 358 F.2d 701 (1966).

95. *E.g. Wells v. People of the State of California*, 352 F.2d 439 (1965). It might be argued that this decision flew in the face of the Supreme Court's 1894 decision in *In re Bonner*, 151 U.S. 242, where a petitioner was discharged on habeas corpus from a prison sentence that he had been sentenced to against a federal statute, which prohibited the particular style of custody in such cases, notwithstanding the fact that a valid sentence could be imposed. In this case, however, the valid sentence was not waiting for the petitioner. It remained for the lower court to actually reimpose a valid sentence in lieu of the invalid one.

96. 390 U.S. 335 (1968).

97. Ibid., p. 336.

98. 291 U.S. 54 (1968).

99. Ibid., p. 55.

100. *See* text accompanying notes 1-85 *supra*.

101. *Peyton v. Rowe*, 391 U.S. 54, 66 (without notes).

102. Ibid., pp. 61-64.

103. Ibid., p. 64.

104. *See Word v. North Carolina*, 406 F.2d 352 (1969).

105. 410 U.S. 484 (1973).

106. Ibid., p. 501.

107. 411 U.S. 475 (1973).

108. Ibid., p. 487.

109. *Van Gildern v. Field*, 498 F.2d 400 (1974).

110. *See Peyton v. Rowe*, 391 U.S. 54, 62, 64.

111. In the case of *Medley*, 134 U.S. 160 (1890), the Court was embarrassed to admit that on habeas corpus it could only totally discharge a convicted murderer who had been *sentenced* according to an *ex post facto* statute.

112. 293 U.S. 131 (1934).

113. Ibid., p. 136. *See also Woods v. Zerbst*, 85 F.2d 313 (1936); *McNealy v. Johnston*, 100 F.2d 280 (1938).

114. *See* text accompanying notes 48-58 *supra*.

115. *United States ex rel. Chilicote v. Maroney*, 246 F. Supp. 607, 609 (1965).

116. *Creek v. Stone*, 379 F.2d 106, 109 (1967).

117. 356 F. Supp. 783 (1973).

118. Ibid., p. 789. *See also Hudson v. Hardy*, 424 F.2d 854 (1970); *Wooley v. Consolidated City of Jacksonville, Florida*, 308 F.2d 1197 (1970).

119. *See*, however, the discussion of *Johnson v. Avery*, 393 U.S. 483 (1969) in Developments, "Federal Habeas Corpus," 83 Harv. L. Rev. 1038, 1082-83. *See Bell v. Wolfish*, 441 U.S. 520, 526-27, n. 6 (1979) (question reserved).

120. *Jones v. Cunningham,* 371 U.S. 236 (1963); *Peyton v. Rowe*, 391 U.S. 54 (1968).

121. *Hamilton v. Craven*, 350 F. Supp. 1251 (1971), *aff'd* 469 F.2d 1394 (1973).

122. *Harris v. Nelson*, 392 U.S. 286 (1969), *reh. den.* 394 U.S. 1025 (1969); *Hamilton v. Craven*, 350 F. Supp. 1251 (1971); *Adderly v. Wainwright*, 58 F.R.D. 389 (1972).

123. *Peyton v. Rowe*, 391 U.S. 54 (1968).

124. 441 U.S. 520 (1979).

125. Ibid., pp. 526-27, n. 6.

-Conclusion-

The Living Constitution:
The Case of Habeas Corpus

This study has raised a number of the most basic normative questions concerning constitutional change: If incorporation of the writ of habeas corpus into the American constitutional system has done nothing to halt the writ's propensity for change, what is the significance of a written constitution? What is the functional difference between the American and English constitutions? Indeed, does the United States also have a "common law constitution?" A second set of questions, that would shift the focus of inquiry from the Constitution to the institutions that interpret it, would ask whether it is legitimate for judges to cause the Constitution to change, when should constitutional change take place, and which factors should guide the change.

The answers to such questions, however, are beyond the scope of this study. Others have argued the legitimacy of constitutional change[1] and a case study of the history of the writ of habeas corpus adds little to the terms of that debate. This study has, however, aided the construction of a model of constitutional change. This conclusion will summarize the contribution of the history of habeas corpus to empirical analysis of constitutional changes short of formal amendment.

AGENCIES OF CONSTITUTIONAL CHANGE

Mr. Chief Justice Marshall in *Marbury v. Madison*[2] held that the judiciary was the final interpreter of the Constitution. In *McCulloch v. Maryland*[3] he reminded posterity that the Constitution was a living document capable of meeting "the various crises of human affairs." Thus from the formative period of the Constitution, the judiciary has been recognized as the premier agency of constitutional change. But, before examining the methods of judicial innovation, it is well to observe that the courts have not been the only agencies of constitutional change. In fact, in the course of the history of habeas corpus, one of "the various crises of human affairs" replaced the court (in the person of Mr. Chief Justice Taney) with the executive department as the supreme interpreter of the Constitution. Although constitutional theory and the best historical evidence compelled the conclusion that the Congress and not the President was intended to be vested with power to suspend the privileges of the writ of habeas corpus, necessity—as perceived by the President—determined the agent of governmental power.

Congress has also played a major role in effecting constitutional change. By gradually extending federal habeas to state prisoners, Congress restructured the concept of federalism. After the Reconstruction period, however, affections for strong central government, symbolized by the Civil War, began to moderate. The issuance of habeas by lower federal courts to release state prisoners became a source of discontent. Congress, therefore, restored the Supreme Court's jurisdiction under the 1867 Habeas Act with the mandate that federal courts should respect state judicial systems. Accordingly, the Supreme Court responded with the exhaustion doctrine.

From these two examples of constitutional innovation by the nonjudicial departments of government it would seem that (1) although the Supreme Court may have the final word on the meaning of the Constitution, actions sometimes speak louder than words; and (2) the words the Court uses to alter the Constitution may be dictated by the other branches, which thus play a major part in reshaping the fundamental concepts underlying the Constitution.

METHODS OF JUDICIAL INNOVATION

The Judiciary has functioned as the primary agent of constitutional change. The most obvious method of constitutional change is for the courts to fill in the gaps of a constitution that does not "partake of the prolixity of a legal code." In *Ex parte Bollman*[4] Marshall had little to guide him. Later Courts, at least, had precedent (itself not easy to understand and covering a unique situation) as well as the text to guide them.

In filling the gaps left by the habeas clause of the Constitution, the Court has looked to the internal logic of the document itself. For example, Marshall's discovery of the "obligation theory" was directed by reasoning that if Congress were not obligated to provide for the writ, "the privilege itself would be lost, although no law for its suspension be enacted." In addition, gaps have been filled by appealing to the political principles underlying the Constitution. *Tarble's Case*[5] moved the meaning of the habeas clause the remaining part of the 180 degree movement begun in *Bollman* by holding that state courts could not issue habeas to release federal prisoners, because such power would threaten the supremacy of the federal government. Similarly, *McCardle's Case*[6] was based upon Taney's inability to believe that the Constitution conferred on the President "more regal and absolute power over the liberty of the citizen, than the people of England have thought it safe to entrust to the crown."

Another method whereby the judiciary has altered the "habeas corpus" of 1787 was by looking to the broad philosophical principle underlying the Constitution and the writ: liberty. Although the Court's jurisdiction under the 1867 Act was withdrawn shortly before its decision in *Ex parte Yerger*,[7] the Court, struggling to find appellate jurisdiction in that case, appealed to the "great and leading intent of the Constitution." In rejecting the concept of custody that steadfastly had been adhered to in the United States for almost a century, Mr. Justice Black—who often expressed his disagreement with the philosophy of "the living constitution"—looked to the "grand purpose" of habeas corpus.

Constitutional change with respect to habeas corpus has been effectuated also by expanding the meaning of the terms of the definition of the writ. The concept of custody was broadened during the last two decades so that habeas corpus could question confinements that were not recognized as such by seventeenth-century English lawyers or eighteenth-century American statesmen. Another example is provided by the development of the concept of jurisdiction, which in *Ex parte Siebold*[9] was not satisfied because the statute under which the lower court acted was unconstitutional and which in *Frank v. Magnum*[10] was held to include certain due process aspects.

Closely related to constitutional innovation *via* expansion of the meaning of the terms of the writ's definition is the formulation and alteration of subsidiary constitutional rules. For example, in *Mapp v. Ohio*[11] the exclusionary rule was adopted by the Warren Court to implement the command of the Fourth Amendment. Recently, the Burger Court in *Stone v. Powell*,[12] expressing concern for finality and comity, held that the exclusionary rule need not be recognized in habeas proceedings where the defendant has had an opportunity for a "full and fair hearing" on his Fourth Amendment claims in a state court. Other examples of subsidiary rules invented and altered by the Court to effect changes in the constitutional law of habeas corpus are the exhaustion and waiver rules.

Since these methods of judicial innovation are interrelated, it is somewhat misleading to separate them. A subsidiary rule like exhaustion, for instance, was the direct result of readjusting notions of federalism. The expansion of the notion of jurisdiction in *Siebold* and *Frank* was inextricably linked to the broadening of the idea of liberty. Similarly, new rules have grown from long-standing rules: the exhaustion requirement has ancestry in the "extraordinary" nature of habeas corpus. Alternatively, new rules have been designed to check already established rules: The "special circumstances" exception to exhaustion allowed fine tuning of the new federalism that followed the Reconstruction period.

CAUSES OF CONSTITUTIONAL CHANGE

THE CHANGING ENVIRONMENT

The most obvious cause of constitutional change is the need to adopt constitutional formulas to situations not contemplated by the framers. In early England, actual physical confinement was the condition that the writ of habeas corpus came to relieve. There, however, release on bail meant release to family or friend and release on parole was not known. When presented with an application for habeas corpus from one held in constraint less than that traditionally subject to habeas relief, the courts had to define the essential nature of the writ.

Closely related was the need to harmonize the instruments of English jurisprudence to the form of government conceived in 1787. Examples of this process include the adjustment of the concept of jurisdiction in *Siebold* to a system where courts exercised the power of judicial review and the manipulation of the subtleties of that concept to a different structure of court hierarchy.

INTRA-GOVERNMENTAL CONFLICT

It is not surprising to find that one of the most significant factors responsible for constitutional change involving habeas corpus was the ongoing political struggle between the agencies of government. A constitution is, after all, a document regulating the distribution of political power. The jurisdictional battles between courts that took place in England from the fourteenth to the seventeenth century were repeated in the United States. The closest parallel to the earlier English battles was the *Ableman* and *Tarble* affair, which turned the meaning of the habeas clause on its head. A century later, the Warren Court developed habeas so that it could be used as a medium for broadcasting its conception of criminal justice to the state courts.

Congress endowed the federal courts with increased habeas jurisdiction after the Civil War, *inter alia*, to insure the efficacy of its policies in the South. When it looked as though the Supreme Court would interfere with its program by means of the newly acquired jurisdiction, Congress revoked the Court's jurisdiction under the Act of 1867. Because a case based on the Act was pending before the Court, Johnson—who had no affection for the Radical Republican program—vetoed the repealing measure. The veto was overridden, and the repealing measure was sanctioned by the Court, thus establishing the principle that Congress can withdraw jurisdiction from the Court. The Court's power under the Habeas Corpus Act of 1867 was restored seventeen years later at the initiative of those who were displeased with the frequent exercise of power by lower federal judges to overturn the decisions of state high courts.

GROWTH OF THE CONCEPT OF LIBERTY

Besides distributing political power, constitutions enshrine fundamental values. These values are devoid of operational meaning, and concepts like federalism and separation of powers are used to put them into effect. It should not be forgotten that federalism and separation of powers are merely instrumental concepts. In the end, the distribution of political power is intended to serve fundamental values. The fundamental value underlying habeas corpus is individual liberty. The idea behind the habeas clause of the Constitution was that by insuring that state courts had power to release prisoners held by the federal government, individual liberty—naturally threatened by centralized government—was secured. The notion that the states were the best protectors of individual liberties was shaken by the Civil War and the federal courts were empowered to issue federal habeas to a larger class of state prisoners than had previously had benefit of the federal writ. During the Fuller Court period, the states were once again viewed as best able to take care of criminal justice. State criminal cases concerned the Supreme Court only when liberties like freedom to contract or possession of property were threatened.[13] With the emergence of the progressive notion of government, process-rights replaced substantive due process as the mechanism for limiting governmental power and safeguarding individual liberty. As procedural due process expanded so did habeas corpus. First, certain due process features were found to be part of the concept of jurisdiction. Later, the Warren Court expanded issues cognizable on habeas corpus to all constitutional, as well as jurisdictional, questions. The Burger Court initially continued that expansion to include some nonconstitutional federal questions. Expansion deeper into nonconstitutional federal questions has recently been stalled.[14] In addition to extending issues cognizable, the Warren Court also expanded the custody concept to broaden the effectiveness of its liberalization of the criminal justice system. That expansion was also initially continued by the Burger Court, though signs of hesitancy appeared during the October 1978 term.[15]

Ultimately, constitutional change is permitted because it has conformed to the fundamental values underlying the Constitution. A court bent on narrowing the availability of habeas corpus can, therefore, take no comfort from the writ's early history. The direction of that court's change, too, must conform to fundamental values.

NOTES

1. *See, e.g.*, Thomas C. Gray, "Do We Have an Unwritten Constitution," 27 Stan. L. Rev. 703 (1975); John G. Wofford, "The Blinding Light: The Uses of History in Constitutional Interpretation," 31 U. Chi. L. Rev. 502 (1964); Charles E. Wyzanski, "History and Law," 36 U. Chi. L. Rev. 237 (1959).
2. 1 Cranch. 137 (1803).
3. 4 Wheat. 316 (1819).
4. 4 Cranch. 75 (1807).
5. 80 U.S. 397 (1871).
6. 7 Wall. 506 (1869).
7. 75 U.S. 85 (1869).
8. *Jones v. Cunningham*, 371 U.S. 236, 243 (1963).
9. 100 U.S. 371 (1879).
10. 239 U.S. 309 (1915).
11. 367 U.S. 643 (1961).
12. 428 U.S. 463 (1976).
13. *See, e.g., Ex parte Young*, 209 U.S. 123 (1908); *Lochner v. New York*, 198 U.S. 45 (1905).
14. *U.S. v. Timmreck*, 441 U.S. 780 (1979).
15. *Bell v. Wolfish*, 441 U.S. 520, 526-27 n. 6 (1979).

-Bibliography-

In addition to the various English and American federal and state court reporters, the following collections were consulted:

ENGLISH

Acts of the Privy Council.
Calendar of Closed Rolls.
Calendar of Inquisitions Misc. (Chancery).
Calendar of Patent Rolls.
Calendar of State Papers (Domestic).
Close Rolls.
Commons Journal.
Curia Regis Rolls.
Lords Journal.
Pipe Rolls.
Placitorum Abbreviatio.
Rotuli Hundredorum.
Rotuli Litterarum Clausarum.
Rotuli Parliamentorum.
Royal Commission on Historical Manuscripts.
State Trials.
Statues at Large.
Statutes of the Realm.
Year Books:
    14 Edward II. Edited by Helen M. Cam. Seldon Society, 1968.
    2 and 3 Edward III. Edited by F. W. Maitland and G. J. Turner. Seldon Society, 1907.
    5 Edward II. Edited by G. J. Turner. Seldon Society, 1947.
    11 Edward II. Edited by John P. Collas and W. S. Holdsworth. Seldon Society, 1942.
    12 Edward II. Edited by John P. Collas and Theodore F. T. Plunkett. Seldon Society, 1953.

14 Edward III. Edited by L. O. Pike. London, 1888.
17 Edward III.
24 Edward III.
 2 Richard II. Edited by Morris S. Arnold. Cambridge, Mass. Harvard
    University Press, 1975.
11 Richard II. Edited by Isobel D. Thornly. Ames Foundation, 1937.
12 Richard II. Edited by George F. Dreiser, Cambridge, Mass. Harvard
    University Press, 1914.
 4 Henry IV.
 9 Henry VI.
22 Henry VI.
39 Henry VI.
 2 Edward IV.
 8 Edward IV.
16 Edward IV.
21 Edward IV.
22 Edward IV.
 2 Henry VII.
13 Henry VII.

EXTRA-JUDICIAL OPINIONS

Wilmot, J. "Opinion on the Writ of Habeas Corpus," 97 Eng. Rep. 29 (1758).
"Concerning Process out of the Courts at Westminster into Wales of Late
    Times and How Anciently," 124 Eng. Rep. 1130.
Privy Council Memorandum of 9 Aug. 1722, 29 Eng. Rep. 646.
Opinion of Attorney General of England William Jones, 2 Va. Col. Dec. B1-
    B2 (1681).

AMERICAN

AMERICAN STATUTES—FEDERAL

Revised Statutes.
United States Code.
United States Statutes at Large.

AMERICAN STATUTES—STATE

The General Laws and Liberties of Connecticut Colony.
Acts and Laws of Connecticut. New-London, 1750.
Laws of Delaware 1700-1797.
Laws of the State of Delaware. New-Castle, 1797.
A Digest of the Laws of Georgia. Philadelphia, 1801.
Compact, Charter and Laws of the Colony of New Plymouth. Boston, 1836.

Acts and Laws Passed by the Great and General Court of Assembly of the Province of Massachusetts-Bay 1692-1719. London, 1729.

Acts and Resolutions of the Province of Massachusetts-Bay.

The Charter and General Laws of the Colony and Province of Massachusetts Bay. Boston, 1814.

Acts and Laws of His Majesty's Colony of Rhode Island and the Province-Plantations in New England in America 1745-1752.

Laws of Massachusetts. Boston, 1807.

Minnesota General Laws.

Acts and Laws Passed by the General Court or Assembly of New Hampshire. Portsmouth, 1729.

Laws of the State of New Jersey. Newark, N.J.: William Paterson, 1800.

Greenleaf, Thomas (ed). Laws of New York.

Acts of the Assembly of New York 1691-1718. London, 1719.

Colonial Laws of New York. Albany, 1894-1896.

Laws of North Carolina.

Laws of the Commonwealth of Pennsylvania. Philadelphia, 1810.

The Charter [and Laws] . . . of Rhode Island. Newport, 1930.

Cooper, Thomas (ed.) Statutes of South Carolina.

South Carolina Statutes at Large.

Hening, William (ed.). Virginia Statutes at Large. New York, 1823.

AMERICAN CONGRESSIONAL MATERIAL

Gales, Joseph (ed.). *The Debates and Proceedings of the Congress of the United States* [Annals]. Washington, D.C.: Gales and Seaton, 1834.

Journals of the American Congress 1774-1788. Washington, D.C., 1823.

Congressional Debates.

Congressional Globe.

House of Representatives Report, No. 730. 48th Congress, 1st Session (1884).

U.S. Code Congressional and Administrative News.

The War of Rebellion: A Compilation of the Official Records of the Union and Confederate Armies. Washington, D.C., 1880-1901.

MISCELLANEOUS—COLONIAL AMERICA

Archives of Maryland. Vols. 34 and 35.

Calendar of State Papers (Colonial).

Journal of the Legislative Council of New York 1691-1743. Albany, 1861.

Massachusetts Historical Society Collections. Series 4, vol. 8 and Series 5, vol. 6.

"The Frame of Government of the Province of Pennsylvania together with certain laws of England." *Minutes of the Provincial Council of Pennsylvania.* Philadelphia, 1851.

MISCELLANEOUS—UNITED STATES OF AMERICA

American State Papers.
Attorney General's Survey of Release Procedures. Washington, D.C.: G.P.O., 1939.
Opinions of the Attorney General.

PAMPHLETS

Alston, Joseph [Agrestis]. *A Short Review of the Late Rebellion at New Orleans.* South Carolina, 1815.
Binney, Horace. *The Privilege of the Writ of Habeas Corpus Under the Constitution.* Vols. 1 and 2, Philadelphia, 1862; vol. 3, 1865.
Breck, Robert L. *The Habeas Corpus and Martial Law.* Cincinnati, 1862.
Brown, David Boyer. *Reply to Horace Binney on the Privilege of the Writ of Habeas Corpus Under the Constitution.* Philadelphia, 1862.
Bullitt, J.C. *A Review of Mr. Binney's Pamphlet on the Privilege of Habeas Corpus Under the Constitution.* Philadelphia, 1862.
Dulany, Daniel Sr. [Cato]. *The Rights of the Inhabitants of Maryland to the Benefits of English Laws.* Annapolis, 1728.
Ingersoll, Charles. *An Undelivered Speech on Executive Arrests.* Philadelphia, 1862.
Jackson, Tatlow. *Authorities Cited Antagonistic to Mr. Horace Binney's Conclusion on the Writ of Habeas Corpus.* Philadelphia, 1862.
———. *Martial Law: What is it? and Who Can Declare It?* Philadelphia, 1862.
Johnson, James F. *The Suspending Power and the Writ of Habeas Corpus.* Philadelphia, 1862.
Kennedy, William. *The Privilege of the Writ of Habeas Corpus Under the Constitution of the United States.* Philadelphia, 1862.
Kent, James. *Introductory Lecture* (1794), printed in 3 Columbia Law Review 330 (1903).
Montgomery, John J. *The Writ of Habeas Corpus and Mr. Binney.* Philadelphia, 2nd edition, 1862.
Myers, Isaac. *Presidential Power Over Personal Liberty,* 1862.
Nicholas, Samuel Smith. *Martial Law.* Philadelphia, 1842.
———. *The Law of War and Confiscation.* Louisville, 1862.
———. *Habeas Corpus—A Response to Mr. Binney.* Louisville, 1862.
Parker, Joel. *Habeas Corpus and Martial Law: A Review of the Opinion of Chief Justice Taney in the Case of John Merryman.* Cambridge, Massachusetts: Welch, Bigelow and Co., 1861.
Parsons, Theophus. Article of 5 June 1861 (*Boston Daily Advertiser*) in Edward McPherson, *The Political History of the United States of*

America During the Great Rebellion. Washington, D.C.: Phillip and Solomons, 1864.

Penn, William. *The Excellent Privileges of Liberty and Property Being the Birthright of Free-Born Subjects of England.* Philadelphia, 1687.

Russell, Lord John. *An Essay on the History of English Government and Constitution.* London, 1823.

Sharp, Glanville. *An Address to the People of England Being a Protest of a Private Person Against Every Suspension of Law that is Liable to injure or endanger Personal Security.* London, 1778.

Sheridan, R. S. *Liberty and Peace.* Speech in House of Commons, 5 January 1795.

Unknown. *Thoughts on the Suspension of the Writ of Habeas Corpus.* London, 1794.

Unknown. *A Modest and Impartial Narrative of Several Grievances and Great Oppressions.* New York, 1610. 3 Doc. Rel. N.Y., 676.

Unknown. "A Narrative of a New and Unusual American Imprisonment." New York, 1707 in Peter Force (ed.), *Four Tracts and Other Papers Relating Principally to the Origin, Settlement, and Progress of the Colonies of North America.* New York: Peter Smith, 1947.

Vaux, Richard. *The Habeas Corpus: Its Death and How it Came by It.* Philadelphia, 1862.

Wharton, George M. *Remarks on Mr. Binney's Treatise on the Writ of Habeas Corpus.* Philadelphia, 1862.

————. *Answer to Mr. Binney's Reply to "Remarks" on His Treatise on the Habeas Corpus.* Philadelphia, 1862.

BOOKS

PRIMARY SOURCES

Attenborough, F. L., ed. *The Laws of the Earliest Kings.* New York: Russell and Russell, 1963.

Bacon, Matthew. *A New Abrigement of the Law.* London, 1832.

Baildon, William Paley, ed. *Select Cases in Chancery.* Seldon Society, 1896.

Ballard, Adolphus and James Tait (eds.). *British Borough Charters 1218-1307.* Cambridge: Cambridge University Press, 1923.

Barnes, Thomas, ed. *Somerset Assize Orders* (1629-1640). Frome: Butler and Tanner Ltd. 1959.

Basler, Roy P., ed. *The Collect Works of Abraham Lincoln.* New Brunswick, N.J.: Rutgers University Press, 1955.

Bateson, Mary (ed.). *Records of the Borough of Leicester.* London: C. J. Clay and Sons, 1899.

Beale, Howard K., ed. *Diary of Gideon Wells.* Boston: Houghton Mifflin Co., 1911.

deBeccaria, Marquis. *Essays on Crime and Punishment.* Dublin, 1767.

Benton, Thomas H. *Thirty Years View*. New York: D. Appleton and Co., 1856.

Blackstone, William. *Commentaries on the Laws of England*. 4 vols. Oxford, 1765-1769.

Bishop, T. A. M. and P. Chaplais, eds. *Facsimiles of English Royal Writs to A.D. 1100*. Oxford: Clarendon Press, 1957.

Bouton, Nathaniel, ed. *Documents and Records Relating to the Province of New Hampshire*. Vol. 1, Concord, 1867.

Boyd, Julian P., ed. *The Papers of Thomas Jefferson*. Princeton, N.J.: Princeton University Press, 1955.

Brodhead, John Romeyn, ed. *Documents Relative to the Colonial History of the State of New York*. Albany, N.Y.: Weld, Parsons and Co., 1853.

Brown, Elizabeth Gasper. *British Statutes in American Law 1778-1836*. Ann Arbor, Mich.: University of Michigan School of Law, 1964.

Care, Henry. *English Liberties, or the Free-Born Subjects' Inheritance*. Edited and additions by William Nelson. 4th edition, 1721.

Chalmers, George, ed. *Opinions of Eminent Lawyers . . . (Great Britain)*. Vol. 1. London: Reed and Hunter, 1814.

Chalmers, George. *Political Annals of the Present United Colonies*. New York: New York Historical Society Collections, 1868.

Chitty, Joseph. *A Practical Treatise on Criminal Law*. Vol 1. London: Samuel Brooke, 1826.

Church, William S. *A Treatise on Habeas Corpus*. San Francisco: Bancroft-Whitney Co., 2nd edition, 1893.

Clay, Charles Travis, ed. *Three Yorkshire Assize Rolls*. Yorkshire Archeological Society, 1911.

Cobbett, William. *Parliamentary Debates of England from Earliest Times to the Year 1803*. London.

Cockburn, J. S., ed. *Somerset Assize Orders (1640-1659)*. Frome: Butler and Tanner Ltd., 1971.

―――. *Calendar of Assize Records: Sussex Indictments (Elizabeth I)*. London, 1975.

―――. *Calendar of Assize Records: Sussex Indictments (James I)*. London, 1975.

―――. *Calendar of Assize Records: Hertfordshire Indictments (Elizabeth I)*. London, 1975.

―――. *Calendar of Assize Records: Hertfordshire Indictments (James I)*. London, 1975.

Coke, Edward. *Institutes of the Laws of England*. London, 1628-1645.

―――. *Second Part of the Institutes of the Laws of England*. London, 1661 and 1671.

―――. *A Little Treatise on Bail and Mainprise*. London, 1635.

Curtis, George Ticknor. *Constitution History of the United States*. New York: Harper and Brothers, 1896.

Davis, Richard Beale, ed. *William Fitzhugh and His Chesapeake World 1679-*

1701: The Fitzhugh Letters and Other Documents. Chapel Hill: University of North Carolina Press for the Virginia Historical Society, 1963.

Douglas, David and George W. Greenaway (eds.). *English Historical Documents.* London: Eyre and Spotteswoods, 1953.

Downer, L. J., ed. *Leges Henrici Primi.* Oxford: Clarendon Press, 1971.

Dunham, William Huse (ed.). *Casus Placitorum and Reports of Cases in the King's Bench.* Seldon Society, 1952.

Easterley, J. H., ed. *The Journal of the Commons' House of Assembly.* Colonial Records of South Carolina, 1945.

Elliot, Jonathan, ed. *Debates of the State Conventions on the Adoption of the Federal Constitution.* Philadelphia, 1861.

Farrand, Max, ed. *The Records of the Federal Convention of 1787.* New Haven: Yale University Press, 1966.

———. *Laws and Liberties of Massachusetts.* Cambridge, Mass.: Harvard University Press, 1929.

Farrer, W. *The Lancashire Pipe Rolls.* Liverpool: Henry Young and Sons, 1902.

Firth, C. H. and R. S. Rait eds. *Acts and Ordinances of the Interregnum 1642-1660.* London, 1911.

Fisher, Sidney George. *The Trial of the Constitution.* Philadelphia: J. B. Lippincott and Co., 1862.

Ford, P. L. (ed.). *Writings of Thomas Jefferson.* New York: Putnam, 1904.

Forsyth, William (ed.). *Cases and Opinions on Constitutional Law, and Various Points of English Jurisprudence.* London: Stevens and Haynes, 1869.

Fowler, Herbert G. *Rolls from the Office of the Sheriff of Bedfordshire and Buckinghamshire 1332-1334.* Archeological Society, 1929.

Fry, Alfred A. *The Writ of Habeas Corpus.* London: Maxwell, 1839.

Gardiner, Samuel R., ed. *The Constitutional Documents of the Puritan Revolution.* Oxford: Clarendon Press, 1906.

Giuseppi, M. S., ed. *Calendar of Manuscripts of the Most Honorable Marquess of Salisbury, Part 19.* Historical Manuscripts Commission, 1965.

Goebel, Julius Jr. and T. Raymond Naughton. *Law Enforcement in Colonial New York.* New York: Commonmwealth Fund, 1944.

Grey, Anchitell, ed. *Debates of the House of Commons.* London, 1765.

Gross, Charles, ed. *Select Cases from the Coroners Rolls 1265-1413.* Seldon Society, 1895.

Hale, Matthew. *A History of the Common Law.* Edited by Charles Runnington. London, 1794.

———. *A History of the Pleas of the Crown.* Philadelphia: R. H. Small, 1847.

———. "Discourse concerning the Courts of King's Bench and Common Pleas." *A Collection of Tracts Relative to the Laws of England.* Edited by Francis Hargrave. Dublin, 1787.

Hall, G. D. G., ed. *Glanvil, A Treatise on the Laws and Customs of England.* Nelson, 1965.

Hamlin, Paul M. and Charles E. Baker. *Supreme Court of Judicature of the Province of New York 1691-1704.* Vol. I. New York: New York Historical Society, 1959.

Harmer, F. E. *Anglo-Saxon Writs,* Manchester: Manchester University Press, 1952.

Hughes, Paul L. and James F. Larkin, eds. *Tudor Royal Proclamations.* New Haven: Yale University Press, 1969.

————. *Stuart Royal Proclamations.* New Haven: Yale University Press, 1971.

Hull, Felix, ed. *A Calendar of the Black and White Book of the Cinque Ports.* Kent Archeological Society, 1965.

Hunnissett, R. F., ed. *Calendar of Nottinghamshire Coroners' Inquest 1485-1558.* Thorton Society, 1969.

Hurd, Rollin C. *A Treatise on the Right of Personal Liberty and on the Writ of Habeas Corpus.* Albany, N.Y.: W. C. Little and Co., 1858 and 1876.

Ingersoll, Edward. *The History and the Law of the Writ of Habeas Corpus.* Philadelphia, 1849.

Jenkinson, Hilary and Beryl R. Formay, eds. *Select Cases in the Exchequer of Pleas.* Seldon Society, 1932.

Jones, Philip E., ed. *Calendar of Plea and Memoranda Rolls of London 1437-1457.* Cambridge: Cambridge University Press, 1954.

Jones, Philip E., ed. *Calendar of Plea and Memoranda Rolls of London 1458-1482.* Cambridge: Cambridge University Press, 1961.

Kelnam, Robert. *Laws of William the Conqueror.* London: Edward Brooke, 1779.

Kent, James. *Commentaries of American Law.* New York, 1836. 12th edition, edited by O. W. Holmes. Boston: Little Brown and Co., 1873.

Kimball, Elizabeth G., ed. *The Shropshire Peace Rolls 1400-1414.* 1959.

————. *Records of Some Sessions of the Peace in Lincolnshire 1381-1396.*

————. *Records of Some Sessions of the Peace in the City of Lincoln 1351-1354 and the Borough of Stamford 1351.*

Labaree, Leonard Woods, ed. *Royal Instructions to British Governors 1670-1776.* New York: D. Appleton-Century Co., 1935.

Leadam, I. S. and J. F. Baldwin, eds. *Select Cases Before the King's Council 1243-1482.* Seldon Society, 1918.

Leiber, Francis. *On Civil Liberty and Self-Government.* 1874.

Madison, Jay, and Hamilton. *Federalist.*

Maitland, F. W., ed. *Select Pleas of the Crown.* Seldon Society, 1888.

————. *Bracton's Notebook.* London: C. J. Clay and Son, 1887.

Marsden, Reginald G., ed. *Select Cases in the Court of Admiralty.* London, 1897.

Maseres, Francis. *The Canadian Freeholder: In Three Dialogues Between An Englishman and a Frenchman....* Vol. 2, London, 1779.

McIlwaine, H. R., ed. *Executive Journals of the Council of Colonial Virginia.* Richmond, Va., 1925.

Montesquieu, Charles de Secondat. *The Spirit of the Laws.* Dublin, 1751.

Moody, Robert E., ed. *Province and Court Records of Maine.* Portland: Maine Historical Society, 1947.

Morris, Richard B., ed. *Select Cases of the Mayor's Court of New York City 1674-1787.* Washington, D.C.: American Historical Association, 1935.

Notestein, Wallace, Frances Helen Relf and Hartley Simpson (eds.). *Commons Debates 1621.* New Haven: Yale University Press, 1935.

Osborne, Bertram. *Justice of the Peace 1361-1848.* Shaftesbury: Sedgehill Press, 1960.

Page, Sir William, ed. *Three Assize Rolls for the County of Northumberland.* Surtees Society, 1891.

Parker, John, ed. *Plea Rolls of the County Palatine of Lancaster.* Chetham Society, 1928.

Parker, Mattie Erma Edwards, ed. *North Carolina Higher-Court Records 1620-1696.* Raleigh, North Carolina: State Department of Archives and History, 1968.

Petersdoroff, Charles. *A Practical Treatise on the Law of Bail.* London: Butterworth and Son, 1824.

Pownall, Thomas. *The Administration of the Colonies.* London, 4th edition, 1768.

Putnam, Bertha Haven, ed. *Proceedings Before the Justices of the Peace in the Fourteenth and Fifteenth Centuries.* Ames Foundation, 1938.

————. *Yorkshire Sessions of the Peace 1361-1364.* Yorkshire Archeological Society, 1939.

Raymond, Lord. *Every Man His Own Lawyer: or, A Summary of the Laws of England.* New York, 1768; Philadelphia, 1769.

Reeves, John. *The History of English Law.* London, 1787 ed. and London: Reeves and Turner, 1869.

Reid, R. R. *The King's Council in the North.* London: Longmans, Greene and Co., 1921.

Richardson, James P., ed. *A Compilation of the Message and Papers of the Presidents (1789-1897).* Washington, D.C.: G.P.O., 1896.

Rigg, J. M., ed. *Select Pleas, Starrs and Other Records from the Rolls of the Exchequer of Jews.* Seldon Society, 1901.

Robertson, A. J., ed. *The Laws of the Kings of England From Edmund I to Henry I.* Cambridge: Cambridge University Press, 1925.

Rushworth, John. *Historical Collections.* London, 1703.

————. *Historical Collections (1640-1644).* London, 1691.

Rutherford, Livingston. *John Peter Zenger, His Press, His Trial.* New York: Dodd, Mead and Co., 1906.

Sanders, George William, ed. *Orders in the High Court of Chancery*. London: A. Maxwell and Son, 1845.

Sanders, William L. and Walter Clark, eds. *Colonial Records of North Carolina*. Raleigh, N.C., 1886-1914.

Sayles, G. O., ed. *Select Cases in the Court of King's Bench*. Vol. 1, 1936; vol. 2, 1938; vol. 3, 1939; vol. 4, 1957; vol. 5, 1958; vol. 6, 1965; vol. 7, 1971. Seldon Society.

Seldon, John, ed. *Fleta*, 1647.

Sillen, Rosamond, ed. *Records of Some Sessions of the Peace in Lincolnshire 1360-1375*. Lincoln Record Society, 1936.

Smith, Joseph H. *Appeals to the Privy Council from the American Plantations*. New York: Columbia University Press, 1950.

Smith, Samuel. *The History of the Colony of Nova-Caesaria or New Jersey*. New Jersey: J. Parker, 1765.

Smith, William Jr. *The History of the Province of New York*. Edited by Michael Kammen, Vol. 1. Cambridge, Massachusetts: Belknap Press, 1972.

Solly-Flood, F. *Abridged History of the Writ of Habeas Corpus Cum Causa as a Remedy Against Unlawful Imprisonment*. MSS Royal Historical Society, 1887.

Stenton, Doris M., ed. *The Earliest Lincolnshire Assize Rolls A.D. 1202-1209*. Lincoln Record Society, 1926.

Stenton, Doris M. *English Justice Before the Norman Conquest and the Great Charter*. London: American Philosophical Society, 1963.

Stephen, Sir James Fitzjames. *A History of Criminal Law of England*. London: Macmillan and Co., 1883.

Story, Joseph. *Commentaries on the Constitution of the United States*. Boston: Little and Brown, 1851.

Stubbs, William, ed. *Select Charters . . . of English Constitutional History*. Oxford: Clarendon Press, 1913.

Taylor, Mary Margaret, ed. *Some Sessions of the Peace in Cambridgeshire in the Fourteenth Century*. Cambridge: Cambridge Antiquarian Society, 1942.

Thomas, A. H., ed. *Calendar of Early Mayors' Rolls . . . of the City of London 1298-1307*. Cambridge: Cambridge University Press, 1924.

———. *Calendar of Plea and Memoranda Rolls . . . of the City of London (1381-1412)*. Cambridge: Cambridge Universty Press, 1932.

———. *Calendar of Plea and Memoranda Rolls . . . of the City of London (1412-1437)*. Cambridge: Cambridge University Press, 1943.

Thomas, Walter Sinclair, ed. *A Lincolnshire Assize Roll for 1928*. Lincolnshire Record Society, 1944.

Thompson, A. Hamilton, ed. *Northumbrian Pleas From De Banco Rolls 1-19 (1-5 Edward I)*. Surtees Society, 1950.

Thorne, Samuel E., ed. *Bracton, De Legibus et Consuetudinibus Angliae.* Cambridge, Massachusetts: Belknap Press, 1968-1977.

Thorpe, B. *Ancient Laws and Institutions of England.* Vol. 1. London: The Commission on Public Records of the Kingdom, 1840.

Thorpe, Francis, ed. *American Charters, Constitutions, and Organic Laws of the States, Territories, and Colonies.* Washington, D.C.: G.P.O., 1909.

de Tocqueville, Alexis. *Démocratie en Amérique.* Paris: Libraire de Charles Gosselin, 1835.

Turner, G. J., ed. *Select Pleas of the Forest.* Seldon Society, 1901.

Twiss, Sir Travers, ed. *Bracton, De Legibus et Consuetudinibus Angliae.* London: Longmans and Co., 1878-1883.

Unknown. *An Essay Upon the Continent of America.* Edited by L. B. Wright. San Marino, Calif.: Huntington Library, 1945.

Vaux, Richard. *Reports of Some of the Criminal Cases on Primary Hearing . . . together with some Remarks on the Writ of Habeas Corpus and forms of Proceedings in Criminal Cases.* Philadelphia: T. and J. W. Johnson, 1846.

Washburn, Emory. *Sketches of the Judicial History of Massachusetts.* Boston: Little and Brown, 1840.

Weinman, Martin, ed. *The London Eyre of 1276.* London Record Society, 1976.

Whitelock, Sir Bulstrode. *Memorials of English Affairs.* London: 1682.

Wilson, James. *Works.* Edited by R. G. McCloskey. Cambridge, Mass.: Harvard University Press, 1967.

Yale, D. E. C., ed. *Lord Nottingham's Chancery Cases.* Seldon Society, 1957.

SECONDARY SOURCES

Adams, George Burton. *The Origin of the English Constitution.* New Haven: Yale University Press, 1912.

American Bar Association. *Report of the Seventh Annual Meeting* (1884).

Advisory Committee on Pre-Trial Proceedings. *Pre-trial Release.* New York: American Bar Association, 1968.

Anthony J. Garner. *Hawaii Under Army Rule.* Stanford, Calif.: Stanford University Press, 1955.

Bailyn, Bernard. *The Origins of American Politics.* New York: Vantage Books, 1965.

Bassett, Joseph Spencer. *The Life of Andrew Jackson.* Archon Books, reprint of 1937 edition, 1967.

Berger, Raoul. *Executive Privilege: A Constitutional Myth.* Cambridge, Massachusetts: Harvard University Press, 1974.

Beveridge, John. *The Life of John Marshall.* Boston: Houghton Mifflin Co., 1919.

Billias, George Althan. *Law and Authority in Colonial America.* Barre, Mass.: Barre Publications, 1965.

Brant, Irving. *James Madison, Secretary of State 1800-1809*. Indianapolis: The Bobbs-Merrill Co., 1953.

Buchanan, A. Russell. *David S. Terry, Dueling Judge*. San Marino, Calif.: Huntington Library, 1956.

Brunet, Ludovic. *De L'Habeas Corpus Ad Subjiciendum*. Montreal: Libraire General De Drait et De Jurisprudence, 1901.

Cam, Helen. *The Hundred and Hundred Rolls: An Outline of Local Government in Medieval England*. London: Methuen and Co., 1930.

Campbell, Lord John. *The Lives of the Chief Justices of England*. Long Island, N.Y., 1894.

Chafee, Zechariah Jr. *How Human Rights Got Into the Constitution*. Boston: University Press, 1952.

Channing, Edward. *A History of the United States*. Vol. 2. New York: Macmillan Co., 1905.

Corwin, Edward S. *The Doctrine of Judicial Review: Its Legal and Historical Basis*. Gloucester, Mass.: Peter Smith, 1963.

Crosskey, William Winslow. *Politics and the Constitution in the History of the United States*. Chicago: University of Chicago Press, 1953.

Crowther, P. W. *The History of the Law of Arrest in Personal Actions*. London: J. and W. T. Clarke, 1828.

De Haas, Elsa. *Antiquities of Bail: Origin and Historical Development in Criminal Cases to the Year 1275*. New York: Columbia University Press, 1940.

Dicey, A. V. *Introduction to the Study of the Laws of the Constitution*. London: Macmillan and Co., 1959.

Duhamel, Jean and J. Dill Smith. *Some Pillars of English Law*. London: Pitman and Sons, 1959.

Fairman, Charles. *The Law of Martial Rule*. Chicago: Callaghan and Co., 1930.

———. *History of the Supreme Court: Reconstruction and Reunion*. New York: Macmillan and Co., 1971.

Fehrenbacher, Don E. *The Dred Scott Case: Its Significance in American Law and Politics*. New York: Oxford University Press, 1978.

Ferris, Forrest G. and Forrest G. Ferris Jr. *The Law of Extraordinary Remedies*. St. Louis, Mo.: Thomas Law Book Co., 1926.

Firth, Charles H. *The House of Lords During the Civil War*. New York: Longmans, Greene and Co., 1910.

Foster, John. *The Debates on the Grand Remonstrance*. London: John Murray, 1860.

Freehling, William W. *Prelude to Civil War: The Nullification Controversy in South Carolina 1816-1836*. New York: Harper and Row, 1966.

Fry, William Henry. *New Hampshire as a Province*. Ph.d. thesis, Columbia University, 1908.

Goldfarb, Ronald. *Ransom: A Critique of the American Bail System.* New York: Harper and Row, 1965.

Gunther, Gerald. *Constitutional Law.* Mineola, N.Y.: Foundation Press, 9th edition, 1975.

Haines, Charles Grove and Foster H. Sherwood. *The Role of the Supreme Court in American Government and Politics 1835-1864.* Berkeley and Los Angeles: University of California Press, 1957.

Hallam, Henry. *The Constitutional History of England.* London: Alex Murray and Sons, 1870.

Haskins, George L. *Law and Authority in Early Massachusetts.* New York: Macmillan Co., 1960.

Henkin, Louis. *Foreign Affairs and the Constitution.* Mineola, New York: Foundation Press, 1972.

Hill, Christopher. *A Century of Revolution 1604-1714.* London: Sphere, 1969.

Hockett, Homer Carey. *Constitutional History of the United States 1826-1876.* New York: Macmillan Co., 1939.

Holdsworth, William S. *A History of English Law.* London: Methuen and Co., 1922.

Holt, J. C. *Magna Carta.* Cambridge: Cambridge University Press, 1965.

Horwitz, Morton J. *The Transformation of American Law, 1780-1860.* Cambridge, Mass.: Harvard University Press, 1977.

Howard, A. E. *The Road From Runnymede: Magna Carta and Constitutionalism in America.* Charlottesville: University of Virginia Press, 1968.

Jenks, Edward. *Laws and Politics in the Middle Ages.* London: John Murray, 1898.

Jensen, Merrill. *The New Nation: A History of the United States During the Confederation.* New York: Vintage Books, 1950.

Jones, W. J. *The Elizabethan Courts of Chancery.* Oxford: Clarendon Press, 1967.

Kutler, Stanley I. *Judicial Power and Reconstruction Politics.* Chicago: University of Chicago Press, 1968.

Levy, Leonard W. *Origins of the Fifth Amendment.* New York: Oxford University Press, 1968.

Maitland, F. W. *The Constitutional History of England.* Cambridge: Cambridge University Press, 1909.

Mathews, John Mabry. *The American Constitutional System.* New York: McGraw-Hill Book Co., 2nd edition, 1940.

May, Thomas Erskine. *A Treatise upon the Law, Privilege, Proceedings and Usages of Parliament.* Shannon, Ireland: Irish University Press, 1971.

McCrady, Edward. *The History of South Carolina Under the Proprietary Government.* New York: Macmillan Co., 1897.

————. *The History of South Carolina Under the Royal Government.* New York: Macmillan Co., 1899.

Meader, Daniel John. *Preludes to Gideon.* Charlottesville, Virginia: Michie Co., 1967.

More, Cresacre. *The Life of Sir Thomas More*. London: William Pickering, 1828.

Morison, Samuel Eliot and Henry Steele Commager. *The Growth of the American Republic*. New York: Oxford University Press, 1954.

Morris, William Alfred. *The Frankpledge System*. London: Longmans, Greene and Co., 1910.

Owsley, Frank Lawrence. *States Rights in the Confederacy*. Chicago: University of Chicago Press, 1925.

Phillips, Harlan B. (ed.). *Felix Frankfurter Reminisces*. London: Secker and Warburg, 1960.

Pollock, F. and F. W. Maitland. *The History of English Law Before the Time of Edward I*. Cambridge: Cambridge University Press, 1968.

Potter, Harold and O. Hood Phillips. *A Short Outline of English History*. London: Sweet and Maxwell, 1933.

Pound, Roscoe. *The Development of the Constitutional Guarantees of Liberty*. New Haven, Ct.: Yale University Press, 1957.

———. *Criminal Justice in America*. New York: Da Capo Press, 1972.

Randall, James G. *Constitutional Problems Under Lincoln*. New York: D. Appleton and Co., 1926.

Relf, Frances Helen. *The Petition of Right*. Ann Arbor, Mich.: University of Michigan Press, 1917.

Robinson, William M. Jr. *Justice in Grey*. Cambridge, Mass.: Harvard University Press, 1941.

Schachner, Nathan. *Aaron Burr*. New York: Frederick A. Stokes Co., 1937.

Scott, Arthur P. *Criminal Law in Colonial Virginia*. Chicago: Chicago University Press, 1930.

Sharpe, R. J. *The Law of Habeas Corpus*. Oxford: Clarendon Press, 1976.

Simpson, Lawrence P. *Law of Suretyship*. St. Paul, Minn.: West Publishing Co., 1950.

Smith, Goldwin. *A Constitutional and Legal History of England*. New York: Charles Scribner's Sons, 1955.

Smith, Joseph H. *Colonial Justice in Western Massachusetts 1639-1702*. Cambridge, Mass.: Harvard University Press, 1961.

Smith, W. Roy. *South Carolina as a Province*. New York: Macmillan Co., 1903.

Spelling, Thomas Carl. *A Treatise on Extraordinary Relief in Equity and At Law*. Boston: Little, Brown and Co., 1893.

———. *A Treatise on Injunctions and Other Extraordinary Remedies*. Boston: Little, Brown and Co., 1901.

Sutherland, Arthur E. *Constitutionalism in America: Origin and Evolution of Its Fundamental Ideas*. New York: Blarsdell Publishing Co., 1965.

Swisher, Carl Brent. *Roger B. Taney*. New York: Macmillan Co., 1935.

———. *The Taney Period 1836-1864*. New York: Macmillan Co., 1974.

Tanner, J. R. *English Constitutional Conflicts of the Seventeenth Century*. Cambridge: Cambridge University Press, 1948.

Taswell-Longmead, Thomas P. *English Constitutional History*. London: Stevens and Haynes, 1875.

Thompson, Faith. *Magna Carta: Its Role in the Making of the English Constitution 1300-1629*. New York: Octagon Books, 1972.

Usher, Roland G. *The Rise and Fall of the High Commission*. Oxford: Clarendon Press, 1913.

van deer Veen, Abraham Niehout. *Des Engelsche Habeas Corpus Act*. Leiden: L. Van Nifterif, 1878.

Vinogradoff, Paul. *Outlines of Historical Jurisprudence*. Oxford: Oxford University Press, 1920.

Warren, Charles. *History of the American Bar*. Cambridge: Cambridge University Press, 1912.

———. *The Supreme Court in United States History*. Boston: Little, Brown and Co., 1935.

Zoline, Elizabeth. *Federal Appellate Jurisdiction and Procedure*. New York: Clark Boardman Ltd., 1928.

ARTICLES

Abbot, Wilbur C. "The Long Parliament of Charles II." 21 English Historical Review 21, 254 (1906).

Amsterdam, Anthony G. "Criminal Prosecutions Affecting Federally Guaranteed Civil Rights: Federal Removal and Habeas Corpus Jurisdiction to Abort State Court Trial." 113 University of Pennsylvania Law Review 793 (1965).

Andrews, Charles McLean. "The Influence of Colonial Conditions as Illustrated in the Connecticut Intestacy Law." *Select Essays in Anglo-American Legal History*. Vol. 1. Boston: Little, Brown and Co., 1907.

Bateson, Mary. "A London Municipal Collection of the Reign of John." 17 English Historical Review 480, 707 (1902).

Bator, Paul M. "Finality in Criminal Law and Federal Habeas Corpus for State Prisoners." 76 Harvard Law Review 441 (1962).

les Benedict, Michael. "Contagion and the Constitution: Quarantine Agitation From 1859 to 1866." 25 Journal of History of Medicine and Allied Sciences 177 (1970).

———. "Preserving Federalism: Reconstruction and the Waite Court." 1978 Supreme Court Review 39 (1979).

Bestor, Arthur. "State Sovereignty and Slavery: A Reinterpretation of Proslavery Constitutional Doctrine, 1846-1861." 54 Journal of the Illinois Historical Society 117 (1961).

Boyte, Sam. "Federal Habeas Corpus After *Stone v. Powell*: A Remedy Only for the Arguably Innocent?" 11 University of Richmond Law Review 291 (1977).

Brennan, William J. "Federal Habeas Corpus and State Prisoners." 7 Utah Law Review 423 (1961).

———. "Some Aspects of Federalism." 39 N.Y.U. Law Review 945 (1964).

Cantor, Milton. "The Writ of Habeas Corpus: Early American Origins and Development." *Freedom and Reform: Essays in Honor of Henry Steele Commager.* Edited by Harold M. Hyman and Leonard W. Levy. New York: Harper and Row, 1967, p. 55.

Carpenter, A. H. "Habeas Corpus in the American Colonies." 8 American Historical Review 18 (1902).

Chitwood, Oliver P. "Justices in Colonial Virginia." 23 Johns Hopkins Studies in Historical and Political Science Nos. 7-8 (1905).

Cohen, Maxwell. "Some Considerations on the Origins of Habeas Corpus." 16 Canadian Bar Review 92 (1938).

————. "Habeas Corpus Cum Causa—The Emergence of the Modern Writ." 18 Canadian Bar Review 10 (1940).

Collings, Rex A. "Habeas Corpus for Convicts—Constitutional Right or Legislative Grace?" 40 California Law Review 335 (1952).

Cover, Robert M. and T. Alexander Aleinikoff. "Dialectical Federalism: Habeas Corpus and the Court." 86 Yale Law Journal 1035 (1977).

Dutton, Henry. "Writ of Habeas Corpus." 9 American Law Register 705 (1862).

De Smith, S. A. "The Prerogative Writs." 11 Cambridge Law Journal 40 (1951).

Douglas, Clarence D. "Conscription and the Writ of Habeas Corpus in North Carolina During the Civil War." Durham, N.C.: Trinity College Historical Papers, 1922.

Duker, William F. "The Fuller Court and State Criminal Process: Threshold of Modern Limitations on Government," 1980 Brigham Young Univ. Law Rev.—(1980).

————. "Mr. Justice Rufus W. Peckham and The Case of Ex parte Young: Lochnerizing Munn v. Illinois," 1980 Brigham Young Univ. Law Review—(1980).

————. "Mr. Justice Rufus W. Peckham: The Police Power and the Individual in a Changing World," 1980 Brigham Young Univ. Law Review—(1980).

————. "The President's Power to Pardon: A Constitutional History." 18 William and Mary Law Review 475 (1977).

————. "The Right to Bail: A Historical Inquiry." 42 Albany Law Review 33 (1977).

Fisher, Sydney G. Jr. "The Suspension of Habeas Corpus During the War of Rebellion." 3 Political Science Quarterly 454 (1888).

Fiss, Owen M. "Foreword: The Forms of Justice." 93 Harvard Law Review 1 (1979).

Fox, Sir John. "Process of Imprisonment at Common Law." 39 Law Quarterly Review 46 (1923).

Friendly, Henry J. "Is Innocence Irrelevant? Collateral Attack on Criminal Judgments." 38 University of Chicago Law Review 142 (1970).

Glass, Albert S. "Historical Aspects of Habeas Corpus." 9 St. John's Law Review 55 (1934).

Gray, Thomas C. "Do We Have an Unwritten Constitution?" 27 Stanford Law Review 703 (1975).

Halbert, Sherrill. "Suspension of the Writ of Habeas Corpus by President Lincoln." 2 American Journal of Legal History 95 (1958).

Hall, Hubert. "An Unknown Charter of Liberties." 9 English Historical Review 326 (1894).

Hart, Henry M. Jr. "The Supreme Court 1958 Term, Forward: The Time Chart of the Justices." 73 Harvard Law Review 84 (1959).

Hazeltine, H. D. "The Influence of the Magna Carta on the American Constitution." *Magna Carta Commemorative Essays.* Edited by Henry Elliot. Aberdeen University Press for the Royal Historical Society, 1917.

Hill, Alfred. "The Forfeiture of Constitutional Rights in Criminal Cases." 78 Columbia Law Review 1050 (1978).

Hitch, Thomas M. "Federal Habeas Corpus: The Concept of Custody and Access to Federal Courts." 53 Journal of Urban Law 61 (1975).

Holtzoff, Alexander. "Collateral Review of Convictions in Federal Courts." 25 Boston University Law Review 26 (1945).

Howard, George E. "Development of the King's Peace." Nebraska University Studies, vol. 1, no. 3 (1890).

Hurnard, Naomi. "The Jury of Presentation and the Assize of Clarendon." 1941 English Historical Review 58.

James, Eldon Revare. "Legal Treatises Printed in the British Colonies and American States Before 1801." *Harvard Legal Essays* (presented to J. H. Beale and Samuel Williston). Cambridge, Massachusetts: Harvard University Press, 1934.

Jenks, Edward. "The Story of Habeas Corpus." *Select Essays in Anglo-American Legal History*, vol. 1. Boston: Little, Brown and Co. 1902.

————. "The Prerogative Writs." 32 Yale Law Journal 523 (1923).

Langbein, Irvin L. "The Jury of Presentment and the Coroner." 33 Columbia Law Review 1329 (1933).

Maitland, F. W. "The History of the Register of Original Writs." 3 Harvard Law Review 97, 167, 212 (1888-1889).

Masters, Edgar L. "Suspension of the Writ of Habeas Corpus." 7 Northwestern Law Review 15 (1912).

Mayers, Lewis. "The Habeas Corpus Act of 1867: The Supreme Court as Legal Historian." 33 University of Chicago Law Review 31 (1965).

McFeeley, Neil. "Habeas Corpus and Due Process: From Warren to Burger." 28 Baylor Law Review 533 (1976).

McKechnie, William S. "The Magna Carta." *Magna Carta Commemorative Essays.* Edited by Elliot Malden. Aberdeen University Press for the Royal Historian Society, 1917.

Michael, Richard M. "The New Federalism and the Burger Court's Deference to States in Federal Habeas Proceedings." 64 Iowa Law Review 233 (1979).

Neuborne, Burt. "The Myth of Parity." 90 Harvard Law Review 1105 (1977).

Oaks, Dallin H. "Habeas Corpus in the States, 1776-1865." 32 University of Chicago Law Review 243 (1965).

———. "Legal History in the High Court." 64 Michigan Law Review 451 (1966).

———. "The Original Writ of Habeas Corpus in the Supreme Court." 1962 Supreme Court Review 153.

Paludan, Phillip. "John Norton Pomeroy, State Rights Nationalist." 12 American Journal of Legal History 292 (1968).

Parker, John J. "Limiting the Abuse of Habeas Corpus." 8 F.R.D. 171 (1948).

Pascal, Francis. "Habeas Corpus and the Constitution." 1970 Duke Law Journal 605.

Pollack, Louis H. "Proposals to Curtail Federal Habeas Corpus for State Prisoners: Collateral Attack on the Great Writ." 66 Yale Law Journal 50 (1956).

Pollock, Frederick. "English Law Before the Norman Conquest." 14 Law Quarterly Review 291 (1898).

Powicke, P. M. "Per Iudicum Parium Vel Per Legem Terrae." *Magna Carta Commemorative Essays.* Edited by Elliot Malden. Aberdeen University Press for the Royal Historical Society, 1917.

Prothers, Dr. G. W. and Colonel E. M. Lloyd. "Presbyterians and Independents." IV Cambridge Modern History. Cambridge: Cambridge University Press, 1906.

Reinsch, Paul Samuel. "The English Common Law in the American Colonies." *Select Essays in Anglo-American Legal History.* Vol. 1. Boston: Little, Brown and Co., 1907.

Reitz, Curtis R. "Federal Habeas Corpus: Impact of An Abortive State Proceeding." 74 Harvard Law Review 1315 (1961).

Round, J. H. "An Unknown Charter of Liberty." 8 English Historical Review 288 (1893).

Sellery, George Clarke. "Lincoln's Suspension of Habeas Corpus As Viewed by Congress." Bulletin of the University of Wisconsin, History Series. Vol. 1, no. 3 (1907).

Shaefer, Walter V. "Federalism and State Criminal Procedures." 70 Harvard Law Review 1 (1956).

Sharer, John D. "Power, Idealism, and Compromise: The Coordinate Branches and the Writ of Habeas Corpus." 26 Emory Law Journal 149 (1977).

Simmons, Robert G. "The Writ of Habeas Corpus." 41 A.B.A. Journal 413 (1955).

Sioussat, St. George L. "English Statutes in Maryland." 21 Johns Hopkins Studies in Historical and Political Science 465 (1903).

———. "The Theory of the Extension of English Statutes in the Plantations." *Select Essays in Anglo-American Legal History.* Vol. 1. Boston: Little, Brown and Co., 1907.

Smith, Joseph H. "The English Criminal Law in Early America." *The English Legal System: Carryover to the Colonies.* Los Angeles: William Andrews Clark Library, 1975.

Sofaer, Abraham D. "Federal Habeas Corpus for State Prisoners: The Isolation Principle." 39 N.Y.U. Law Review 78 (1964).

Spritzer, Ralph S. "Criminal Waiver, Procedural Default and the Burger Court," 126 University of Pennsylvania Law Review 473 (1978).

Sutherland, Donald. "Mesne Process upon Personal Action in Early Common Law." 82 Law Quarterly Review 482 (1966).

Tague, Peter W. "Federal Habeas Corpus and Ineffective Representation of Counsel: The Supreme Court Has Work To Do." 31 Stanford Law Review 1 (1978).

Tarrant, Catherine M. "To 'ensure domestic Tranquility': Congress and the Law of Seditious Conspiracy, 1859-1861." 15 American Journal of Legal History 167 (1971).

Thompson, Seymour D. "Abuses of the Writ of Habeas Corpus." 18 American Law Review 1 (1884).

Turner, William Bennett. "When Prisoners Sue: A Study of Prisoner Section 1983 Suits in Federal Courts." 92 Harvard Law Review 910 (1979).

Tushnet, Mark V. "Judicial Revision of the Habeas Corpus Statutes: A Note on *Schneckloth v. Bustamonte*." 1975 Wisconsin Law Review 484.

Unknown. "Writ of Habeas Corpus." 3 William and Mary Quarterly 147 (1895).

Van Alstyne, William W. "A Critical Guide to *Ex parte McCardle*." 15 Arizona Law Review 229 (1973).

Vinogradoff, Paul. "Magna Carta, Clause 39." *Magna Carta Commemorative Essays.* Edited by Elliot Malden. Aberdeen University Press for the Royal Historical Society, 1917.

Wade, H. W. R. "Constitutional and Administrative Aspects of the Anisminic Case." 85 Law Quarterly Review 198 (1969).

Walker, Robert S. "The Constitutional and Legal Development of Habeas Corpus." Oklahoma State University Publications, 1960.

———. "The American Reception of the Writ of Habeas Corpus." Political Science Research Reports. Department of Political Science, Oklahoma State University, 1961.

Warren, Charles. "New Light on the History of the Judiciary Act of 1789." 37 Harvard Law Review 49 (1923).

Wiecek, William M. "The Reconstruction of Federal Judicial Power. 1863-1876." 13 American Journal of Legal History 333 (1969).

Wofford, John G. "The Blinding Light: The Uses of History in Constitutional Interpretation." 31 University of Chicago Law Review 502 (1964).

Wurts, John. "Law of Habeas Corpus." *Modern American Law.* Vol. 1. Edited by Eugene Allen Gilmore and William Charles Wermuth. Chicago: Blackstone Inst., 1917.

Wyzanski, Charles E. "History and Law." 36 University of Chicago Law Review 237 (1959).

Zeigler, Donald H. and Michele G. Hermann. "The Invisible Litigant: An Inside View of Pro Se Actions in the Federal Courts." 47 N.Y.U. Law Review 157 (1972).

COMMENTS AND NOTES

COMMENTS

"Availability of Federal Post-Conviction Relief in Light of a Subsequent Change in the Law." 66 Journal of Criminal Law and Criminology 117 (1975).

"Criminal Procedure—Federal Habeas Corpus Relief for State Prisoners." 1977 Annual Survey of American Law 123.

"Effect of Supreme Court Change in Law of Exhaustion of State Remedies Requisite to Federal Habeas Corpus." 113 University of Pennsylvania Law Review 1303 (1965).

"Federal Habeas Corpus." 83 Harvard Law Review 1038 (1970).

"Federal Habeas Corpus and Fourth Amendment Claims." 41 Albany Law Review 172 (1977).

"Habeas Corpus: A New Look at Fourth Amendment Claims." 16 Washburn Law Journal 528 (1977).

"Habeas Corpus: Still As Great As When It Was Writ?" 43 Brooklyn Law Review 773 (1977).

"Protecting Fundamental Rights in State Courts: Fitting a State Peg into a Federal Hole." 12 Harvard Civil Rights-Civil Liberties Law Review 63 (1977).

"The Unpredictable Writ—the Evolution of Habeas Corpus." 4 Pepperdine Law Review 313 (1977).

NOTES

"Constitutional Law—Criminal Procedure—Circuits Split Over Application of *Stone v. Powell's* 'Opportunity for Full and Fair Litigation.'" 30 Vanderbilt Law Review 881 (1977).

"Constitutional Law—Federal Habeas Corpus Relief Is Barred for State Prisoners' Fourth Amendment Claims." 8 Texas Tech. Law Review 446 (1976).

"The Custody Requirement for Habeas Corpus in the Federal Courts." 51 California Law Review 228 (1963).

"Exclusionary Rule Need Not be Applied in Federal Habeas Corpus Review of State Convictions." 28 Mercer Law Review 567 (1977).

"The Fourth Amendment Exclusionary Rule and Federal Habeas Corpus." 37 Louisiana Law Review 289 (1977).

"Habeas Corpus—Power of Courts to Determine that the Danger Requiring Suspension of the Writ has Passed." 92 University of Pennsylvania Law Review 107 (1943).

"Habeas Corpus—Restraint in Violation of Federal Law—Federal Collateral Relief Not Available For State Prisoners Who Have Had An Opportunity for Full and Fair Litigation of Fourth Amendment Claims in State Courts." 53 North Dakota Law Review 263 (1976).

"Habeas Corpus—Suspension of the Writ by Executive or Military Order." 43 Columbia Law Review 408 (1943).

"Limitation Placed on Federal Habeas Corpus Jurisdiction in Fourth Amendment Cases—A Further Erosion of the Exclusionary Rule." 22 Loyola Law Review 856 (1976).

"*McCardle*." 50 A.B.A. Journal 500 (1964).

"Modest Proposal: Habeas Corpus, the Exclusionary Rule and the Supreme Court." 7 Memphis State Law Review 85 (1977).

"Shutting the Federal Habeas Corpus Door." 31 University of Miami Law Review 735 (1977).

"*Stone v. Powell* and the New Federalism: A Challenge to Congress." 14 Harvard Journal on Legislation 152 (1977).

NEWSPAPER

Independent Gazetteer (25 February 1789), Philadelphia.

-Index-

ABOUT THE AUTHOR

William F. Duker received his Ph.D. from the University of Cambridge. He is a contributor to various legal periodicals.